Comparative Community Politics offers
fresh insights on how local governments
work; on how decisions are made, policies
developed, and the issues of federalism/
localism/decentralization are resolved. Data
for comparisons were drawn from American,
Eastern and Western European communities
and are presented here in original essays
by a distinguished multinational group of
scholars, addressing themselves to such
questions as:

- What are the variations in public
  policy emerging from differences in
  the social, political and economic
  characteristics in varying communities?

- What are the theoretical and methodological problems in cross-national
  research on local communities?

- How do we deal with variations in the
  degree of local community autonomy
  in different national systems?

- How can we best study community
  decision-making in different local and
  national political systems?

- What are the similarities and differences between the attitudes of citizens
  and their elected officials? Between
  local public officials and party
  activists?

- What theory best suits the study of
  community decision-making in
  socialist countries?

The contributors also share a desire to put
U.S. patterns of community power and
decision-making into a broader world
perspective. This comparative focus enriches
the volume's theoretical contributions,
while the broad variety of methodological
approaches offers both substantive and
technical insights to scholars and researchers.

COMPARATIVE COMMUNITY RESEARCH

COMPARATIVE COMMUNITY POLITICS

Edited by

TERRY NICHOLS CLARK

The University of Chicago

SAGE Publications

Halsted Press Division
JOHN WILEY & SONS
New York—London—Sydney—Toronto

Distributed by Halsted Press, a Division of
John Wiley & Sons, Inc., New York

Printed in the United States of America

Library of Congress Cataloging in Publication Data

Clark, Terry N.   comp.
    Comparative community politics.

    Selection of papers presented at 3 conferences held
in Grenoble, France, Sept. 9-11, 1968, Milan, Italy,
July 1-3, 1969, and Varna, Bulgaria, Sept. 14-19, 1970.
        1. Local government--Addresses, essays, lectures.
    2. Community power--Addresses, essays, lectures.
    3. Comparative government--Addresses, essays, lectures.
    I. Title.
JS91.C58   320.3   72-98030
ISBN 0-470-15858-1

FIRST PRINTING

To

Sidney Stein, Jr., *Godfather Extraordinary*

CONTENTS

COMPARATIVE COMMUNITY POLITICS

PREFACE

This volume grows out of concern with the extent to which earlier studies of community power and decision-making, largely undertaken in the United States, may be extended to other countries—in the case of these papers, especially European countries. From many standpoints the twenty-five year history of community decision-making studies in the United States provides a remarkable illustration of what not to do.[1] There are abundant examples of confused definitions of basic concepts, poor and incompletely reported empirical work, unprofitable debates among researchers, and noncumulativeness of substantive findings. The researcher interested in working on analogous problems outside the United States thus may easily conclude that he should not imitate the errors of the Americans; but what should he conclude beyond this? What lessons may he draw from the errors as well as the positive advances of research efforts in the United States in order to understand better another country? This is one side of a concern that led to some of the work reported in this volume. The other side relates to the degree to which patterns of community power and decision-making isolated in the United States will take on greater perspective through comparison with patterns in other countries.

As social scientists, most students of community decision-making are concerned with elaborating theories to help explain what they observe; and as the generality of the theories can best be gauged by the degree to which they help explain observations in many differing situations, cross-national comparisons can enhance considerably the value of work in any single national setting.

One issue recurrently discussed is where to begin. In a country where little previous work on local politics and community decision-making has been completed, what kinds of information are most productively studied? The researcher may be tempted to generalize from the results in other countries. But one must guard against the ever-present danger of premature transfer of experience. Some things simply have to be investigated again in almost each national setting. Given the many technical complications, not to mention the considerable costs, of mounting a large-scale comparative study of community decision-making in a country where little previous research has been completed, it is often useful at least initially to work with the materials already available. These are generally of several types, each of which is amenable to different, but mutually complementary, kinds of analysis.

(1) Impressionistic materials of various sorts may be analyzed. Observations by perspicacious travelers and commentators—De Tocqueville remains a classic example—as well as newspapers, novels, and biographies of mayors and leading community actors can serve as valuable sources. For example, Edouard Herriot, for many years mayor of Lyon as well as a national politician, left three volumes of autobiographical memoirs dealing largely with his political activities. Especially for historical studies, materials of this sort are often the most important single type of source. Today, unfortunately, fewer such biographies seem to be written.

(2) Legal materials, including the basic laws relating to community activities, the records of judicial proceedings, and textbooks and manuals prepared from such materials, seem expecially valuable in countries which have inherited traditions of specifying the legal competencies of various governmental units in great detail. It would be most valuable to complete a careful mapping of the various functions which local communities in different countries of the world are legally authorized to perform. And inside countries, like the United States, where legal competencies vary considerably in different states and communities, such a mapping could be equally illuminating.

(3) Census-type reports have been available for most countries of the world for at least the last few decades, and in many Western European countries they date from the early nineteenth century. Censuses in several European countries are more frequent and in many respects more complete than in the United States, and thus provide especially rich ore to mine. Political scientists and sociologists have been less active in exploiting census-type materials than economists and geographers, although there have been important signs of change in this respect in recent years. The efforts to establish ecological data banks including data from census sources (published and unpublished), survey studies, and other materials seem especially promising.[2] Given the availability of such data, and the increasing degree to which relatively complex analysis has been facilitated by recent computer technology, one may hope for more numerous as well as more sophisticated studies based on census-type materials in future years.

(4) Proceedings of community institutions are relatively few and incomplete for most cities in the United States, and thus have been seldom used in American studies; but in many European countries, highly detailed records are kept of meetings of city councils, special commissions, and other institutions involved in significant community decisions. The types of analyses of legislative behavior used for national and international bodies deserve to be applied to local bodies where the data merit the effort.

(5) Materials on particular local activities, such as housing, education, transportation, public works, welfare, cultural affairs, economic development, etc., are often numerous and relatively accessible, especially in the more centralized European countries. Generally compiled by the individual ministries

charged with activities in the particular sector, such materials—ranging from legal and institutional discussions, to survey studies, to policy statements—can be valuable as a complement to the largely quantitative census-type sources. In countries where planning in these various sectors has become reasonably institutionalized, the raw data, as well as some of the preliminary analyses, are likely to be especially useful. Of course, this raises in turn the degree to which decisions in particular sectors remain the province of local, regional, or national authorities; but the experience in even as centralized a country as France suggests that the analysis of materials and activities from a few basic sectors can yield valuable results.

(6) Original data collection concerning particular types of decisions in one community or a sample of communities can build on analysis of the above types of materials. Just how useful it is to draw upon materials of each of these types depends of course on the relative completeness of the materials as well as the particular patterns of decision-making in any given country. But it would seem that more general use of such materials to complement one another would save time and energy in future studies, and help provide a historical and comparative perspective absent from many case studies. Even if case studies in a few communities are planned, it is often useful to perform some basic analyses with the available census-type data before selecting communities for study.[3] If one is focusing on economic development, housing construction, or community governmental budgets as outputs, for example, correlations of these with other variables can be examined for a large sample of communities, and regressions performed to isolate some of the most important other community variables associated with the particular outputs. Then the sample can be drawn so as to include communities that rank differently on the variables isolated. One may be constrained to select communities in a particular region for administrative or financial reasons; but some variation is likely among communities within any given region, and in any case the researcher in this way can become conscious of the characteristics of the communities which he selects in the national perspective.

The same basic procedure, at least in certain sectors and national settings, can also be employed as a rough measure of the extent of local autonomy as well.[4] For example, if the national government provides support for units of housing per capita throughout the country, but certain communities fall well above and below this figure, the causes of the patterns of deviation from the norm constitute an interesting problem to explain. Local patterns of decision-making are likely to be more important than in decisional areas where output levels are more uniform throughout the country—although, of course, such conclusions can only be drawn after careful investigation of the particular sector.

Clearly important lessons can emerge from analysis of many different types of data; there is no single methodology that leads to good research. But a direct corollary of this statement is that any single approach tends to constrict the researcher in certain ways. To obtain the perspective that can derive from more than one approach, therefore, it is often useful to utilize several of these approaches simultaneously. Care must be taken not to overextend the resources available; but each of the above approaches can be utilized with differing levels of intensity, comprehensiveness, and cost. In the United States, for example, the Comparative Study of Community Decision-Making involves analysis of certain impressionistic materials, census-type data, materials about particular local activities, interview data from a national sample of fifty-one communities, and more intensive case studies in two communities nearby Chicago. The Yugoslav materials presented here derive from both case studies in two communities and comparative studies in seventeen communities. The Grenoble team has moved back and forth between census-type reports, materials on particular local activities, case studies in individual communities, and a comparative study of seventeen communities (Roig et al., 1970). Eclecticism, at least in methodology, seems to be becoming a more general practice.

The papers in this volume largely emerge from the activities of the ISA Committee for Community Research. This Committee grew out of the Committee for Comparability in Community Research, which was founded in 1964 in an effort to bring together researchers working on analogous studies throughout the world so that they might, through mutual contact, achieve more cumulative results.[5] From the outset, a goal of the Committee has been to assist in the confrontation of findings in different national settings so as to help move toward more general theories. The International Sociological Association has provided important institutional support for these activities. A session of the Committee was held at the Evian World Congress of the ISA in 1966. After the Evian Congress, a Working Group on Community Research was established under the ISA Committee on Political Sociology, and in early 1969 it was formally recognized as an autonomous Research Committee of the ISA.

The Committee helped organize three conferences where drafts of several of the papers in this volume were presented. The first was a planning conference, held in Grenoble, France, at the Institute of Political Studies of the University of Grenoble on September 9, 10, and 11, 1968, arranged in conjunction with Charles Roig and J. L. Quermonne and supported by the Ford Foundation and the Grenoble Institute of Political Studies. Participants included:

Laura Balbo, Scuola di Formazione in Sociologia, Milano, Italy.

Michel Bassand, Centre de Recherches en Anthropologie Régionale, Geneve, Switzerland.

Guy Bourassa, Department of Political Science, University of Montreal, Montreal, Canada.

Terry Nichols Clark, Department of Sociology, University of Chicago, Chicago, Ill.

Peter Jambrek, Institute of Sociology and Faculty of Law, University of Ljubljana, Yugoslavia.

Janez Jerovsek, Institute of Sociology, University of Ljubljana, Ljubljana, Yugoslavia.

Charles Roig, Institute of Political Studies, University of Grenoble, Grenoble, France.

Mme. Biarez, Mlle. Souchon, and Messrs. Mingasson, Jobert, Nizard, Quermonne, Tournon, Michel, and Kukawka, Institute of Political Studies, University of Grenoble, Grenoble, France.

The major focus of the Grenoble meeting was on research designs of community decision-making studies in European settings. Such questions as involvement of higher levels of government in local communities and selection of issue areas and outputs were discussed, as were problems of questionnaire construction, informant selection, sampling, and other technical matters. Experiences in Switzerland, Yugoslavia, Canada, Italy, the United States, and France were compared.[6]

Nine months later, some of the Grenoble participants as well as others presented papers in Milan summarizing their various studies on community power and decision-making. This International Conference on Community Decision-Making was held July 1-3, 1969 in conjunction with the Scuola di Formazione in Sociologia, supported by the Ford Foundation, royalties from Committee publications, the *Scuola,* and The New Atlantis.[7] Presentations were made as follows:

Michael Aiken, University of Wisconsin, Madison, Wis., "Comparative Urban Research and Community Decision-Making."

Laura Balbo, Scuola di Formazione in Sociologia, Milano, Italy, "Perception of Community Issues and Political Demand: A Study of Decision-Making in a Southern Italian Community."

Terry Nichols Clark, Department of Sociology, University of Chicago, Chicago, Ill., "An Interchange Model of Community Leadership."

Mattei Dogan, Centre d'Etudes Sociologiques, Paris, France, spoke on the political consequences of community size.

Pierre Grémion, Centre de Sociologie des Organisations, Paris, France, "La structuration du pouvoir au niveau departemental" (published as a separate monograph by Copedith, Paris, 1969).

Peter Jambrek, Institute of Sociology and Faculty of Law, University of Ljubljana, Ljubljana, Yugoslavia, "Some Methodological Problems of Cross-National Comparison of Community Decision-Making: The Case of Yugoslavia and the U.S."

Janez Jerovsek, Center for Community Studies and Industrial Sociology, School of Sociology, Political Science and Journalism, Ljubljana, Yugoslavia, "The Structure of Influence in the Yugoslav Commune" (in absentia).

Mark Kesselman, Department of Public Law and Government, Columbia University, New York, N.Y., and Centre Universitaire Experimental de Vincennes, France, on "Research Choices in Comparative Local Politics."

William Kornblum, Department of Sociology, University of Chicago, Chicago, Ill., "The Yugoslav Communal System: Decision-Making in Housing and Urban Development" (in absentia).

Juan J. Linz, Departments of Sociology and Political Science, Yale University, New Haven, Conn., spoke on community power and decision-making in Spanish communities. See his *Local Elites and Social Change in Rural Andalucia* (Paris: OECD, 1967) and a forthcoming volume in Spanish.

Zdavko Mlinar, School of Sociology, Political Science and Journalism, Ljubljana, Yugoslavia, "Actualization of Community Potentialities for Development."

Kenneth Newton, Department of Political Science, University of Birmingham, Birmingham, England, "Profile of a Local Political Elite: Businessmen as Community Decision-Makers in Birmingham, 1838-1966."

Charles Roig and C. Mingasson, Institute of Political Studies, University of Grenoble, Grenoble, France, "Recherche sur la structure du pouvoir local en milieu urbain."

Erwin Scheuch, Institut für Vergleichende Sozialforschung, University of Cologne, Cologne, Germany, spoke on studies of regional planning and community decision-making in Germany.

Jörgen Westerståhl, Statsvent. Institutionen, University of Goeteborg, Sweden, "The Communal Research Program in Sweden."

Jean-Pierre Worms, Centre de Sociologie des Organisations, Paris, France, discussed "Les institutions régionales et la société locale" (published in Paris by Copedith, 1968).

Other participants included:

Guido Martinotti, representing the International Sociological Association and the New Atlantis.

Angelo Pagani, representing the Scuola di Formazione in Sociologia and the International Sociological Association.

Alessandro Pizzorno, Scuola di Formazione in Sociologia, Milan, Italy.

Charles Tilly, Center for Advanced Study in the Behavioral Sciences, Palo Alto, Calif. and Department of Sociology, University of Michigan, Ann Arbor, Mich.

A selection of the papers presented in Milan was published in a special issue on "Comparative Research on Community Decision-Making" of the new Italian journal, the *New Atlantis,* volume 1, number 2 (Winter, 1970).[8]

The third meeting of the Committee was held at the Seventh World Congress of the International Sociological Association in Varna, Bulgaria, September 14 to 19, 1970. There were twenty-seven regular participants who presented papers, commented on each other's research, and discussed issues of cross-national comparison at a roundtable session. Support for the Varna sessions from the International Sociological Association and the National Science Foundation is gratefully acknowledged. Many of the regular participants had attended the two earlier conferences. Michael Aiken agreed to serve as chairman of a Working Group on Cross-National Research for the Committee.

The first paper in this volume, by Clark, deals with an issue that has been raised recurrently at international conferences: how to deal with variations in the degree of local community autonomy in different national systems.

The next three papers focus on details of local community structure and politics in particular countries. K. Newton illuminates several dimensions of English local government by specific comparisons with communities in the United States. Thomas Anton suggests that Swedish communities may best be studied as elements of a reasonably integrated national system. Mark Kesselman seeks to isolate some of the peculiarities of French local government by detailing differences between local public officials and party activists.

Part II includes four papers dealing with processes of decision-making in four different countries. Westerståhl summarizes some of the results from one of the largest community research projects undertaken anywhere in the world. He presents some striking findings concerning similarities and differences between the attitudes of citizens and their elected leaders. Peter Jambrek suggests the need for a theory of political development distinctive to socialist countries, and outlines some basic propositions for such a theory which he tests with data from a study of 16 Yugoslav communes. Like Jambrek, Erik Cohen is concerned with the impact of political and economic development on local community autonomy and decision-making. These studies of Yugoslavia and Israel both document the leading role played by local political officials, and suggest that the impact of higher-level administrators has decreased in the last two decades. Considering a longer time period, Charles Tilly challenges received sociological theory concerning the pathological nature of urban violence. He suggests, in conjunction with painstaking empirical analysis of French historical materials, that urban disorders may often be better interpreted as an extension of established community decision-making processes.

Part III deals with variations in public policy that emerge from different configurations of social, political, and economic characteristics of communities. Michael Aiken and Robert Alford consider variations in community output levels of three major programs funded largely by the American federal government. Seen in international perspective, their study demonstrates the considerable autonomy of American communities in influencing even nationally supported programs. Pusić pursues an approach similar to Alford and Aiken using data from Yugoslav communes. The richness of the Yugoslav census makes it possible for him to consider community structural correlates of a variety of political outputs. Robert Fried deals with variations in such policy outputs as budgetary expenditures, public housing, and policemen and teachers per capita in Germany, Switzerland, and Austria. His basic concern is to compare the impact of these outputs exercised on the one hand by the dominance of various political parties, and on the other by socioeconomic characteristics of the communities. All three studies in this section provide striking examples of how much analysis can be completed using almost exclusively census-type published information.

Part IV includes three papers that deal with theoretical and methodological problems in cross-national research on local communities. Mark Kesselman reviews the conceptual bases for cross-national comparisons of communities, stressing the involvement of the national government in local affairs. Delbert Miller suggests the use of an "institutional approach" in cross-national comparisons, and reviews its application in four countries he has studied. Ostrowski and Teune consider the fundamental problem of selecting the appropriate level of a society to study in order to understand systematic variations in policy outputs. Their discussion of the relative saliency of cities, regions, and nation states, and the solutions they propose for analysis at these different levels, deserve careful consideration.

Most papers in the volume are published here for the first time. Support for individual papers is acknowledged by each author; the editor, however, wishes to thank the Barra Foundation for its generous assistance in preparing the volume.

$-T.N.C.$

NOTES

1. See Friedman (1970) for a review of recent research in the United States and Clark (1973).
2. See, for example, Rokkan (1966) and Dogan and Rokkan (1969).
3. For one approach, see Roig et al., 1970.
4. This idea is developed by Ostrowski and Teune, this volume.
5. On the Committee, see Clark (1968: ch. 22) and the Committee Newsletters.
6. Reports on the Grenoble meetings are contained in "International Conference . . ." (1968) and "Réunion de travail . . ." (1968).
7. See also "International Conference . . ." (1969).
8. A free copy of the issue may be obtained by writing to Marsilio Editori, Piazza de Gasperi 41, 35100 Padova, Italy.

REFERENCES

CLARK, T. N. [ed.] (1968) Community Structure and Decision-Making: Comparative Analyses. San Francisco: Chandler.
––– (1973) Community Power and Policy Outputs. Beverly Hills: Sage Publications.
Conference on Community Decision-Making (1969) PS II (Fall): 697-698.
DOGAN, M. and S. ROKKAN [eds.] (1969) Quantitative Ecological Analysis in the Social Sciences. Cambridge: MIT Press.
FRIEDMAN, P., (1970) "Community decision-making in the U.S.: a review of recent research." The New Atlantis, 1 (Winter): 133-142.
International Conference on Community Decision-Making (1969) The American Sociologist 4 (November): 370.

––– (1968) Urban Research News 3 (December 28): 1-2.

MERRITT, R. and S. ROKKAN [eds.] (1966) Comparing Nations: The Uses of Quantitative Data in Cross-National Research. New Haven: Yale Univ. Press.

Réunion de travail consacrée à la structure du pouvoir local dans différents pays (1968) Centre d'Etude et de Recherche sur l'Administration Economique et l'Aménagement du Territoire, Institut d'Etudes Politiques, Université de Grenoble. (mimeo)

ROIG, C., C. MINGASSON, P. KUKAWKA (1970) "Social structure and local power structure in urban areas, analysis of 17 French townships." New Atlantis 1 (Winter): 65-84.

ROKKAN, S. [ed.] (1969) Comparative Research across Cultures and Nations. Paris and The Hague: Mouton.

––– [ed.] (1966) Data Archives for the Social Sciences. Paris and The Hague: Mouton.

Chapter 1

Community Autonomy in the National System:
Federalism, Localism, and Decentralization

Terry Nichols Clark

Local communities are not closed systems. The obviousness of the assertion may lead one to question the necessity to emphasize it; it is, after all, a traditional theme in studies of local government in much of the world. The theme is new, however, for most observers of local American communities, as well as for many observers in other national systems working from a social scientific perspective. Social scientific analyses have tended to emphasize social bases of political cleavage, party organization, power and informal decision-making patterns, and the local sources of public policy variation. They have not dealt with national-local relations so directly as has research conducted under the rubrics of public law and public administration, the history of governmental institutions, and public finance. The first set of themes has been emphasized by social scientists, especially those oriented toward North America; the second set has been more salient for legal scholars, historians, and institutional economists, more frequently working in European universities. But this dichotomy, only partially valid for the past, seems to be breaking down even more at present. This is clearly the case outside the U.S. It is increasingly true for studies of American communities.[1] The vast scale of urban renewal programs, anti-poverty efforts, and model cities are only a few salient examples of the rapid growth of American "federalism."

Because of the recency of concern with national-local relations by many social scientists, however, we have few coherent theories and little precise

AUTHOR'S NOTE: *It is a pleasure to acknowledge support from the Barra Foundation, the National Science Foundation, and the Urban Institute. The author, however, assumes sole responsibility for the text. This is research paper 24 of the Comparative Study of Community Decision-Making.*

empirical work in this area. The aim of this paper is to present a series of propositions linking what appear to be some of the major variables influencing local community autonomy.[2] Some propositions are clearly elementary, and others verge on the tautological; given the absence of research in the area, however, it seems important to state explicitly a set of basic hypotheses. Especially where cross-national comparisons are likely—and they seem especially fruitful in this particular area—the availability of a checklist of basic hypotheses can help prevent overlooking the obvious, and important, variables.

Limits for the propositions are difficult to establish. Most supporting examples are from Western Europe and the United States, mainly at the present time, but occasionally from earlier historical periods, going as far back as the middle ages. Presumably the more societies outside these limits are similar to those inside them, the more applicable are the propositions. What is distinctive about the West has been debated enough that we might best not broach the subject. But as there have been considerable variations within these general limits, it seems useful to list certain assumptions necessary for most of the following propositions:

(1) The existence of a national state and subsidiary local community governments.

(2) A national administrative structure responsible for certain activities within the local communities.

(3) Local political leaders selected acording to criteria that tend to reflect, in some general fashion, the preferences of local community citizens.

(4) Selection of local and national political leaders through constituency elections are essential for a few but not all propositions.

(5) Local and national political party structures.

(6) Some degree of national integration of the economy, but possible local autonomy in economic affairs.

(7) A few propositions assume a mixed public-private national economy; most do not.

(8) Local communities within the national system differ in their degree of local autonomy as well as on other basic socioeconomic characteristics.

Many of the propositions relate to four general factors, and are prefixed by a capital letter corresponding to that factor: devolution (D), resources (R), localism (L), and local political power (P). Relationships among these general factors are summarized in the conclusion.[3]

LOCAL COMMUNITY AUTONOMY

This is our basic dependent variable. It might be defined in the following way. Consider the set of all *community decisions*—i.e., decisions which involve choices among alternative goals relating to maintenance or modification of institutions or facilities that involve the majority of community residents.[4] Individual decisions are thus excluded as are decisions involving only narrow sectors of the community. If all community decisions were made by actors residing within the local community, we would consider the community entirely autonomous. But as autonomy usually varies along a continuum, we may define local community autonomy as the tendency for a large proportion of community decisions to be made by actors residing within the local community.

This definition necessitates several remarks. It does not specify the criteria by which decisions are made. That is, a representative of an administrative bureaucracy or national corporation may reside within a local community and simply enforce national imperatives at the local level. The best solution here may be to consider the decision as local to the degree that the local representative of the larger structure is free to select among alternatives. If national legislation, as is sometimes the case in Yugoslavia, for example, virtually determines a choice among alternatives for the local community, then local representatives do not make autonomous community decisions in the area. But if the larger structure only constrains the local representative to the extent that he must, for example, balance his books at the end of the year, then a wide range of choices may lead to community decisions as defined here. Most decisions, at some stage, will normally pass through an authoritative decision-making body, probably part of the local government, but this is not necessarily the case.

To operationalize the concept, some manner of sampling community decisions is almost obligatory. Criteria for sampling have been discussed elsewhere, and will be passed over here except to mention that one basic criterion is importance. When only a few decisions may be studied, it is often more revealing to study those ranking high on existing criteria of importance (cf. Clark, 1968: 67 ff.). Perhaps the most straightforward procedure is then to study the involvement of significant actors in the specific decisions sampled, and to classify actors according to local or nonlocal residence. Local community autonomy would then be measured by the proportion of local residents who are significantly involved in the sample of decisions.[5] A second measure, not necessarily the exact inverse of the first,[6] would be the proportion of national governmental actors involved. Variations of these essential procedures have been used in studying local decision-making in the United States, France, and Yugoslavia (cf. Clark, 1971; Roig et al., 1970; Jerovsek, 1970; Jambrek, this volume).

In the absence of such original fieldwork, however, more crude indicators might be considered. The traditional approach is of course in terms of legal provisions regulating activities of the local community. Doubtless the legal structure provides the fundamental core around which informal variations take place, although in some cases these may be considerable.[7]

Another measure is the ratio of local governmental revenues and expenditures to total governmental revenues and expenditures.[8] The simplicity of this measure is appealing, although many would question the result that Sweden and the United Kingdom are more decentralized than the United States (see Anton and Newton, both in this volume). Doubtless more careful procedures could generate better measures of the extent of autonomous local expenditures and revenues, as well as the proportion of funds deriving from higher levels that still permit some freedom of choice at the local level (see Ostrowski and Teune, this volume, for discussion of procedures for moving in this direction).

A further crude but simple measure is the amount of time spent by local officials dealing with actors from higher levels of government (Segal and Fretschler, 1970). Frequency and duration of contacts of local actors with persons in different national institutions (parliament, political parties, various ministries, etc.) have also been used (Roig et al., 1970). Transactions flows of communications from the local community to the national government and other units could also be utilized (cf. Jacob and Toscano, 1964).

Issues of operationalization of community autonomy could be pursued much further, as could problems of operationalization of many concepts discussed below. We shall largely avoid doing so, however, as our present concern is to formulate a general set of propositions rather than to develop specific procedures for testing them.

What then are the sources of local community autonomy? To this issue we now turn, considering first variables associated with the national society, and then characteristics of the local community: natural physical resources, social and economic resources, institutions supporting localism, the attraction and retention of local elites, and local political power.

NATIONAL SOCIETAL FACTORS

To begin with characteristics of national societies is important to help suggest the most general structures influencing local community autonomy.[9] But it is also to begin with the variables most difficult to conceptualize and measure precisely, and with those which have been the subject of the least serious study. Propositions at this level are also frequently the most difficult to test, for they virtually necessitate cross-national comparison. By contrast, many propositions in subsequent sections deal with relationships that may be tested within a single national context.

A general proposition subsuming a number of more specific factors is the following:

(1) D: *The greater the devolution*[10] *of authority to the local level in a particular institution, the greater the local community autonomy.* The most

important institutions directly affecting local community decisions are political and administrative institutions, but this proposition emphasized that community decisions can also be affected by local autonomy in economic, religious, and other institutions. There would seem to be a general "strain toward consistency" in terms of the extent of devolution across institutional structures. If major decision makers of the governmental administration, for example, are concentrated in the capital, business institutions will tend to locate their headquarters there as well. Clearly it is inadvisable to posit any generally independent or dependent institutional structures. For present purposes, however, many of our propositions focus on the impact of nongovernmental institutions on government and politics.

Let us stress initially perhaps the most obvious structural support for local community autonomy, or its converse:

(2) D: *The more centralized are the national governmental administrative structures, and the more competent the officials with which they are staffed, the less autonomous is the local community.* We have included in Proposition 2 two variables that need to be held separate in comparisons between more and less developed countries, or between countries where the ability of the civil service to attract competent persons significantly varies. For example, France and the Soviet Union have occasionally served as models for national centralization for other countries. But problems of staffing (as well as technology, geographic and linguistic barriers, and other factors) have sometimes made impossible the centralization of authority indicated on the organizational charts. For example, totalitarian regimes have only been possible in societies with reasonably advanced technology and efficient administrative infrastructures. Certain authoritarian regimes might have become more centralized if the means to do so had been available; but their leaders were constrained by the difficulties of staffing and administering national bureaucratic structures (cf. Linz and De Miguel, 1966). In past historical periods, problems of creating and maintaining a loyal and efficient civil service have of course been absolutely central to national integration (Eisenstadt, 1963). Until very recently in most countries, difficulties of communicating with outlying areas almost precluded highly centralized administrative structures.

Beyond these fundamental quasi-technological problems, however, several specific institutional arrangements influence the nature and extent of administrative devolution. Structures that aggregate and articulate interests are clearly fundamental.

(3) D: *The more centralized and unified, ideologically and organizationally, are the national political party or parties, the less autonomous is the local community.* The American Democratic and Republican parties are often cited as examples of especially decentralized and nonideological parties. Their broad and heterogeneous social bases, their ability to reformulate policy positions for

subregions (and subcommunities!), and their weak bureaucratic structures are certainly conducive to local community autonomy. Even though some local candidates run for office under national party labels, they often diverge considerably from national party positions on particular issues. And candidates within the same party in different cities may have little in common besides the party name.

Certain national factors contributing to two-party systems of large but weak national parties correspondingly help maintain local autonomy:[11] a presidential system in contrast to a parliamentary system, and constituency representation instead of proportional representation (cf. Lipset, 1963: 286-317). Multiparty systems tend to develop parties with more distinct social bases and sharper ideological orientations; their greater unity and centralization decrease local autonomy. One-party systems, ceteris paribus, might be expected to encourage even greater internal diversity within the party, but seldom are other things equal. If a one-party system is to remain just that, the party must often remain nonresponsive concerning local demands. And one-party systems tend to be found in countries that are also more ideologically and organizationally mobilized. Parties can significantly contribute to mobilization of the population, but such mobilization remains a separate variable:

(4) D: *The greater the (national) social mobilization of the population, the less the local community autonomy.* The mass media, the political style of leaders, and the content of the dominant political ideology are just a few of the many factors behind social mobilization (Deutsch, 1961). Although the concept is less precise than we might desire, it captures a sufficiently important dimension of the political process to retain as a separate independent variable. Many observers of developing areas have suggested that national mobilization, and the dissolution of often primordial local ties, is an important step toward national integration and political and economic development (e.g., Wallerstein, 1961). Without going into these widely debated issues, we point out that two countries that have enjoyed remarkably rapid economic growth—Yugoslavia and Israel—have both witnessed, simultaneously, a considerable increase in local community autonomy (see Cohen, Jambrek, both in this volume).

National mobilization as a policy is often urged, or attempted, because of the strong centripetal tendencies of ethnic, regional, racial, linguistic, religious, and economic cleavages of the population. National mobilization around a common ideology, in such societies, can be attempted as a functional alternative to social homogeneity. Where greater social homogeneity is already present, however, the emphasis on social mobilization can be less strong. But homogeneity of the population may well diminish the social differences which often help maintain demands for local autonomy. Thus,

(5) D: *The more socially homogeneous the population of a society, the less the community autonomy.* The Scandanavian countries have often tended

toward national solutions of problems, and Sweden in particular has been able literally to dissolve large numbers of local governmental units without substantial local opposition—in part, it seems, because of the considerable social homogeneity (cf. Westerståhl, Anton, both in this volume). Yugoslavia, on the other hand, is divided by profound social differences. The efforts of the Yugoslavs even to outdo the Russians in creating a nationally centralized state in the immediate postwar period was not a little related to internal problems of social heterogeneity. Such centralization was not greeted by universal enthusiasm. But the considerable devolution to the local community in the 1950's, reversing the earlier policy, was far from a compromise with the social differences dividing the country. On the contrary, because these cleavages were most strongly associated with the republics, devolution to local communities tended to mute the republican cleavages. Both of the policies represent, in a sense, enforced reactions against the simple logic of our Proposition 5, which might be reformulated to read that the boundaries of political autonomy tend to coincide with social divisions of the population. In the governmental rearrangements currently (early 1971) being discussed, Yugoslavia may well move in the direction of this reformulated Proposition 5, reinforcing the republican governments while reducing community autonomy.

The most fundamental social divisions, of course, frequently have economic overtones. Regional concentration of wealth, as in Katanga or Slovenia, has its community counterpart in the exclusive American suburb. The nationalizing influence of capitalism, as analyzed by Marx, might be introduced in comparisons between Yugoslavia and the U.S. (Meister, 1970). Put in slightly different terms, geographic separation between the means of economic production and consumption of goods is small in Yugoslavia. Factories and most means of production are controlled largely by residents of the community within which they are located. Exclusive American suburbs, on the other hand, are often those with the least amount of local economic production—a separation between production and consumption made possible by the national structure of the property system. Among socialist countries, however, Yugoslavia is virtually unique in its emphasis on the local community; socialism per se, certain ideologues to the contrary, thus need not imply a particular geographic relationship between production and consumption.

These considerations also suggest that the impact of the economy on local autonomy must be specified separately for production and consumption. If financial institutions are considered an element of the means of production, and the geographic location of capital is largely assigned to the location of financial institutions (rather than with owners of capital), then

(6) D: *The more nationally centralized are the means of economic production, the less the community autonomy.* Local management of local industries certainly helps promote local autonomy (Aiken and Mott, 1970: 60-67,

170-193, 487-526). The dependence of local enterprise on local finance also tends to support local norms of operation: an individual's community reputation can be an important determinant of the capital available to him from local financial institutions. Local consumption of wealth further reinforces local autonomy, but we will consider this point below.

The degree to which economic activities are tied to a market, especially a national market, is also important in influencing the national concentration of political power. The more elements of the economy (peasant agriculture, other subsistence activities) that remain largely outside the national economy, the greater the local concentration of decision-making.

Note that Proposition 6 does not distinguish between private and public control at the national level. It suggests merely that the greater the concentration of the economy, the less the local autonomy. If the private sector remains dominated by many different corporations, and limits are imposed on development of monopolies, then the leading actor at the national level will tend to remain the state. The general dependence of local communities on the national government will then be such that control of local activities by the national government (military bases, national industries, etc.) is likely to decrease local autonomy more than if the same activity were that of a national private corporation.

Correspondingly,

(7) D: *The greater the involvement of the national government in the (national and local) economy, the less the local community autonomy.* These first seven propositions have all been variations of the devolution idea of Proposition 1. We turn now to different types of factors. One idea which is difficult to express or measure with precision, but is clearly important in influencing local autonomy, is the following:

(8) *The more firm and more clearly demarcated are the national boundaries of a society, the less autonomous are its local communities.* Firm national boundaries are those restricting international communication and exchanges involving trade, tourism, etc. Firm legal and economic boundaries over time tend to become culturally significant as well. It remains outside our present concerns to consider the dynamics of such processes; from the standpoint of local community autonomy, what principally matters is the final result (see Deutsch et al., 1957; Etzioni, 1966, for two discussions of sources of national commitment). However, peaceful international relations and low tariffs are among the factors weakening national boundaries and thus facilitating contacts between local communities and foreign countries. The more such international contacts develop, normally, the less salient are those with the national society. Given weak enough national boundaries, local communities may even be able to bargain with more than one national society for military loyalty, tax rates, and other matters. The free cities developing in late medieval Europe were such examples.

A variable often associated with others, but which deserves some consideration in its own right, is the size of the country.

(9) *The larger the country, in territory and in population, the stronger the local community autonomy.* The relative, and optimal, population size of cities relative to nations has of course been the subject of much debate (Duncan, 1951; Clark, 1970), and although advanced technology has created new possibilities for centralized administration, there remain many problems associated with the sheer demographic burden which nations often resolve by delegating authority to subsidiary levels of government. Territorial dispersion of population, especially in the past, hindered communication and thus fostered local autonomy. A large, and often heterogeneous, geographic territory also gives rise to social demands for differential treatment in subregions (e.g., irrigation versus snow removal). These provide an additional strain to delegate authority to lower levels.

If the size of local communities were constant across countries, then the size of the national population would determine the number of local governmental units. But clearly this is not the case. Hence,

(10) *The larger the number of local communities in the society, the less their autonomy.* France is an extreme example, with some 38,000 communes—although the principle of divide and conquer has been applied outside France as well. Related to the number of distinct units is their relative overlap with other socioeconomic cleavages.

(11) *The more similar are the lines of social cleavage in the local community to those at the national level, the less the local autonomy.*[12] This proposition recalls our observations about party structure. Especially where representation is based on different geographic criteria from the local community, or on different or additional nongeographic criteria (Stände, size of property holdings, etc.), the national cleavages will tend to remain distinct from those at the local level. A national government seeking to weaken the national significance of a particular social group may divide it into several different local units. While such gerrymandering may reduce the national significance of the social group, it may simultaneously give rise to more self-conscious and powerful local groupings.

Fragmentation at the top, however, is just as possible as fragmentation below. Where national authority is divided between executive, legislative, and judiciary, or when parliaments are so divided as to make majorities tenuous and unstable, the possibilities for local community autonomy increase:

(12) *The more fragmented is the national leadership, the more autonomous are the local communities.* Fragmentation among national administrative structures is also an important consideration. Where leading civil servants remain generalists and shift across ministries, common administrative solutions are likely to emerge. Without some means of integration, however, each ministry may deal separately with local communities, which opens the way for entreprenurial local

leaders to play off one ministry against the other, and tends to prevent several ministries from enforcing common solutions on the local community.

Sometimes associated with fragmentation of national leadership, but nevertheless distinct, is its degree of legitimacy:

(13) *The more legitimate the national government is with the national population, the less the local community autonomy.* Short of a loss of legitimacy, the national government may still not represent the values of local community citizens as effectively as the local government. Such patterns of cultural distinctiveness are further considered below.

Local Community Characteristics. We turn now from basically national characteristics to those of local communities. Our focus henceforth is not on aspects of the national system shared by all local communities, but on characteristics differentiating particular communities from each other.

NATURAL RESOURCES

An idea that will be used in several resource propositions (prefixed with an "R") is the following:

(14) R: *The greater the resources available to the local community.*[13] *the greater its autonomy.* Here our referent is primarily natural physical resources. Close proximity to such production resources as wood, coal, and good land, and to transportation resources like rivers and seacoasts, were fundamental before development of modern transportation. More recently, physically pleasing surroundings, both to attract (especially affluent) residents, mobile economic enterprises, and tourism, have also become more important. The absence of natural disasters, such as earthquakes and floods, makes an area both more attractive and less dependent for assistance from higher levels of government. Given attractive surroundings, the community may also be in such demand that it can exclude less desirable social groups or activities (e.g., heavy industry), whereas a less physically attractive community may have difficulty simply retaining its population.

Another factor is communication, which has many complex effects on local autonomy, some opposed to each other. One effect related to the natural resources is

(15) R: *The closer the physical location of the local community to the national capital, the less its autonomy.* Proximity facilitates communication, and in turn more easy access by national government to the local community, and vice versa.[14]

SOCIAL AND ECONOMIC RESOURCES

Our basic resource proposition (Proposition 14) applies to social and economic as well as to natural resources.

(16) R: *The greater the social and economic resources available to the local community, the greater its autonomy.* Clearly resources ary many and diverse.[15] Those most fundamental for community autonomy are resources in demand by the national system, and in particular by the national government. Resources in great demand may be exchanged for power. Such basic resources are a strong economy and a large and talented population (convertible into votes and lobbying efforts) which is relatively homogeneous, or at least not seriously divided by cleavages on local issues. If social cohesion regarding national issues is also present, more effective bargaining with the national government is possible. As such resource exchanges are largely dependent on political variables, however, we defer further discussion to the section on the local political structure.

Economic backwardness of a community can weaken its autonomy, especially if it sinks to a level where its citizens and outsiders feel it needs special assistance. Poorer communities in Yugoslavia tend to request and receive greater economic assistance from higher levels of government. They also are less autonomous in their decision-making patterns (Jerovsek, 1970; Jambrek, this volume). The less affluent Yugoslav republics (Macedonia, parts of Serbia) are also those that tend to favor national integration, standardized national criteria for social assistance, and less community autonomy in decision-making.

INSTITUTIONS SUPPORTING LOCALISM

The availability of resources constitutes a potential for local autonomy; the extent and nature of their activation, however, depend on the values of local residents. Three interrelated propositions stress the importance of local values for resource allocations:

(17) D,L: *The more distinctive are local institutional structures, the greater the local cultural distinctiveness.*

(18) L: *The greater the local cultural distinctiveness, the less the mobility of local elites.*

(19) L: *The greater the local cultural distinctiveness and the less the mobility of local elites, the stronger the emphasis on local values by local decision makers.*

We focus initially on specific factors involved in Proposition 17 before turning to those of 18 and 19.

Some factors supporting localism involve local resources, although the pattern of influence may not be the same as that of the above sections. One, however, is quite similar to earlier propositions:

(20) L: *The more the community economic and financial institutions are locally owned and managed, the greater the local cultural distinctiveness.* With greater local control, local criteria will tend to enter business operations, and in turn be reinforced in nonbusiness aspects of community affairs.

Localism of course is an essentially particularistic criterion for decision-making, and eventually must conflict with those activity patterns relying heavily on universalistic criteria. The core of particularism has traditionally been the family. Continued emphasis on familism is reinforced where the family and economic institutions remain closely interdependent—family inheritance of land is the classic example. Extreme emphasis on the family, however, conflicts with community loyalty. But extended family loyalties can shade into ethnic solidarity, which is a level of generality of value commitment that can blend into strong community solidarity (Suttles, forthcoming).

(21) L: *The more ethnically homogeneous the community population, the stronger the local cultural distinctiveness.* We might also specify that ethnic groups with few or weak ties in the rest of the national society, or other national societies, will tend to be more attached to the local community.

Similar to ethnicity in its effects is common residence:

(22) L: *The lower the in- and outmigration of population of the community, the greater its cultural distinctiveness.* Strong attachment to a geographic area can also be reinforced through particular occupations. For example, peasants are often more attached to their land than others. More generally,

(23) L: *The more the occupational activities of the population depend upon specifics of the local geographic area, the greater the local cultural distinctiveness.* Rainfall, soil, topography, and climate, and their interactions with particular crops, are of fundamental importance for peasants. Especially when they understand little about the relations among these variables, peasants are understandably disinclined to leave a region where long experience has taught them the appropriate mix of elements for successful farming.

Community size is related to cultural distinctiveness through a number of variables. The overall relationship seems to be the following:

(24) L: *The size of the community population is related in curvilinear fashion to local cultural distinctiveness.* What are some of the intermediary linkages between community size and cultural diversity? Very small towns are not able to perform many functions for their inhabitants. Loyalties in such instances may be primarily to family or small neighborhood groups. Increasing size often implies greater population density, and

(25) *The more dense the population, the greater the social interaction.* As size and density increase, so do, generally, the functions performed by the community for its residents (Clark, 1968: ch. 4). In addition,

(26) L: *The more functions performed by the community for its residents, the greater the social interaction of community members.*

Further,

(27) L: *The greater the social interaction at the community level, the greater the affective ties among community members.*[16]

And,

(28) L: The greater the affective ties among community members, the greater their cultural distinctiveness. With increases in population size and density, however, other changes tend to occur which eventually reverse the initial positive relationships. Population growth is frequently the consequence of inmigration; and migrants are often socially distinct from former residents of the community. Hence,

(29) L: *The larger the community, the more socially diverse its population.*

And,

(30) L: *The more socially diverse the population, the less culturally distinctive is the community.* Social diversity, however, is only in part a function of differential inmigration. Intricately linked with social diversity are the factors leading to and generating further population expansion. Among the most fundamental of these is the division of labor.

(31) L: *Increases in population size, density, and interaction tend to generate social and cultural differentiation.* Durkheim (1933) and others have, of course, discussed this process in general theoretical terms. The particular point at which the effects of size will tend to reverse themselves are obviously dependent on a wide range of factors: possibilities for outward mobility, the available technology, the skills of the population, and many more. In the mid-twentieth-century United States, however, the effects of size seem to reverse themselves at about 50,000. Public opinion studies have shown that the relative homogeneity of beliefs and intolerance for nonconformity is greatest (in the United States) in towns of 10,000 to 50,000 (Key, 1963: 110 ff.). Above 50,000 the effects of size seem to begin to operate in the opposite direction.

(32) L: *The presence of local mass media and other institutions maintaining local culture, especially religious and educational institutions, leads initially to local cultural distinctiveness.* The presence of at least some community institutions creating, maintaining, and diffusing culture helps reinforce the loyalties of local residents (cf. Janowitz, 1967). Too great a proliferation of such institutions, however, eventually works in the opposite direction, for several reasons. The dynamics of competition, especially among newspapers, can lead to differentiation of the local cultural products to appeal to different subgroups of the population. A single newspaper, on the other hand, often seeks to appeal to at least some degree to all sectors of the local population to maintain and extend its circulation (cf. Clark, 1969a). Considerable development of cultural activities, and a heightened awareness of these among the local population, are eventually

likely to move them in a cosmopolitan direction—to attract persons from outside the community (to visit, to study at local universities, to apprentice with local cultural leaders, etc.), and to lead to demands for more extralocal culture. Advanced cultural activities tend to become antagonistic to strong local loyalties (Clark, 1969b).

A central element in this process is education.

(33) L: *Increases in education of community inhabitants initially increase local cultural distinctiveness, but subsequently lead to the opposite.* A minimal education can provide a stronger sense of attachment to the local community than none at all. And doubtless more advanced educational institutions could be designed to emphasize localism above most other concerns. But education as it has existed in at least most of the West has, at its higher levels, tended to disparage local, at least local community, concerns. The point at which the effects of education changed direction was very roughly the end of primary school in traditional European systems, and the beginning of college in the American system—although obviously we are subsuming many complex relations under a single heading. It would be valuable to study more carefully the many effects of education in relation to loyalties to different levels of society (see Ozouf, 1963, for a preliminary effort).

Consideration of effects of advanced education leads to a focus on the community elite. Attraction and retention of a talented elite can be particularly valuable for enhancing local autonomy: the national government is more likely to be responsive to the desires of a talented elite, the elite will be more skillful in negotiating with national figures, and in general it will tend to make more effective use of the mass media and other available resources. At any one time, only a small portion of the community elite may be involved in such activities. But the availability of a pool of elite members which can provide replacement of more active members, as well as general status which they bring to the community, and the knowledge that they could potentially act as an effective pressure group if necessary, all contribute to local autonomy.

As Proposition 18 made explicit, factors encouraging local cultural distinctiveness generally help retain an elite. Certain community characteristics, however, are particularly important for elite members. Attractive housing and living conditions, better-than-average schools, and the availability of superior consumer goods are standard items of elite consumption. Few elites are static, however; possibilities for continuing social and economic advancement are essential to maintain a dynamic elite. Communities dominated by a family oligarchy, as was reputedly the case of the "X" family in Middletown (Lynd and Lynd, 1937), will tend to discourage potential elite members from remaining in residence.

(34) *Possibilities for upward mobility must remain open to retain talented younger persons in the community, or to attract others from outside.* On the

other hand, a certain elite cohesiveness is valuable for concerted community action.

The appropriate balance among the variables of Propositions 17, 18, and 19 is critical to retain an effective local elite. Too much cultural distinctiveness can become stifling for leaders whose talents transcent facilities of the local community. For the elite in particular, the linear proposition about cultural distinctiveness changes direction at higher levels. This is especially the case for integration with the national system. National contacts are essential for desirable goods and services unprocurable locally. National newspapers and other media must not be entirely excluded from the local community. Communication and transportation to the rest of the society must be sufficient to permit access to information and resources essential for business and professional activity as well as for personal consumption. The educational and cultural institutions must not be too parochial, and something besides peasant folklore, local history, and regional food must be occasionally available. Too much cohesion will drive out talented leaders, but too complete integration into the national society, which may retain them at the local level, can lead to their acting without reference to the local community. Loyalties will shift toward other centers of attraction. A classic example is the manager of a national industry, who spends only a few years in any community and whose loyalties belong to his company. This example and related factors have been treated already. We might suggest additionally that

(35) *A local elite is likely to become more involved with a wide range of community issues if the elite includes representatives of several social sectors.* A business oligarchy is less likely to become broadly involved in community affairs than a community elite including religious leaders, free professionals, educators, civic leaders, labor representatives, etc. Such a heterogeneous elite will be in greater contact with a range of potential issues, and more sensitive in dealing with them, than a narrower elite.

There is also likely to be an interaction effect involving community, and elite, wealth.

(36) *More affluent elites and communities will be even more inclined to support a wide range of charitable, civic, and other community projects if the elite includes several social sectors.* An elite forced to devote considerable energy to meeting minimal needs for food and shelter, and to holding down the lower classes, finds it difficult to undertake more general civic projects.[17]

The propositions about cultural distinctiveness suggest that differentiation from the national system will generally foster community involvement of the local elite and prevent its attraction elsewhere. Different patterns of social and political cleavage at the local from the national level reinforce the same tendency (see Proposition 11). Like many others, however, this tendency reverses itself at the extreme.

(37) L: *Given sharp enough disparity between the basic cultural concerns and operating assumptions at local and national levels, a local parochialism can generate situations leading to less community autonomy.* Declining industrial centers in the United States that resist federal assistance for ideological reasons may hasten their decline and eventual subservience to the national government. Communist-controlled cities in France and Italy, on the other hand, have generally been astute at administering programs with remarkable efficiency (Fried, forthcoming). One consequence of such conduct, of course, is the absence of scandal or questionable situations which would occasion more involvement by national inspectors in the local community. But such distinct and visible opposition to general policies of the national government often severely hinders local autonomy and strains local resources.

Where more values are shared by the local and national government, local leaders tend to have more easy access to the national (especially political) leadership. This in turn can generate support for local projects that might otherwise be difficult to obtain. When resource exchanges in the political arena are involved, however, the situation changes once again. The range of possibilities for exchange, and exchange "prices" of resources for different actors, provide definite advantages to those closer to the national leadership. But here we enter into considerations of political leadership, the subject of the next section.

LOCAL POLITICAL STRUCTURES

Certain legal elements of the political structure vary across communities within a national system. Many of these relate to powers of leading political officials. Our most general proposition in this area is the following:

(38) P: *The greater the legal powers of local political officials in general (i.e., in matters other than local autonomy), the greater the local community autonomy.*[18]

Some of the most basic legal arrangements affecting the power of local political officials relate to the terms of office.

(39) P: *The longer the period for which local political leaders hold office, the greater their power.* Time in office permits, among other things, creation of local loyalties and informal exchange relations with higher officials. In addition to time, a certain freedom of action is important.

(40) P: *The greater the scope of legal authority of the local political leader(s) (for appointments, taxation, establishment of budgets, etc.), the greater their power.* These matters are clearly fundamental. Powers of taxation, especially over more lucrative sources of local wealth (personal and business income, commercial sales, property, etc.) make available liquid assets to

exchange for local support and eventually enhanced community autonomy.[19] Yugoslav communities in this respect are among the most powerful in the world, for they have powers of taxation on personal and business income, in addition to the more usual items (Meister, 1970.) Authority over appointments permits patronage, but these immediate benefits are significant for only a limited proportion of community inhabitants—although they may constitute an essential corps for party maintenance, grass-roots work, etc. Local leadership can be far more responsive to local citizen demands if it is also empowered to determine budgetary allocations. This is not the case when the central budget items are administered directly by higher levels of government, or externally determined by precise legal formula and similar controls. Again, responsiveness to local citizen preferences enhances local support, which in turn can be converted into community autonomy.

Certain legal patterns influence local political power; others influence local loyalties.

(41) L: *The more local criteria (e.g., local residence) are stressed as requirements for local political office, up to the point that competent leaders are excluded, the greater the community autonomy.* Long contact with local affairs tends to reinforce the distinctive orientation of community leaders. But localism can be restrictive. If lifetime community residence, including local education, were required of political leaders, for example, the pool of talents would almost certainly be diminished.[20] In addition to narrowing the pool of leadership, localistic requirements can curtail the experiences of candidates who could use their greater knowledge of activities elsewhere to enhance local autonomy. The French mayor, for example, often can best enhance his commune's autonomy by maintaining close and frequent contact with selected Parisian ministries and national political leaders (Kesselman, this volume). This can be achieved by frequent trips to Paris if the mayor's major political post is his mayorship. The French institution of *le cumul,* however, permits mayors simultaneously to hold national political positions—Edouard Herriot of Lyon and Jacques Chaban-Delmas of Bordeaux have been two mayors who did not even restrict themselves to sit in the National Assembly, but also served as Prime Minister. Holding such an important national post clearly opens vast resources that could potentially be channeled to their local communities. But national office simultaneously brings considerable nonlocal commitments. Thus,

(42) P: *Local community autonomy will be enhanced if local political leaders can participate in extralocal decisions affecting the local community (through membership in commissions, holding higher offices, etc.), up to the point where the marginal gains in resources exceed the marginal gains in extralocal commitments which must be assumed by the leader.* Insofar as time must be spent away from activities beneficial to his community, the opportunity costs incurred by a leader in not spending the same time for the community may

be a substantial element of average and marginal extralocal commitments. But as is the case with formulations of this sort in economics, measuring marginal gains in resources and commitments is far from straightforward.

Let us turn now from legal to extralegal political factors enhancing local autonomy. A basic proposition here is a variation of others concerning resources (Propositions 14, 16, 38):

(43) R: *The greater the resources available to local political leaders, the greater the local community autonomy.* Certain natural and socioeconomic resources of the community (as considered above) are accessible to local political leaders, but many others are not. For centuries political leaders have sought means to gain access to natural and socioeconomic resources in their jurisdictions. Devising legal structures permitting liberal taxation and other governmental activities, as considered in Propositions 38, 39, 40, and 42, is clearly one means to increase political resources. But given that most local politicians, most of the time, are not able significantly to influence the basic legal structures within which they operate, what alternatives are open to them, and what extralegal characteristics facilitate or hinder their tasks?

The general processes of extension and consolidation of power have been analyzed, of course, for some time. The necessity for empire builders to develop support structures outside traditional kinship and ethnic groupings is paralleled by the need for the urban political leader to work around higher-level legal structures. One recurrent theme (cf., for example, Weber, 1968: vol. 3; Eisenstadt, 1963) is the importance of a committed staff of followers, at the city level often in the form of a political machine (which fascinated Weber for its solution to many problems he had analyzed elsewhere; see Weber, 1946: 107 ff.). By providing a minimal level of material goods, and occasional services, for persons in great need of the essentials of existence, and by asking in return only remembrance on election day, skillful machine politicians were able to mobilize a considerable support structure. Control of access to local political office then made feasible extraction of considerable resources, especially from local economic sources in need of some form of political authorization or support. Their contributions could in turn be applied to extend the influence of the machine.

The same general process may be employed by local political leaders in dealing with higher-level officials. A local leader in control of considerable resources can make these available to candidates for higher political office. He can endorse, underwrite campaign costs, provide staffing and technical assistance, and help bring out a favorable vote, especially in primaries but also in the final election. Once elected, such officials normally remain concerned with the welfare of the leader's local community. They can provide resources through national programs that are distributed at the local level to strengthen further the position of the local machine. Mayor Richard Daley of Chicago has been one of the most successful local leaders in America with such tactics. The central role of the Chicago Democratic machine in selecting state and Congressional leaders has been legendary. With the decline of machines in other major cities of the United States, however, Daley's ability to influence selection of presidential candidates, and to gain national support for policies favoring his city, have been even further enhanced. Although the Chicago Democratic Party is an extreme example, the principle it illustrates seems to be more general:

(44) P: *The stronger the local party structure supporting the local political leader(s), the greater the local community autonomy.* Of course a political party is only one type of support mechanism. At a slightly higher level of generality, we may suggest that

(45) P: *The more centralized the community decision-making structure, the greater the autonomy of the local community.* In France or Italy, the control of the Communist Party may be dominant in individual cities, although the Communists obtain a smaller proportion of the national vote in those two countries than does the Democratic Party in the United States. In all three countries, however, the influence of local decision-makers on national politics depends on a system of national organizational contacts outside the legal structures of government. If Mayor Daley can offer gentle suggestions through personal contacts or the U.S. Conference of Mayors, French and Italian local Communist leaders can contribute local resources to their national parties to help make national strikes and other partisan activities very real political weapons.

Involvement of local leaders in national party-type activities, however, is analogous to their involvement in higher political offices:

(46) P: *Local community autonomy will be enhanced by greater involvement of local political leaders in national organizations (parties, voluntary organizations, etc.) up to the point where the marginal gains in resources exceed the marginal gains in extralocal commitments.* Even though linkages with higher governmental levels may increase opportunities for political leaders to bargain for their communities, these same linkages can simultaneously decrease the distinctiveness and salience of the local leader with his citizens. The same may be said for linkages with metropolitan groups or decentralization efforts; insofar as involvement with these efforts decreases local citizen support (within existing political boundaries), local political leaders will tend to avoid them.

The sources of support for political leaders are obviously many and diverse; but they are of less concern to us here than their consequences:

(47) P: *The greater the citizen support, especially as manifested in elections, for the local political leader, the greater his bargaining ability, and the greater the local community autonomy.* The "economic theory of democracy" stresses the central role of citizen preferences in determining the behavior of political leaders (Downes, 1957; Davis et al., 1970). It also assumes, in many versions,

that political leaders have perfect knowledge of citizen preferences (Stigler, 1971). Practical politicians, however, devote years to internalizing the hierarchical ranking and relative intensities of basic citizen preferences. The simple variable of time is fundamental in the process; even astute leaders can commit egregious errors if they have not become sufficiently familiar with local public opinion. Long residence in a community can help generate such knowledge, but time spent in office is likely to lead to even more extensive and continual involvement with various citizen's groups. Thus,

(48) *The longer the period in office of local political leaders, the greater the community autonomy.* Time in office, of course, implies far more than familiarity with citizen preferences. Familiarity with potentially available resources can also come only with time; and experience in dealing with higher levels of government is not always rapidly acquired. Long tenure permits cumulative acquisition of contacts and contraction of debts from junior political and bureaucratic officials. Legal restrictions may impose outer boundaries on the period of incumbency, but a strong party structure and other resources can help extend time in office up to those limits.

CONCLUSION

Let us review the relationships among the basic variables we have analyzed. Six general sets of variables were considered that directly or indirectly influence local community autonomy (see Figure 1). General propositions were labeled with capital letters, and lower-level propositions following from them were indicated with the same notation. The more general propositions help clarify relationships among the variables in Figure 1. National factors were linked to local political power and to local community autonomy primarily through variations of a devolution proposition:

D = *The greater the devolution of authority to the local level in a particular institution, the greater the local community autonomy.* The basic institutions considered were the national governmental administration (2),[21] political parties (3), and the means of economic production (6), (7).

Natural resources and social and economic resources were linked to local community autonomy largely through the potential influence they made available to local elites in dealings with the national government. For both sets of variables, the basic idea was

R = *The greater the resources available to the local community, the greater its autonomy* (14), (16). But in order for local elites to mobilize community resources they must retain a minimal loyalty for local concerns; they must not become too cosmopolitan. Several institutional mechanisms maintaining the loyalties of community elites were considered: autonomous economic activity

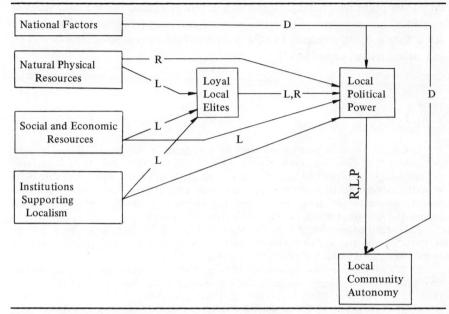

Figure 1: RELATIONSHIPS AMONG BASIC VARIABLES

(20), ethnic homogeneity (21), length of residence (22), community-specific occupational patterns (23), population size (24), and density (25), the presence of mass media and other cultural institutions (32), educational patterns (33), and possibilities for upward social mobility (34). The guiding ideas in the section centered on localism:

L = *The more distinctive are local institutional structures, the greater the local cultural distinctiveness, the greater the localism of the community elites, and the more their actions enhance community autonomy.* Given the availability of basic resources to a community, and a loyal local elite, use of these resources depends largely on the local political structure. Local political leadership can enhance community autonomy most effectively if it is powerful in a wide range of issue areas.

P = *The greater the power of the local political leadership in general (i.e., in matters other than local autonomy), the greater the local community autonomy.* Power derives from legal structures which help consolidate local leadership: long periods of office for local officials (39), and considerable authority in appointments, taxation, and the establishment of budgets (40). Local criteria for local office (e.g., residential requirements) help maintain the localism of community leaders (41). Participation of local leaders in extracommunity decisions (through membership in commissions, etc.) increases local autonomy up to the point where marginal gains in resources exceed the marginal gains in extralocal commitments (42). Other factors reinforcing powerful local leadership are a strong party structure (44), a centralized decision-making structure (45), and strong citizen support (47).

NOTES

1. Certain American political scientists have analyzed the interpenetration of levels of government (e.g., Grodzins, 1966; Martin, 1965; Derthick, 1970), and "fiscal federalism" has increasingly attracted the attention of economists (e.g., Hirsch, 1970; Margolis, 1970; Musgrave, 1965). Social scientists concerned with international comparisons have been virtually forced to pay attention to these phenomena (e.g., Maas, 1959; Fesler, 1965; Daland, 1969; Walsh, 1969; Institut d'Etudes Politiques, 1970).

2. It might be mentioned in passing that a number of the relationships discussed here in terms of the national-local context have direct analogues at the subcommunity or neighborhood level within individual cities (see Clark, 1970).

3. The propositions may be assumed to be stochastic, generally sequential, irreversible, substitutable, and contingent statements of causal relationships among variables (see Clark, 1968: 92 ff; Zetterberg, 1963: 11-34; Blalock, 1969: esp. 1-48).

4. Cf. Clark (1968: 21-22) for further discussion of delimiting community decisions.

5. The definition of "significant involvement" could vary with the research instruments used, as long as consistency across decisions and communities was maintained.

6. Because, of course, of possible involvement of actors from adjoining communities, intermediary levels of government, and nongovernmental national institutions.

7. By law, American communities often appear to have very little autonomy. According to "Dillon's rule," they may undertake only those functions that have been explicitly granted to them. Many states have granted such detailed city charters that there would seem to be little room left for local autonomy. Consider, for example, the following regulations from the charter of Nashville, Tennessee: "In the event any regular member of the Fire Department, above the rank of pipeman or ladderman, shall be temporarily absent from his duties without pay, because of illness or disability, the chief of the Fire Department, subject to the approval of the Mayor, shall designate any regular member of the Fire Department from a lower rank to perform the duties of such member during his absence, and the members so designated shall receive the rate of pay of the absent member during said member's absence and until he returns, or the position has been permanently filled under the general provisions of this Charter" (quoted in Banfield and Wilson, 1963: 65).

8. Such "decentralization scores" for 45 countries have been computed by Paulo Reis Vierira, presented in Sherwood (1969).

9. We understand by characteristics of national societies those global and structural properties which do not apply to any single community, as well as aggregate or "analytical" properties based on performing some mathematical operation on properties of individual communities (see Lazarsfeld and Menzel, 1961, on general property types).

10. By "devolution" we refer to the tendency to shift the locus of decisions toward the local level of a national system. The close meaning of such related terms as "deconcentration" (see Walsh, 1969: 157) and "decentralization" (Clark, 1970) suggests the appropriateness of designating this general proposition with a "D." Such a "D" will precede more

specific propositions which may be derived from Proposition 1. The same convention will be followed for other propositions.

11. See Riker (1964) for a suggestive discussion of the importance of a two-party system for maintaining federalism.

12. See, however, Proposition 37.

13. Here and in subsequent propositions concerning resources of the local community, the statement should be understood in national context; i.e., "the greater the resources available to the local community" implies in comparison with those available to other communities, and to the national society.

14. On the other hand, good transportation and communication retain elites who need access to the capital and the rest of the country. This, in turn, can increase local autonomy—as discussed following Proposition 34.

15. A consideration of some of the most valuable for community decision-making is contained in Clark (1968: ch. 3). See also Coleman (1971).

16. Cf. inter alia, Homans (1961).

17. John Walton's work (forthcoming) comparing patterns of elite involvement in Mexican cities tends to support Propositions 35 and 36.

18. Power, decision-making, and related concepts are elaborated in Clark (1968: ch. 3).

19. The remarks here and elsewhere concerning exchanges of various material and symbolic resources for local power and autonomy build on earlier work on exchange theory and resources (see esp. Clark, 1968: ch. 3; Coleman, 1971).

20. Just how restrictive such legislation must be before the marginal gains to community autonomy are lost obviously depends on specifics of the local community (e.g., population size, number and nature of local educational institutions, etc.), and of the national society (relative migration rates, ease of national communication, etc.).

21. The number in parentheses refers to the number of the proposition.

REFERENCES

AIKEN, M. and P. E. MOTT [eds.] (1970) The Structure of Community Power. New York: Random House.

BANFIELD, E. C. and J. Q. WILSON (1963) City Politics. Cambridge: Harvard Univ. Press.

BLALOCK, H. (1969) Theory Construction. Englewood Cliffs, N.J.: Prentice-Hall.

CLARK, T. N. (1972) "The structure of community influence," pp. 283-314 in H. Hahn (ed.) People and Politics in Urban Society. Beverly Hills: Sage Publications, Urban Affairs Annual Reviews 6.

——— (1971) "Community structure, decision-making, budget expenditures, and urban renewal in 51 American communities," pp. 293-313 in C. M. Bonjean, T. N. Clark, and R. L. Lineberry (eds.) Community Politics. New York: Free Press.

——— (1970) "On decentralization." Polity 2 (Summer): 508-514.

——— (1969a) "A comparative study of community structures and leadership." Presented at the annual meeting of the American Political Science Association, New York, September.

——— [ed.] (1969b) Gabriel Tarde on Communication and Social Influence. Chicago: Univ. of Chicago Press.

——— [ed.] (1968) Community Structure and Decision-Making: Comparative Analyses. San Francisco: Chandler.

COLEMAN, J. S. (1971) Resources for Social Change. New York: Wiley Series in Urban Research.

DALAND, R. T. [ed.] (1969) Comparative Urban Research. Beverly Hills: Sage Publications.

DAVIS, O. et al. (1970) "An expository development of a mathematical model of the electoral process." American Political Science Review 64 (June): 426-448.

DERTHICK, M. (1970) The Influence of Federal Grants. Cambridge: Harvard Univ. Press.

DEUTSCH, K. (1961) "Social mobilization and political development." American Political Science Review 55: 493-514.

——— et al. (1957) Political Community in the North Atlantic Area. Princeton: Princeton Univ. Press.

DOWNS, A. (1957) An Economic Theory of Democracy. New York: Harper and Row.

DUNCAN, O. D. (1951) "Optimum size of cities," pp. 759-772 in P. K. Hatt and A. J. Reiss, Jr. (eds.) Cities and Society. New York: Free Press.

DURKHEIM, E. (1933) The Division of Labor in Society. New York: Macmillan.

EISENSTADT, S. N. (1963) The Political Systems of Empires. New York: Free Press.

ETZIONI, A. (1966) Studies in Social Change. New York: Holt, Rinehart and Winston.

FESLER, J. W. (1965) "Approaches to the understanding of decentralization." Journal of Politics 27 (August): 536-566.

FRIED, R. (forthcoming) "Communism, urban budgets and the two Italies."

GRODZINS, M. (1966) The American System. Chicago: Rand McNally.

HIRSCH, W. (1970) The Economics of State and Local Government. New York: McGraw-Hill.

HOMANS, G. (1961) Social Behavior: Its Elementary Forms. New York: Harcourt, Brace and World.

Institut d'Etudes Politiques (1970) Aménagement du territoire et développement régional. Grenoble: Institute d'Etudes Politiques.

JACOB, P. E. and J. V. TOSCANO [eds.] (1964) The Integration of Political Communities. Philadelphia: J. B. Lippincott.

JANOWITZ, M. (1967) The Community Press in an Urban Setting. Chicago: Univ. of Chicago Press.

JEROVSEK, J. (1970) "The structure of influence in the Yugoslav commune." New Atlantis 2 (Winter): 31-47.

KEY, V. O., Jr. (1963) Public Opinion and American Democracy. New York: Alfred A. Knopf.

LAZARSFELD, P. F. and H. MENZEL (1961) "On the relation between individual and collective properties," pp. 422-440 in A. Etzioni (ed.) Complex Organizations. New York: Holt, Rinehart and Winston.

LINZ, J. J. and A. de MIGUEL (1966) "Within-nation differences and comparisons: the eight Spains," pp. 267-320 in R. L. Merritt and S. Rokkan (eds.) Comparing Nations. New Haven: Yale Univ. Press.

LIPSET, S. M. (1963) The First New Nation. New York: Basic Books.

LYND, R. S. and H. M. LYND (1937) Middletown in Transition. New York: Harcourt, Brace and World.

MAAS, A. [ed.] (1970) Area and Power. New York: Free Press.

MARGOLIS, J. [ed.] (1970) The Analysis of Public Output. New York: Columbia University Press.

MARTIN, R. (1965) The Cities and the Federal System. New York: Atherton.

MEISTER, A. (1970) Ou va l'autogestion yougoslave? Paris: Anthropos.

MUSGRAVE, R. A. [ed.] (1965) Essays in Fiscal Federalism. Washington, D.C.: Brookings Institution.

OZOUF, M. (1963) L'école, l'église, et la république. Paris: Armand Colin.

RIKER, W. (1964) Federalism. Boston: Little, Brown.

ROIG, C. et al. (1970) "Social structure and local power structure in urban areas, analysis of 17 French townships." New Atlantis 2 (Winter): 65-84.

SEGAL, M. and A. L. FRETSCHLER (1970) "Emerging patterns of intergovernmental relations," pp. 13-38 in The Municipal Yearbook. Washington, D.C.: International City Management Association.

SHERWOOD, F. P. (1969) "Devolution as a problem of organizational strategy," pp. 60-87 in R. T. Daland (ed.) Comparative Urban Research. Beverly Hills: Sage Publications.

STIGLER, G. (1971) "Economic competition and political competition." University of Chicago. (unpublished)

SUTTLES, G. (forthcoming) The Social Construction of Communities. Chicago: Univ. of Chicago Press.

WALLERSTEIN, I. (1961) Africa: The Politics of Independence. New York: Random House.

WALSH, A. H. (1969) The Urban Challenge to Government. New York: Praeger.

WALTON, J. (forthcoming) "The politics of urban development in Mexico."

WEBER, M. (1968) Economy and Society. New York: Bedminster Press.

――― (1946) Essays in Sociology. New York: Oxford Univ. Press.

ZETTERBERG, H. L. (1963) On Theory and Verification in Sociology. Totowa, N.J.: Bedminster.

APPENDIX
SOME EMPIRICAL EVIDENCE

This appendix reports the results of a very tentative analysis of some empirical materials in light of the above propositions. The data come from a study of fifty-one American communities. As empirical details of the study have been reported elsewhere (Clark, 1969a, 1971, 1972)[1] we note here only that interviews were conducted in a sample of 51 cities by a representative of the National Opinion Research Center. One set of questions, the "ersatz decisional series," inquired about the influence of different actors in four issue areas: the election of the mayor, air pollution control activities, anti-poverty activities, and urban renewal programs. (The last two issue areas were restricted to federally-supported programs.) Questions were adapted to the specifics of each issue area, but in general they inquired about who initiated a proposal, who supported it, who opposed it, who mediated among the competing groups, and who prevailed in the decision.

There was generally no provision in the interview schedules either to include or to exclude actors from outside the community. When all schedules were sent to Chicago, an inductive code was developed to include the social status of every actor mentioned by each of the informants in each city.[2] There was a total of seventy-three such statuses, fourteen of which were for essentially extracommunity statuses, as listed in Table 1.

For each status, s, an influence index, I_s, was computed.[3] Statuses with the highest mean influence index scores for all fifty-one cities were mayor, newspaper, and various business statuses. The low scores in Table 1 sharply portray the minimal involvement of extracommunity actors in at least the four issue areas studied.[4] In most communities these extralocal actors were not mentioned at all; they appeared in only about ten cities. The ten cities where Officers of Federal Administrative Agencies were mentioned are listed, with their influence scores, in Table 2. These simple marginal findings may be the most compelling to some readers: federal governmental officials are simply quite minor actors for many aspects of American community affairs. Obviously many

AUTHOR'S NOTE: *I am grateful to Kristi Andersen and Wayne Hoffman for assistance with data processing.*

TABLE 1
MEAN INFLUENCE INDEX SCORES FOR SELECTED STATUSES

Status	n Communities with Score Above Zero	Mean Influence Index Score
Newspaper	51	66,000
Mayor	40	43,800
Officers of federal administrative agencies	10	4,700
U.S. senator or congressman	8	3,610
Other federal officials	1	314
State governor	5	2,350
State legislators	6	2,120
Officers of state administrative agencies	8	4,080
Members of county legislative body	8	4,080
Officers of county administrative agencies	11	6,470
Members of county boards, commissions, and committees	11	4,100
Other federal, state or county governmental officers	8	2,820
State Democratic chairman or committeeman	2	785
County Democratic chairman	2	863
State Republican chairman or committeeman	1	294
County Republican chairman	3	942

national influences may affect local communities too indirectly to appear in these measures. Still, considered in cross-national perspective, these findings show remarkably little influence of extracommunity actors in local matters, even though two of the issue areas are federally funded programs.

With positive scores for only about ten communities, sampling error is such that all relationships must be interpreted with considerable care. Given the small amount of data, and the general definition of community autonomy used in the above text, we combined the influence scores for all of the extracommunity actors in a single index, the ECA Index. To examine empirical relationships that might be considered in conjunction with our several propositions, we computed simple Pearson product-moment correlation coefficients between the ECA Index and selected community characteristics. As the data were not assembled to test these particular propositions, however, only some of them could be examined, and then only in most approximate fashion. With these limitations in mind, let us consider the findings in conjunction with our above propositions.

Devolution. The general devolution idea was examined with measures of the involvement of the federal government in local community affairs. No significant

TABLE 2
INFLUENCE INDEX SCORES FOR OFFICERS OF FEDERAL
ADMINISTRATIVE AGENCIES

Berkeley, California	1,720	Long Beach, California	9,520
Buffalo, New York	1,160	Memphis, Tennessee	3,330
Hamilton, Ohio	1,320	Palo Alto, California	1,470
Indianapolis, Indiana	1,470	San Francisco, California	1,960
Irvington, New Jersey	1,060	Waco, Texas	1,350

relationships were found, however, between the ECA Index and urban renewal expenditures per capita in the community (−.003) or a factor score based primarily on the number of persons in the community employed by the military (−.025).[5]

Natural Resources. In general, natural resources probably decline in their relative explanatory importance with increasing economic development, as does physical location in particular with improved transportation and communication. Indeed, Proposition 15: *The closer the physical location of the local community to the national capital, the less its autonomy* was not supported. Influence and the region in which each community was located correlated as follows: Northeast, −.001; South, .238; Midwest, −.257; West, .077. It seems doubtful that distance from Washington is a significant element of these relationships, however; they are probably in part linked to the greater role played by state and county governments in the South, according to state law. The Midwest relationship may well be related to religious and national background characteristics, to which we turn shortly.

Social and Economic Resources. Here the basic idea was summarized in Proposition 16: *The greater the social and economic resources available to the local community, the greater its autonomy.* Several measures of social and economic resources were available, the most obvious, perhaps, being income per capita of the community inhabitants; it correlated −.312 with the ECA Index, nicely supporting the proposition. So did a .218 relationship of the ECA Index with the percentage of the community population with incomes under $3,000. Weak but in the expected direction was a −.115 relation with the assessed value of the taxable property in the community. Other measures, however, did not show the same relationship—total number of inhabitants (.032), median education (−.006), and more than a dozen measures of local budgetary expenditures per capita were not significantly related to the ECA Index. There are of course many confounding elements in these relationships. One of the most important is the tendency for many current federal programs to be directed toward social problems (especially related to poverty and housing) which are more intense in larger cities with disadvantaged populations. Such programs naturally involve federal (and often state and county) officials, and thus counteract the simple resource proposition; it still may hold, but can only be subjected to meaningful empirical test after introducing more controls than we have been able to here. Problems of curvilinearity between educational level of the population and local involvement have been discussed.

Institutions Supporting Localism. Several propositions can be considered here in conjunction with our empirical results. One idea is implied in Proposition 11: *The more similar are the lines of social cleavage in the local community to those at the national level, the less the local autonomy.* If we consider not simply social cleavage, but also the issue of more general cultural indentification with the national society by local inhabitants (touched on in Proposition 13), we would gather that ethnic and religious groups with some cultural distinctiveness would tend to seek to encourage autonomy in their local communities. This pattern seems generally supported by the relationships between religion and national background of community inhabitants and the ECA Index (see Table 3).

Proposition 22: The lower the in- and outmigration of population in a community, the greater its cultural distinctiveness, when operationalized with percent population change from 1950 to 1960 and the ECA Index, was not supported. The correlation was −.129. This simple census measure may be too tenuously related to our cultural distinctiveness idea to be meaningful.

Our data were simply too crude to attempt any meaningful consideration of Propositions 24 through 31 concerning population size, density, interaction, and

TABLE 3
CORRELATIONS BETWEEN RELIGIOUS AND NATIONAL BACKGROUND
VARIABLES AND THE EXTRACOMMUNITY ACTOR INDEX[a] (in percentages)

Protestants	.178
Catholics	−.118
Jews	−.201
Irish	−.016
German	−.205
Polish	−.179
Mexican	.247
Italian	−.019
Central European (German, Polish, Czech, Austrian, Hungarian, Yugoslav)	−.293
Northern and Western European (UK, Ireland, Norway, Sweden, Denmark, Netherlands, Switzerland, France)	−.053

a. The figures on religious affiliation are estimates by the National Council of the Churches of Christ; the national background figures are for persons born in the particular country, or one or more of whose parents were born in that country (foreign stock in the U.S. census designation). See Clark (1971, 1972) for further details.

localism. We might mention here simply that there was no simple linear relationship between the ECA Index and population size (.032) or population density (−.071).

Proposition 32 concerning local mass media suggested the importance of local newspapers. Although our data were not well adapted to test this proposition as many communities had only a single newspaper and publisher, the ECA Index still correlated .267 with the number of daily newspapers and .184 with the number of publishers. Cause and effect may be difficult to disentangle here, but if the presence of competing newspapers is taken to indicate a lack of cultural homogeneity, then general support is provided for our reasoning.

Local Political Power. The basic ideas of Propositions 38 through 40 concerning the legal powers of local political officials were operationalized using an Index of Mayoral Authority, including the mayor's term of office, appointive and veto powers, etc. It correlated only −.079 with the ECA Index. An Index of Reform Government, based on the number of reform characteristics present (city manager, at-large elections, nonpartisanship) also showed no significant relationship with the ECA Index (−.042).

Surprisingly, the measures of mayoral power (based on issue-specific reputational items) and mayoral influence (based on the same ersatz decisional series used to construct the ECA Index) showed no relationship to the ECA Index. Almost none of the other power or influence measures for other actors was consistently related to the ECA Index, with the exception of the influence measures for businessmen. An index combining the scores for influence in the mayoral election of the chamber of commerce and five types of businessmen, for example, correlated .445 with the ECA Index. A similar measure for business influence in the poverty program correlated .274. Despite these relationships, businessmen, in most of our cities, do not seem to be overwhelmingly important actors. Their involvement here in conjunction with extracommunity actors may tend to occur along with a general fragmentation of influence in the community. This interpretation is supported by a strong relationship between the ECA Index and economic diversification (.409) and, more modestly, our basic measure of decentralization of decision-making (.166). These last findings seem consistent with Proposition 45.

To test our propositions in meaningful fashion it would be necessary to collect additional data directly related to the involvement of extracommunity actors, and the structural sources of variation in their involvement. And, of course, many propositions can only be tested with historical or cross-national comparisons. With the mounting interest in the importance of extracommunity actors in local communities, however, we hope that other systematic empirical investigations of these issues will follow shortly.

NOTES

1. References are included at the end of Chapter 1.

2. Eleven informants were interviewed in each community; information from seven was utilized to compute the influence index.

3. The index consisted of the total number of mentions of the status, s, by each of the seven informants, i, in each of the four issue areas, a, divided by the total mentions for all statuses, t. Or algebraically,

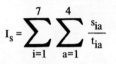

$$I_s = \sum_{i=1}^{7} \sum_{a=1}^{4} \frac{s_{ia}}{t_{ia}}$$

4. Contrast the scores for extracommunity actors in Yugoslavia, computed in roughly similar fashion, in the paper by Jambrek (this volume).

5. If standard statistical assumptions were met, simple correlations of .230 would be significant at the .05 level and correlations of .320 significant at the .01 level. In keeping with the very tentative nature of this appendix, we consider all findings only as suggestive for more careful future work.

Part I

COMMUNITY STRUCTURE AND POLITICS:

CASE STUDIES

Chapter 2

Community Decision Makers and Community Decision-Making in England and the United States

K. Newton

I

Each unit within the English system of local politics has a readily identifiable center of decision-making, with formal authority being largely consolidated within a single body of elected and appointed public officials. By comparison, the local government system of the United States is noncentralized and fragmented, and each local government area within the system is similarly noncentralized and fragmented, with formal authority being dispersed among a relatively large number of official, semi-official and nonofficial bodies. These primary characteristics of the systems very strongly affect the way in which the local decision-making processes work in the two countries; they also have a marked effect on the social composition of the decision-making bodies. Indeed, one could say that the whole nature and style of community decision-making in the two countries is entirely different. However, before abstract differences of political style can be discussed it is necessary, first of all, to expand and explain the two opening sentences of the paper, for they are central to an understanding of the contrasts in community decision-making and decision makers in England and the United States.

AUTHOR'S NOTE: *This is a revised version of a paper prepared for the Committee on Community Research meeting at the Seventh World Congress of Sociology, Varna, Bulgaria, Sept. 14-19, 1970. It forms part of a larger study of political processes and decision-making in Birmingham which is financed by the Social Science Research Council. The author wishes to express his thanks to Dr. J. D. Stewart, Dr. R. Chapman, Professor Oliver P. Williams, Mr. W. Hampton, Mr. L. J. Sharpe, and Professor M. Aiken, whose criticisms and comments on earlier drafts have greatly improved the quality of this version.*

There are, of course, marked differences between and within different types and levels of city government in both countries. In the United States there are so many different types of formal structure and modes of informal operation that almost any generalization about city government and politics must be subject to important qualifications and exceptions. Similarly, in England there are different types of local governments, with different political structures, practices and traditions. The Scottish and Welsh systems of local government also differ in some respects from the English. These variations between cities are undoubtedly important, and yet the fact that each and every city has a unique configuration of political characteristics does not preclude the possibility that some have similar characteristics, or that city government in the United States as a whole may exhibit a different range of common characteristics from that shown by city government in England. At one level, every urban political system in England and the United States is uniquely individual; at another level, English city government and politics has a set of common characteristics which can be compared with a different set shared by most American cities. In fact, for reasons which will shortly become clear, one important difference between city government and politics in England and the United States is the relative uniformity of the former by contrast with the great variety of the latter. American cities may be run according to the weak or strong mayor-council plan, the commission or council-manager plan, or a federated metropolitan plan. All the largest English cities, except Greater London, are run by county borough councils all of which have similar formal political structures, almost identical powers and functions and roughly the same modes of political operation. As one American study of six English cities has showed, "The processes of decision-making in all six communities were surprisingly similar" (Peterson and Kantor, 1970: 6). This makes it possible to generalize about them without doing too much violence to the differences which undoubtedly distinguish one from the other. Further, there are strong similarities in certain aspects of the government and politics of all urban areas of England, Scotland and Wales so that what is said here about English city politics also applies, broadly speaking, to the politics of most cities and large towns in Scotland and Wales.

The most obvious and probably the most important single difference between city government and politics in England and the United States concerns the number of local government units. Government of urban America is broken up into a vast number of separate local units. Banfield and Wilson (1963: 76) have pointed out that "The American city is not governed by a single hierarchy of authority in which all lines are gathered together at the top in one set of hands. On the contrary, from a purely formal standpoint, one can hardly say that there is such a thing as a local government. There are a great many of them. Or, more aptly, bits and pieces of many local governments are scattered around the local scene." The New York Metropolitan Region is a good example of the atomization of American city government. Wood (1961: 1) has called its government "one of the great unnatural wonders of the world" and has observed that the Region "governs itself by means of 1467 distinct political entities (at latest count), each having its own power to raise and spend the public treasure, and each operating in a jurisdiction determined more by chance than design. . . . The responsibility to maintain law and order, educate the young, dig the sewers and plan the future environment remains gloriously or ridiculously fragmented." New York may be an example of extreme atomization of the formal political structure but, even so, it is not far removed from many other urban areas whose governments are broken up into a large number of separate units each of which, in turn, is further subdivided and cut across by a number of even smaller units. It has been calculated that there are over ninety thousand units of local government in the United States, including about eighteen thousand municipalities, seventeen thousand townships, and thirty-five thousand school districts, as well as a further eighteen thousand special districts handling such services as water supply, fire protection, and sewage.

In vivid contrast to this gigantic mosaic, the whole of England outside Greater London, with its population of more than thirty-five million has fewer local government units (1,210) than the New York Metropolitan Region alone. As far as the government of urban England is concerned a two-tier system operates. County borough councils form part of the top tier and control most of the larger cities in the country (population, 1,000,000 to 33,000). The rest of the country is divided into forty-five county councils, some of which are predominantly rural and which fall outside the scope of the present discussion. Urban areas within the counties are controlled partly by the county councils and partly by one of two types of second-tier authority. These are the 227 noncounty boroughs (population, 100,000 to 1,600) and the 450 urban district councils (population, 123,000 to 1,700).[1] In addition to this range of general purpose councils, there are a few special purpose authorities, but, again in contrast to the American pattern, these are comparatively few in number and the vast majority are concerned with a whole region covering several cities, rather than with an area within a single city. In most regions there are special purpose authorities to control services such as water, hospitals, gas, electricity, and some aspects of the police force.

American city politics is fragmented in the further sense that the formal political structure of each urban area provides for a multiplicity of independent centers of power. There is no single center of formal power from which all important decisions of city government emanate. Instead, the formal political structure of each city may be composed of tens, hundreds, or even more than a thousand independent or semi-independent authorities, each dealing with its own particular area or service, in its own particular way, and each jealously guarding its rights and duties against the encroachment of other authorities. In

England, on the other hand, most of the formal power of city government is concentrated in the hands of the elected representatives of the city council and the permanent officials who serve them. The term "city council" is synonymous with "local government" in England because the council is the local government as far as the bulk of the population is concerned. Councils, to quote an official source, "carry out all the main functions of local government within their areas" (Central Office of Information, 1964: 17). The important word here is "all," for the supremacy of the city council within its own area is a fact of both theory and practice. Sociologists and political scientists have found that the council is unquestionably the center of community decision-making. In his comparative study of "American City" (Seattle) and "English City" (Bristol), Miller (1958a, 1958b) found that the council of Seattle was small and weak and tended to arrive at decisions only after a variety of community organizations had fought out the issue among themselves. But in Bristol, as Miller points out, the council is the center of decision-making in the community and pressure groups play a rather secondary or supplementary role. Another community power study, of Bath, a city near Bristol, also found that the council was unquestionably the center of decision-making powers and that no other community organization, the local Chamber of Commerce included, had the ability or the resources to challenge its decisions effectively (Green, 1967). In both Bristol and Bath community power was centralized and concentrated on the council, and there is no reason to believe that these two city governments are different in any significant way from any other in England (see, e.g., Birch, 1959; Stacey, 1960: 38-56; Bealey et al., 1965; Jones, 1969; Friend and Jessop, 1969).

Closely bound up with the division of American city government into myriad units is the second major characteristic of the system—its considerable decentralization and local autonomy. By comparison with English cities, those in the United States are *relatively* free to conduct their own affairs without close control or supervision by a higher authority. This statement may seem thoroughly inconsistent with all that the textbooks have to say about city-state relations but it is, nevertheless, valid as a generalization based on a comparison of English and American city government. American cities are not autonomous by any means. "Dillon's rule," the limitations set by various forms of city charter (including the misnamed "home rule" charter), and the financial supremacy of the States, all ensure that cities are subject to state legislatures. As Banfield and Wilson (1963: 65) put it, "Dillon's rule" means that "a city cannot operate a peanut stand at the city zoo without first getting the state legislature to pass an enabling law, unless, perchance, the city's charter or some previously enacted law unmistakably covers the sale of peanuts." A similarly strict law of *ultra vires* determines precisely what English city governments can and cannot do, but, in addition, a close control is maintained over how it is done, when it is done, where it is done, and how much it costs to do it.

Central control of English and American city government has been compared in the following way (Marshall, 1967: 67, 69):

> All the features of central control and influence known in Europe can be found in the United States—legislation (e.g., fixing minimum tax rates), prior approval to actions, power over appointments, orders, regulations, inspections, transfer of functions, financial assistance, with strings attached, reports, informal advice and assistance. But the intensity of control, though varying from state to state, is far less than in England despite a tendency for it to increase. Local authorities and also boards and commissions are comparatively free to carry on their services as they wish, except in the case of education which is subject to more stringent supervision. The police, fire, water and sewage services, for instance, are little controlled once they have been established. . . . The prescriptions from the federal government are general and very different from the meticulous orders, regulations and circulars to which we [in England] are accustomed. Local officials in conversation say openly that many of the detailed controls can be 'got round.' . . . On our standards American local authorities are not closely controlled.

The existence of tens of thousands of local government units in the United States makes it virtually impossible for either state or federal government to exercise anything but the most general supervision over local government activity, even if more than this were thought to be desirable, which is certainly not the case. The reverse pattern is found in English city government which is controlled to a much greater degree by the national government. This does not mean that English city government is the mere agent or servant of national government, for it has been shown (Alford and Boaden, 1969) that the county boroughs are still independent of central government in many ways. The fact remains that English city government is relatively tightly controlled by central government by comparison with state or federal government control over city governments in the United States.

So far, it has been argued that American and English city government differ in two important respects. The first refers to the locus of authority and the number of separate units involved in the government of each city, and the second refers to the degree to which each city government is centrally regulated by state or national government. In other words, the first distinction is concerned with the degree of central political control within each individual city, and the second with the degree of central political control of all city governments by a higher political authority at the regional (state), or national (federal) levels. A combination of these two forms of political control yields four types of city government.

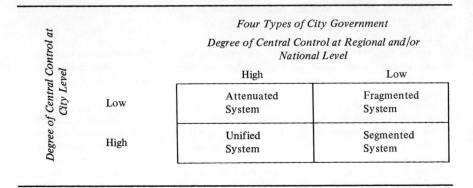

THE FRAGMENTED SYSTEM

This type of city government system consists of many separate local government units in each city, none of which is closely controlled by a higher political authority either at the city level itself or at the regional or national level. The weak mayor-council cities of the United States are a particularly good example of this kind of system, since in these cities "each department is likely to move in its own direction with no one empowered to coordinate. The effect of all these independent agencies is to make city government into a series of many little governments rather than one. There is one city government for parks, another for libraries, another for airports, another for sewage disposal, and so on" (Adrian and Press, 1968: 190). The commission plan is also likely to produce a fragmented form of city government in the United States. In some cases commission cities are even more fragmented than weak mayor-council cities (Adrian and Press, 1968: 201). In general, fragmentation of city government and politics is more characteristic of the United States than England, although there are exceptions. Some American city governments are highly fragmented in theory but less so in practice. These cities have found that a multiplicity of poorly coordinated government units are ill-suited to the needs of modern urban society and so a process of informal centralization of power has taken place, usually focused upon the mayor and his staff, which makes the cities more akin to the segmented than the fragmented type.

THE SEGMENTED SYSTEM

This type of city government is more or less centralized under a single authority at the city level, but each individual city government is relatively free of control by higher authority of regional or national government. The clearest example of this form of city government in England and North America is probably provided by Metropolitan Toronto. The metropolitan federations of Nashville and Miami are rather milder forms of segmented city government. These types of city government may be termed "segmented" because they function as distinct political systems, each with one overall political authority which is separate from, and also relatively free of control by higher authorities of regional or national government. The inadequacies of the weak mayor-council plan have encouraged many of the larger cities in the United States to develop strong mayor-council systems which are also an example of segmented city government systems. The council-manager plan may result in either a fragmented or a segmented system depending on how successful the council and manager are in exercising a relatively united control over the normal range of local government functions.

THE UNIFIED SYSTEM

The unified form of city government combines a relatively high degree of central control within each city with a relatively high degree of centralization of all city governments at the regional or national level. English city government is a clear example of this type since it is controlled and regulated to a great extent by national government and since there is one general purpose authority in each city which, although closely regulated by national government, is the main authority responsible for most local government activity in its own area. The unified type of city government will be found in the United States only where a strong mayor-council city, or a metropolitan federation, or a locally centralized council-manager city is closely controlled by its state legislature. Insofar as this is rare, the unified form of city government is an exception to the rule in the United States and, therefore, the contrast between English and American city government lies in the difference between the unified system on the one hand, and the fragmented and segmented systems on the other.

THE ATTENUATED SYSTEM

The attenuated type of city government is one in which the government of each city is divided into many separate units, none of which is centrally controlled at the city level, but each of which is closely controlled at the national level. Although this combination of central control at the national level but not at the city level is a theoretical possibility, it is rarely found in practice. It may exist in totalitarian or highly centralized states where the central government is careful to prevent the left hand of city government from knowing what the right hand is doing, but as a type of city government it is not found in either England or the United States, and may be set aside as far as the present discussion is concerned.

This fourfold typology is based upon differences in degree rather than differences in kind. All city governments are controlled to some extent by their national governments. If they were not they would be city-states, not city governments. At the other extreme, it is virtually impossible to find an example of such total and complete control of city government that it becomes nothing more than a local branch of national government. Almost all city governments have some autonomy in one sphere of action, and they all have some measure of influence over their own affairs, irrespective of how rigidly they are controlled by a higher authority. Similarly, there are few cities which give total control of every aspect of local government to one central authority in the city just as there is usually one central body or person with some sort of general authority, even though it may be minimal in theory and practice.

Although the typology is based on quantitative rather than qualitative differences, it is probable that each of the four types of city government will display different clusters of characteristics. For example, a country or region with a fragmented system will probably display a wide variety of city political structures and processes, each city or area developing its own specialties according to its own politics, history, and socioeconomic conditions. This has happened in the United States. On the other hand, the unified system of city government will tend to be fairly uniform in operation, if not in appearances. The control exercised by central government over city government will tend to result in the reproduction of national political structures and processes at the city level with similar parties, governmental structures, pressure group activity, decision-making processes and even, perhaps, power structures. This, it could be hypothesized, is what has happened in England. In the fragmented system, local politics will be contained within the system, whereas in the unified system a certain amount of local politics will be acted out at the national level, within national political institutions, because decisions are made partly at the national and partly at the city level. Thus, the parties and pressure groups of fragmented and segmented systems have no incentive to go outside the system.

In the unified system one is more likely to find a homogeneous political pattern in which parties and pressure groups are local branches of national organizations and in which local political organizations are obliged to operate at both local and national levels. The autonomy of the segmented system may also result in higher rates of participation, as expressed in voting turnout, pressure group activity, and party membership by contrast with the unified system where control is split between city and national government and where local political activity is less decisive than in the segmented system. Local participation is probably lowest of all in the attenuated system, because control is in the hands of national institutions and because there is no possibility of any one local political action having a decisive effect on the whole local system. This is all speculation, however, and the purpose of the rest of this paper is to explore the threefold typology of city governments in England and the United States in order to throw some light on the causes and consequences of each system.

Several formal constitutional factors help to account for the unification of English city government systems and their fragmentation in the United States. First and foremost is the organization of English local government by a strong national government. At the beginning of the nineteenth century there were no unified local authorities with general powers in England, but a whole series of independent local boards and authorities, often with similar or overlapping functions, with powers to deal with particular problems. Ths result has been described as "a chaos of areas, a chaos of franchise, a chaos of authorities, and a chaos of rates" (Central Office of Information, 1964: 1). Gradually, legislation passed by central government removed the vast majority of these independent and ad hoc bodies and gave their powers to elected councils each of which came to hold general responsibility for the administration of public services in its own area. Thus formal power of local government and decision-making in each city was unified under the control of a single set of elected representatives.

Each council now forms part of an integrated and relatively uniform pattern of general purpose local government units, each of which controls, within its own area, the vast majority of local government services, including education, housing, roads, fire services, libraries, parks, local taxation, sanitation, town and country planning, entertainments licensing, street lighting, and many other services. Central government plays a role of immense importance, so important that it is difficult to overestimate it, in each of these areas of local affairs, but even so it is correct to say that insofar as decisions are made locally, they are made by the council. In the United States, on the other hand, city government does not mean one or even a small handful of local authorities but a bewildering complexity of different authorities, each dealing with its own particular area or service. As one English observer of American city government has put it, "In an American city hall one never finds the range of work to be found in an English county borough, a point to be continuously borne in mind by observers used to a more streamlined system" (Marshall, 1967: 65).

The fragmentation of American city government is also a consequence of the separation of executive and legislative powers, particularly in the strong mayor-council and council-manager systems. In English city government, as in national government, there is no separation of powers. What may be loosely termed the "executive" of city government in England emerges out of the majority group on the council in much the same way as the Prime Minister and his colleagues of the inner cabinet emerge out of the majority party in the House of Commons.[2] Unlike the strong mayor-council cities of the United States, the English Mayor or Lord Mayor is not vested with executive powers, but performs the ceremonial role of civic figurehead. Many of the most powerful figures in the world of English city politics have not been, and have never wanted to be, Lord Mayor of their city. The sources of power are elsewhere.

Just as central government played a critical role in creating a relatively small number of general purpose local authorities in England in the nineteenth century, so it continues to play an equally critical, though more latent, role in maintaining the concentration of centers of responsibility in twentieth-century city government. It does so by means of the large amounts of money which it passes to local government. Although difficult to calculate with any precision it has been estimated (Humes and Martin, 1969: 188) that approximately sixty percent of municipal income comes not from local tax-raising efforts but from central government grants and subsidies. And, of course, central government likes to keep a close watch on how this money is spent. This means that for the ease of administration and supervision it likes to deal with the smallest possible number of local government units, and with only one responsible body within each individual authority. Local and central government finance would be impossibly complex if local government were divided and subdivided into tens of thousands of small parts. As long as central government continues to play an important part in city government, any tendency towards atomization of this kind will be resisted by enormously strong economic pressures. Pressures of a similar strength have not been exerted on city governments of the United States, although it is likely that they will increase with the development by the federal government of urban aid programs, anti-poverty programs and others.

Another major factor which helps to concentrate power in English city politics is the party system which exists in a more or less well-developed form in all large cities and in most large towns. The Conservative, Labour, and Liberal parties all have local organizations; these provide the majority of active participants in local politics and the supporting structures for party groups on the council. The two main parties contest a very high proportion of all elections in urban areas and control a large majority of council seats. For example, in Birmingham, the second largest city, the Conservative and Labour parties have fought every election in the city for the past thirty years, and this means contesting thirty-eight or thirty-nine wards each year. Control of the council has been fought for by the two main parties ever since 1945. The party system which operates in most city councils is not unlike that of the House of Commons, although with lower stakes, party discipline is sometimes weaker and the organizational and ideological foundations are less firm. Nevertheless, the party system of English city politics does have the important effect of aggregating interests and of mobilizing and organizing groups of people behind two or three political organizations, each of which is willing and able to take control of decision-making authority. When council opinion is thus unified into two or three power blocs, the chances of outside groups effectively challenging council decisions are reduced considerably. Community groups have to try to work through and with the party groups and the administration. Community groups cannot overcome them (without very considerable and sustained effort) and they cannot afford to ignore them. A good illustration of the power of the council and the relative weakness of outside groups is provided in a study of the politics of comprehensive education in three British cities and of the role played in the issue of educational pressure groups. Even when the situation was conducive to the influence of teachers' pressure groups, their impact on plans for reforming the educational system was modest. As the author of the study (Peterson, 1969) concludes, "Local politicians are more isolated from group pressures in Great Britain than in the United States." It is the concentration of effective power within the majority group on the council that shields majority group members from the influences of the pressure-group system.

In most American cities the party system is less fully developed than in England and in some of them it plays a negligible role. In such cases the community and its decision-making bodies are not organized into a small number of strong political parties, but into a large number of groups based primarily on religious, occupational, industrial, status, ethnic, color or class differences. Each of these groups may attempt to influence issues which are of interest to them and they may well compete or cooperate with others in doing so, but there is less likely to be a relatively stable coalition of forces such as one finds organized into city politics by the party system in England. To this extent the American city is more likely to play a more direct and also a more obvious role in community issues. As Williams and Adrian (1963: 312) found, "organised recruitment and campaigning for city council members leads to concentration of much decision-making in the council. Without such organisation, the professional administrators and the interest groups fill the void." This is certainly not to say that parties are absent from city politics in the United States or that pressure groups are absent from city politics in England. It does mean that decision-making powers in England are centralized and concentrated by the party system, which is relatively well developed, while in the United States they are decentralized and fragmented by the pressure-group system, which is given more room to flourish by virtue of the loosely organized party system.

The formal constitution of English local government, together with its complementary party system, are mainly responsible for making the city council the center of community decision-making, but there are other factors at work as well. Rarely is the referendum used as a decision-making mechanism in England. Invariably, decisions are taken by the elected and permanent officials of the council and, no matter how controversial, the issue is only very very rarely thrown back into the community arena for the whole electorate to make its will known directly. In the cities of the United States decision-making powers are not infrequently given back to the electorate when a referendum is held. Over a quarter of the cities studied by Crain et al. (1969: 92) decided to put the fluoridation issue to a vote by referendum. In addition, local election primaries are not held in England, party candidates for local elections being selected by a very small group of local party officials and activists. Moreover, since a majority of wards rarely change hands between parties, selection as a candidate for the right party virtually guarantees eventual election, and this puts a great deal of influence into the hands of the small selection panels which choose candidates. Little work has been done on this aspect of candidate selection, but the system in most cities seems roughly similar to that used to select Parliamentary candidates (cf. Ranney, 1965; Paterson, 1967). The primary, where it is used in America, gives the electorate a greater measure of direct influence over who is to stand in local elections, and to this extent power is distributed over a broader cross-section of the community, rather than being concentrated in the hands of a small handful of local political activists. Nor do English cities use the initiative or the recall which are other mechanisms used in America designed to transfer power from the hands of a few elected officials to those of the whole electorate.

Paradoxically, the broad base of popular support necessary for election to the average American city council seems to paralyze rather than encourage political action. It has been found that some American councilmen have been unwilling to act as political leaders and innovators because this may jeopardize their future electoral success. Adrian (1958) has written that "while a councilman might concentrate upon a particular aspect of municipal policy, it was found to be dangerous for him to seek to make some specific issue a *cause celebre*. If he chose to do so, he immediately subjected himself to greater public attention and scrutiny than was the case for the typical councilman, and he risked defeat on the issue which could in turn have disastrous political consequences for him. There is danger in leadership, relative safety in conformity and anonymity. The study indicated that councilmen were aware of this." (See also Altschuler, 1967: 362-363). The situation of council members in England is quite the reverse. They are continually taking up issues and fighting political battles, because they have the security and protection of their party organizations and party lable—providing, of course, that their stand is not flatly contradictory to their party's general policy. When election time comes around the council member's individual record will count for little. What really matters is his party label and his party organization. Thus, while the American councilman is nervously side-stepping political controversy, and attempting to thrust it back into the community, his English equivalent has nothing to lose by making the council chamber a real political battleground.

It does not follow that the typical English council member invariably responds to the demands of outside groups. He may well be a crusader for causes but he is likely to pick his causes with care, as the study of the politics of comprehensive education (cited above) shows only too well. However, individual council members are free, within fairly broad limits laid down by their party group, to campaign on issues about which they feel strongly. Aldermen are even more independent than councillors because they come up for reelection not every three years but every six years, and they are elected to office not by the electorate as a whole but by their colleagues on the city council. This form of indirect election gives the council even more power for it means that the council itself is responsible for the election of one-third of its own membership. The tradition has grown up of electing aldermen only from among sitting councillors so that they have had the seal of popular approval stamped upon them at one time or another. Even so, once elected to the aldermanic bench there is no reason in principle to fight a popular election ever again, and it is possible to remain on the aldermanic bench for anything up to thirty or forty years. This fact endows the alderman with considerable latitude in choice of political action.[3]

In fact, council members are even more independent than this analysis suggests, for recent research has shown that local factors and local party records are not the main determinants of local election results. As noted earlier, local parties almost invariably form an arm, or are supporters, of the national Conservative, Labour, Liberal, and Communist parties. What determines the election success of any given local party and its candidates is not their particular record in community politics but the record of their national party in national politics (cf. Gregory, 1969; Morris and Newton, 1970; Fletcher, 1967). The Labour Party recently lost control of the vast majority of city councils not because each individual city Labour party fell into disfavor but because the Labour Government was unpopular. The fact that local election outcomes are not determined by local factors but by national ones means that the actions of elected representatives in English local government have little or no effect on their performance in elections. This gives them considerable freedom of political movement and consequently the system is conducive to the most controversial issues being raised, discussed, and fought out within the council by council members, rather than such issues being dropped like hot potatoes into the laps of community leaders outside the council. It must be pointed out, however, that this point is a rather academic one because it seems that most elected representatives are not aware of their freedom from "the law of anticipated reactions" and believe that their own political behavior will affect very directly their reelection or rejection at the next election (cf. Gregory, 1969).

Whether or not they appreciate the full extent of their freedom from electoral constraints, council members in England are sure of the fact that they and only they are the popularly elected officials in the city—they and only they are the elected representatives of the people and, therefore, they have the right to exclusive control of public policy. This contrasts with the system in many American cities whereby not only is the council popularly elected but also a broad range of other officials besides. The "long list" allows for the election of mayors, treasurers, clerks, assessors, auditors, attorneys, departmental heads, school boards, and other special purpose boards and agencies. Each elected official or board forms a separate little center of power which is legitimated by the fact of popular election. This leads to situations which are, to say the least, rather strange in English eyes:

> "Here, for example, is an account given by Councillor Thomas A. Sullivan of his experience as chairman of a sub-committee to review a city budget of more than one hundred million dollars:
>
> "The first witness at my first hearing was the police commissioner.
>
> "Commissioner," I said, "would you like to give us the broad outlines of your program for the year ahead?"
>
> "No," he said, "I would not."
>
> "That was the tone of most of the hearings . . . " [Banfield, 1966: 41].

The concentration of community leaders and decision makers within local councils in England is further facilitated by the fact that councils are large. The largest of them (Liverpool) has one hundred sixty members, while county boroughs (with a population of thirty-three thousand or more) have, on average, fifty-seven members (Committee on the Management of Local Government, vol. 5: 1967: 538). The councils of most cities are certainly large enough to contain representatives of all the most important community groups and organizations. Study of council members has also shown that they have an astonishingly broad range of contacts with community groups (cf. Committee on the Management of Local Government, vol. 2: 1967: ch. 6; Rees and Smith, 1964: 58-59), so that in most local authorities a wide range of political views and the positions of a broad variety of community organizations can be expressed during council debates and committee meetings. This is in contrast with city councils in many American cities which, on average, have five, seven, or nine members (Banfield and Wilson, 1963: 88). As a consequence, a majority of community organizations may be predisposed to act outside the official political forum of their community. Pressure-group activity is generally a great deal more visible in America than in Britain, though it is not necessarily any more important for that reason.

Groups which are represented among the elected members of the council can gain representation as co-opted members of council committees. The practice of co-opting a small number of representatives of leading community organizations onto a few local government committees is widespread in England and Wales. An American observer (Smallwood, 1965: 105) has noted that "the British have been considerably more open than is generally the case in the United States in incorporating many of their groups directly into the very heart of the executive process." One survey (Committee on the Management of Local Government, vol. 5: 1967: 559) found that seventy-eight of the larger cities in England and Wales co-opted members onto their local authority committees, and that the total number of co-optations was only a little short of three thousand. As the report points out, "Co-option to committees aims at broadening the basis of council decisions and in some cases at associating relative outside interests in their work. It acknowledges a need to bring into deliberation members of the public who have a special contribution to make, either because of their expert knowledge or as spokesmen of groups of the community which are closely affected by council decisions and which might otherwise be inadequately represented." Co-option is not of great importance in community decision-making in England; nevertheless it is a factor, however small, which helps to concentrate rather than disperse influences on the decision-making process.

No account of the factors which contribute towards the concentration of decision-making power in English city politics could be complete without a discussion of the committee system. As all the textbooks state, English city government is government by and through committees. Moreover, the deliberations of the vast majority of committees are not accessible to either the press or the general public, which gives committee members more independence to bargain, compromise and take up unpopular positions than if their every word was exposed to public scrutiny and criticism. Decisions made by committees in private must be ratified by the whole council, which meets in public, but, as one source (Humes and Martin, 1969: 103) puts it, "Many English local committees act in an apparently independent fashion, with council approval of their action appearing to be an almost forgone conclusion." It is indeed true that most committee decisions are accepted by the council with little or no discussion, but this is only half the story. Control of the committee system is at the heart of majority group control of the council. In most cases the policies to be pursued by the party group on the council are discussed in each group's caucus meeting by all members of the group plus a few other members of the borough party. These meetings are secret because political parties are private organizations. Once they have made up their minds about an issue each party will pursue its policy in council and committee according to agreed tactics. The majority party can get its own way because it holds a majority of committee places including the committee chairmen, as well as a majority on the whole council. And since it holds a majority on the whole council, the minority party or parties will rarely find it tactically fruitful to force a vote. The council therefore leads back to the committees which, in turn, leads back to the party system, and the end result is the centralization of all policy and decision-making through the internal organization of the majority party. Since the majority party can only retain control of the council and its committees by ensuring that it presents a solid front to the opposition on most important issues, it must have either a strong, natural cohesion, or else a well-developed set of formal and informal rules designed to maintain party discipline. In either case, effective power is concentrated within a single organization and is centralized to the extent that the party organization is centralized. The party groups on some councils maintain a centralized system of party discipline and policy-making which is the envy of all but the most diehard Stalinists.

Another factor is worth mentioning here. In the United States the mass media are predominantly localized with each area having its own radio and television stations, and its own newspapers. The local press seems to be a particularly important center of influence in American cities and in many of them rank second in importance only to the mayor (Clark, 1969). In England the mass media are mostly centralized on London, although very recently a number of local radio stations have been established. At the moment they are too new to have become much of a force in the community. The press is also centralized and the majority of city dwellers read not a local morning paper but one of the national dailies. It is true that a small handful of the larger cities like Birmingham, Glasgow, Sheffield, and Leeds have their own morning newspapers which offer editorial comment and leadership on important community issues, but the vast majority of local newspapers appear in the evening or the weekend, dealing with local social gossip and devoting little space to systematic coverage of serious community issues. Thus another important center of power outside the council is absent in English city politics but present in America.

Lastly, one could point to cultural differences between England and the United States which have helped to shape different types of political structures in the cities. A strong tradition of local self-government has always expressed itself in forcible ways in the United States and is more deeply embedded in the political "ethos" of city government than in England. It could be argued that England is altogether too small and too continuously urbanized to sustain much of a preference for local autonomy or to make this the most practical form of governing cities. Centralized planning and regulation were accepted as necessary evils or as blessings long before the Labour Party encouraged ideas of socialist planning and central control of local government. At the same time, feelings of deference towards the independent authority of the government was probably a great deal more widespread during the formative years of modern English city politics and helped shape a political structure which concentrated power and authority in relatively few hands. The participant political culture of the United States combined with a tradition of local autonomy resulted in a more open and less hierarchical system, with a multiplicity of access points for popular intervention at all its levels. These differences in culture and structure have helped to produce different forms of city government in England and the United States and yet the differences in actual operation of the systems are curious, even paradoxical, in that they are not the ones that seem, at first glance, to be appropriate to a unified system of city government on the one hand, and a segmented and fragmented system on the other.

II

The English pattern of city government seems, on the face of it, to be hierarchical, closed, and elitist. The concentration of local political power in the council, the relative independence of council members once elected, the importance of the party system in organizing one main center of influence within the council and limiting influence of community organizations outside it, and the absence of strong, localized mass media, all contribute towards its hierarchical and elitist appearance. One and only one group is empowered to take important decisions in the city. There are other groups both inside and outside the council and although they may contest issues in an attempt to influence the majority group and its leaders, they are not ultimately able to make final decisions, while the majority group is well placed to ignore or overrule their political demands. Political attention is focused on the leading members of the majority group in the council who form the peak of the local pyramid of power and influence. In this sense, English city government is hierarchical and elitist. Moreover, since there is no formal center of power of any importance outside the council, no elected officials other than council members themselves, no incentive for powerful cliques of community leaders to exercise themselves outside the official decision-making bodies, and few powerful local newspapers, or TV or radio stations, there is one dominant political arena in the community and one main access route to it. To become influential the political actor must go through the council and capture the interest and sympathy of the majority group and the administration. On a bipartisan issue a minority group might suffice, but in any case no channel of political activity which does not pass through the council is likely to be notably effective. In the sense that there is one center of political activity and few access routes to it, the English system of city government is relatively closed.

In contrast to this, the system of city government in the United States seems to be pluralistic, open, and sensitive to public opinion. This is particularly true of the fragmented type of city government. Its many centers of independent power mean that political decision-making takes the form of bargaining between many different groups and interests. The fact that decisions may be influenced, if not actually made, by many different bodies in many different places also means that there are different political arenas with different access points to them. The American system of government, as Dahl has strongly emphasized (1967: 326) has a multiplicity of access points at all its levels. If a group fails to achieve its goal on its first attempt at one level, it can try again at a different point in the political system. In this sense the system is an open one. A multiplicity of decision-making centers encourages a multiplicity of interest groups, and the formation of these centers of power creates still more decision-making centers. Insofar as this type of fragmented political system is enclosed at all, it is enclosed by a highly porous political boundary which enables group influences to pass from one part of the system to another so that influences from all quarters eventually filter throughout the system and pervade the overall character of policy outcomes. To this extent the fragmented type of city government is sensitive and responsive to the changing moods of political opinion. These characteristics have been strongly emphasized in the pluralist literature on American community power structure.

The contrast between English and American forms of city government and politics is not nearly as stark as this analysis suggests. There are social and political processes at work which make English city government less elitist and closed, and equally strong influences which make American city government less open and pluralistic than many American observers have claimed. As so often happens, formal differences in structure are modified by informal processes, and organizations which seem dissimilar on paper and in theory, turn out to be not so very different in practice. The purpose of the second half of this paper is to explore some of these differences and similarities. To do this effectively it is necessary to distinguish rather more carefully between different types of American city government and to employ rather more actively the distinction between fragmented and segmented systems. The discussion will start with an examination of community decision-making bodies in England and the United States.

With a few rare exceptions, published studies indicate that political decision makers at most level of Western society tend to be drawn very heavily from the high-status, older, and male sections of the community. Conversely, the least well-represented social groupings are the young, those with low status, and females. Explanations for this pattern are not difficult to find and do not need elaborating here, but there are also indications that the pattern can be very strongly modified, or, in some cases, totally reversed by the interaction of class and party factors in political recruitment.

In their study of four cities, Williams and Adrian (1963: 78) found that manual workers made up only eight, four, eight, and twenty-four percent of council members. Underrepresentation to a similar degree has been found in other studies (Adrian and Press, 1968: 64-65). It is quite clear from the considerable work to date, city councils of England are not made up of a cross section of the adult population, but they do seem to contain an appreciably larger proportion of manual workers than in the United States. In Birmingham, manual workers comprised almost a third of the Labour group of the council in 1966 and, as the majority group, Labour controlled the council and all its important positions (Morris and Newton, 1969). Miller (1958b) found that 32 percent of Bristol city council was made up of labor and trade union leaders, which, as he points out, was considerably more than in Seattle or Atlanta. Miller's findings have been confirmed by a follow-up study showing that

Bristol had many more labor and union leaders among its decision makers than six American and two Mexican cities (D'Antonio et al., 1961: 328).

Miller explains these differences in terms of two factors—the different occupational prestige systems of England and the United States, and the different council-community power complex in the two countries. The English community, he states (1958b: 13-14) accords the businessman lower status than in America and is, therefore, less likely to select him for a community leader. Banfield and Wilson (1963: 246) opt for a very similar explanation to account for the businessman's importance in American city politics. Three things may be said about this explanation. First, it is of highly dubious validity since there is little evidence to suggest the British evaluate businessmen that much lower than the Americans. Indeed, businessmen are still the most heavily overrepresented occupational group on the local authority councils of English cities (Committee on the Management of Local Government, vol. 2: 1967: 20-24; Morris and Newton, 1970). Second, it does not explain why manual workers, and trade union and labor leaders are better represented in England, unless, of course, one is prepared to argue that they are given higher status and prestige in this country than in America. Third, there are more simple and more powerful explanations of the differences between England and America.

The first is the party system which, as has already been said, operates in almost all urban areas in England and Wales. Particularly important is the fact that the Labour Party being a left-wing, socialist party, recruits manual workers into its ranks, some of whom rise to political positions of considerable authority. This is particularly true in local politics where, using the Labour Party ladder, working-class political activists can rise to high office and become not just council members but committee chairmen or council leaders. Epstein (1967: 199) has examined at some length the effects of "class distinct party systems" on political recruitment in Western societies and concludes that the Socialist working-class party is distinctive in recruiting a share of its leaders from the working class. As Epstein points out, the party system in the United States is not so clearly divided along class lines and, as a result, proportionately few positions of political importance are filled by people of low socioeconomic status (see also Rokkan and Campbell, 1960; Matthews, 1954: 47-48). To the extent that party organizations of most American cities are more diffuse and more class heterogeneous than are those in England, they are less likely to recruit manual workers to positions of authority. The small proportion of American cities with a well-developed, class-distinct party system is likely to recruit more manual workers than usual (for example, "Delta"—one of four cities studied by Williams and Adrian, 1963: 78), but these are the exceptions rather than the rule.

Bias against individuals of low socioeconomic status in the United States is further strengthened in nonpartisan cities where, as Adrian (1952) has found, elections favor those wealthy enough to pay their election expenses and whose high socioeconomic status makes them conspicuous to the community. Working-class candidates must rely heavily on party finance, party organization, and a party label to make them meaningful to the electorate. Their chances for electoral success are reduced drastically if political parties are debarred in theory and in practice from elections. In addition, there is evidence that nonpartisan elections bring out a disproportionately middle-class, Republican vote, thereby weighing the balance still further against working-class parties and candidates (Salisbury and Black, 1963; Williams and Adrian, 1959; Lineberry and Fowler, 1967; Lane, 1961: 270). Dye (1969: 276-277) has summarized the electoral consequences of the nonpartisan ballot:

"nonpartisanship reduces the turnout of labor, low income, ethnic, Democratic voters, and consequently, increases the influence of well educated, high income, white, Anglo-Saxon Protestant, Republican voters, who continue to come to the polls in nonpartisan elections. In addition, nonpartisanship means the recruitment of candidates will be left to civic associations, or ad hoc groups of one kind or another, rather than Democratic or Republican party organizations. This difference in recruitment and endorsement practices tends to give an advantage to middle class, white, Protestant candidates. Candidates from minority groups are rarely put forward and endorsed by newspapers and influential civic associations."

Nonpartisanship is unheard of in England, even though some of the smaller towns have a relatively underdeveloped party system. More than two-thirds of all American cities with a population of fifty thousand or more are officially nonpartisan.

At-large elections add further to the bias in favor of high-status parties and candidates, while ward-based elections tilt the balance slightly towards manual-worker candidates and parties. Williams and Adrian (1963: 77, 146) pick out a number of reasons for this. First, ward-based elections overcome the handicap of nonvoting among low social strata. In working-class wards it does not matter whether 10 percent or 90 percent of the population votes as long as the majority votes for the working-class party. Second, ward-based elections can be cheaper than at-large elections. The working-class party can choose to fight on its own ground, and is not forced to make a more expensive community-wide campaign. And third, the residence requirements of some ward-based elections mean that some candidates will be drawn from working-class areas and are less likely, therefore, to be the usual sort of professional and upper-class election candidate. While at-large elections are common in the United States, local elections in the larger English cities are ward-based. Moreover, the number of wards is generally much larger in Britain than in those American cities which use ward-based elections, so that a city the size of Birmingham (with just over a million population) is split into thirty-nine wards, about a third of which are solidly working class and normally return a Labour candidate.

Nonpartisanship and at-large elections usually go together but neither is universal practice even in the medium- to small-sized cities where they predominate. Many of the largest cities like Chicago, Detroit, and San Francisco are nonpartisan in theory but not in practice. Nonpartisanship is also generally part of the council-manager and commission form of government, whereas the larger cities which more usually have mayor-council governments are generally partisan in their electoral arrangements. In terms of the recruitment of community decision makers, therefore, the English pattern of unified city government is most closely approached by the segmented form of system as typified in the United States by the larger, partisan, mayor-council cities. It must also be remembered that cities are smaller in England, so that, size for size, a large proportion of American cities are nonpartisan and, to this extent, are likely to elect a relatively small number of working-class citizens to positions of authority.

Besides its effects on the class composition of community decision-making bodies, the free play of a well-developed class distinct party system has consequences for the recruitment of other sections of the population to positions of political authority. Women are not generally found in large numbers at any level of the political hierarchy in Western societies. In none of the eight cities studied by Williams and Adrian (1963: 78) and by Alford (1969: 154) did women form more than 11 percent of the council, and the average figure was nearer 5 than 10 percent. Half the councils had no women on them at all. Less than 7 percent of council members in Los Angeles county in 1957 were women (Huckshorn and Young, 1960). Adrian and Press (1968: 249) also refer to the extremely small number, and point out that until fairly recently even such large cities as Los Angeles and Milwaukee had no women council members at all (see also Jennings, 1964: 40). Women are certainly underrepresented on city councils in England, but less so, it seems, than in the United States. They make up 12 percent of council members in all local authorities, but the figure is appreciably higher in urban than in rural areas. In London (Sharpe, 1962: 37) and Birmingham (Morris and Newton, 1969) about one in five council members is female. In Wolverhampton (Jones, 1969: 377), Sheffield (Hampton, 1970: 188), Banbury (Stacey, 1960: 44), and Leeds (Sharpe, 1967: 141) the ratio is slightly higher.

In the main, women city council members in English cities seem to be recruited by the low-status, left-wing Labour Party. This is so partly for economic and partly for social and ideological reasons. The high-status Conservative Party can usually find enough financially independent or self-employed males to fill its election slates. Indeed, in the upper-class house the man may well be better able to pursue a part-time political life than his wife who may feel the need to stay at home with the children. In the working-class house, however, the man must be a full-time breadwinner, and it is his wife who is better able to spare time for politics. Besides this, the selection committees of the Labour Party are more in favor of female emancipation than those of the Conservative Party (Paterson, 1967: 45; Ranney, 1965: 198). In fact, women candidates for the Birmingham Labor Party are more likely to be given a safe seat than men, but in the Conservative Party the opposite is true. In contrast to this situation, the class heterogeneity of the two main American parties is more likely to result in top political vacancies being filled by more affluent men, and thus the American system offers fewer opportunities for women to become community decision makers. There is also a faint suggestion in the literature that the class-distinct party system is likely to recruit proportionately more young adults, but the comparative evidence is so slim that this must remain a most tentative suggestion. The figures for working-class and female community decision makers are fairly clear, however, and show that English cities are more likely to give political weight to these two social groupings by comparison with nonpartisan American cities.

The presence or absence of a well-developed party system (class distinct or otherwise) may also affect the locus of community decision-making, especially the extent to which council members are effective decision makers. One study of British local politics has pointed out that the power of elected representatives over the administration is much weakened when the former are not organized into unified party groups. The study concludes that "In the absence of groups and strong, long serving committee chairmen, much of the co-ordination of present policy and even thinking about future policy has passed into the hands of the Rural District Officials" (Bealey et al., 1965: 339). Another study suggests that appointed officials may have more influence over policy formation when they work in a city with a loosely organized party system (Bulpitt, 1967: 92). Suggestions along the same lines are to be found in the literature about American city politics. Williams and Adrian (1963: 297-300) found that when council politics was not structured along party lines, administrators tended to act as policy makers (see also Wood, 1958: 162-163; Fiellin, 1962, and for a similar observation about state legislatures, see Zeller, 1954: 204-205). It seems from these studies that a unified party group on a council can act as an important counterbalance to the power of permanent officials, although many other factors no doubt blur and confuse the pattern. However, to the extent that American cities have generally less well-developed and more fluid party systems, it can be tentatively hypothesized that their appointed local government officials will be more influential in decision-making processes than the administrators of city government in England. As before, the contrast lies between cities whose lack of a party system helps to create a fragmented form of government and those whose party systems help create a unified or segmented form of government.

It could be argued that the social composition of decision-making bodies and the locus of decision-making powers are less important than the extent to which the system is open and pluralistic in its operations. It might be argued, for instance, that irrespective of who is charged with final responsibility for decisions, the fragmented type of city government is one which permits more grass-roots participation, more citizen control over elected officials, and a freer and more open interplay of group interests in determining policy outcomes. While this might carry some weight as an argument about the theory of fragmented government, it is less plausible as a description of its practice. Fragmented government is so ill-adapted to the problems of modern urban life that it has, in many cases, undergone a metamorphosis into something better adapted, but far from fragmented. This response to formal fragmentation of community decision-making structures consists in organizing and centralizing the pieces through informal, but nonetheless highly effective political methods. Banfield's account of how this is done in Chicago is well known. In fact, the Chicago system is informally centralized to such a degree that "the heads of the Democratic machine had ample power to decide almost any matter" (Banfield and Wilson, 1963: 244). The Chicago system starts with the ideal that everybody in general and nobody in particular should have decision-making power, but it ends with the fact that power in the city is virtually monopolized by a small group of professional politicians who control the Democratic machine. The problems caused by extreme decentralization in the name of an open, pluralist political system are cured, in this case, by going to an extreme centralization.

Chicago is occasionally regarded as an exception to rules of American city politics, but it is not clear that it forms a minority of one in its centralization of political power. The number of comparable depth studies of other large- and medium-sized cities is still rather small; no clear pattern seems to emerge from cities that have been examined carefully. New Haven, presented by Dahl as a good example of pluralist democracy, has a highly centralized political executive with considerable autonomy in certain matters. The whole urban redevelopment program was "the direct product of a small handful of leaders" (Dahl, 1963: 114). The elaborate structure of citizen participation in the program was, furthermore, "deliberately *created* by Mayor Lee" (Dahl, 1963: 133). On another occasion the Mayor's new city charter was passed by the Board of Aldermen, although a majority of them opposed it in private, because all but three of them had an income dependent on the city administration, and particularly on the Mayor (Dahl, 1963: 251-253). The Mayor was instrumental in changing the total power structure of the city from one composed of petty sovereignties to an executive centered coalition in which he was "a member of all the major coalitions, and in each one of them he was one of the two or three men of highest influence" (Dahl, 1963: 200). All this does not show that New Haven was as highly centralized as Chicago, nor does it suggest that Mayor Lee could do anything he liked. It does suggest that, like Chicago, New Haven's formal decentralization had been overcome to some degree and that power over some important matters was centered on one individual and his staff, rather than on one body of elected representatives. In this respect New Haven seems to differ only in degree but not in kind from Chicago, and to this extent the cherished faith in grass-roots autonomy, resulting from a decentralized power structure, needs a careful reexamination. Indeed, it has been suggested that the conclusions of the elitist and pluralist schools are not substantially different (see, e.g., Alford, 1969: 194; Rosenbaum, 1967; Newton, 1969).

It would be unwise to push this line of argument too far and claim that the majority of American cities were centralized in this manner, for it is undoubtedly true that numerous small- and medium-sized cities in the United States can be correctly classified as having fragmented power structures. These are mainly cities which were successfully captured by the reform movement which aimed to take political power out of the hands of a small number of professional politicians and put it into those of the mass of decent citizens. In such systems, organized groups and citizens were to be given many opportunities to influence decisions at various stages of the policy process. This, at least, was the theory even if it is not quite how it came to operate in practice. In the first place, the reformed system of fragmented, open government was set up on the principle of the economic market place in which every interested party would bargain in a spirit of free enterprise and open competition. The system was designed to be pluralist in the sense that groups which organized themselves to protect their own interests would be able to play an influential part in the political process. The flaw in the pleasant logic of the argument is that such a system of "free enterprise" politics tends to degenerate into a process of natural selection through survival of the fittest. The system is indeed pluralist in the sense that organized groups are free to compete with each other for influence, but it is also elitist in the sense that the poorly organized or the unorganized are unlikely to be strong enough to compete on equal terms, so that ultimately this section of society becomes politically poverty-stricken in the same way as it becomes financially poverty-stricken in the economic world. Pluralist theory thus becomes a tautology which states that the competition of organized and influential groups demonstrates the presence of competing interests which are organized and influential. Those who are unorganized or influential are generally left out of the picture.[4]

There is further evidence to show that nonpartisan cities also put minority and working-class groups at a disadvantage in deciding actual policy outcomes in terms of "who gets what?" A recent research report (Lineberry and Fowler, 1967) produces data which suggest that "reformed institutions maximize the power of the middle class" and that "the electoral institutions of reformed governments make public policy less responsible to the demands arising out of social conflicts in the population." Reformed cities seem less responsive to their socioeconomic cleavages than unreformed cities, and impose a further set of formal political disadvantages on top of the already extensive informal social disadvantages of minority and working-class groups.

The significance of this conclusion is much reduced when it is placed alongside the finding that reformed cities tend to have less marked socioeconomic cleavages than other cities. Some of its significance is restored, however, by two other observations. First, although it may be true that reformed cities tend to have a smaller proportion of nonwhites, foreign born, old, and manual workers than unreformed cities (cf. Schnore and Alford, 1963; Sherbenou, 1961; Kessel, 1962), it is still true to say that they generally have such groups in their populations and that nonpartisanship weighs heavily against the political aspirations of these minority groups. Second, the finding that reformed cities tend to have a homogeneous population has itself been questioned on the basis of data which suggest that "with the exception of race, reformed cities appear somewhat more homogeneous than unreformed cities. While the differences in homogeneity are more clear-cut than class differences, this hardly indicates that reformed cities are the havens of a socially homogeneous population" (Lineberry and Fowler, 1967). It seems that more work is required to establish the homogeneity or heterogeneity of reformed cities but meanwhile it seems fair to conclude that the reformed type of city government operates in such a way as to counteract many of the pluralistic qualities which are, in theory, inherent in this form of city government.

The English form of city government manages to escape at least some of the political dangers. It is formally centralized so that it is not faced with Chicago's problems. On the other hand, it does not compound the disadvantages of the already disadvantaged in the same way as do nonpartisan cities. The English form of unified city government is centralized at the city level to a high degree but not so rigidly as to deny the possibility of a certain measure of genuine pluralism. On the contrary, the system allows a broad range of groups, organizations and sectional interests an official access to the decision-making process by giving a relatively large number of them the opportunity to get their representatives or spokesmen elected or appointed to the most important public body in the city. The system is pluralist in the sense that the structure permits in a passive way a set of organized group interests to emerge within it. This guarantees some sections of the population a certain minimum representation in community decision-making. The system is also pluralist in a more positive and active way in that councils have institutionalized a political division between parties which represent, in a very general way, the middle-class and the working-class interests of the city. The class-distinct party system, together with ward-based elections and the internal arrangements between parties in the council, ensure that working-class representatives are elected to the council and play a part in it, especially when there is a Labour majority, as, indeed, there often is. The fact that there is one main line of social division between middle and working class in English society simplifies the task of creating a body which represents the larger and most important social groups. And the fact that this social division is paralleled by a political division between the Labour and Conservative parties further simplifies the party political task of interest aggregation. This is a more difficult and complex task in the United States where social divisions run not only along class lines but along religious and ethnic lines, as well.

One could not conclude from this that all or even most interests and social groupings are represented on the council of the average English city, although it is fair to say that there are fewer formal bars against working-class participation and more informal incentives for working-class participation than in the average American city. The class struggle is traditionally the most important battle in English politics and it has been successfully institutionalized in the majority of English cities. However, groups which are defined as being outside this struggle are overlooked and excluded from the pluralist system to the same extent as they are in America. Colored immigrants are the most significant group of this kind, the poorest and most deprived are another. To say that nothing formally prevents these groups from entering pluralist politics is not to deny that powerful social forces of an informal nature operate against this happening. Pluralism is a "natural" outgrowth of some sections of society, especially the middle-class sections, but it is an "unnatural" development in others which must be actively encouraged rather than passively permitted. Nonpartisanship, it appears, actively discourages working-class participation in pluralist politics, partisanship in most American cities passively permits it, while the class-distinct party system actively encourages it to some extent.

A good example of the emergent elitism of reformed city government in the United States and of the element of built-in pluralism of English city politics lies in the role of trade unions in community decision-making. English trade unions are an integral part of the Labour Party at national and at local levels, and the class-distinct party system, combined with ward-based elections, virtually guarantees some trade unionists a voice on the local council. Trade union representatives are also generally co-opted onto a handful of public bodies and committees in any large city. Besides this, research into Birmingham politics has shown that the leadership group of the Labour council members was constantly receiving delegations of trade unions wishing to make representations and influence decisions. When the Labour group forms a majority on the council, as it did between 1952-1965, the trade union movement has direct access to the most powerful group of men in the community and, indeed, can turn to its own members of this powerful group. In the smaller and medium-sized reformed cities a number of important channels of influence are cut off for the working class. In a study of nine large cities (Banfield, 1966: 12), it is said that labor groups have little political influence. The same could not be said for any large English city.

Another example occurs in a comparison one might make of the way in which the fluoridation issue has been handled on either side of the Atlantic. In the United States, the cities with a centralized form of government were able to react in a positive way in either rejecting or accepting the measure, whereas the less centralized cities were more frequently helpless to do anything in the face of the anti-fluoridation campaign (Crain et al. 1969). Fragmentation, sustained by nonpartisanship, resulted in one small but vociferous group being able to block all fluoridation measures. The outcome of this political struggle was not a "pluralist compromise" (a compromise in this, as in many other political battles, is not possible), but one in which one section of the community registered an outright victory over another. The victory is not guaranteed in the long run, but, to twist a famous phrase, in the long run we can all get rotten teeth. The contrast with the way in which fluoridation was handled in one English town is interesting (Brier, 1970). As in the American examples it was favored by a wide range of medical officials, both publicly and privately employed. As in many American cases the final decision was against fluoridation in a firm and decided way; the issue was not allowed to die or fade away because official bodies were frightened to take hold of it, as it was in some nonpartisan cities in the United States. The issue was decided by the elected members of the council and not by outside pressure groups. The elected officials were successful in overruling the wishes of paid administrators in the public health and other departments. In addition the majority group was so predominantly working class in outlook, if not in social composition, that "middle class minority views tend to be disregarded because councillors are representatives of the working class majority and their contacts with alternative values are restricted" (Brier, 1970: 154). Lastly, the safe majority of the Labour group on the council seems to have limited the power of administrators and given more power to the elected representatives of the majority group. Thus, fluoridation was rejected but not as a result of the pressure group activities of community organizations; the decision was taken by the working-class majority group on the council against the wishes of their professional advisors. These comparisons rest upon a single case study but they illustrate and confirm the points made earlier in the paper.

The danger to pluralist democracy in the English system lies in the tendency for council members to have too much independent power and autonomy of action. A well-organized and disciplined party with a safe majority is in an excellent position to ignore the pleas or demands of other groups inside and outside the council. In one study of three English cities it is reported (Peterson, 1969) that the majority groups virtually ignored the wishes of teachers unions on the comprehensive schools issue. The working-class members of Hull county borough were able to ignore the advice of their professionally qualified, medical administrators. In some cases it is as though council members are so convinced that they represent public opinion that they refuse to acknowledge the legitimacy of outside demands. As one councillor is quoted as saying (Brier, 1970: 162), "We are the responsible people who must take the decision, not those who are jogging our elbow."

CONCLUSION

The picture which emerges from this series of paired comparisons of English and American city politics is clear in parts but unclear in others. It is clear that the formal structure of city government is entirely different in the two countries. In theory, American city government is fragmented and decentralized. This gives government an open and unstructured appearance which makes it look as if the entire community forms the political arena and not just a few institutions within it. Anybody or any group can enter the arena in order to fight a political battle. There are no formal barriers to jump, or gates to pass through, or structures to penetrate. The group struggle proceeds unconstrained by rigid political structures or institutions and power is decentralized to such an extent that this group struggle is the power structure. This aspect of city politics has been heavily emphasized by those who point to the pluralist nature of American city politics. But, as so often happens, this formal structure is modified by actual operation. In the case of Chicago, the formal structure has been totally transformed by a very high degree of informal centralization. The open, fragmented, and pluralist structure has become a closed and centralized one which concentrates extensive power for independent political action in the hands of a few individuals. The same process of centralization has occurred in New Haven to a greater extent than Dahl is prepared to recognize, although it is not clear exactly how far Mayor Lee was able to centralize his city nor is it clear how typical New Haven is of other American cities.

At the other extreme from Chicago are the smaller, nonpartisan cities. These are decentralized in theory and in practice but they are not necessarily pluralistic for this reason. Nonpartisanship has built in a bias against working-class and minority-group influence. It was, after all, a device used by reformers to destroy the corruption of working-class machine politics, and it has been successful in its creation of a political system which favors middle-class control. Nonpartisan cities are not, therefore, as open or pluralistic as they might be, even in their formal structure because their no-party politics puts some groups at a disadvantage. In general, these formal disadvantages are superimposed on groups which are already disadvantaged by lack of money, time, political skills, competence, and so on. The political arena of the fragmented, nonpartisan city is indeed open, but it is more open to some than to others. In this situation pluralist, free enterprise politics is largely middle-class politics.

English city government is highly centralized and is organized from start to finish along partisan lines. The class-distinct party system helps to recruit and to give political power to those groups which are disadvantaged by the machinery of nonpartisanship. This is almost universally true of working-class and trade union interests, although it is not the case for minority colored groups. The dangers to pluralist democracy in English city government lie not so much in the exclusion of working-class groups from political influence but in the exclusion of some community groups, working or middle class, from centers of influence. The system is centralized to such an extent that the majority group on the council can often afford to ignore the demands of organizations outside the formal machinery of city politics. In this respect English city government has greater affinities with the larger, more centralized, partisan, mayor-council cities of the United States than with smaller, nonpartisan, mayor-council or commission cities.

NOTES

1. Technically speaking, this paper is concerned only with the seventy-nine English county boroughs, but much of what is said about them applies also to the urban counties and to the larger noncounty boroughs and urban districts.

2. In order to distinguish party organizations of the whole community from party organizations within the council, the latter are generally called "party groups." By the political executive I mean the much smaller number of elected officials within the majority group who, like the inner cabinet at Westminster, are at the very center of the formal decision-making apparatus and who perform a leadership and policy-initiating role within the council. By the administration (a term used later in the paper), I mean the bureaucratic machinery, staffed by appointed, permanent officials, whose role it is to carry out the policies agreed upon by the elected members of the council.

3. Aldermanic seats have been abolished by local government reform taking effect in 1974.

4. I have argued this theme at greater length elsewhere—(1969: 215-219). See also Kariel (1966: 103-113).

REFERENCES

ADRIAN, C. R. (1958) "Leadership and decision-making in manager cities." Public Administration Review 18: 208-213.

——— (1952) "Some general characteristics of nonpartisan elections." American Political Science Review 46: 766-776.

——— and C. PRESS (1968) Governing Urban America. New York: McGraw-Hill.

ALFORD, R. R. (1969) Bureaucracy and Participation. Chicago: Rand McNally.

——— and N. BOADEN (1969) "Sources of diversity in English local government decisions." Public Administration 47: 203-223.

ALTSHULER, A. A. (1967) The City Planning Process: A Political Analysis. New York: Cornell Univ. Press.

BANFIELD, E. C. (1966) Big City Politics. New York: Random House.

――― (1960) "The political implications of metropolitan growth." Daedalus 90 (Winter).

――― and J. Q. WILSON (1963) City Politics. Cambridge: Harvard Univ. and MIT Presses.

BEALEY, F. et al. (1965) Constituency Politics. London: Faber and Faber.

BIRCH, A. H. (1959) Small Town Politics. Oxford: Oxford Univ. Press.

BRIER, A. P. (1970) "The decision process in local government: a case study of fluoridation in Hull." Public Administration 48: 153-168.

BULPITT, J. G. (1967) Party Politics in English Local Government. London: Longmans.

Central Office of Information (1964) Local Government in Britain. London: H.M.S.O.

CLARK, T. N. (1969) "An interchange model of community leadership." Presented at the International Conference on Community Decision-Making, Milan, Italy, July.

Committee on the Management of Local Government (1967) The Local Government Councillor, vol. 2; Management of Local Government, vol. 5. London: H.M.S.O.

CRAIN, R. L. et al. (1969) The Politics of Community Conflict. Indianapolis: Bobbs-Merrill.

DAHL, R. A. (1967) Pluralist Democracy in the United States. Chicago: Rand McNally.

――― (1963) Who Governs? New Haven: Yale Univ. Press.

D'ANTONIO, M. et al. (1961) "Institutional and occupational representations in eleven community systems." American Sociological Review 26: 440-446.

DYE, T. R. (1969) Politics in States and Communities. Englewood Cliffs, N.J.: Prentice-Hall.

EPSTEIN, L. D. (1967) Political Parties in Western Democracies. London: Pall Mall.

FIELLIN, A. (1962) "The functions of informal groups in legislative institutions." Journal of Politics 24: 72-91.

FLETCHER, P. (1967) "The results analysed," in L. J. Sharpe (ed.) Voting in Cities.

FREEMAN, L. C. (1968) Patterns of Local Community Leadership. Indianapolis: Bobbs-Merrill.

FRIEND, J. K. and W. N. JESSOP (1969) Local Government and Strategic Choice. London: Tavistock.

GREEN, B.S.R. (1967) Community Decision-Making in Georgian City. Bath: Ph.D. dissertation. Bath University of Technology.

GREGORY, R. (1969) "Local elections and the rule of anticipated reactions." Political Studies 17: 31-47.

GOODALL, L. (1968) The American Metropolis. Columbus, Ohio: Charles E. Merrill.

HAMPTON, W. (1970) Democracy and Community: A Study of Politics in Sheffield. London: Oxford Univ. Press.

HUCKSHORN, R. J. and C. E. YOUNG (1960) "A study of voting splits on city councils in Los Angeles county." Western Political Quarterly 13: 479-497.

HUMES, S. and E. MARTIN (1969) The Structure of Local Government. The Hague: International Union Local Authorities.

JENNINGS, M. K. (1964) Community Influentials. New York: Free Press.

JONES, G. W. (1969) Borough Politics. London: Macmillan.

KAPLAN, H. (1967) Urban Political Systems. New York: Columbia Univ. Press.

KARIEL, H. S. (1966) The Promise of Politics. Englewood Cliffs, N.J.: Prentice-Hall.

KESSEL, J. H. (1962) "Governmental structure and political environment." American Political Science Review 56: 615-620.

LANE, R. E. (1961) Political Life. New York: Free Press.

LINEBERRY, R. L. and E. P. FOWLER (1967) "Reformism and public policies in American cities." American Political Science Review 61: 701-716.

LOCKARD, D. (1963) The Politics of State and Local Government. New York: Macmillan.

MARSHALL, A. H. (1967) Local Government Administration Abroad, vol. 4. Committee on the Management of Local Government. London: Her Majesty's Stationary Office.

MATTHEWS, D. R. (1954) The Social Background of Political Decision-Makers. New York; Doubleday.

MILLER, D. C. (1958a) "Decision-making cliques in community power structures: a comparative study of an American and an English city." American Journal of Sociology 64: 299-310.

——— (1958b) "Industry and community power structure: a comparative study of an American and English city." American Sociological Review 23: 9-15.

MORRIS, D. S. and K. NEWTON (1970) "Turnout in local elections." Birmingham Faculty of Commerce and Social Science Discussion Paper F.8.

——— (1969) "The occupational composition of party groups on Birmingham council: 1920-1966." Birmingham Faculty of Commerce and Social Science Discussion Paper F.3.

NEWTON, K. (1969) "Critique of the pluralist model." Acta Sociologica 12: 209-223.

OSTROM, V. et al. (1961) "The organization of government is metropolitan areas: a theoretical enquiry." American Political Science Review 55: 831-842.

PATERSON, P. (1967) The Selectorate. London: MacGibbon and Kee.

PETERSON, P. E. (1969) "The politics of comprehensive education in British cities: A re-examination of British interest group theory." Delivered to the Sixty-Fifth Annual Meeting of the American Political Science Association, New York, September 2-6.

——— and P. KANTOR (1970) "Citizen participation, political parties and Democratic theory: an analysis of local politics in England." Delivered to the Sixty-Sixth Annual Meeting of the American Political Science Association, Los Angeles, September 8-12.

RANNEY, A. (1965) Pathways to Parliament. London: Macmillan.

REES, A. M. and T. SMITH (1964) Town Councillors. London: Acton Society Trust.

ROKKAN, S. and A. CAMPBELL (1960) "Citizen participation in political life: Norway and the United States of America." International Social Science Journal 12: 69-99.

ROSENBAUM, A. (1967) "Community power and political theory: a case of misperception." Berkeley Journal of Sociology 1967: 91-116.

SALISBURY, R. H. and G. BLACK (1963) "Class and party in partisan and non-partisan elections." American Political Science Review 57: 584-592.

SAYRE, W. S. and H. KAUFMAN (1965) Governing New York City. New York: W. W. Norton.

SCHNORE, L. and R. R. ALFORD (1963) "Forms of government and socioeconomic characteristics of suburbs." Administrative Science Quarterly 8: 1-17.

SHARPE, L. J. (1967) Voting in Cities. London: Macmillan.

——— (1962) A Metropolis Votes. London: The London School of Economics and Political Science.

SHERBENOU, E. L. (1961) "Class, participation, and the council-manager plan." Public Administration Review 21: 131-135.

SMALLWOOD, F. (1965) Greater London: The Politics of Metropolitan Reform. Indianapolis: Bobbs-Merrill.

STACEY, M. (1960) Tradition and Change. Oxford: Oxford Univ. Press.

WILLIAMS, O. P. and C. R. ADRIAN (1963) Four Cities. Philadelphia: Univ. of Pennsylvania Press.

——— (1959) "The insulation of politics under the nonpartisan ballot." American Political Science Review 53: 1052-1063.

WOLFF, R. P. (1960) "Miami metro." Reprinted in P. B. Coulter (ed.) Politics of
   Metropolitan Areas. New York: Thomas Y. Crowell.
WOOD, R. C. (1961) 1400 Government. Cambridge: Harvard Univ. Press.
——— (1958) Suburbia: Its People and their Politics. Boston: Houghton Mifflin.
ZELLER, B. (1954) American State Legislatures. New York: Thomas Y. Crowell.

Chapter 3

The Pursuit of Efficiency: Values and Structure in the Changing Politics of Swedish Municipalities

Thomas J. Anton

The fundamental difficulty behind cross-national studies of community politics is that "community" means different things in different national settings. The organization of local units, the scope of activities controlled or influenced by local units, and the subjective meanings attached to such activities by participants all vary considerably from one country to the next. Foreign scholars quickly discover these problems as they attempt to study and interpret events in one setting in terms of analytic frames of reference taken from another.[1] How they solve these difficulties depends largely on what part of social reality is of most interest to them. In what follows I am most interested in understanding policy-making that takes place in Swedish localities. For that purpose it is not enough merely to do away with American analytic assumptions. It is also necessary to come to grips with environmental, cultural and structural characteristics of the Swedish setting—to construct a map, as it were, of what is going on. As will be apparent, such an effort raises different, but equally fundamental, questions about the purposes of cross-national community research.

THE ENVIRONMENT OF LOCAL POLITICS IN SWEDEN

In a land full of paradoxes for foreigners, a first step in understanding is to realize that local politics is not what it appears to be. Indeed, at this moment it is quite impossible to say with very much precision what local politics is, for, since 1952, the Swedes have been engaged in a restructuring of local units that can only be described as revolutionary. Legislation implemented in that year reduced the number of local governments from 2,500 to 1,000, while at the same time reducing the number of elected local officials by several thousand. Complaints about this extraordinary change began almost immediately and led, in 1962, to another legislative decision, not to retract the earlier reform, but to extend it even further! According to the second reform bill, the number of local units in Sweden will be reduced to 274—roughly one-tenth the number that existed in 1950—with the reduction phased so as to be completed by the middle of this decade. Currently existing localities have been allowed a certain amount of freedom to work out their own procedures for amalgamation as well as their own time schedules, so that the pace of structural change varies from one area to the next. But all local units either have completed, or are in the process of completing, final arrangements for a new national system of 274 local governments.[2] When the final goal is reached, local units will be much larger than they were, on the average, the number of elected local officials will be greatly reduced and, presumably, patterns of local politics will be quite different.

Just how "different" such patterns will be is extraordinarily difficult to judge, in part because the more-or-less constant reshuffling of structural boundaries during the past twenty years hampers any attempt to establish a "base line" from which to estimate differences, and in part because structural reshuffling has been accompanied by equally significant changes in the scope of local responsibilities. A major local responsibility was eliminated in 1965, when local police forces were replaced by a national police system.[3] Changes of the opposite kind have been far more significant, however. Pursuing an active policy of "decentralization" the national government during the last few years has gradually shifted major responsibilities to local units.[4] Major readjustments have also taken place in the absence of national legislation. In the Stockholm area, for example, an entirely new unit of government—the Greater Stockholm Council— came into existence on January 1, 1971, leaving the city of Stockholm with roughly two-thirds of its former number of employees as a consequence of program reassignment.[5] Though not dictated by national legislation, this change reflected the growing national interest in bringing about change, not only for local units, but also for the next highest units of government in Sweden—the counties (län).[6]

Massive and continuing structural change, then, has been undertaken simultaneously with equally significant changes in local responsibilities, usually producing an expansion in those responsibilities. Expanding those responsibilities has meant, among other things, that local government investments increased by more than 300 percent in the period 1946-1963, primarily for housing, and that local investments have continued at an extremely high level.[7] Indeed, it is difficult to travel through the major urban areas—Stockholm and

Gothenburg—without concluding that those areas are little more than gigantic construction zones. Expansion has also meant the creation of thousands of new administrative positions, concentrated in far fewer units, through a process of change that is not yet completed. Finally, though these processes have taken place throughout Sweden, they are most concentrated and most noticeable in and around the largest urban areas. Clearly enough, Swedish local politics has been, is, and will continue to be, a "turbulent field."[8]

Simple recitation of these developments is enough, I should think, to suggest the kinds of difficulties researchers are likely to face in studying Swedish community politics. American researchers in particular are bound to suffer severe intellectual pain as they attempt to stuff whatever they learn about local politics into their own political and analytical boxes. Coming from an environment in which local boundaries appear to have hardened into geologic formations, at least around our large cities, an American scholar's first reaction is likely to be an expression of wonderment at the ability of Swedes to change so much so quickly. Reminding himself of all those local politicians whose jobs have been eliminated, he will probably conclude that the national government must have rammed structural change down local throats. At this point, Swedish self-consciousness about a "tradition of strong local government" or "local independence" will begin to appear curious, to say the least. Yet another American abroad will have found reason to challenge the utility of treating community politics as something separable from larger political-administrative environments. As Swedes themselves might say, "det går inte"—it doesn't work.

But if American-type assumptions about the political significance of local government in relation to national political control do not work, what does? It is clear enough that national directives have had a decisive impact on Swedish local government during the past twenty years, but a closer look at the process of structural reform destroys the easy conclusion that national politicians "rammed" anything down local throats. For one thing, the distinction between "national" and "local" politicians is not very meaningful. The parliaments which have enacted structural reform legislation have included an exceptionally large percentage of active local politicians, not least because one of the two chambers has been made up entirely of representatives selected by the county councils. Moreover, the first series of reforms was in fact initiated by local officials, while the second was not only a product of continuing local complaints, but was to a large extent guided by representatives of the local government interest organization, Kommunförbundet. Finally, it is of more than slight interest to note that the great majority of elected local officials—i.e., those who would lose their jobs through structural change—supported rather than opposed the reforms.[9] Bear in mind also that fundamental structural changes, such as the new metropolitan government for Stockholm, were initiated by city and suburban politicians quite independent of pressure from the national government. If the assumption of municipal independence is not analytically useful, then, neither is the assumption of totally centralized control. Indeed, it may well be that local politics in Sweden cannot be at all profitably analyzed in terms of legally established or changed boundaries.

American analytic modes are certain to cause as many difficulties as political assumptions, particularly if applied uncritically. Consider, to begin with, the "systems analysis" that has become popular in recent years, producing a number of studies measuring the relationship between community characteristics, political systems, and policy outputs.[10] This style of analysis treats the political system as coterminous with legal municipal boundaries and typically measures relationships at only one point in time. Though hardly faithful to the real world, these procedures permit analysts to draw suggestive conclusions about the policy implications of different kinds of systems, operating in measurably different environments. And since the boundaries defining the "systems" are relatively stable, there are grounds to believe that many conclusions offered have more than temporary significance. In a world of rapidly changing municipal boundaries, however, empirical systems are constantly being reshaped. The consequence is that measurements taken at one point in time are necessarily ambiguous, since it is impossible to say whether such measurements represent the past, present or future systems: in short, we are not able to say what systems are being represented by such analysis.[11] To be sure, this kind of analysis can be attempted despite these difficulties, provided one is careful to specify the time period during which a given system or systems existed, but such specification will very likely confine the analytical utility of potential conclusions within severely limited bounds. To be useful, systems analysis of this kind requires relative stability, but the fundamental characteristic of Swedish local government is change.

Though not peculiar to systems analysis, the problem of finding appropriate indicators to represent important political variables is especially troublesome, precisely because "policy output" measurements are central to the analysis. The concept of policy output often carries the assumption that the policy source is the local unit. But, as I have pointed out, much of what is now being done by Swedish localities involves responsibilities more or less recently assigned to them by national legislation. Moreover, roughly 80 percent of expenditures by local units are devoted to activities mandated by the state—however old or new the mandate.[12] Disentangling local from national sources or policy in any precise way is probably impossible, though conceivably an effort of this kind might be rewarding.

Even apparently clear-cut measures of policy can be quite superficial. Local governments are now responsible for the bulk of new apartment construction in Sweden, and it is easy enough to obtain figures that show the number of new apartments built annually by each commune.[13] Among those communes that have constructed the largest number of new apartments, however, such figures are far less revealing, politically, than figures which report differences in housing administration. Apartments administered by what Americans would call cooperatives (bostadsrättsföreningar) require large down payments, sometimes reaching or exceeding the equivalent of $10,000, and thus attract the relatively affluent middle and upper classes. Apartments administered by public companies or foundations, on the other hand, are typically rental apartments that attract working-class residents. Local governments have considerable latitude to choose between these kinds of organizations, and thus influence the class composition of future residents. Since social class is closely related to partisan affiliation, these choices become extremely important for local politics.[14] Subtleties of this kind are impossible to detect with the naked eye (all apartment buildings look very much the same) and would be completely hidden if "total apartments built" were the only indicator of policy output used. Here, as always, the fundamental problem is knowing what to measure, and it can only be solved through awareness of the environmental conditions that give significance to available numbers.

The older, and now less popular, tradition of "community power" research is equally difficult to transplant into a new setting. Analytically, that tradition was dominated by a fixation on the structural problem of centralization or dispersion of influence. What made this question researchable was the development of techniques to estimate participation in community decision-making. The normative "bite" of the problem, on the other hand, was structured by cultural norms emphasizing the desirability of maximum citizen participation, the separability of public and private spheres of action, and the illegitimacy of private control of public action. Neither the norms nor the research technique are especially relevant in Sweden, however.

Asking people to identify participants in local decision-making is bound to prove frustrating. Since only a handful of people are involved, only a handful are likely to have usable information to offer, but to these people, questions about participation are likely to seem naïve. Answers to questions phrased as broadly as those used in Floyd Hunter's now classic inquiry[15] would almost certainly include a few blank stares, together with a great many references to persons whose official positions designate them as formal leaders. Though it might be obvious that respondents have little specific information to justify their nominations, further study would probably confirm their statements—thereby presenting the researcher with the interesting question of how people who seem to know nothing can nevertheless produce accurate information. The answer, of course, lies in the widespread assumption that those who hold official positions do in fact constitute the principal community decision makers. The accuracy of this assumption, in turn, is due, first, to representation structures which traditionally have included all organized interests in the work of public decision-making and, second, in the extremely broad scope of local authority which in practice guarantees that no major decision—whether it be of primarily individual, business, or strictly public concern—can be made without some form of public participation.[16] Asking knowledgeable persons (i.e., participants) who makes decisions is thus asking them to state the obvious. Reconstruction of specific decisions, though a different technique, leads to the same conclusions: tiny elites centered around the principal public officials, but including representatives of all interests, make all community decisions; the mass of local citizens have few opportunities to participate and thus do not participate; therefore power is effectively centralized in Swedish communes.

This conclusion, so incendiary in the United States, produces little more than a "so what" response in Sweden, where evaluative norms are quite different. A long tradition of government by high-status noblemen or otherwise privileged officials is reflected today in the acceptance of government as an "expert" occupation, capable of being performed only by those who have been specially trained to do the job. Lacking expertise themselves, citizens do not expect to participate in the work of government, except for the obligation to vote periodically, and see nothing particularly upsetting in having decisions made by an elite. The important issue for Swedes is not how decisions are made, but what effects decisions have. Thus, lack of housing, jobs, day-care centers, classrooms, hospital facilities and so on are issues in Swedish communes; who makes decisions is not an issue. Furthermore, participation by business or financial elites in decisions made by public authorities is regarded as perfectly appropriate, even when such decisions involve profit-making possibilities for such elites. Employees of banks and construction companies, for example, are usually represented in communal councils, and often hold key positions in the council committees that make decisions about construction and finance. Far from compromising the quality of official decisions, participation by private or corporate employees is regarded as adding to the expertise available to the local government. The assumption seems to be that all interests, public and private, are in the same boat, and thus have an equal right to pull on the public oars.[17]

The preceding argument yields one obvious conclusion, which is that attempts to compare Swedish to American or other local units across national boundaries, given present levels of information, are hazardous. This point is emphasized dramatically by the turbulence of the Swedish setting, where old units disappear and new units come into existence literally before the researcher's eyes.[18] But the conclusion would remain even if organizational change were not taking place for, again and again, cultural patterns of belief and evaluation, along with national patterns of intergovernmental relationships, must be referred to in order to account for activities taking place at the "local" level. To be sure, one can focus on the locality and draw implicit or explicit comparisons between such units in two or more countries. The result of such an exercise, however, is little more than a series of statements explicating the various reasons why strict comparisons cannot be made. Since those reasons, in Sweden at least, have to do with national rather than local characteristics, understanding the politics of local units (*not* local politics) implies some prior understanding of the national political system.

This is clearly not an appropriate occasion to attempt anything like comprehensive analysis of the Swedish political system, but I would like now to offer some observations about two aspects of that system which I think are especially important to the activities that take place in Swedish localities. The first might be called the "framework of understanding," by which I mean the ideas that Swedes use to organize their perceptions and evaluations of government, including local government. The second can be thought of as the "framework of behavior," by which I mean the patterns of interaction that appear repeatedly in Swedish public decision-making. One framework will be recognized as an aspect of Swedish political culture;[19] the other as an aspect of Swedish political structure.[20] What follows will be based to some extent on guesswork, since data to justify some of my conclusions are not always available, but I proceed in the hope, not only that my guesses will be reasonably intelligent, but also that they will permit a more systematic presentation of ideas that were merely hinted at above.

A FRAMEWORK OF UNDERSTANDING

Let us begin by recalling again what has been taking place in Sweden during the past two decades. At an individual level, thousands of people have been leaving small towns and moving to the largest cities, where jobs in industry, commerce and government increasingly have been concentrated. At the governmental level—and largely because of this massive shift in population—more than 2,000 municipalities have been eliminated and replaced by totally new units, created by combining several of the older units into new "Kommunblocks." Individuals have left their former places of residence voluntarily, in search of work and enjoyment, while officials formerly holding public office have voluntarily agreed to changes whose effect has been to eliminate both their municipalities and the offices they held in those municipalities.[21] The voluntary nature of these individual and official decisions justifies, I think, the inference that Swedes do not attach much significance to local boundaries. Though a number of traditional "company towns" still exist in areas far from the largest cities, many have disappeared as factories or lumber mills have shut down, thus reducing the importance of the municipality as a source of work. Nor is the municipality an important source of social status: only a handful of visibly upper-class communities exist, and some of those have been absorbed into larger units in the process of structural reform.[22] Not being associated with important social values, community is not highly valued in Sweden.

The consequences of this low affective investment in community are clearly visible in the Stockholm area where—again with the exception of two or three upper-class suburban municipalities—identification with or commitment to municipal units seems almost nonexistent. Residential turnover in the new suburbs that have been developed during the past two decades is high,[23] while studies of residential satisfaction have repeatedly shown that place of residence is of minimal interest to Swedes.[24] What counts most is, first, convenience—that is, access to work and entertainment—and second, quality of housing—that is, modernity, time-saving household equipment, and size (Dahlstrom, 1951; Birgersson, 1973). Given a choice between poor- and high-quality housing, Swedes would—and do—move from wherever they are located to another location. And, given a choice between high quality but poor convenience and poor quality but high convenience, Swedes would—and do—prefer convenience: many Stockholmers, for example, would happily exchange an apartment in a modern, well-planned suburb for an apartment in the middle of their beautiful but noisy and polluted city, provided, of course, that their work-place was in the city. Most Stockholmers, it should be added, do not have such choices to make. With 185,000 persons registered in the housing queue (1971 figures), and six years as a typical waiting period for an offer of an apartment, Stockholmers often are forced to choose between accepting an apartment in an inconvenient location or remaining in an apartment whose inconvenience or inadequacy was the principal cause of their becoming registered in the first place.[25] And this, too, hinders municipal identification, particularly in the new suburbs, most of whose residents arrived there less by choice than by compulsion.

Like citizens, Swedish official policy makers have had no commitment to existing municipalities. For them, the Swedish tradition of strong local government required that most such governments be eliminated, precisely because most of them had become incapable of providing the convenience and services that citizens had come to expect and that they, as officials, felt were minimally necessary. Among officials, then, the Swedish tradition has emphasized "strong" rather than "local" and has led to changes based upon careful calculations of the minimum population and tax base necessary to support decent housing, schools and commercial services.[26] It is important to note, too, the significance of an ideology of equal opportunity that has prevailed among representatives of the governing social democratic party. According to this ideology, no child should be penalized—in terms of inadequate schools or career possibilities—simply because of the accident of being born in an area that has lost population and resources to the more fortunate portions of the country.[27] To maintain equal opportunity the government has shaped tools to equalize local financial resources and job opportunities, as well as restructuring local governments into administrative units with sufficient strength to properly use these tools.

A citizenry without powerful affective attachments to municipalities per se, then, has been led by officials with equally weak commitments to existing boundaries, but with powerful ideological interest in reducing disparities in life chances arising from rapid urbanization. For both of these groups municipalities have been appraised, not in terms of what they are, or have been, but in terms of what they can do: their administrative and financial competence. Those whose competence has been found wanting have been eliminated, with few strong voices of protest to be heard. Those that remain after 1975 will be large and well-financed units, staffed with large numbers of administrators to meet the convenience and service demands of the local citizenry. In Sweden's "service democracy," to borrow a phrase from Professor Jörgen Westerståhl (1956) municipalities have become predominantly service-oriented organizations.

But just as "strong" has been more important than "local" in Swedish thinking, "service" has been far more important than "democracy." The preceding discussion should have made clear that the value of "democratic participation" has not been given much weight in the reorganization of Swedish municipalities, whose affairs will increasingly come to be dominated by the appointed administrators who replace elected officials. Understanding this general disinterest in participation is always confused by Sweden's well-publicized record of extraordinarily high turnout in general elections. This record is clear and impressive,[28] but it conceals the fact that Swedes have virtually no opportunities to participate in public decision-making apart from voting. At the municipal level, for example, there is no opportunity for referenda on important issues, and no tradition of public hearings on controversial or noncontroversial matters to gather impressions of public opinion. Nor is there a very strong tradition of citizen pressure groups, organized around specific issues or outside regular party or other organizational channels, to protest or support public decisions.[29] Indeed, it is virtually impossible for such groups to form except in an ad hoc way, for local decision-making takes place in the various committees established by the local council, and the meetings of these committees are not open to the public. Protests do occur, of course, but they are seldom effective in changing decisions already made and, over time, such protests seem only to reinforce prevailing patterns of citizen apathy.[30]

Some portion of this general nonparticipatory orientation is probably due to a reasonably high level of satisfaction among Swedes with the level and quality of the services they receive. By any standard, these services must be judged to be very high, particularly by a population which includes a large percentage of persons over the age of fifty. Such persons are in a position to recall how poor Sweden was thirty to forty years ago and to know by their own experience the extent of the progress made since then. Beyond satisfaction, however, it remains true that most Swedes do not see the work of government as something in which they either can or should be involved. The popular conception of government as an expert undertaking emphasizes knowledge or special information as the principal criterion of legitimate public participation at the same time that it dampens the expression of opinion not grounded on fact. There seems to be, in addition, the feeling that citizens are busy enough with their own problems and interests—earning a living or enjoying their free-time activities—to devote much time to politics. Swedish citizens live in a highly organized society but they are highly privatized as individuals. Finally, when it comes to local politics in particular, Swedes tend to believe that activities at this level are far less interesting and significant than national politics.

Fortunately, there is now a fair amount of evidence to support these conclusions. Recent surveys in thirty-six Swedish communes of three size classes (0-8,000, 8-30,000 and 30,000+), for example, revealed that an average of only 38 percent of the respondents indicated a "high interest" in politics.[31] Since those reported as having "high interest" include both a small proportion who indicated that they were "very interested" and a larger proportion who said they were "quite interested," this average of "high interest" persons probably overstates the level of interest considerably. It certainly overstates the level of interest in communal politics for, according to the same study, an average of only 22 percent of the respondents indicated a "high interest" in local, as opposed to national, politics (Örtendahl, 1969: 85) What even this figure can mean may be judged by what these respondents know and what they do. Though they get a fair amount of information about politics, most of it concerns national rather than local politics, and they thus have considerable difficulty on local questions. An average of only 10 percent of respondents in these communes correctly identified the local tax rate, only 8 percent could name a local issue in the 1966 campaign, and less than 3 percent, on the average, could identify a local issue put forward by at least two parties in that campaign (Örtendahl, 1969: 155, 118). Moreover, while 15.5 percent said they were members of a political organization and 59 percent indicated membership in some nonpolitical organization, only 4.1 percent remembered being present at a party meeting where local issues were discussed, and only 6.5 percent were in organizations that discussed local questions (Örtendahl, 1969: 42-45). When they discussed such questions at all, they did so in the home (75.5 percent), among friends (64 percent), or at the place of work (73 percent). These latter figures are almost certainly misleading, however, since the great majority of respondents were unable to name even one local issue that had been discussed among family, relatives and work-comrades (Örtendahl, 1969: 63-67).

Though hardly unambiguous, such figures do suggest a population with not much interest in politics, more interest in national than in local politics, and little political connection to either the parties or organizations, for which Sweden is so well known. Additional support for such conclusions may be drawn from a recent study of 647 officials in the Swedish cities of Norrköping, Karlskoga and Skellefteå. Four hundred sixty-four of these officials were members of the Swedish Association of Industries and 183 were associated with the Swedish Municipal Employees Association. The purpose of the study was to compare the political activity of the two groups and to identify the factors contributing to or preventing, such activity. All these individuals are middle class and the industrial officials especially make up a group whose political participation in local affairs has been the subject of so much American speculation. Consider, now, some conclusions drawn from this work. Among the 464 industrial officials, 8.6 percent indicated that they were or had been members of "some political organization" in the preceding three-year period, and 3 percent indicated that they were or had been members of "some state or local agency" during the same period. Among the local employees, the respective figures were somewhat higher—12.6 percent and 11.5 percent—though not spectacularly so, considering their employment (Bolmgren, 1970: 25). Asked to indicate the most significant hindrances to greater political activity, 40.5 percent of the industrial officials and 31.1 percent of local officials named "other vacation interests" followed by "job responsibilities" (15.7 percent, 17.5 percent), "family requirements" (5.6 percent, 7.1 percent) or some combination of these (26.3 percent, 26.9 percent) (Bolmgren, 1970: 27). Clearly enough, neither of these groups participated very much, and both placed a higher value on more privatized nonpolitical action. Since these individuals were white-collar officials, presumably with time to participate if they had the desire, I think we can imagine the situation among the more hard-pressed members of the working classes in each town.

What emerges is a portrait of a people who have little attachment to community, little interest in politics, and even less interest or participation in local politics. The municipality is viewed primarily as a provider of convenience (i.e., access to job) and service, and evaluated in terms of its ability to provide both. Absent either or both of these provisions Swedes willingly abandon one locality for another if they can; if they cannot, they are most likely to suffer or complain privately, for they are not easily mobilized for collective action outside established party and organization structures and, in any case, are far more interested in privatized activities than in collective action. For most Swedes, influencing public decisions is either impossible, because they do not think of themselves as competent, or unnecessary, because they believe public matters are being handled well enough by those whose job it is to look after the public interest.

A FRAMEWORK OF BEHAVIOR

Merely to point to ways of understanding and evaluating local politics, while necessary, is hardly sufficient. Orientations of the kind discussed above may be more or less temporary, particularly in a society that is changing so rapidly. Moreover, the more lasting kinds of orientations do not simply exist, as though permanently fixed, in mid-air; they are maintained by persons acting out political-institutional roles which have the effect of reinforcing some patterns of action, while denying legitimacy to others. I want, now, to examine some of these patterns and draw out some of their implications for local politics in Sweden.

The obvious point of departure here is the party system, whose major participants during the last several decades have been five party organizations. On the left, the Social Democratic Party has been consistently supported by 45-50 percent of the electorate, while the Communist Party has typically been able to draw the support of 4-6 percent of the electorate. The right, or "bourgeois" vote has been divided between the centrist Liberal and Center (formerly agrarian) parties and the more openly conservative Moderate (formerly "Right") Party.[32] This pattern of support has enabled the Social Democrats to retain power continuously since 1932, giving them a powerful hold on the machinery of government (Stjernquist, 1966). Of more significance for my purposes, however, is the fact that all of these parties are national parties, built up from local party organizations which carry the same names and which follow policies determined by the national leadership. Thus the same organizations that compete for national electoral support also compete for support from the various local electorates. From time to time, specifically "local" parties appear, usually organized around some special local interest, but these are few, short-lived, and seldom significant.[33] The result, not unexpectedly, is that local issues tend to be submerged in political conflict that focuses on issues of national significance. This result will be even more pronounced in the future because of the constitutional change initiated in September 1970. Beginning with the election held at that time, and continuing in the future, elections to national and local offices are to be held on the same day, at three-year intervals.[34]

This is not to say that local issues are insignificant, or that they are handled the same way in every commune. Such issues are extremely important to the daily welfare of Swedish citizens and they are handled differently, if only because social-democratic control of the national government has not been matched by similar local power. A great many communes have been, and are, led by bourgeois coalitions, though of course such power may be more difficult for the bourgeois parties to win under the new electoral system.[35] But two consequences of this nationalized party system are extremely important for local politics. One is that such issues of local significance as may exist are difficult, if not impossible, to perceive by average citizens.[36] Here, an additional hindrance is the practice of giving proportional representation to all local party groups in committees of the local councils, where decisions are actually made. Thus a social democratic voter in a commune controlled by the bourgeois parties may dislike a public decision, but if he pursues the matter (recall that committee meetings are not open to the public), he will discover that members of his own party participated in making that decision. Unless the decision has strong ideological overtones, his party representatives will not have opposed it and will not be likely to agitate the decision into an "issue." Local decisions thus appear to citizens as products of unanimity among local politicians, despite the supposedly different points of view represented by local parties. The second consequence, following from the first, is that a great deal of citizen sophistication is required to act upon issues that have been determined to be locally significant. The social democratic voter in the above case might, as a consequence of his dissatisfaction, decide to vote for the communist or one of the bourgeois parties in the next local election to punish his own party representatives, but he might still want to cast his ballot for Social Democracy at a higher level. Conceivably this would be a "sophisticated" response, but the evidence is that very few Swedes vote this way.[37] Since they do not, local issues are seldom decisive in deciding local electoral outcomes.

Operating in environments where citizen knowledge, interest and participation is low, and where it is difficult or impossible to identify or act upon "local" issues, communal political elites are relatively free from constraints that might be imposed by the local citizenry. They are, on the other hand, severely constrained by the necessity of securing approval and/or assistance from other elites in a complex, but well-integrated structure of national organizations. The first such organization is the national government itself, which exerts commanding influence over both what localities do, and the resources available for local actions. Detailed national legislation obliges municipalities to carry out certain responsibilities (education, social service, housing and planning, etc.) in specified ways. And, in keeping with the national policy of equalized opportunities, the state grants general financial assistance to communes with inadequate tax resources as well as categorized assistance for special programs. The effect of these obligations and contributions is to remove much discretionary power from local authorities (recall that something like 80 percent of local budgets is devoted to these obligatory programs).[38]

Municipalities are, of course, free to act in any area that is not regulated by national legislation. They can, for example, own and operate utility of transportation companies, housing and land development companies, recreation facilities, municipal theatres, and so on. Moreover the national government has no formal authority to interfere with local tax rates, which are set independently by each commune.[39] Clearly, wealthier municipalities are in a position to exercise a great deal of discretionary power by offering a wide variety of services supported through public taxes. Even here, however, national influence is felt, for major discretionary programs often require heavy capital investments, and borrowing by public agencies is subject to national review. For this purpose, as well as to supervise obligatory programs, a representative of the national government is located in each county and provided a staff capable of reviewing the actions taken by local governments in the area.[40] In practice, then, no major action can be taken by a local government without the knowledge, and in most cases the explicit approval, of the national government.

Other national structures focus less on supervision than on the provision of technical and financial assistance to municipalities. The League of Cities (Kommunförbundet) maintains a large staff, operates a well-known school for local officials and publishes a magazine to keep local officials up to date on new legislative and judicial requirements. The League is also an important participant in national policy determination as well as an easily available source of technical assistance to communes with difficult problems to solve.[41] Two large cooperative housing organizations—HSB and Svenska Riksbyggen—account for roughly a third of all new housing construction in Sweden, maintaining large central staffs that work closely with local officials—in one case (HSB) through local affiliates of the national organization.[42] Locally controlled public housing companies account for another third of new construction and they, too, operate with the assistance of a national organization.[43] Salary scales for local workers are set in national negotiations between the central labor organization (LO) and the central employer's organization on the one hand, while official salary scales are set in national negotiations between the central white-collar unions (TCO, SACO) and the state.[44] Money to finance the large building projects undertaken by so many Swedish communes recently is provided by the few large national banks or, increasingly, from the burgeoning general pension fund created a decade ago[45]—all according to detailed regulations laid down by the State but administered by the communes. Merely to recite this very partial list of national organizations that are necessarily and continuously involved in the work of local units should be enough to indicate how exceptionally limited in descriptive significance the word "local" is in Sweden. Constraints arising from a localized electorate may be relatively insignificant, but the constraints arising from the need to secure consent or cooperation from a variety of nationally organized structures are very powerful indeed, and in some cases (i.e., wage negotiations), totally beyond local influence.

Perhaps it is now possible to understand, however imperfectly, some of the structural sources of citizen apathy. The costs of learning about local activities, in an environment where elections are dominated by national issues, are extremely high. Even when successful, such efforts to find out what is going on are likely to produce little reinforcement, since what is "learned" will consist of knowledge about the extraordinary number of organizations, including national organizations, directly involved in local affairs, the complexity of the negotiations required to bring about local action, and the difficulty of establishing responsibility for actions taken in so many different settings, by so many different actors. And if, as will surely be the case, discovering who is responsible is discovering that some national bureaucrat, labor official or bank president made the decision or decisions, the citizen will have some reason to throw up his hands in frustration, for how can he, as a local citizen, influence such actions? The same question will raise itself if a local official is discovered to be responsible, for the only weapon available to citizens—the vote—will have little impact on that official. And creating other weapons will be extremely difficult among a population that has, perhaps, anticipated his own experience. From a citizen point of view, certainly, attempts to influence local decisions will be very much like punching a ball of dough: the system absorbs every blow without ever changing its character.

But what, in fact, is its "character"? How does a system composed of so many public, semi-public and private actors, at all levels of authority, manage to work? One answer, of course, is that sometimes it doesn't work. A new suburb (or new town) is built for 40,000 people, but contains no fire station: the result is a $10 million loss in Scandinavia's largest furniture store. A four-lane super-highway connector is built to relieve pressure on the streets of central Stockholm, but the only exit from the highway is a single traffic lane leading onto an already overburdened city street. Two giant hospitals are planned for essentially the same location. One is begun but the other, after an expenditure of $10 million for land clearance, is halted.[46] This sort of list could be expanded, but it would prove little, except that Swedes are like other people. For in spite of examples such as these, the system functions well enough. How?

That the system, of necessity, works slowly should be obvious. Though mobilization for quick action sometimes occurs, the need to secure agreement among large numbers of officials for any major local action typically requires a good deal of time first, for lengthy informal negotiations leading to an acceptable proposal, second, for official studies of the proposal, and third, for more discussion leading to acceptance of the proposal or some modified version of it. Swedes themselves often complain about the slowness of policy-making, but the process has at least this great virtue: by the time a decision is made most conceivable objections or alternatives have been so well-aired that implementation of the decision finally reached becomes noncontroversial (see Anton, 1969c, for a more general discussion of this point).

It should also be emphasized that the system is one of elite interaction. While the number of elite participants for any given decision is likely to be large, neither participants nor common citizens expect any interference from outside citizen groups to take place. A wide range of potential uncertainty is thus eliminated, leaving the more manageable problem, for officials, of learning what persons, in what agencies or firms, have what authority or resources that are necessary or helpful in what range of problems. Such learning naturally takes time, but top-level government personnel change slowly (expertise cannot be developed overnight) and local officials also tend to have long tenure.[47] Even longer tenure can be expected as the new communes create more full-time positions to manage their increasing work load. Thus, over time, local officials develop clear solutions to the problem: who to see about what, and use that information to structure regularized channels of interaction between themselves and their organizational counterparts at the national level.

Part of what officials learn in this process is that some problems simply have no short-cuts, that some red tape is too entrenched to cut. I suspect that it is such knowledge that has led so many communes to establish what I think of as "avoidance structures"—that is, organizations created outside of the existing organizational system to solve problems that have no solution within it. One problem that has been especially onerous to the more rapidly urbanizing communes has been the necessity to secure national government approval for loans to support heavy capital investment in housing, land, etc. To avoid this difficulty a great many communes—including virtually all suburban communes around Stockholm—have created private stock companies, particularly for land development. All the shares in such companies are held by the commune, and all board members are local officials, but these companies are legally private, and thus may borrow large sums from banks without securing national approval.[48]

Another problem for such communes arises from the Swedish Constitution, which requires that records of all public transactions be made immediately available for public inspection (a major reason, incidentally, why there is justice in the observation that Swedish government floats on a sea of paper (Pierre Vinde, 1967: 26, discusses this provision). This requirement applies not only to official directives or minutes of meetings, but also to transactions such as correspondence between officials. The obstacles thus created for localities anxious to buy land for new housing, industrial parks or recreation areas can easily be imagined, and the common technique for overcoming them, once again, has been the creation of private stock companies, whose transactions need be reported only in the form of annual reports. Unquestionably the most significant company of this type is the city of Stockholm's land acquisition company, AB STRADA. Created in 1954, this company began slowly, but in the period 1960-1967 alone, it purchased 77,500 acres of land in and around Stockholm. This was 21,500 acres more than the city had purchased in the preceding 55 years, when AB STRADA did not exist. Purchases of this magnitude have enabled Stockholm to exert strong control over urban growth as well as to earn substantial sums of money through land and apartment rentals. City officials now take considerable pride in their successes as land speculators and there is little doubt that Stockholm's success has contributed to the spread of such companies to other localities.[49]

Note that such organizations are not designed to hide anything from other members of the governing elite. Indeed, for reasons to be discussed shortly, they could not hide very much from other elite representatives. Such organizations do, however, permit local officials to hide their activities from citizen scrutiny, particularly in those cases where citizens may own desirable property that local officials wish to buy. Above all, however, they are designed to permit public authorities to get around systematic restrictions on their behavior built into the existing organizational structure. Similarly ad hoc organizations are created for other purposes as well: a special company may be created to avoid state salary limitations, a nonprofit foundation may be created as still another way of avoiding borrowing limitations, and so on. Proliferation of such organizations must constitute a further note of confusion for citizens, while also aggravating the problem of coordination among more and more organizational elites—or so it would seem.

For officials, at least, these appearances are deceptive, due to an extraordinary degree of overlapping among elites. I have already pointed out that many local officials sit in the Riksdag, but that is only one form of overlapping.[50] One Stockholm social democrat is an elected member of the City Council, member of the Council's Executive Board, Managing Director of the largest Stockholm housing company, member of the Finance Committee of the new Greater Stockholm Council, and regular participant in the various study commissions appointed by the national government to research policy proposals in housing and urban problems.[51] A suburban politician is an elected member of the communal council, the county council and the Riksdag, while serving as local school superintendent. Another is vice chairman of the local Building Board, President of the local HSB organization and member of the Council, while simultaneously employed full-time by a company responsible for much of the new construction in the commune.[52] In addition to overlap, circulation among elites is common. Officials knowledgeable in one area often pursue their expertise in a number of organizations working in that area. An official may move from a private construction company, to a local public housing company, to the head office of HSB, to the National Building Board, and back again, in a game of musical chairs in which positions change while function remains the same. If there is anything that can be observed as a behavioral coordinating device, the circulation of overlapping elites is it.[53]

One may question, of course, whether there is any need for an explicit coordinating device in such a system, for overlapping and circulation in effect produce a situation in which everyone more or less knows what everyone else is doing. Officials involved in activities of municipal significance come from many organizations, but they know each other and are often involved in each other's work. The official world is unlikely to be disturbed by public pressures, so that officials can be confident that the only support they need is support from others like themselves. Reasonably long tenure in office provides plentiful opportunities to develop that support by developing personal relations, and once developed, such relations can structure the processes through which major local policies are developed. What is done is done more through common understandings than through directives, more through the nuances and subtleties of interpersonal relations than through formal—and thus observable—procedures. Confusing and largely impenetrable from the outside, from the inside it must be a tight little world.[54]

CONCLUSION: TWILIGHT OR DAWN IN
SWEDISH LOCAL POLITICS

To study local politics in Sweden, I hope it is now clear, is not to study "local" politics at all; it is to study those aspects of a nationalized system of political interactions which define and structure activities of significance to local units. Getting at those interactions is an immensely complicated task, but we cannot be too wide of the mark if we begin by paying attention to what can be observed in the environment. Immense shifts of population from rural to urban areas can be observed; a massive and continuing reorganization of local unit boundaries can be observed; a huge volume of construction—for schools, apartments, hospitals, streets, etc.—in urban areas can be observed; more recent efforts to create incentives for greater investment in declining rural regions can be observed. For citizens and officials alike, these are significant activities. Understanding how, when, and why they occur will tell us a great deal about the politics of local government in Sweden.

Understanding such activities in Sweden, however, requires some prior appreciation of their significance to the actors involved as well as the structures through which action is taken. Because Swedish politics is so nationalized, actions taken at the local level will be perceived and justified in terms that are commonly held throughout the country, and initiated through structures that operate nationally. In this sense, local boundary changes may be interpreted to represent an effort to bring the administration of public programs to a level of rationalization and centralization that already exists in the party, interest group, industrial and financial sectors of society. Public desires for convenience, matched by official concern for "service," has motivated an attempt to create a system of local units whose principal function will be to administer national policy directives. In this sense, too, the changes that have seemed so remarkable may turn out to be more apparent than real: the same values will be served by the same kinds of people, but presumably in a more rational and efficient way.

But the pursuit of efficiency has its own costs. The future politics of local government in Sweden will involve fewer and fewer elected officials, and more and more bureaucrats. It seems reasonable, then, to expect that central organizational directives will increase in significance as special local concerns decrease. This will surely produce considerable strain, particularly as the new communes establish stable political interests and alignments based on their redrawn boundaries. Pressures to decentralize currently existing structures of decision-making are already apparent and it may well be that the changes of the past two decades will lead to increased political as well as administrative strength at the local level. In that event, the recent history of local politics in Sweden will be merely a prelude to even greater and more interesting changes to come. Except for those scholars who slavishly devote themselves to static modes of analysis, the uncertain outcome of present developments in Sweden's local governments will present a worthy challenge for research.

NOTES

1. Rosenthal, 1968; see also, Mark Kesselman's chapter in this volume.

2. Donald R. Niemi (1966) provides an excellent account of these developments.

3. For an up-to-date review of problems of police organization see *Statens offentligan utredningar 1970: 32* (The Police in Society). Hereafter, these reports of Swedish Royal Commissions will be cited in abbreviated form, i.e., *SOU 1970: 32*.

4. A recent review of these activities can be found in *SOU 1968: 47*.

5. The politics of this reform is analyzed in Anton, 1969a.

6. Studies reflecting this interest include *SOU 1967: 20, SOU 1967: 23* and *SOU 1968: 47*.

7. Ingvar Hjelmqvist, "Local government finance in Sweden," (mimeo) provides these and other interesting figures.

8. I have borrowed this term from Robert Alford and Michael Aiken (1970: 105), who use it in their very interesting article.

9. Plans for both the 1952 and 1962 reform were circulated among all localities for their comments and/or counter-proposals. Of the communes which reacted to the government's proposals, only 15 percent were clearly opposed to the first and only 27 percent were clearly opposed to the second reform, with opposition heavily concentrated among the smallest communes on both occasions. See Niemi (1966: 41 and 163) for the figures.

10. Alford and Aiken (1970) provide an excellent review of many of these studies.

11. In 1970 we might have taken such measurements in 848 communes. On January 1, 1971, however, the total number of communes was reduced to 464, and 190 of these will disappear by 1974! See the unsigned editorial "464 Kommuner 1971" in Kommunal tidskrift 11 (June, 1970: 658-659).

12. Niemi (1966: 111-112) reviews a study which points out that the tendency has been for communes to exercise full control over a declining proportion of their resources. That proportion was 18 percent (an average of six studies communes) in 1958. For reasons to be discussed below, we can assume that the proportion is far smaller today.

13. Such reports are issued periodically by the National Central Bureau of Statistics, Stockholm.

14. A heavy vote for the Social Democratic Party among renters in one Stockholm suburb was reported in Anton (1969b: 263).

15. "If a project were before the community that required decision by a group of leaders—leaders that nearly everyone would accept—which ten on the list of forty would you choose? "

16. Representation of all organized interests is in effect guaranteed by the "remiss" system, according to which all proposals of more than minor significance are circulated to representatives of all organizations in the commune prior to action that affects the interests of such organizations. The empirical significance of this system was shown in a recent survey of organizations in 36 Swedish communes. Sixty-three percent of the organizations in those communes reported that they had "supporters" in the various agencies of the communal governments (Sven-Runo Bergqvist, 1969). Communes are also required to place their own representatives on the boards of the various housing cooperatives (bostadsrättsföreningar) organized by groups of individuals. And housing companies not only must build according to physical plans laid out by communes, but they must also submit their financial plans—including profit calculations—to the communes for approval of state construction loans.

17. While there is no good survey data to support these conclusions, the material cited above, note 16, provides powerful indirect support, as does the material offered below on cultural perspectives.

18. I began some work on political structure and policy outputs in the 28 Stockholm-area communes in September 1970; on January 1, 1971, the number of such communes was reduced from 28 to 8.

19. For an examination of more general aspects of Swedish political culture, see Anton (1969c).

20. Structure seen from the local perspective is analyzed in Anton, 1969b. A brief but useful analysis of national structures is provided in Nils Stjernquist, 1966.

21. Many local officials, particularly from the smaller communes, have resisted these changes, and there have been a fair number of disputes between officials of communes being joined together, particularly over the question of which commune should be designated as the new "central place" of the "kommunalblock." In the main, however, the changeover has proceeded smoothly, with little of what Americans might call "die-hard opposition."

22. Danderyd and Djursholm, two of the most obviously upper-class residential suburbs north of Stockholm, were joined together on January 1, 1971.

23. During the 1960s one new suburb was adding roughly 3,000 inhabitants per year to its total population. At the same time, according to the chairman of the Building Board, some 3,000 people were leaving the commune each year, producing a turnover of some 6,000 persons every year! See Anton (1969b) for a review of the development of this suburb. A more recent study reported that, in another suburb " . . . 20 percent of the flats and townhouses were changing hands every year" (Birgersson, Häggroth, and Wallin, 1973: 3).

24. An early but still-relevant study of this type is Edmund Dahlström, 1951.

25. It should be added here that Swedes include "high cost" in their definition of inconvenience and are thus unwilling to expend a very high proportion of their income on housing. Despite the thousands registered in the queue, for example, some 2,000 two-bedroom apartments were without tenants in 1968, many of them in Skärholmen, the "new town," where rentals ranged from $160 to $180 per month. In 1970 such apartments were available in distant suburbs for $100 to $120 per month, but many were nevertheless empty. A similar situation prevailed in Gothenburg, Eskiltuna, Köping and other cities. By late 1973, Stockholm's daily newspapers were reporting more than 5,000 apartment vacancies in the city.

26. In answer to the question, "How can communal democracy be encouraged? " Prime Minister Palme recently responded as follows: "A major issue for communal democracy ... is our capacity to create communes that are sufficiently strong to meet popular demand for better conditions." *Kommunal tidskrift* 14 (September 1970: 814). For a good review of the rationale behind communal reform in Sweden, see Niemi (1966: 135-159).

27. Niemi (1966) reviews this ideology and its application.

28. Since World War II, the turnout in Swedish parliamentary elections has ranged from 77.4 percent (1958) to 89.3 percent (1968). See Stjernquist (1966: 408) and Bo Särlvik (1970).

29. Bergqvist (1969: 108-112) shows activity by ad hoc groups to be insignificant.

30. Noninvolved citizens can observe that such protests fail on matters of significance and succeed, if at all, in matters of trivial importance. An example of the former was the extended protest over the new town, Skärholmen, which was opened on September 3, 1968. That protest was fundamental enough—it attacked design, costs and environmental quality—but it began in the summer of 1968, two or three months before the new town was opened, and some six to eight years after such protests might have had some effect. An example of the latter is the recent protest over the destruction of some large elm trees in Kungsträgården, a beautiful green park in downtown Stockholm, to make way for a planned subway station. Even if the trees are saved, the fundamental character of the planned subway extensions will remain unchanged, giving passengers of the future nothing but underground walls to look at during their trips into the city. Thomas Michélsen, a columnist for *Dagens Nyheter,* has written the following insightful commentary on the matter (November 21, 1970): "How is it possible to plan what for the most part is such a massive deterioration of the travel environment without having citizens of the region rise up in protest? The most important trick is to concentrate attention on details so that the whole is concealed. A typical example is the elms in Kungstragården. A huge storm of protests and petitions is blown up over the planned but technically unnecessary cut-down. The issue is: a kiosk in the subway or trees in the park? Interest is concentrated on a little part, a small outrage. But the whole, the total burial (of the subway system) continues to be planned without hindrance" (see *Dagens Nyheter,* November 21, 1970).

31. Those of us interested in Swedish community politics owe a great debt to the "Community Research Group," led by Professor Jörgen Westerståhl of Gothenburg University, but including scholars from each of the Swedish universities. This group has been working for the last five years and, while much of its work has not yet been published, when it is we will have the first comprehensive look at Swedish community politics ever attempted. Professor Westerståhl has given a brief description of the work of his group in The New Atlantis, op. cit., and I have already cited one of the unpublished dissertations produced by the group—Bergqvist, 1969. In what follows I will be using data from other works in this series, but since I have special purposes here, the reader should be cautioned that the full significance of this research project can only be appreciated by examining the studies themselves, both those that are unpublished and those that will shortly be available in print. Here, the reference is to Claes Örtendahl, 1969: 84.

32. Bo Särlvik of Gothenburg University has been the foremost student of Swedish political parties. See, in addition to his already cited article, Särlvik, 1966.

33. This is a tentative conclusion based on work now under way in the Stockholm region.

34. It should also be noted that the Riksdag became a unicameral parliament on January 1, 1970, thus eliminating the ability of county councils to elect members to one house.

35. Since 1945 control of local councils has been relatively evenly divided between bourgeois and socialist coalitions. After the 1966 elections, however, bourgeois party

coalitions had a majority of council seats in 542 municipalities, as opposed to socialist majorities in 292 units (Board, 1970: 223-224; Hancock, 1972: 96-98).

36. In the six groups of communes, of different size classes, examined by Ortendahl, the average percentage of respondents who could identify a local issue in the 1966 campaign were as follows: 0.0, 3.2, 3.5, 6.3, 7.9 and 12.6. Another survey of the same respondents taken around the time of election day revealed that these percentages had increased somewhat, although in one case the percentage actually declined, from 7.9 to 6.3 (Ortendahl, 1969: 119).

37. Niemi (1966: 90-91) examined the relationship between percentage of votes cast for the Social Democratic Party in local and national elections in 20 communes over the period 1936-1962. Six pairs of elections were used, producing the following Coefficients of Correlation: .977, .981, .996, .989, .986, and .996. More recent evidence of the predominant role of national, rather than local, party identification can be found in Lennart Månsson, 1968: 123.

38. A useful introduction to some of these relationships, in English, is Per Langenfelt (1964).

39. The rate referred to is an income tax rate, since local property taxes are insignificant in Sweden. The local rate applies uniformly to all local residents who earn income that is taxable. For most Swedish communes, the 1971 local tax rate was between 20 and 25 crowns per hundred crowns of taxable income.

40. This official is called the Landshövding—or County Governor—and the office is one of the most prestigious in Sweden. The amount of prestige attached to the office may be gleaned from a recent appointee who, in accepting appointment, experienced an income reduction of more than 250,000 crowns. Hancock (1972: 96) presents information about the persons appointed to these positions since 1945.

41. The League, in fact, operates a consultant organization with offices in major cities around Sweden.

42. Svenska Riksbyggen was formed by construction unions in order to stabilize employment, as well as provide housing. HSB is an association of individuals who, through savings deposited in a HSB organization, create the financial conditions necessary to provide them with housing administered through a cooperative organization.

43. SABO, the national organization, had about 300 local affiliates in 1968. In fact, these public housing companies have been increasing their share of new construction over the past decade. See Ella Ödmann and Gun-Britt Dahlberg (1970: 185-186).

44. TCO is the central organization of white-collar workers. SACO is the central organization of academically trained workers. For a useful discussion of interest organizations in Sweden, see Hancock (1972: 146-169).

45. The rapid growth of the General Pension Fund (APF) and the increasing application of the Fund to housing loans has been sketched out recently in Magnus Roos, Allmänna pensionsfonden och obligationsmarknaden" (unpublished seminar paper, mineographed, Stockholm University, 1970).

46. All these events have been reported in *Dagens Nyheter,* September-December, 1970.

47. Between 1950 and 1966 there was no change in political control in 16 of the 28 Stockholm-area municipalities. In 5 others, there was only one change during that period.

48. There is no good study of such organizations, but numerous examples of how they work can be found in Jonason (1970).

49. Speculation, of course, often involves concealment of true motives. Stockholm officials have been both adept at this form of activity and proud of it. Hjalmar Mehr, a leader in these activities, has been quoted as follows: "Thus, we buy earth. That's one of the biggest political tricks that's been done. We don't say what and where. We talk about recreation uses and we've bought land at recreation prices" (quoted in Passow, 1970: 184).

50. See Hancock (1972: 95) for figures on local representation in parliament.

51. American students of community politics may compare this official, Albert Aronson, to Edward Logue, as described by Robert Dahl (1961). Some data for such a comparison can be found in David Pass (1969: 218-229).

52. The holding of multiple positions is characteristic of Swedish politicians at all levels and can be carried to great extremes. For example, the first Chairman of the Finance Committee of the new metropolitan government for Stockholm is reported to have resigned eight managing directorships and more than thirty "part time" responsibilities in order to concentrate his attentions on Metro. Even at that, he managed to retain six other positions in addition to the Finance Committee Chairmanship. See *Dagens Nyheter*, January 7, 1971.

53. I use "behavioral coordinating device" here to distinguish overlapping from the formal coordination provided by the "remiss" system, noted earlier. See note 16, above, and Hancock (1972: 156-159).

54. Jonason (1970: 71) offers a number of good examples of how this "tight little world" operates. In one of them, a small commune in the south of Sweden hired the consulting firm K-Konsult (owned by Kommunförbundet) to help plan an area of vacation-type houses. The firm's office was in another city, which happened to be the location of all county offices (controlled by the Landshövding), which meant that the planning consultant was in very close contact with the county officials whose approval of any plan would be necessary. The builder was located in yet another city but the builder's architect was also in close contact with the planning consultant, with whom he had worked for some time. Plans for the area were developed initially by the builder, reviewed and changed somewhat by the planning consultant, and approved by the county authorities without even being sent to the commune for which the plan was made.

REFERENCES

ALFORD, R. and M. AIKEN (1970) "Comparative urban research and community decision-making." New Atlantis 1 (Winter).

ANTON, T. J. (1969a) "Incrementalism in utopia: the political integration of metropolitan Stockholm." Urban Affairs Quarterly 5 (September): 59-82.

——— (1969b) "Politics and planning in a Swedish suburb." Journal of the American Institute of Planners 35 (July).

——— (1969c) "Policy-making and political culture in Sweden." Scandinavian Political Studies 4: 88-102.

BEGGQVIST, S. (1969) "Kommunerna och organizationerna." Ph.D. dissertation. Uppsala University.

BIRGERSSON, B. O., S. HAGGROTH and G. WALLIN (1973) Att Leva i Salemstaden. Stockholm: Statens Institute för Byggnadsforskning.

BOARD, J. B., Jr. (1970) The Government and Politics of Sweden. Boston: Houghton Mifflin.

BOLMGREN, T. (1970) "Industritjänstemännens faktiska samhällsengagemang 1969." Stockholm University. (unpublished)

DAHL, R. (1961) Who Governs? New Haven: Yale Univ. Press.

DAHLSTROM, E. (1951) Trivsel i Söderort. Stockholm: Stockholms Kommunalförvaltning.

HANCOCK, M. D. (1972) Sweden: The Politics of Post-Industrial Change. Hinsdale, Ill.: Dryden Press.

JONASON, A. (1970) Byggherrarna. Stockholm: Wahlström and Widstrand.

LANGENFELT, P. (1964) Local Government in Sweden. Stockholm: The Swedish Institute.

MANSSON, L. (1968) "Rikspolitiska attityder—kommunalpolitik." Ph.D. dissertation. Gothenburg University.

NIEMI, D. R. (1966) "Sweden's municipal consolidation reforms." Ph.D. dissertation. University of Chicago.

ÖDMANN, E. and G. DAHLBERG (1970) Urbanization in Sweden. Stockholm: Government Publishing House.

ÖRTENDAHL, C. (1969) "Politisk kommunikation—politisk information." Ph.D. dissertation. Uppsala University.

PASS, D. (1969) Vällingby and Farsta—from Idea to Reality. Stockholm: National Swedish Building Research.

PASSOW, S. S. (1970) "Land reserves and teamwork in planning Stockholm." Journal of the American Institute of Planners 36 (May).

ROOS, M. (1970) "Allmänna pensionsfonden och obligationsmarknaden." Stockholm University. (unpublished)

ROSENTHAL, D. B. (1968) "Functions of urban political systems: comparative analysis and the Indian case," in T. N. Clark (ed.) Community Structure and Decision-Making: Comparative Analyses. San Francisco: Chandler.

SARLVIK, B. (1970) "Voting behavior in shifting 'election winds': an overview of the Swedish elections 1964-1968." Scandinavian Political Studies 5: 241-283.

——— (1966) "Political stability and change in the Swedish electorate." Scandinavian Political Studies 1: 188-222.

STJERNQUIST, N. (1966) "Sweden: stability or deadlock? " pp. 116-146 in R. A. Dahl (ed.) Political Opposition in Western Democracies. New Haven and London: Yale Univ. Press.

VINDE, P. (1967) The Swedish Civil Service. Stockholm: Ministry of Finance.

WESTERSTAHL, J. (1956) in Dagens Nyheter (August 4).

Chapter 4

Political Parties and Local Government in France: Differentiation and Opposition

Mark Kesselman

INTRODUCTION

A growing body of literature is beginning to challenge assumptions about the extent of centralization in France. The power of French local officials and institutions can be inferred from diverse indicators: the dilution or defeat of national efforts at regional and local administrative reforms, alliances between local and national officials in opposition to national goals, the failure of the ruling Union des Démocrates pour la République (U.D.R.) to penetrate local government. The most dramatic example of the power of local notables and institutions was the defeat of the April 1969 referendum called to reform regional government and to weaken the Senate, a bastion of local power; the defeat of the referendum precipitated President de Gaulle's resignation from office (see Avril, 1971; works by Grémion and Worms; Kesselman, 1970, and my other article in this volume; Lipmanson, 1971; and Médard, 1970).

The diverse findings of varied literature suggest the persistence of a local political subsystem in France with relatively great autonomy from the national sphere. The precise character of the two spheres will not concern us here. Rather we will be concerned with the relatively neglected subject of the relationship between political parties and local government in France. An examination of their tenuous and complex linkages furthers understanding of how the local

AUTHOR'S NOTE: *An earlier version of this paper was presented to the 1972 Annual Meeting of the American Political Science Association, Washington, D.C. I am grateful for the financial assistance of the John Simon Guggenheim Foundation, the National Science Foundation (Grant GS-2537), and the Institute on Western Europe, Columbia University.*

subsystem continues successfully to resist Gaullist efforts to "nationalize" political life under the aegis of the Gaullist movement.

The partisan aspect of French local politics has rarely been studied. Research on the politico-administrative system of local politics has ignored partisan linkages; studies of French political parties devote little attention to the local organizations of political parties, even less to the linkage between political parties and local government. (This was a major theme to emerge from a colloquium on local factors in French political life, see Mabileau, 1972. For studies of French political parties and activists, some of which examine grassroots politics, see Ambler, 1968; Bernard and LeBlanc, 1970; Charlot, 1966, 1970; Dreyfus, 1972; Hunt, 1970; works by Kesselman; Simmons, 1969, 1970; Wilson, 1971. For studies of French local public officials and politics, see Berger, 1969; Bon and Ranger, 1972; Gilli, 1968; Hayward and Wright, 1971; Longpierre, 1970, 1972; Souchon, 1968; Verdès-Leroux, 1970, 1971.)

Although distinct, the spheres of local government and political parties do not exist in isolation from each other. Political parties have long attempted to "colonize" local governments in France. The most prominent examples include the red belt about Paris, where cities have been ruled by Communist mayors without interruption (except during the Occupation) since the 1920s (Platone, 1967). Other cities of diverse political persuasions have also been ruled by the same local administration for long periods. Examples include Arras, Lille, Nice, Rennes, Strasbourg, and Toulouse. A mining town in the southwest recently celebrated its seventy-fifth straight year of Socialist rule.

On the national level, political parties and politicians frequently try to mobilize local officials for their own ends. The Association des Maires de France, a voluntary association grouping most French mayors is—although officially nonpartisan—frequently divided by conflicts among members over government policies. Most political parties, including the Centre Démocrate, Communist Party, Socialist Party and Gaullists sponsor their own associations of local officeholders. Many politicians hold local and national office simultaneously: two-thirds of French deputies, for example, are also local elected officials (Médard, 1972).

National politicians often try to build a following among local elites. In the 1969 presidential campaign, Socialist candidate Gaston Defferre wrote to local officials throughout France seeking their support. After his election as deputy from Nancy in 1970, Jean-Jacques Servan-Schreiber announced that his future political efforts would be directed to organizing local officials against the Gaullist government.

Political party leaders assign high priority to capturing local office. A leader of the U.D.R. stated that he considered it of "capital importance" to increase Gaullist control over local governments. "One of our grave mistakes at first was not considering the local level as important. Now we realize our error. We need troops, cadres. We're trying to develop an organization. And look at the Communists. They exercise a veritable dictatorship in the communes they rule. Once they conquer a town hall, they never lose it."[1] The Gaullists deployed enormous efforts before the 1971 municipal elections to increase their hold over local government.

In a survey of local leaders of the U.D.R. and Socialist Party, the results of which will be presented below, significant proportions of grass roots party leaders and members designated winning local elections as the most important task of the local (federation) party organization. Party activists ranked obtaining local offices third among seven possible goals for the local party federation, outweighing in importance, for example, participation in presidential election campaigns.

There are attractive incentives inducing political parties to compete for control of local governments in France. First is the sheer volume of local governments: nearly 38,000 municipal governments exist in France—one for every commune—and each ruled by a municipal council, ranging in size from 9 to 37 members (the municipal councils of Lyon, Marseille and Paris are larger), and a (far more powerful) mayor elected by the municipal council from among its ranks. The total number of municipal councilors in France exceeds 450,000! In addition, each of France's 95 départements has a general council, composed of approximately 30 general councilors. General councilors are popularly elected, one from each canton in a département (the canton groups a number of communes). There are about 3,000 cantons in France; hence, 3,000 general councilors. Although their legal powers are slight, general councilors are powerful figures in provincial France. Most cumulate offices by running for mayor of a commune in their canton.

The experience, prestige and sheer number of French local officials is immense. Whatever powers local governments possess, political parties could hardly ignore the existence of grass-roots elites.

Moreover, local governments have a good deal more power than is commonly supposed. Their positive powers are great, despite severe limitations imposed by financial constraint. Perhaps more important, local approval (and often sponsorship) is needed for many public investments: over half the public works in France are sponsored by local governments. Therefore, local governments are powerful because of their ability to obstruct change. Further, given the rapid urbanization that has recently occurred in France, urban governments are becoming increasingly prominent.

Local governments are also powerful indirectly. They serve as the first link in the French administrative structure and have privileged relations with the much praised, much feared (but never ignored) bureaucracy (Grémion, 1970; Worms, 1966). Control of local governments assures favorable access to the administration, a critical consideration since the central government has extensive legal and financial control over local government.

Local control also provides a redoubt to which parties can retreat when defeated elsewhere. MacRae has shown how, in the Fourth Republic, when General de Gaulle temporarily withdrew from party politics in 1953, those Gaullist deputies who were also mayors stood a better chance of being reelected in 1956 (MacRae, 1967: 54). At the present time, the Gaullist U.D.R. has relatively few such strongholds, compared to its position of dominance nationally. Far weaker than the U.D.R. at the national level, opposition parties survive despite repeated defeats in legislative and presidential elections because they control so many departmental councils and town halls.

Despite manifold reasons why one would expect political parties to be well entrenched in French local governments, however, the reverse is more nearly true: most local governmental officials are not cardcarrying members of a political party and most local governments are ruled by coalitions of diverse forces, rarely by a local branch of a national political party.

Data from a survey of regional party leaders and members and local public officials throughout France will be analyzed here in an attempt to understand the relationship between political parties and local governments in France.

In each of six départements, interviews were conducted during the winter 1969-1970 with local public officials and political party activists. Approximately twenty general councilors per département were interviewed as well as twenty mayors per département: ten from rural communes (under 2,000 population) and ten from urban communes. Interviews were also conducted with political party leaders and rank and file members in the six départements from two political parties, the Socialist Party (Parti Socialiste, P.S.) and the Gaullist Party (U.D.R.). Leaders were defined as members of the federation executive committee of each party at the departmental level. The federation executive committee, composed of members elected by local party organizations as well as members ex officio (e.g., the party's deputies in the département), runs the party at the regional level. Party members were selected from lists of the party membership in each département furnished by local party secretaries and national party headquarters.

More than six hundred local officials were interviewed; questions concerned recruitment, current political issues, and the functioning of local parties and local government. The data obtained provide a unique opportunity to study the connection between party activists and local governmental officials in France.[2]

The first finding from the survey suggests a relative lack of penetration by political parties at the lowest reaches of local government and far more success at the next higher level: the general council, particularly in urban areas.

While most local officials have partisan preferences, only a moderate number are currently party members. There is a strong divergence of general councilors and mayors regarding partisan affiliation: several times more general councilors than mayors are party members.

TABLE 1
PARTISAN AFFILIATION OF LOCAL PUBLIC OFFICIALS[a](in percentages)

	Presently Enrolled Party Members	*Once Enrolled in a Party, but not Presently*	*Party Sympathizers*	*Non-Partisan*	*%*	*(n)*
General Councilors	61	13	20	6	100	(110)
Mayors	26	22	39	14	101	(106)
Rural General Councilors	28	13	44	16	101	(28)
Urban General Councilors	74	13	4	9	100	(78)
Rural Mayors	19	22	40	19	100	(58)
Urban Mayors	33	21	33	13	100	(48)

a. Here and elsewhere, percentages may not total 100% because of rounding errors. Where information is not available, the cases are not presented in the table. Mayors were selected from a sample stratified by size of commune. General councilors were not selected from a stratified sample; those living in rural and urban communes are listed separately to permit comparison.

The distinction is significant between party membership and mere party preference or identification (the term used in American voting studies carried out by the Survey Research Center). Enrolling in a party requires an active public and psychological commitment. The French government establishes statistics showing the partisan preferences of local officials (see Kesselman, 1970; Simmons, 1969; Verdès-Leroux, 1970 for analyses based on these figures). But statistics on local officials' party preferences are a poor indication of the extent of actual membership. A majority of mayors and one-third of the general councilors are party sympathizers or ex-members of a party but not currently party members. The data presented here, the first which provide information on actual membership, suggest a complex picture: While parties are well represented among the lower middle reaches of the elected political elite in France, they have made little headway at lower levels. Overall, with the important exception of urban general councilors, the proportion of currently enrolled party members among local officials is not great.

From the opposite perspective, a different picture emerges from calculating the proportion of the party activist sample who simultaneously hold local elected office.

These figures suggest, paradoxically, that political parties, especially at the level of the regional leadership (and the Socialist Party in particular) are thoroughly entrenched in local office. Whereas parties are likely to contain many members holding local office, local governments are less likely to be run by mayors with a partisan affiliation. Although there is significant overlap between officials who run local governments and officials who run political parties in

TABLE 2
LOCAL OFFICES OCCUPIED BY PARTISAN ACTIVISTS[a] (in percentages)

	Municipal Councilor	Assistant Mayor	Mayor	General Councilor	Activists Having at Least One Post	(n)
Socialist Leaders	18	12	13	15	46	(108)
Socialist Members	17	3	4	2	24	(90)
U.D.R. Leaders	14	7	13	15	41	(115)
U.D.R. Members	8	3	1	2	12	(96)
Total						(409)

a. Each figure refers to the proportion within the partisan sub-group who occupy the given local office. All mayors and assistant mayors are necessarily municipal councilors, since the occupants of the first two positions are filled from among the third. A given respondent will only be counted once, according to the highest position he fills among these three. However, the *cumul* permits general councilors to be elected to lower office, and those general councilors who are also municipal councilors, assistant mayors, or mayors are tabulated twice.

France, political parties have failed to recruit most grass roots elites. If many party activists are local officials, a large proportion of local public officials are not enrolled in a political party. The party system in France reaches down only to the intermediate level of the general council and urban centers.

While it is impossible to infer the flow of influence between the sectors of political parties and local government from these figures, it appears (partly on the basis of data to be presented below) that the balance of power between local government and political parties may be in favor of the former. What the data presented here indicate is that while local governmental office is a chief source of power for political parties, many local governments escape partisan control.

An additional point to be noted (which will be explored below) is that the great disparity in strength between the Socialist Party and U.D.R. nationally is not reflected in these data: more Socialist than Gaullist activists hold local office.

This paper examines the complex variations among partisan activists and local officials in France. In certain respects the two groups are quite distinct; in other respects, however, the internal differences within the two groups of officials are greater than the contrasts between them.

Comparison between partisan activists and local officials suggests that the two groups share many socioeconomic characteristics and differ on others. More significant is that the two groups appear to be recruited to politics by different processes and that those local public officials who are also party members appear less integrated into the party than are other party activists. Comparison will also be made, within the local elected official sample, between those who are (or were at some time) members of a political party and local officials (whom we will designate nonpartisan) who have never belonged to a political party.

A related question, given the Gaullists' great success nationally, will be their relative inability to capture local office or gain the allegiance of local elites. Comparison within the group of elected officials will thus also focus on contrasts between Gaullist sympathizers and opponents. (The indicator used will be reported vote at the second ballot of the 1969 presidential elections: pro-Pompidou [the Gaullist candidate] versus pro-Poher or abstention.) Although the Socialist Party is in tatters nationally, its local strength remains great (greater, in fact, than that of the U.D.R.). Indeed, the Socialist Party was chosen for close study and comparison with the U.D.R. because it represents a typical party from the Fourth Republic that, although soundly defeated by the Gaullists since 1958, continues to survive—in large part because of its persistence locally. What light do the data presented here shed on the Socialist Party's success in local politics and the Gaullists' weakness?

RECRUITMENT

Party and local governmental officials in France are recruited from highly diverse sectors. Variations in their socioeconomic backgrounds are only partially associated with their present organizational positions; it is not by socioeconomic factors that party and local governmental spheres in France are differentiated.

The Urban-Rural Cleavage. Village mayors are the most distinct group studied. They are mostly from farming backgrounds, nearly half are farmers themselves and most have low incomes. They are highly stable geographically: their ties to the communes they govern usually go back one generation and frequently two. Most are elderly, with three-fifths over 60 years old, which (coupled with the other factors above) helps explain why the majority have not progressed beyond elementary school.

Although rural mayors may appear marginal in French politics, by their numbers they are more nearly representative of French grass roots elites than all other groups analyzed: the vast majority of the 38,000 communes in France are rural. (For a portrait of village mayors see Kesselman, 1967.)

The urban-rural cleavage remains significant in other ways. Elected officials are generally rurally based. The vast majority of French communes are rural. Political parties, which are predominantly urban-based, thereby encounter an additional obstacle in their efforts at recruiting local elected officials. As was indicated, rural local officials (both mayors and general councilors), are far less apt to join a political party than are their urban colleagues. From another perspective, only 11 percent of Socialist activists and 20 percent of Gaullist

TABLE 3
SOCIOECNOMIC CHARACTERISTIC OF LOCAL OFFICIALS AND PARTY ACTIVISTS (in percentages)

	General Councilor	Rural Mayor	Urban Mayor	Socialist Leader	Socialist Member	U.D.R. Leader	U.D.R. Member
Father's Occupation							
Farmer	25	56	19	13	21	10	19
Worker	16	11	17	28	35	6	17
Salaried, Commercial	39	21	48	48	39	55	57
Professional	21	11	17	11	6	30	8
%	101	99	101	100	101	101	101
Respondent's Occupation							
Farmer	10	40	10	4	7	4	7
Worker	27	21	23	9	23	2	16
Salaried, Commercial	19	18	23	45	54	23	57
Professional	44	21	44	42	16	71	20
%	100	100	100	100	100	100	100
Education							
Primary	28	61	30	24	63	18	54
Secondary, Technical	36	32	32	31	25	28	29
University	37	7	38	45	12	54	17
%	101	100	100	100	100	100	100
Income (francs per month)							
<1,750	20	61	23	24	57	12	39
1,750-3,999	48	27	37	38	37	36	50
4,000+	32	12	40	38	6	52	12
%	100	100	100	100	100	100	101
Age							
Below 40	5	3	0	24	23	15	26
40-59	56	38	42	57	37	68	56
60+	40	59	58	19	40	17	18
%	101	100	100	100	100	100	100
Geographic Mobility							
Intergenerational[a]	37	41	37	22	21	14	20
Intragenerational[b]	53	53	48	44	50	38	42

a. Each entry refers to percentage of respondents who live in same commune where their father was born.
b. Each entry refers to percentage of respondents who live in same commune where they were born.

TABLE 4
PLACE OF RESIDENCE OF PARTY ACTIVISTS, BY PARTY AND LEADERSHIP
POSITION (percentage living in rural communes)[a]

	Socialist Leaders	Socialist Members	U.D.R. Leaders	U.D.R. Members
Party Activists Exercising Elected Office	16	27	26	40
Party Activists Not Exercising Elected Office	7	4	12	20
(n)	(105)	(90)	(114)	(96)
Total n (405)				

a. Each figure represents the percentage of the subgroup (e.g., Socialist leaders also exercising elected office) who live in a rural commune.

activists live in rural areas. The divergence in the geographic center of balance between urban-based parties and rural-based local governments can be seen when the place of residence of partisan activists who also occupy local public office is compared with partisan activists who do not.

Vertical and Horizontal Stratification. Yet in many respects (occupation, education, and income), vertical differences are more significant than horizontal ones. There is a convergence among higher level groups (leadership groups for the two parties and general councilors within the local governmental sphere) that occurs across party-local governmental lines. Thus, traditional measures of social rank are associated with political stratification and cross-cut party-local governmental institutional boundaries (for an extended analysis of political recruitment patterns of the partisan activist group, which reaches the same conclusion regarding socioeconomic factors, see Kesselman, 1973).

French local officials are a highly diverse group. Village mayors are traditional rural notables; urban mayors and general councilors rank among the moderately successful members of French provincial society but, although they are a political elite by virtue of their elected mandate, they are less likely than Gaullist leaders, who are substantially higher in status than all other groups, to be found among the economic and social privileged in these areas.

Compared to party activists, local public officials are somewhat older, more rurally based, more stable geographically, and thus, apparently, more traditional. They resemble Socialist leaders (also a traditional group, judging by their low rate of geographic mobility) in regard to occupation, education, and income, but resemble Gaullist activists by their rural backgrounds.

Religion, Local Government, and the Party System. Religion unites local officials and Gaullist party activists even more strongly. Local public officials are

TABLE 5
RELIGIOUS PRACTICE OF LOCAL ELITES (in percentages)

	Proportion Attending Parochial School For at Least Part of Their Education	Proportion Attending Church at Least Occasionally	n(ca)
Socialist Leaders	10	36	(106)
Socialist Members	14	40	(89)
U.D.R. Leaders	41	90	(115)
U.D.R. Members	42	83	(95)
Rural General Councilors	25	86	(32)
Urban General Councilors	30	66	(76)
Rural Mayors	29	89	(56)
Urban Mayors	29	77	(45)
Partisan General Councilors	25	66	(79)
Nonpartisan General Councilors	38	90	(29)
Partisan Mayors	26	58	(47)
Nonpartisan Mayors	31	96	(54)

apt to have been educated in parochial schools and to attend church at least occasionally, They appear quite religiously observant, resembling Gaullist party activists in this respect and diverging sharply from Socialist Party activists.

Within the ranks of French local elected officials, religious and partisan cleavages converge: partisan local officials are less religiously observant than non-partisan local officials.

Coupled with the high proportion of local governmental officials who are religiously observant, this finding corroborates the symmetrical relationship that has been observed between religion and politics in France. Unlike other Catholic countries, such as Italy and the Benelux countries, a strong Christian Democratic party has never really taken hold in France. Instead, political parties appear to flourish where the Church is weak (and vice versa).

The high proportion of U.D.R. activists who are religiously observant challenges the traditional pattern. Among the ways in which the U.D.R. is atypical of French political parties is its appeal to traditional religious milieux. Our data suggest that the U.D.R. may be bridging the gap between organized religion and organized politics in France.

If the party system has traditionally been a secular preserve, religious practice does not serve as a barrier to filling local governmental office. Quite the contrary. The high proportion of local governmental officials who are religiously observant suggests a further difference between party and local governmental sectors. The differences between the two spheres is associated with the urban base and leftward orientation of organized parties, in contrast to the rural base and conservative orientation of French local government. Here again, the U.D.R. represents a contrast to other French parties.

POLITICIZATION

If few socioeconomic differences distinguish local governmental officials as a whole from activists of both parties, the two groups diverge sharply in regard to the process of politicization. Differences in politicization within the group of elected officials are especially consequential for the question of joining a political party.

One measure of politicization was whether respondents recalled having discussions about politics with their father. Local officials were less likely than partisan activists to report having had such discussions. Rural officials, both mayors and general councilors, were especially unlikely to discuss politics.

Politics was not explicitly "in the air" during the childhood of local officials. Although they were later to participate extensively in public affairs, they were not prepared for such participation as a result of discussions with parents. The decision to participate in a political party, on the other hand, was clearly related to such discussion in childhood.

The hypothesis that discussions with one's father were more influential in encouraging participation in partisan politics than in local public affairs is borne out by comparing local officials who joined a political party with those who did not.

Twice as many partisan as nonpartisan local officials recalled having political discussions with their father. While such discussions seem to have facilitated

TABLE 6
POLITICAL DISCUSSIONS WITH FATHER BY LOCAL ELITES (in percentages)

	Proportion Recalling at Least "Fairly Frequent" Discussions About Politics with Father[a]	(n)
Socialist Leaders	59	(98)
Socialist Members	48	(85)
U.D.R. Leaders	54	(108)
U.D.R. Members	36	(83)
Rural General Councilors	35	(31)
Urban General Councilors	53	(75)
Rural Mayor	27	(51)
Urban Mayor	39	(46)

a. Each entry refers to the proportion of the subgroup recalling at least fairly frequent discussion. The question asked: "Did you talk about politics with your father: very frequently, fairly frequently, rarely, or never?"

TABLE 7
POLITICAL DISCUSSIONS WITH FATHER BY PARTISAN AND NONPARTISAN
LOCAL OFFICIALS (in percentages)

	Proportion Recalling at Least "Fairly Frequent" Discussions About Politics with Father	(n)
Partisan General Councilor	55	(77)
Nonpartisan General Councilor	31	(29)
Partisan Mayor	49	(43)
Nonpartisan Mayor	24	(54)

entry into a political party, their absence was not a bar to running for local governmental office.

Another finding suggestive in understanding the different paths to politicization followed by local public officials and partisan activists derives from the age at which respondents reported first evincing interest in public affairs.

Public officials generally reported reaching political awareness at a much later age than partisan activists.[3] While most of the latter group reported an interest

TABLE 8
AGE OF POLITICAL ELITES' FIRST POLITICAL INTEREST[a] (in percentages)

	Below Age 17	17-23	24+	%	(n)
Socialist Leaders	52	31	18	101	(107)
Socialist Members	36	38	25	99	(90)
U.D.R. Leaders	27	29	43	99	(114)
U.D.R. Members	21	37	41	99	(96)
Rural General Councilor	3	25	72	100	(32)
Urban General Councilor	22	28	50	100	(78)
Rural Mayor	9	12	79	100	(57)
Urban Mayor	21	25	54	100	(48)
Partisan General Councilor	21	30	49	100	(81)
Nonpartisan General Councilor	3	21	76	100	(29)
Partisan Mayor	27	29	45	101	(49)
Nonpartisan Mayor	4	9	88	101	(56)

a. The question asks, "How old were you when you began to be interested in politics [for party activists] or public affairs [for public officials]?"

in politics by their late teens (somewhat later for Gaullist activists), public officials were not politically aware until their mid-twenties or later. The urban-rural factor is again prominent, with rural mayors and general councilors unlikely to report political interest originating early in life. It would seem that while late politicization did not preclude running for public office, it did discourage joining a political party.

Such an hypothesis is corroborated by comparing the age of first political interest for local officials who joined a political party and for nonpartisan local officials. Virtually none of the nonpartisan officials had developed political interest by their mid-teens; four-fifths did not develop political interest until their mid-twenties or after. Partisan local officials are politicized younger, similar to party activists: over half developed political interest before their mid-twenties.

The data suggest that an early interest in politics was associated with the decision to join a political party but not to run for local office. What was there about an early interest in politics that fostered participation in a political party? What was there about not reaching political awareness until well into adulthood that discouraged joining a political party?

One might infer that an antipathy for political parties apparently developed among those not politicized young. Without the offsetting factor of early politicization, the natural tendency was to remain distant from political parties. The distaste for political parties and partisan politics prevalent in French political culture does not extend to local governmental affairs: late politicization does not constitute a barrier to running for local public office. But unless familiarity with politics occurs early, one is likely to adopt the prevailing detachment from political parties.

What kinds of factors, on the other hand, encourage local officials to enter public life? Were political stimuli largely absent, especially for those who did not join a political party, or were they simply different from the stimuli motivating partisan activists?

One way in which politicization occurred for public officials was through direct example. Given the small proportion of public officials who report being politicized young, it is surprising to find that a relatively large proportion of local officials (about 20 percent) have fathers who exercised political responsibilities (usually rural mayors). Both mayors and general councilors outrank all four groups of partisan activists on this measure; few differences existed between partisan and nonpartisan local officials.

Moreover, unlike the rest of the French electorate (but similar to partisan activists), most local public officials recall their father's political preference (tendance). Whereas Converse and Dupeux (1966: 280) report that only 25 percent of the electorate recall their father's political preference, three times more local officials (74 percent) reported such recall, a figure not far from the

79 percent of partisan activists who recalled their father's tendance. Whatever anti-partisan influences exist in the backgrounds of local officials do not preclude ready identification of parental political preferences.

Thus, politics was present in the homes of many who ran for public office, but in a more diffuse way than for partisan activists. The data only hint at the different processes of becoming politically involved. There was an apparent absence of explicit references to politics in the childhoods of nonpartisan officials. Although the lack of discussions with parents about politics and the lateness of interest in politics is related to the reluctance to join a political party, the fact that many public officials had fathers with political responsibilities and most could recall their father's political preference probably facilitated their entry into local public affairs.

VIEWS ABOUT POLITICAL PARTIES

One might hypothesize that, no matter how strong the anti-partisan current present in the childhood of local officials, they might still join a political party if the incentives were sufficiently attractive. However, local officials generally have a low regard for political parties. Their apparent lack of confidence in parties' abilities to deliver benefits probably represents a formidable obstacle in the parties' efforts to recruit them.

Several measures suggest that local officials neither view political parties with great favor nor perceive them as providing great benefits. One clear indicator of the (un)importance of party affiliation is the fact that a large minority of local officials have never belonged to a political party. The reason is not that the party makes heavy demands on how local officials should run local affairs: only one-fifth of the local officials belonging to a political party reported that the party issues directives *(consignes)* to them. When partisan local officials consider that their party is intervening unduly in their proper domain, they may ignore the party altogether (usually with impunity) or bolt. In the spring of 1970, for example, the Socialist mayor of Mulhouse (in Alsace) quit the party because he felt its new political strategy was hindering his activity. (The party's inability to retaliate can be inferred from the fact that he was reelected at the first ballot of the 1971 municipal election despite the presence of an opposing Socialist slate.) The main reason such cases are rare is because of weak party discipline. (The Communist Party probably represents an exception to this and much of our analysis here. However, research on Communist local officials, a fascinating subject, is nearly nonexistent. See Platone, 1967; Tiersky, 1972.)

Yet party membership does provide benefits in some cases. Among local officials who have belonged to a political party, 49 percent of general councilors and 30 percent of mayors rated the advantage of party membership as very high.

The most important reason is the electoral support party membership brings. A mayor from the Southwest said, "There is a strong Socialist tradition at Monesties and it isn't certain the voters would follow me if I changed party." For a Socialist from the North (a Socialist stronghold), party membership increased his electoral standing: "Socialism is a party which voters respect."

Another reason frequently given was the favorable access party membership facilitated: for a Gaullist from the North, "Belonging to the same party as the deputy increases the chance of my having my requests granted." The importance of controlling local office was suggested by a Socialist from Marseille who clearly considered that he belonged to the governing party, no matter what the national election returns, because the mayor of Marseille (Gaston Defferre) is Socialist. For this Socialist general councilor, "the governing majority to which I belong enables me to gain tangible results." And a classic advantage, cited by a general councilor who belonged to the classic party using this tactic (the Radical Party) was: "My political affiliation, if it doesn't give me any direct benefit, permits electoral alliances which wouldn't be possible for a candidate from another party."

Yet exactly how helpful is party membership? It appears that political parties control neither candidate selection nor electoral competition. Responses are suggestive to a question concerning the importance of the party for the electoral victory of those local officials who were party members.

Many partisan mayors rated their party's help at election time as of slight importance. More general councilors dismissed their party's help than rated it very important. Indeed, many local officials reported in interviews that party membership could be a downright liability for municipal elections (for a description of grass-roots anti-party sentiment, see Tarrow, 1971).

Thus, even for elected officials who are party members, the impact of their partisan affiliation may not be great. When local officials were presented with a list of possible reasons why they obtained the nomination and were later elected to local office, personal notoriety ranked highest. Partisan and ideological

TABLE 9
IMPORTANCE OF PARTY FOR PARTISAN LOCAL OFFICIALS' ELECTORAL VICTORY[a] (in percentages)

	Very Important	Fairly Important	Unimportant	%	(n)
General Councilor	26	33	41	100	(66)
Mayor	16	0	84	100	(32)

a. Rural and urban mayors are grouped together because of the small number who are party members. The question asks: "During the election to the general council [or municipal council] do you estimate that your party's role was: very important, fairly important, or unimportant?" The question was asked only of local officials belonging to a political party.

TABLE 10
REASON FOR CHOICE AS CANDIDATE IN LOCAL ELECTIONS (in percentages)

	Occupation[a]	Notoriety[b]	Ideological and Partisan[c]	%	(n)
Rural General Councilor	20	50	30	100	(30)
Urban General Councilor	17	42	42	101	(72)
Rural Mayor	13	66	21	100	(53)
Urban Mayor	7	64	29	100	(45)
Partisan General Councilor	13	44	43	100	(75)
Nonpartisan General Councilor	30	44	26	100	(27)
Partisan Mayor	17	50	33	100	(48)
Nonpartisan Mayor	4	80	16	100	(50)

a. Profession; union or professional association activity.
b. Local resident; already exercised elected mandate; considered a prominent personality in region.
c. Represent a particular doctrine; active militant; supported by national party leaders.

reasons ranked far lower in importance for mayors and somewhat lower for general councilors. Even for the partisan group, personal notoriety continued to play a larger role than ideology.

The lack of importance of the party label can be seen from responses to another question, which asked about the specific mechanisms by which local officials obtained the nomination for local office. Nearly all mayors reported a political party designation to be of negligible importance. Even among partisan general councilors, the group most frequently citing the party mechanism as the means of gaining the nomination, only 55 percent stated that the party's designation played a decisive role.

In municipal elections, where a party label is rarely influential, a candidate for mayor may be nominated by the candidates for municipal council of a given slate. More frequently, in fact, the initiative comes from the candidate for mayor: he organizes and heads a slate of candidates for the municipal council. His position at the top of the list *(tête de liste)* means that if his slate is elected to the municipal council, he will in turn be elected mayor by his colleagues. (Mayors are indirectly elected in France: by the municipal council from its ranks.) Although partisan factors are important in the composition of municipal slates and an intricate process of ticket-balancing *(dosage)* occurs, local party officials rarely control the process or even select which of their members will be chosen for an electoral list. Moreover, slates of candidates usually represent political coalitions. Only 10 percent of general councilors, 12 percent of rural mayors, and 17 percent of urban mayors (often Communist) stated they were planning to form a single-party ticket in the next local election. Local tickets do not even bear the name of a national political party. Thus, the importance of political parties in the local electoral process is minimal (for a more extended description, see Kesselman, 1967: part III).

Coalitions are necessary in a multiparty situation, given the majoritarian features of the two-ballot electoral law used in French local elections. But an equally compelling reason—probably more influential in reducing the value of partisan affiliation for local officials—is the antipathy of the French electorate to party labels.

As has been true in the United States for some periods, particularly in small cities, an ideal in France is to minimize political party involvement in local governmental affairs. One of the most frequent responses of nonpartisan local officials, when asked why they do not join a political party, is that such involvement is foreign to their activity as local officeholders and that partisan involvement would antagonize voters. Presumably, being too prominently identified with a political party would alienate more voters than it would attract. Examples of anti-partisan feeling, common among French electors (see Tarrow, 1971) were also evinced by local officials in explaining why they did not join a party. One mayor stated, "I believe that in a small village like this one, instead of engaging in politics, which divides, one should unite people and remain detached from parties—which I have done ever since I was mayor beginning in 1944, for 26 consecutive years. I believe I should be mayor for everyone and not just for a clan." (For an analysis of this approach, which I have called the "rhetoric of apolitisme," see Kesselman, 1967.) According to a Gaullist sympathizer from the Paris region, "When one joins a party, one becomes a marionette. One is obliged to obey the directives of the party. I prefer to remain free." Another Gaullist from the same area agreed: "A mayor must be free to govern all his citizens without *arrières pensées.*" A Radical sympathizer from the Southwest refused to join a party "to avoid becoming imprisoned, for when one is in a party, one must follow the group. That is contrary to my fashion of viewing things. I prefer to remain outside (m'abstenir)."

Mayors active in a political party appeared to experience embarrassment at being questioned about both party and local governmental activity during the same interview: apparently they compartmentalized the two. (General councilors probably make the transition more easily, since partisan factors are more relevant to general council activity, e.g., election of officers.)

All this is not to minimize the frequency or significance of the overlap between various functions. Individuals with multiple affiliations help coordinate and integrate the activity of diverse organizations. Thus, for example, one gentleman interviewed was a member of his Socialist federation executive committee, a former member of the national executive committee of the Socialist Party, a mayor of an important city in the département, general councilor (and vice president of the general council and leader of the Socialist Party faction in the general council), and a senator from the département as well.

Yet the *cumul* also increases the chance of role conflict. In the case just cited, the senator ran in municipal and senatorial elections on a slate grouping the Socialist and third force centrist parties against the Communist Party; but at the level of the general council, the Socialist and Communist parties formed a coalition against the Socialists' allies from these other elections!

Dissonance is usually resolved by minimizing partisan involvement. Thus, when questioned about his Socialist Party activity, the senator replied, "I'm not as active in the party now as I used to be. It's better not to be because I have to deal with members of the prefectural and national administration and it's better not to be too prominently identified with a party." Moreover, his alliance with the Communist Party in the organization of the general council was dismissed as an electoral tactic, born from sheer necessity. (Hayward and Wright, 1971: 289, cite public opinion data which show that about one-fourth of the electorate opposes local officials simultaneously holding the position of deputy.)

Possibly in an attempt to reduce their public identification with a party, local officials who belong to a party are usually less active than other members. In answer to a question asking whether they would accept a higher post in a political party if it were offered to them, partisan local officials proved far less willing than party activists to accept greater party responsibilities. While the older age of local officials who belong to a party makes such an answer more likely, it also reduces their potential contribution to the party (for an analysis of the power exercised by local officials within French political parties, see Kesselman, 1972b).

An additional factor opposing immersion in party affairs is the sheer demand of administering a local government. Local officials devote most of their free hours to local government; they are not given a salary as local officeholder and they often exercise an occupation at the same time.

All these factors, probably above all the lack of concrete benefits a party can deliver, lead local officials, even those who are nominally party members, to keep their distance from political parties. Local officials who belonged to political parties were asked to assess the relative importance of their party and public position by assigning a score from 0-100: zero signified that the party post was relatively unimportant and the public position all-important; 100 signified that the party post was all-important and the public post unimportant; 50, that the two posts were of equal importance. (Gradations were also permitted.) Thus, the higher the figure, the more important the party position. The mean score for general councilors who belonged to a political party was 40; for mayors, 31. Virtually no local officials who belong to a political party rate their party position as more important to them than their elected office.

The data presented here offer eloquent testimony to the unimportance of party affiliation for local officials. Many have never belonged to a party; others were once members and have resigned. For local officials who are currently party members, priority appears to be given to public office rather than party position.

GAULLIST LINKS TO LOCAL GOVERNMENT

Since coming to power in 1958, the Gaullist regime has won nearly every national political contest: Its two defeats—May 1968, in the streets, and April 1969 (when the first referendum of the five submitted since 1958 was rejected)—were both swiftly followed by resounding triumphs. In June 1968, the U.D.R. won an absolute majority of seats in the National Assembly, the first time such a feat had occurred in this century. In April 1969, General de Gaulle's resignation of the presidency after public rejection of the referendum he sponsored, ended with the victory of the Gaullist candidate, Georges Pompidou, in the presidential election several weeks later.

Yet the Gaullists remain unable to translate their national political strength into success at the grass roots. Most town halls, from small *mairies* to the *hôtel de ville* of the largest cities, remain occupied by opponents of the U.D.R. After three general municipal elections in the Fifth Republic, the U.D.R. is far from obtaining a share of local power commensurate with its national strength. If political parties have colonized local governments and local officials to only a moderate extent, the U.D.R. has proved especially unsuccessful. Prior to the 1971 municipal elections, a mere 7 percent of all French mayors were Gaullist sympathizers, only 2 of the 31 cities with more than 100,000 population had Gaullist mayors (Verdès-Leroux, 1970: 978). By contrast, a majority of French deputies belonged to the U.D.R.

The U.D.R.'s failure to woo local elites is especially evident among partisan local officials: only 10 of the 67 general councilors and 3 of the 27 mayors in the sample who are presently party members belong to the U.D.R. To the extent that political parties have penetrated the ranks of French local public officials, parties opposing the U.D.R. are particularly likely to predominate.

An additional point suggesting the extent of Gaullist weakness locally is that a far smaller proportion of partisan local officials (those presently belonging to a party or belonging in the past) voted for Georges Pompidou in the 1969 presidential election than voted for his opponents.

What is the temporal and causal sequence among the variables: does the fact of being partisan lead to opposition to the U.D.R.? Or, conversely, are those with Gaullist preferences predisposed to remain nonpartisan while opponents of the U.D.R. are more likely to join a political party?

De Gaulle's repeated attacks on the "parties of the past," his aim of being above parties and his disdain even for his own party cannot have failed to alienate members of opposition parties and to discourage even local officials

TABLE 11
PARTISAN AFFILIATION OF LOCAL OFFICIALS BY VOTING PREFERENCE
IN PRESIDENTIAL ELECTIONS

	Pompidou		Opponents of Pompidou		Total	
	% →	% ↓	% →	% ↓	%	(n)
Partisan General Councilor	21	46	79	88	100	(81)
Nonpartisan General Councilor	69	54	31	12	100	(29)
Total %		100		100		
n		(37)		(73)		(110)
Partisan Mayors	30	30	70	59	100	(47)
Nonpartisan Mayors	58	70	42	41	100	(55)
Total %		100		100		
n		(46)		(56)		(102)

favorable to Gaullism from joining the U.D.R. (The concept of political parties is so unpalatable to Gaullists that their own is officially designated a "union," not a party, and is informally referred to by members as "le mouvement.") The government's aggressive local fiscal, tax, and administrative reform proposals also antagonized local officials; joining the U.D.R. may have appeared to a local official as betrayal.

Factors examined above suggest that the characteristics which local officials share with Gaullist (rather than Socialist) activists are the very ones which minimize the chance of joining any political party, e.g., rural residency and an absence of explicit politicizing influences in youth. For example, no general councilor favorable to Pompidou's candidacy developed an interest in politics by age 17, compared to one-fourth of the general councilors opposed to Pompidou. General councilors favorable to Pompidou were nearly twice as likely as other general councilors not to develop an interest in political affairs before their mid-twenties (81-44 percent, respectively). Likewise, local officials opposed to Pompidou's candidacy were far more likely to recall discussing politics at home in their youth.

It is reasonable, therefore, that the causal sequence is in both directions. The very ideological, socioeconomic, and social-psychological reasons which might impel a local official toward membership in the U.D.R. also impelled him away from joining a political party in the first place. Conversely, being a party member was likely to mean rejecting the Gaullist regime.

The U.D.R.'s failure to attract partisan local officials is not without consequence. For example, in the April 1969 referendum on regional reform (whose defeat cost de Gaulle the presidency), being a partisan local official appreciably increased the probability of opposing the proposal. Whereas a small

TABLE 12
LOCAL OFFICIALS' VOTE IN APRIL 1969 REFERENDUM (in percentages)

	Proportions Voting:		Refuse to Answer, Abstention	%	(n)
	Oui	Non			
Rural General Councilors	41	56	3	100	(32)
Urban General Councilors	17	74	9	100	(78)
Rural Mayors	49	42	9	100	(55)
Urban Mayors	25	60	15	100	(48)
Partisan General Councilors	15	78	7	100	(81)
Nonpartisan General Councilors	48	45	7	100	(29)
Partisan Mayors	25	67	8	100	(48)
Nonpartisan Mayors	49	36	16	100	(55)

plurality of nonpartisan local officials endorsed the referendum, large majorities of partisan local officials opposed it.

The U.D.R. might be content simply to derive support from rural mayors and other nonpartisan local officials but for the fact that these officials are relatively inactive politically compared to partisan local officials. In the referendum and presidential election campaigns of 1969, partisan local officials gave advice far more frequently than did nonpartisan officials. More than twice as many partisan as nonpartisan local officials addressed public meetings during the campaigns.

The consequence of the differential political proclivities and political activity of partisan officials compared to nonpartisan officials (along with the unpopularity among local elites of the issue posed in the 1969 referendum), was that local officials opposing Pompidou in the presidential election were more active than were his supporters.

The difficulty caused the U.D.R. by the low repute in which it is held by local officials is thus compounded of the fact that there are fewer local officials favorable to the party than opposed and that those local officials who are favorable are less active politically. The net effect is for the U.D.R. to suffer from the efforts of local governmental officials. Of the 109 general councilors interviewed, only 5 reported delivering public speeches favorable to the April 1969 referendum or to Georges Pompidou in the election campaign following the referendum's defeat; by contrast, 44 general councilors reported delivering speeches opposing the referendum or Pompidou's candidacy. Small town mayors on both sides were generally inactive: among the 58 interviewed, 4 spoke for the Gaullist cause, 4 for the opposition. Among urban mayors, who are more active and more powerful than village mayors, the tendency was also to oppose the U.D.R.: of the 11 urban mayors interviewed who delivered speeches (among the 48 urban mayors in the sample), 10 spoke in behalf of the opposition, 1 in

TABLE 13
LOCAL OFFICIALS ASKED FOR ADVICE AND ADDRESSED PUBLIC MEETINGS
IN POLITICAL CAMPAIGN (in percentages)

	Proportion Asked for Advice	Proportion Who Addressed Public Meetings During Campaign	n(ca)
Socialist Leaders	78	51	(107)
Socialist Members	32	6	(87)
U.D.R. Leaders	78	59	(115)
U.D.R. Members	63	9	(96)
Rural General Councilors	61	19	(32)
Urban General Councilors	74	56	(77)
Rural Mayors	40	14	(57)
Urban Mayors	67	23	(48)
Partisan General Councilors	76	54	(80)
Nonpartisan General Councilors	55	21	(29)
Partisan Mayors	69	33	(49)
Nonpartisan Mayors	38	5	(56)
Pro-Pompidou General Councilor	68	14	(37)
Anti-Pompidou General Councilor	72	61	(72)
Pro-Pompidou Rural Mayor	38	13	(32)
Anti-Pompidou Rural Mayor	48	17	(23)
Pro-Pompidou Urban Mayor	71	7	(14)
Anti-Pompidou Urban Mayor	64	30	(33)

behalf of the U.D.R. Overall, 58 of the 68 local officials who campaigned were opponents of the U.D.R.

Part of the reason that local officials favorable to the U.D.R. do not campaign more actively in its behalf is that they are not as apt to be integrated into an organizational network which would foster campaign work. As was noted, a far smaller proportion of U.D.R. supporters among local officials are members of a party than is the case for opponents of the U.D.R. In addition, when party members were asked to rate the importance of party membership, local officials belonging to the U.D.R. were less apt to regard their party affiliation as valuable for local office.

Given the U.D.R.'s power nationally, it might appear surprising that few local officials are attracted to the party. Yet local officials who do belong to the U.D.R. see party membership as being of little benefit—less, indeed, than local elected officials from other parties regard the value of their party affiliation. The mean party-public office score for Gaullist general councilors was 32, compared to 41 for anti-Gaullist general councilors. (There are too few Gaullist mayors for meaningful comparison.) Thus, local officials belonging to the U.D.R. rated the importance of their party position lower than did local officials belonging to opposition parties.

The U.D.R. is engaged in numerous efforts to increase its municipal strength. A drastic change occurred after de Gaulle's resignation as President. The theme of *ouverture* in the 1969 presidential campaign was intended to placate local elites. Not least among the benefits the U.D.R. derived from gaining the centrist Centre Démocratie et Progrès (C.D.P.) as an ally was the party's strong links to local government.

President Pompidou and Jacques Chaban-Delmas (prime minister from 1969-1972 and mayor of Bordeaux, France's fifth largest city), spoke frequently and warmly of the importance of local public officials. The government consulted local officials when launching new administrative reforms and, unlike previous proposals, made ratification of the new plan contingent on approval by local officials.

At the same time, the U.D.R. was not unrealistic enough to think that it could recruit many incumbent notables. In preparing for the March 1971 municipal elections, the U.D.R. hesitated between trying to obtain a share of power in existing ruling coalitions by forming alliances with a broad array of parties (an approach proposed by Roger Frey, a chief Gaullist strategist), or running electoral slates of its own to capture exclusive control. Its weakness was evident by its choice of the former strategy. Yet implicit recognition that incumbents were not apt to join the Gaullist bandwagon was symbolized by the U.D.R.'s sponsorship of regional party schools in 1970 for future Gaullist candidates in municipal elections.

The Gaullists engaged in meticulous preparations for the 1971 municipal election, at the highest level, in an attempt to improve their municipal position. (The following report is based on the fine analyses of Bon and Ranger, 1972, and Heyward and Wright, 1971.) Prior to the election, a series of meetings was held, presided over by the prime minister and attended by the minister of the interior, minister responsible for relations with parliament, and administrative and parliamentary leaders of the government parties (U.D.R., Républicans Indépendants, and Centre Démocratie et Progrès). The aim of the meetings was to eliminate dissension within the governing coalition and reach agreement on a common slate of candidates representing the three parties for elections in large cities. The electoral situation was examined case-by-case in every French city over 30,000 and many smaller ones as well—over five hundred in all. At previous municipal elections in the Fifth Republic, the three parties frequently competed. Indeed, the U.D.R. was often opposed by coalitions of the two other parties allied with Socialists and Radicals. In 1970-1971, the time devoted by the highest governmental officials to reaching a mutually satisfactory dosage suggests the value they placed on a favorable electoral outcome.

However, the massive efforts within the Gaullist camp were largely unsuccessful. Although the Gaullist coalition gained votes in the municipal election, compared to the preceding municipal election of 1965, its advance came principally from the "opposition right" closest on the political spectrum. The major source of opposition (on the left), as well as traditional local notables continued to resist the Gaullist attack (Bon and Ranger, 1972: 236). Even in alliance with parties having strong ties to local government (the R.I. and P.D.M.), the Gaullist movement has not outdistanced opposition parties at the local level. The U.D.R.'s share of the 192 cities over 30,000 population rose from 28 to 30, but, since its allies' share dropped from 50 to 43 cities, the Gaullist movement lost ground overall.[4]

The toughness and resilience of the French local political infrastructure is further suggested by the fact that, when the U.D.R. has succeeded in gaining grass roots strength, it has mostly had to do so by coopting traditional local notables and thus losing its distinctive character. The result is that, like traditional French parties, it has become in part a captive of local notables (for a case study of this process in Lorraine, see Bonnet, 1972). The 1971 municipal election results thus suggest that the pattern evident from the survey data presented here will continue to prevail at least in the medium range.

CONCLUSION

We have come full circle in examining some linkages between partisan activists and local public officials. Parties are eager to colonize local government but multiple factors make such colonization difficult. Local administration (as local politics is significantly termed in French) and party politics are considered distinct activities; the intrusion of partisan factors into the conduct of local affairs is regarded as illegitimate. Partisan involvement may be a handicap in running local government; local public officials who belong to a political party are less integrated in the party than are other party members. Above all, local officials do not see what benefits party affiliation will have for the exercise of their local governmental position—which lies outside the party's control and which the party cannot be of much help in obtaining in the first place.

Principal findings presented here include:

(1) A relative lack of partisan entrenchment at the lowest levels of French local government (mayoral ranks); a far higher degree of partisan entrenchment at the next higher level (general councilors), with a generally greater partisan reach in urban as compared to rural areas.

(2) A small proportion of rank and file party members and nearly half of regional party cadres hold local public office.

(3) There do not appear to be major socioeconomic differences between the two groups of partisan activists and local elected officials; rather, differences are greater between

those of differing partisan affiliation and those occupying different hierarchical positions.

(4) However, partisan and public officials diverge sharply in regard to the politicization process. Compared to elected officials, party activists were exposed to more salient political stimuli in youth, were more ideologically inclined, and were politically conscious at an earlier age.

(5) The detachment local public officials evince toward political parties appears related to the meager support parties furnish and their relative unimportance in the recruitment and local electoral process.

(6) When there is a cumulation of functions (the same individual holding both a party and public office), partisan affiliation is regarded as less important than the public office occupied.

(7) The ruling U.D.R. is only moderately entrenched at the local level. Despite religious affinity between local public officials and Gaullist activists, the prevailing situation puts the U.D.R. at a relative disadvantage: most elected officials at the grass roots are unfavorable to the U.D.R.; most local elected officials who are party members belong to parties in opposition to the U.D.R.

The analysis suggests a stable system of differential spheres of local government and political parties in France. Local government remains largely distinct from national politics and relatively resistant to colonization by political parties. Municipal government remains outside the control of political parties, although the next level (the general council) has a more partisan basis. Moreover, the lines of cleavage are quite different in national and local politics. Above all, the U.D.R. continues to prove unable to convince local officials of the benefits it can provide. Few local elected officials are U.D.R. members; many more are neutral, opposed to the U.D.R., and members of opposition parties. The trend does not seem to be toward the disappearance of local distinctiveness but toward the persistence of differentiation and even opposition between the two spheres.

A complex set of factors makes it likely that political parties will fail to strengthen their links appreciably to French local government. The kind of factors which foster partisan affiliation are not apt to be prevalent among French local elites. There is little evidence that new elites—including those who reached power in the municipal elections of 1965 and 1971—are more favorably disposed to party affiliation (see Berger, 1969, and Verdès-Leroux, 1971).

In light of the fact that, in many respects, nonpartisan local officials resemble the Gaullists, it is paradoxical that the existing situation favors the opposition. However, the fluid and multiparty situation which prevails locally—more similar to the Fourth than the Fifth Republic—makes it difficult for any one party to gain power by itself in most cities. The U.D.R. has made but slight headway in controlling local government. Although there are slow trends toward a congruence of local and national political forces in France, the future remains very much open. Meanwhile, the Fourth Republic persists at the municipal level long after the republic's demise.

NOTES

1. From an interview conducted with the assistant to the administrative secretary of the U.D.R. in the winter 1970.

2. The number of officials interviewed include:

Socialist Party leaders	108	General Councilors	110
Socialist Party members	90	Rural Mayors	58
U.D.R. leaders	115	Urban Mayors	48
U.D.R. members	96	n=	625

Rural communes contain less than 2,000 population; urban communes are considered by the French government to be communes with more than 2,000 population. Establishing a higher threshold would have precluded carrying out statistical analyses because of the small number of large cities in the départements studied.

When leaders and members from the two parties are combined, they will be referred to as partisan (or party) activists. (This does not imply all are necessarily active within their party organization.) Mayors and general councilors will be referred to as local officials, local public officials, or as local governmental officials; those local officials who reported ever having been a member of a political party (past or present) will be called partisan local officials; and local officials who have never belonged to a political party will be termed nonpartisan local officials.

I am grateful for the generous cooperation of P.S. and U.D.R. officials at national and departmental headquarters, party activists and local public officials. The survey was carried out by SOFRES and the help of Pierre Weill, political director of SOFRES, is gratefully acknowledged.

3. In order to maximize comparability, the questions posed to the two groups were slightly different. Partisan activists were asked at what age they became interested in "problèmes politiques," whereas the question to local officials asked about interest in "affaires publiques." The reason for the latter formulation was it was feared the term "political problems" might antagonize local officials, who frequently deny involvement in politics (for an analysis of these nuances, see Tarrow, 1971). Given the less restrictive formulation of the question put to local public officials, their later politicization becomes even more striking.

4. Observers who consider the 1971 municipal elections a victory for the U.D.R. usually base their analysis only on cities over 30,000, whereas, as Verdès-Leroux (1970) showed, it is in smaller cities that the opposition to Gaullism was (and remains) particularly strong. Moreover, it is surely significant that the Gaullist alliance is far from controlling the majority of town halls in France after three municipal elections spanning nearly two decades in the Fifth Republic (a period when the Gaullists were continuously in control at the national level).

REFERENCES

AMBLER, J. S. (1968) "The Democratic Union for the Republic: to survive de Gaulle." Rice University Studies 54 (Summer): 1-51.

AVRIL, P. (1971) "La modernisation politique et le systeme local français." Analyse et Prévision 12 (November): 1319-1328.

BERGER, S. et al. (1969) "The problem of reform in France: the political ideas of local elites." Political Science Quarterly 84 (September): 436-460.

BERNARD, A. and G. Le BLANC (1970) "Le parti socialiste S.F.I.O. dans l'Isère." Revue Française de Science Politique 20 (June): 557-567.

BON, F. and J. RANGER (1972) "Bilan des élections municipales de Mars 1971 dans les villes de plus de 30,000 habitants." Revue Française de Science Politique 22 (April): 213-237.

BONNET, S. (1972) Sociologie Politique et Réligieuse de la Lorraine. Paris: Armand Colin.

CHARLOT, J. (1970) La Phénomène Gaulliste. Paris: Fayard.

——— (1967) L'U.N.R., étude du pouvoir au sein d'un parti politique. Paris: Armand Colin.

CONVERSE, P. E. and G. DUPEUX (1966) "Politicization of the electorate in France and the United States," pp. 269-291 in A. Campbell et al., Elections and the Political Order. New York: John Wiley.

DREYFUS, F. (1972) "Les instances locales des forces politiques nationales," pp. 53-66 in A. Mabileau (ed.) Les Facteurs Locaux de la Vie Politique Nationale. Paris: Pédone.

GILLI, J. P. (1968) "Le maire et l'exercise de ses fonctions dans le département des Alpes-Maritimes." Revue Française de Science Politique 18 (June): 467-507.

GREMION, P. (1970) "Introduction à une étude du systeme politico-administratif local." Sociologie du Travail 12 (January-March): 51-73.

——— and J. WORMS (1970) "L'état et les collectivités locales." Esprit 38 (January): 20-35.

——— (1968a) Les Institutions Régionales et le Société Locale. Paris: Centre de Sociologie des Organisations.

——— (1968b) "La concertation régionale, innovation ou tradition? " pp. 35-60 in Institut d'Etudes Politiques de Grenoble, Aménagement du Territoire et Développement Régionale, I. Paris: La Documentation Française.

HAYWARD, J. and V. WRIGHT (1971) "The 37,708 microcosms of an indivisible republic: the French local elections of March 1971." Parliamentary Affairs (Autumn): 284-311.

KESSELMAN, M. (1973) "The recruitment of rival party activists in France." Journal of Politics 35 (February): 2-44.

——— (1972a) "Changes in the French party system." Comparative Politics 4 (January): 281-301.

——— (1972b) "Systèmes de pouvoir et cultures politiques au sein des parties politiques Français." Revue Française de Sociologie 13 (October): 485-515.

——— (1970) "Overinstitutionalization and political constraint: the case of France." Comparative Politics 3 (October): 21-44.

——— (1967) The Ambiguous Consensus: A Study of Local Government in France. New York: Alfred A. Knopf.

LIPMANSON, D. L. (1971) "Protest versus traditional local rule in France." Presented at the annual meeting of the American Political Science Association, Chicago.

LONGPIERRE, M. (1970) "Permanence des conseillers généraux et renouveau des traditions administratives départementales," pp. 3-34 in Institut d'Etudes Politiques de Grenoble, Aménagement du Territoire et Développement Régionale, III. Paris: La Documentation Française.

MABILEAU, A. (ed.) (1972) Les Facteurs Locaux de la Vie Politique Nationale. Paris: Pédone.

MacRAE, D., Jr. (1967) Parliament, Parties, and Society in France, 1946-1958. New York: St. Martin's.

MEDARD, J. F. (1972) "La recherche du cumul de mandats par les candidats aux élections législatives sous la Cinquième République," pp. 139-159 in A. Mabileau (ed.) Les Facteurs Locaux de la Vie Politique Nationale. Paris: Pédone.

——— (1970) "La recherche sur la vie politico-administrative locale en France." Presented at the Congress of the International Political Science Association, Munich.

PLATONE, F. (1967) "L'implantation municipale du parti communiste dans la Seine et sa conception de l'administration communale." Paris: Mémoire, Institut d'Etudes Politiques.

SIMMONS, H. G. (1970) French Socialists in Search of a Role, 1956-1967. Ithaca, N.Y.: Cornell Univ. Press.

——— (1969) "The French socialist opposition in 1969." Government and Opposition 4 (Summer): 294-307.

SOUCHON, M. (1968) Le Maire, Elu Local dans un Société en Changement. Paris: Cujas.

TARROW, S. (1971) "The urban-rural cleavage in political involvement: the case of France." American Political Science Review 65 (June): 341-357.

TIERSKY, R. (1972) "The Communist movement in France: 1920-1971." Ph.D. dissertation. Columbia University.

VERDES-LEROUX, J. (1971) "L'idéologie communale des élus locaux." Espaces et Sociétés (March): 169-183.

——— (1970) "Characteristiques des maires des communes de plus de 2,000 habitants." Revue Française de Science Politique (October): 974-990.

WILSON, F. L., III (1971) The French Democratic Left, 1963-1969: Toward a Modern Party System. Stanford, Calif.: Stanford Univ. Press.

WORMS, J. (1966) "Le préfet et ses notables." Sociologie du Travail 7 (July-September): 249-276.

Part II

PROCESSES OF DECISION-MAKING

Chapter 5

Decision-Making Systems in
Thirty-Six Swedish Communes

Jörgen Westerståhl

BACKGROUND

Political systems must continually adapt themselves to technical, economic and social changes. "Adaptation" here involves not only a passive accomodation to this development, but also adaptive measures which in their turn can modify the trend of the development. Since an essential feature of this development is the increasing specialization of individual and group work functions, it becomes an important element in the adaptive measures taken by a political system to take over duties which the individual or the family used to be responsible for: that is, to expand social services in their widest sense.

The adaptive measures taken by a political system can, in principle, be said to consist of two types. On the one hand there are those whose aim it is simply to cater to new social needs which have arisen; on the other, there are those whose purpose it is to adjust the actual structure of the political system.

The problems of adapting are just as great for the national (federal) political system as for its subsystems at the regional (state) and local levels. What characterizes the traditional form of the local political system as it has emerged from its historical development, is the great variation to be found in its ability to solve the problems actualized by a developing society. This variation involves the financial and personnel resources at the disposal of the local units, but it is also a matter of their actual "clientele," that is, the availability of consumers to a certain service. For example, if a compulsory school is to be able to offer a

AUTHOR'S NOTE: *This is a revised version of a paper prepared for delivery at the 1970 Annual Meeting of the American Political Science Association, Biltmore Hotel, Los Angeles, September 7-12.*

degree of course differentiation so as to reach a desired standard, there must be enough school children to make such a differentiation seem reasonable.

There are various ways of coming to grips with this situation of a growing need for social services combined with widely differing prospects for the local political systems to meet these needs. One solution is for the federal or state unit to take over those responsibilities which the local units are no longer considered capable of managing. It becomes then a question of shifting certain responsibilities from a lower to a higher level. Since the service must be offered locally anyway, it might be necessary for the higher administration to build up a new local one. Another possibility is for the local units to cooperate in managing those functions which each unit by itself is too small to cope with. A third way out is to reorganize the entire local structure into sufficiently large self-supporting units. In practice this will usually mean guaranteeing that no local unit fall below a certain minimum of population, resources, etc.

Sweden has largely settled for the third solution. Of course a transfer of responsibilities has occurred. But it has been made in both directions, and the net result has rather been an increase in responsibilities carried out by the local governments. Since 1955, local government investment in, and consumption of, the gross national product has been greater than that of the central government. It should be observed at this point, however, that the duties of the local government have in many areas been specified in detail by the central government. The method involving cooperation between the local governments has also been tried, but the need for such cooperation decreases, at least temporarily, when the smaller units disappear.

Up until the early 1950s, there were about 2,500 local government units (communes) in Sweden. Well over 100 of these were urban communes while most of the small local communes coincided with the local parishes of the state church of Sweden. Through a decision of the Riksdag (the Swedish national legislature), smaller rural communes were combined or reapportioned into larger units. By 1952, the number of communes had been reduced to less than 1,000.

Ten years later it was already evident that this reform did not go nearly far enough. In 1962 the Riksdag decided that the communes should be grouped into blocks. The communes within these blocks which, from the very beginning, had no important decision-making powers, were gradually to combine to form new large communal units. At first it was assumed that the final amalgamation would be entirely voluntary. Now a deadline for 1974 has been set for the completion of the consolidation within the blocks at which time there will only be about 250 communes left. This means that the number of communes will have decreased to about 10 percent of the original figure in a little over 20 years.

The motivation for both reforms has been explained in terms of the communes' need for sufficient resources if they are to be able to offer their inhabitants a satisfactory standard of service. One of the objects stated in the

1952 reform was that each commune should be large enough to afford a qualified administrator (minimum pop. 3,000); according to the old system, the communes were administrated by unsalaried elected representatives. The 1962 reform directed itself particularly to the new nine-year school system (minimum pop. 8,000).

There is, however, an interesting difference between the two decisions. The 1952 reform was carried out quite mechanically. Two or more rural communes were simply combined until the desired minimum size was reached. The 1962 decision put into effect a completely new view of communal organization. The old difference between town and country, which originated in the Middle Ages, was to be abolished as well as, insofar as this was possible, the differences in social services offered by urban and rural areas. The entire local organization was recast according to the principle that social services should be concentrated at a main natural gathering center of a certain area. This meant, then, adapting the administrative reapportionment of communal districts to natural regions. The new communes were to be built around a center and to constitute this center's area of influence (i.e., the central town commune and its peripheral communes).

A theoretical model for the new communal apportionment is presented in Figure 1. The figure shows the areas of influence, and their theoretical border lines, of three hypothetical urban areas, C1, C2, and C3, of which C2 was considered to have the highest degree of centrality and C1 the lowest.

Against this background, it seemed a rewarding research project to investigate the effects upon the mechanism of communal self-government in Sweden of societal changes in general, and in particular, of the program of communal reapportionment.

RESEARCH ORGANIZATION

Other reasons for selecting and investing heavily in this particular research project were the desire to promote cooperation between the political science departments of the various universities, and to develop empirical research methods. From a theoretical point of view, it seemed especially interesting to study and compare a large number of communes—i.e., a large number of political systems functioning within a common frame—since this increased the possibility of coming to grips with what lies behind the differences between the various systems.

After several conferences and preliminary investigations, the political science departments of the five Swedish universities presented a request for funds to the Tri-Centermial Fund of the Bank of Sweden, for a five-year research project called "Communal Self-Government—Communal Apportionment." Full-scale work was started on the project in 1966, and the Foundation has laid a total of

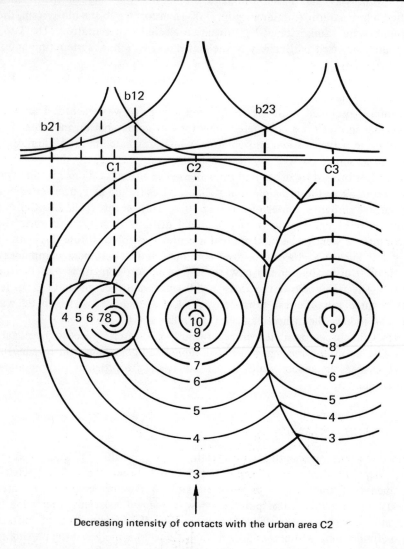

Decreasing intensity of contacts with the urban area C2

Figure 1: THEORETICAL MODEL FOR COMMUNAL APPORTIONMENT

over 5 million Sw. Cr. (about $1 million) at our disposal by means of annual appropriations to continue until the beginning of 1971. A smaller sum has been calculated for the closing phase.

The project is led by a board consisting of one representative for each of the political science departments. In addition to the general responsibility for carrying out the project, the board has direct control over budgetary matters, appointments, and the authorization of dissertation subjects.

The immediate responsibility for the overall planning of research is held, under the board, by a program director and the directors of the various projects. Each respective board member functions as a kind of area director at each university. In principle, personnel and financial resources have been distributed equally among the five university departments. The scope of the budget has made possible the appointment of three to five research assistants (with a certain turnover) to each department.

Since most of the research work covers a sample of communes spread all over the country, they have been distributed to the various departments according to location. In this way, each department has chiefly been responsible for keeping in touch with "its" communes, regardless of project type.

The research is being done mainly in the form of "licentiat" and Ph.D. dissertations. The total number of dissertations is expected to reach 40 (18 have been completed). Over 700 undergraduates have participated in the gathering and preparation of the data.

It has been the endeavor of the board in those projects where there are several doctoral candidates (this is true for most of them), to distribute the dissertation subjects among the various departments. We have refrained from the obvious solution of letting each department work in its particular area of specialization, because of our desire to promote a unified approach within the whole research project. On the whole, the exchange of views within the project has been extremely lively. Approximately one-tenth of costs has gone to cover conferences, meetings between the researchers, and visits to the communes under study.

As is evident from this description, the work of the project has also functioned as a graduate training program.

THE VALUE APPROACH

The general purpose of the research program is therefore to attempt to determine how local self-government is influenced by society as a whole and particularly by changes in apportionment decided on.

In deciding on more precise questions to be selected within this framework we chose not to begin from a definite group of hypotheses which may be

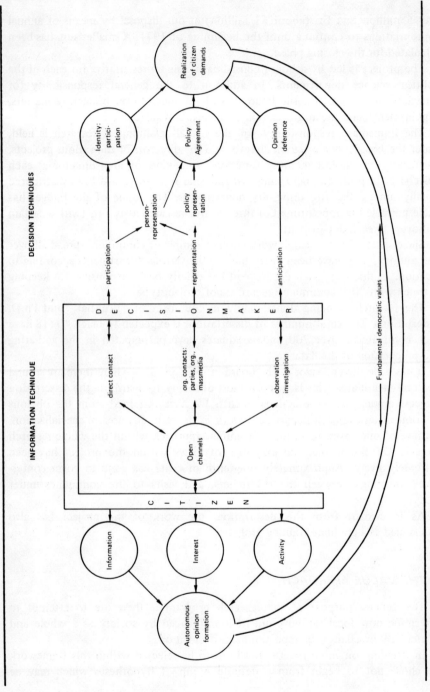

INFORMATION TECHNIQUE

DECISION TECHNIQUES

Realization
of citizen
demands

Identity:
partici-
pation

Policy
Agreement

Opinion
deference

person-
representation

policy
represen-
tation

participation

representation

anticipation

D E C I S I O N M A K E R

Fundamental democratic values

direct contact

org. contacts:
parties, org.,
massmedia

observation
investigation

Open
channels

C I T I Z E N

Information

Interest

Activity

Autonomous
opinion
formation

Figure 2: THE DEMOCRATIC VALUE

assumed to influence local self-government. We chose instead a broader approach and began by going through what has been said about local self-government in different national commissions, parliamentary protocols and in open discussion during the last decade in Sweden: why is local self-government desired; what positive values have been connected with local self-government in this debate?

The reason for choosing this approach was partly one of practical politics. We wished to create the best possible guarantees that we have taken up such questions as are generally regarded as relevant. Our results could in this way best be thought of as being suited as a basis for political decision-making. The fact that all political parties assert that they are positively interested in local self-government also enters into the picture.

It soon became obvious that the values connected with local self-government in open debate could be grouped under two headings, related to democracy and efficiency. The purpose of the research can therefore be summed up as concerning *how the possibilities of providing for democratic values and efficiency values within local self-government are influenced primarily by changes in apportionment.*

The term "values" is used in many different senses.[1] It is here used to mean that which is given a value—an object, a situation, a relationship, etc.—and which therefore in this case should be connected with local self-government. Even if the evaluation itself contains a subjective element, the realization of the values is nevertheless something which can be objectively measured.

Before the values could be measured extensive preliminary work was required. This work comprised three main separate steps. The first was to extract statements on the value of local self-government from public discussion. These statements are made in various actual connections and the values are described in many different ways and more or less completely. It therefore became necessary as a second step to attempt to systematize and delimit the values appearing in the debates. As a third step there followed the real work of operationalization.

Task number two, the systematizing and delimiting of the values, is in principle the most difficult task. This work can be illustrated by the attempt to systematize the democratic values which we finally decided on (Figure 2).

Behind this diagram lie two essential notions.[2] Firstly it is assumed that the fundamental democratic value consists of two main elements, of which one is concerned with the realization of citizen demands and the other one with autonomous opinion formation. Secondly it is assumed that the provision of these fundamental democratic values is dependent on various democratic techniques which in their turn are connected with different values. It is this complexity in democratic value which the diagram attempts to come to terms with.

Provided the diagram is largely realistic—i.e., covers important parts of the prevailing conceptions of democracy—it is suitable as a basis for operational analysis. Perhaps the most practical value of the diagram will be to prevent the investigations from being biased towards one or two partial aspects of democracy (compared with the American community power literature, with its strong concentration on participation value).

Concerning efficiency values it may be briefly stated here that by efficiency is meant the achievement of goals at minimum cost. The communes are not only organs for self-government in the sense of local citizen activity but they can also be regarded as organs for decentralized administration. From the viewpoint of the national political system the communes appear as subsystems. The political activity of the communes is therefore limited on the one side by personnel and financial resources and on the other side by the boundaries set by the government for communal activity or what might be called central state steering.

SAMPLE OF COMMUNES

How shall one predict the effect of apportionment changes on democracy and efficiency values? Two ways seem to present themselves. The first involves studying those communes which are already of the type which future communes will be. However, the new communes will be to an important extent of a type which now has no real counterpart. The second and more essential way is therefore to study generally the pattern of causes which affects democracy and efficiency values with special observation of such conditions as are directly changed by apportionment changes.

The best way of studying causal connections is, as is well known, through experiment. However, it has not been possible to carry out experiments in the real sense in this case just as in most other social science investigations. The causal-analytical approach we chose was, however, given a form which can be described as quasi-experimental.

Although there is very comprehensive statistical information available for all Swedish communes, it was clear from the start that we must collect important data and that we must therefore make use of a sample of communes. We chose, with the help of statistical expertise, a system of sampling which was judged as being the most suitable for causal analysis but on the other hand not very suitable as a description of Swedish communes. This last point means, for example, that one cannot state with satisfactory precision how common a particular characteristic is in all of the Swedish communes. This choice of approach is naturally not without problems. Politicians, for example, are often concerned primarily with descriptive data.

The following sample procedure was used. To begin with, Sweden's communes were divided into three separate groups. In the first group were communes which are part of the three metropolitan areas (population M); in the second, communes which are undergoing changes—that is, communes which were affected, wholly or partially, by communal mergers 1/1 1967 (population C); and in the third group, the remaining communes—that is, the majority of the communes (population A).

From population A, 36 communes were drawn using a modified "grecco-latinsquare-design." As basic selection variables, size and density of population were chosen (see below). Furthermore, the political situation was also considered (communes where the Social Democrats had/did not have a majority according to the 1964 election results), as well as geographical position and location within the block of communes. From the figures in Table 1, the commune sample construction appears in relation to the two basic variables. The numbers within parentheses indicate how many communes there actually are within the combined size-density of population classes. As is apparent, six communes have been taken from each such class whenever the real numbers permitted. The three largest cities—Stockholm, Göteborg and Malmö—have in some studies been added to the A-sample. Six communes have been taken from the C-sample.

The majority of the investigations have been carried out within the sample. The choice of the two basic stratification variables, size and density, depended on various considerations. It is first and foremost these two variables which were directly influenced by the decided apportionment changes. For the political decision makers it is these variables which are directly open to manipulation. Everything further indicated that these two variables were basic in the sense that many other variables followed these in their variation. Our preliminary investigations also indicated the importance of being able to simultaneously check for both size and density.

Naturally, it would have been desirable to take into account further variables in the sample procedure, e.g., the rate of population increase and economic structure. Our experience hitherto does not, however, suggest that any of these variables should be given priority before the basic stratification variables.

When the sample was constructed, we had no possibility to take into account any administrative variables. A simple but essential administrative variables'

TABLE 1
THE MAIN SAMPLE

		Size of Population		
	% Inhabitants in Densely Populated Areas	I 0-8.000	II 8.000-30.000	III 30.000+
A	90-100	6 (36)	6 (42)	6 (17)
B	30- 90	6 (332)	6 (50)	— (1)
C	0- 30	6 (305)	— (2)	—

TABLE 2
NUMBER[a] OF FULL-TIME LOCAL GOVERNMENT PERSONNEL PER 1,000 INHABITANTS IN THE A-SAMPLE COMMUNES—MEAN VALUES

	I	II	III
A	4,3 (4,3)	7,3 (7,)	8,6 (8,9)
B	3,2 (3,0)	5,9 (4,7)	
C	2,7 (2,3)		

a. Figures within parentheses denote the corresponding distribution within all communes.

relationship to size and density is illustrated in Table 2. The number of full-time local government personnel per 1,000 inhabitants in the various size and density classes can therefore be regarded as a kind of test of the assumptions of the fundamental importance of the stratification variables. Note that the table underscores precisely the importance of being able to check simultaneously for both size and density.

An important condition in connection with the analysis of causal conceptions is, in accordance with the quasi-experimental approach, that the whole population of Sweden's communes be treated as a sample from an imaginary infinite population of communes, within which each subgroup be deemed to have arisen under similar conditions. The communes are chosen on the basis of certain characteristics, or rather a combination of certain characteristics. These characteristics are, theoretically speaking, not "Swedish." Even if all Swedish communes had been used in the groups compared the conclusions would not have been "certain" in the same sense as a description of all Swedish communes can be certain.

THREE EXAMPLES OF FINDINGS

As previously said there are already 18 dissertations in which the findings from this research project are presented. There is therefore a considerable amount of material to choose from. The examples which have been used here have the advantage of not needing extensive presentation of institutional details. In a sense which will be treated in the final section it can be said that all findings may be regarded as preliminary.

A. Citizen Interest in Communal Problems (Claes Ortendahl, Uppsala). In connection with the municipal election of 1966, 1,800 voters were interviewed in the 36 communes of the A-sample (approximately 50 voters per commune).

It was assumed that discussion on local government matters would form the last link in a chain of information from the local authorities to the voter level. Information is made available to the voters through the press, parties and organizations, and is further divulgated step by step through conversation

TABLE 3
MEAN PERCENTAGE OF VOTERS WITH HIGH DISCUSSION FREQUENCY INDEX

	I	II	III
A	38,1	36,0	29,3
B	30,0	28,7	
C	23,5		

between voters. We further assumed that there exists a process of communication in the other direction, from the voters to the local representatives in the commune and that discussions form the first step in communication.

The appearance of discussions on communal problems is measured through a number of interview questions treating partly how often discussions occurred, partly the subjects of discussion in the various types of groups. On the basis of these questions a scale was constructed forming a basis for dividing the voters into two groups: those who often and those who seldom discussed local problems.

In Table 3 is indicated what proportion of voters in the communes selected often discussed local problems. It appears that in the small densely populated communes (IA) about 35 percent of voters discuss local problems frequently. With diminishing degree of density and with increase in size this proportion is reduced.

We have sought for an explanation of these tendencies in terms of the voters' social contacts with people who have information about the commune. Two types of such contacts have been particularly studied. The first of these is personal contact with the local representatives. The second is contact through membership in parties and organizations.

It is of course the case that the proportion of the population which is directly involved in local government is significantly greater in small communes than in large ones. Membership in political and other voluntary organizations of various kinds has also a tendency to be greatest in the small communes.

In Table 4 voters with a high discussion frequency index have been divided into four groups in each cell according to a combination of characteristics "acquantance with representatives" and "membership of organizations." Some results from an analysis of these four groups will be presented here. Firstly, we can see that among those who are not members of organizations contact with representatives hardly plays any significant role. On the other hand, we can see that contact with representatives has great importance among those who are members of organizations. In all cells of the sample matrix we can note that those who are members of organizations, whether they are acquainted or not with local representatives, discuss communal problems more than those who are not in organizations.

It seems that through this analysis we have to some extent managed to

TABLE 4
MEAN PERCENTAGE OF VOTERS WITH HIGH DISCUSSION FREQUENCY
INDEX: ACQUAINTANCE WITH LOCAL REPRESENTATIVES AND
MEMBERSHIP OF ORGANIZATIONS

	I		II		III	
Organization Membership	Yes	No	Yes	No	Yes	No
Contact with Representatives						
A Not acquainted	32,9	15,1	24,6	17,5	18,1	11,3
Acquainted	42,9	13,9	36,4	17,9	35,2	11,7
B Not acquainted	23,8	10,1	30,9	14,2		
Acquainted	38,4	13,9	34,8	9,9		
C Not acquainted	15,3	14,8				
Acquainted	25,6	21,3				

explain why discussions occur particularly often in the small communes and less often in large communes. It can further be noted that the two factors which influence the occurrence of discussions—contact with representatives and membership of organizations—will be considerably influenced by the merging of communes. When the total of representatives is reduced, contact situations between voters and the voted are also reduced. Other investigations within the project also suggest that the proportion of voters who are members of organizations will be reduced by a merging of communes. This would mean that the proportion which discusses communal problems will diminish after a merging, which therefore in turn has the consequence that the conditions for a well-operating communal democracy are, from this point of view, negatively influenced.

B. Representation (Lars Strömberg, Gothenburg). Two types of representations are considered here, policy representation and person representation. By policy representation is meant the extent to which in various matters the attitudes of the elected representatives reflect the attitudes of the voters, by person-representation the extent to which the personal characteristics of the elected representatives (for example, social background, income, occupation, education, and so on) reflect those of the voters. Information about the voters is taken from the above-mentioned interviews and about the elected representatives in the communes from a questionnaire sent out in the autumn of 1968 to all councillors in the 36 communes in the A sample and in the city of Gothenburg, in all more than 1,200 people. In each commune about 50 voters and between 20 and 80 councillors.

To illustrate how the degree of person-representation varies between different types of communes we have chosen to compare the education of councillors and electorate, and to limit ourselves to the portion of the group with only

TABLE 5
EDUCATION OF SOCIALIST AND NON-SOCIALIST COUNCILLORS AND VOTERS
(mean percentage per commune with elementary school education within the respective groups)

	I		II		III		Gothenburg	
	Non-soc.	*Soc.*	*Non-soc.*	*Soc.*	*Non-soc.*	*Soc.*	*Non-soc.*	*Soc.*
A								
Councillors	19,5	35,9	7,9	32,2	5,7	18,4	0,0	11,8
Voters	54,4	75,9	39,3	77,6	43,6	66,3	37,9	58,0
B								
Councillors	27,3	47,2	22,3	27,3				
Voters	66,3	82,9	56,9	67,7				
C								
Councillors	27,4	59,5						
Voters	69,6	85,0						

elementary school education. In Table 5 both voters and councillors have been divided into two groups—socialists and nonsocialists—and for each group the percentage with only elementary school education is noted. Of the five Swedish parties it is principally the Social Democrats, together with the numerically small Communist party, who account for the socialists, and the three more or less equally large parties, Conservatives, Peoples party and Center party (formerly Agrarians), for the nonsocialists.

It is clear from this table that there are very great differences between socialists and nonsocialists at both council and voter level. The other point of comparison between on the one hand socialist councillor and voter and on the other nonsocialist councillor and voter, that is the person-representation within the socialist and nonsocialist blocs, shows on the whole that differences are of roughly the same order. For the socialist parties, however, the differences increase in large and more densely populated areas, while the nonsocialist parties show the opposite tendency. It may be mentioned that supporters of the Center party, which is included in the nonsocialist group, have a considerably lower level of education among both their voters and their councillors than the other nonsocialist parties. The difference between socialists and nonsocialists would be much greater if the Center party were taken out of the analysis.

One conclusion that could be drawn from this material is that the councillors form an educational, social and economic elite in comparison with the electorate, but that at the same time the party system works efficiently in that it reflects the essential differences in the electorate.

Perhaps the most fundamental questions of political attitude concern the legitimate scope of public operations, how much it should be allowed to cost and how society, working on a limited budget, is to decide on priorities. We used

TABLE 6
POSITIVE ATTITUDE TO LOCAL SPENDING AMONG SOCIALIST AND NON-SOCIALIST COUNCILLORS AND VOTERS (mean percentage per commune within respective groups of those prepared to raise local taxes)

	I		II		III	
	Non-soc.	*Soc.*	*Non-soc.*	*Soc.*	*Non-soc.*	*Soc.*
A						
Councillors	15,5	24,0	19,0	62,0	20,8	63,8
Voters	15,0	19,3	13,5	20.3	15,6	16,3
B						
Councillors	23,7	53,2	21,6	52,4		
Voters	25,3	23,0	17,3	29,1		
C						
Councillors	11,0	32,1				
Voters	19,5	30,2				

questions in each of these areas to study the policy representation of the voters by their councillors.

The first question was about the attitude of voters and councillors to expenditure, that is principally their positiveness towards a rise in local taxes in order to meet various claims on the local purse. We have chosen here to make a distinction between socialists and nonsocialists in the same way as in the previous table.

It would be pointed out first that among voters, if one does not distinguish between socialists and nonsocialists, there is a systematic tendency in the direction of decreased positiveness towards local spending with increasing size and density of commune population. Resistance is lowest in the sparsely populated communes and highest in the largest towns investigated. Among councillors there is, however, an even more clearly marked tendency in the opposite direction. Resistance to spending decreases with increasing size and density of population.

From Table 6, however, it can be seen that with a division into socialist and nonsocialist these differences show themselves in reality to be a function of the fact that socialist councillors are decidedly readier to spend public funds, or if you like are more radical, than their nonsocialist colleagues. It can also be seen that the socialist councillors are considerably less policy-representative of their voters than are the nonsocialists according to the measuring technique used here. Just as with person-representation, the party system functions at the local level in such a way that differences of opinion among the electorate are reflected and reinforced among councillors.

In the interviews carried out at the time of the 1966 local elections, voters were also asked about their attitude towards local services. Those interviewed

TABLE 7
COMPARISON BETWEEN VOTERS AND COUNCILLORS CONCERNING HIGHEST
PRIORITY AMONG LOCAL SERVICES

	I		II		III	
	Voters	*Councillors*	*Voters*	*Councillors*	*Voters*	*Councillors*
A	Housing Work Day nurseries	Housing Work Day nurseries	Housing Home help Day nurseries	Housing Work Day nurseries	Housing Home help Old people's homes (Day nurseries)	Housing Work Day nurseries (Old people's homes)
B	Work Roads, Streets Housing (Day nurseries)	Work Day nurseries Housing	Housing Day nurseries Home help (Work)	Housing Work Old people's homes		
C	Work Day nurseries Home help	Work Day nurseries Housing				

were invited to express their opinions on the large number (12) of areas of local service and to explain with reference to each of these areas if they thought the commune "should do more than now," if on the whole they thought "things were all right as they were," if they thought the commune "should decrease its efforts" or if they "had no opinion on the matter." Similar questions were put to councillors in the questionnaire.

The table shows which service areas received the highest number of "should do more" ratings among voters and councillors. It is clear from the table that in all types of commune there is a high level of agreement between voters and councillors as to which areas should receive the highest priority. A closer analysis shows that this agreement seems to be greatest in cell 1 A but that with increasing size of commune and, to some extent, a decrease in population density it decreases somewhat.

Even if the results shown here are only provisional, it is already clear that the elected representatives differ from the voters of all parties and in all types of commune, both economically, socially and educationally, and that these differences increase with increasing size of commune. The traditional assumption, however, that an elite of this type would be conservative in economic matters was not found to be true. The results point rather in the opposite direction if we control for party. Social Democrats in the largest communes differ considerably, for example educationally, from their supporters among the electorate, but they are even so much more radical than the latter in the sense of being readier to spend public money.

The close agreement between voters and councillors on the question of priorities in the local services may appear remarkable, not least in view of the results of other investigations of voters' scant knowledge of local political matters and of the weaknesses of local elections as a measure of voters' wishes. Several explanations can be considered. One might be that many community problems are so clearly geographically limited and of such a local character that all parties both on the council and among the electorate are agreed upon priorities and measures or, to express it differently, the elected representatives form policywise a truly representative cross-section of the whole electorate.

C. A study in local government decision-making in a risk-taking situation (Lennart Brantgärde, Gothenburg). The Swedish party system is, in common with that of the majority of West European countries, to a high degree built up around the existing socioeconomic structure. This means that to some extent the local strongholds of the five national parties are found in different types of commune. The Center party, for example, is strong in the rural communes, while the Social Democrats find their greatest support in the densely populated industrial areas. A reapportionment of communes along the lines described in the introduction would, therefore, inevitably have considerable effect on the relative strength of the parties at the local level. In the study presented here a leading objective has been to clarify what consequences this may have for local decision-making and choice of strategy in the implementation stage of the consolidation reform.

Before the government finally decided on the nationwide consolidation plan, according to which the revision of boundaries during the 1960s was to take place, all the communes in the country were given several opportunities during the period of nearly two years that this plan was under discussion to put forward points of view (orally and in writing) about the overall structure of the plan and about the scope and composition of their own new block in particular. Shortly before the government fixed the terms of the consolidation plan, the communes were given the opportunity to state formally their standpoint with regard to a proposal for a consolidation plan. This investigation is based on an analysis of these standpoints. It is a total investigation and is not limited to the A-sample.

According to this proposal, which was drafted by the regional administrative districts (länsstyrelserna), certain communes would be designated central town communes, others peripheral communes.

The Decision Situation

Communes and party groups have thus to consider a given block which can be analyzed with respect to its probable consequences for a series of communal action parameters such as (a) proximity to services (variable = distance in km to central town), (b) availability of services (variable = central town's centralization index), (c) cost of public services (variable - differences in local tax within the block), (d) party majority in the block (variable = distribution of votes in latest local elections). The possibility is open to politicians of predicting the consequences of the block proposal with almost complete certainty. Since only a limited number of block proposals can apply to an individual commune, the commune can calculate what the optimum block might be. The individual commune can, therefore, consider the block proposal in the light of its own local political objectives (value-factors or utility-factors). For peripheral communes (about 600) there are four strategy options in the decision situation.

(1) Approve the proposal.

(2) Reject the proposal and try to achieve status of central town commune.

(3) Reject the proposal and try to cooperate with another central town.

(4) Reject the proposal and try generally to change the composition of the block.

On the other hand, since the decision makers are aware that the basic principles have been laid down by the Swedish Parliament in democratic fashion, the probability of realizing communal objectives which diverge from the provisional plan will be dependent on the compatibility of these objectives with the principles of the reform (probability factor).

Probability functions for success with various strategies can in general be deduced from the principles or the short-term objectives of the reform are in no way absolute, the probability of success is seldom zero, especially since the communes should be free to influence the government's assessment of the principles when the consolidation plan is ratified. This is obviously the same thing as to influence probability. The demarcation of "reasonable" probability is, therefore, somewhat imprecise, but even so essential differences occur between the different strategies. To achieve the status of a central town commune (strategy 2), the commune should include a densely populated town with a high centralization index and should have an index at population change of more than 100. Considerably more modest requirements apply if one simply proposes a merger with another central town (strategy 3) or an alteration in the composition of the block (strategy 4). In these cases the only requirement is that the peripheral commune should have a functional affinity with the central town. The probability factor may in this way consist of one or more components depending on the number of reform principles involved. The relation between conflict and probability can thus be expressed more formally as follows:

$$\text{if } PS_i = P, \text{ then the degree of conflict} = 1 - P$$

where PS_i = the probability of success with strategy i.

This assumption has a parallel in Atkinson's (1957) motivation theory model. In our model the assumption forms a basis for characterizing the decision-making situation as a risk-taking situation, where the outcome can be predicted under risk or under limited certainty.

The Basic Model

We can now formulate the basic hypothesis for the whole study.
Provided conflicting interests between national and local levels, local decision-makers, in order to avoid an open and formal conflict, tend to provide for local objectives if and only if reasonable probabilities exist for the success of their proposal.
This hypothesis can more formally be stated as follows:

$$SP_i = GV_i \times (PS_{iP_1} \times PS_{iP_2} \times ... \times PS_{iP_n}),$$

where SP_i = strategic potential of strategy i; GV_i = net value for strategy i with respect to local objectives; and PS_{iP_1} = the probability of success with strategy i with respect to principle 1. It may be clarifying to make some references to other models in decision-making theory. Thus: "strategy potential" corresponds to the concept of "weighted valence" in the aspiration model presented by K. Lewin et al. (1944) as well as to the concept of "resultant motivation" employed by Atkinson, the SEV-model suggested by W. Edwards (1955) and the "choice potential" in N. T. Feather's model (1959). It is also seen that PS bears resemblance to "expectancy" (Atkinson) and "probability" (Lewin et al., Edwards, Feather) just as GV corresponds to utility (Edwards) "incentive value" (Atkinson) "valence"(Lewin et al.), and "attainment attractiveness" (Feather) in these related theoretical models. In our model it is presumed (just as in Edward's SEV-model) that the value-factor is completed independent of the "probabilities," an assumption that is eminently reasonable in view of the fact that we are dealing with a group decision made by a socialist or a nonsocialist majority.

A multiplicative model and theory should be tested empirically with the aid of techniques which allow interaction between the independent variables. A suitable analysis program in such a situation is the AID program developed by Morgan and Sonquist. We conclude this presentation by describing the tree-analysis generated by the aid of this technique. As a dependent variable a dummy variable has been selected for the choice of strategy 2 among peripheral communes (achieve status of central town commune).

As will be seen, two "probability variables" have been used in the first splits, while an "objectives variable," such as change in party majority has not been introduced until a later stage. If one controls for the probabilities of success

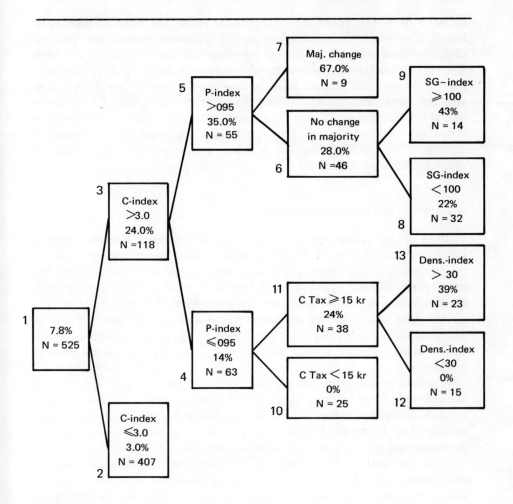

Variables:

1. C-index = index of centralization (Sven Godlund).
2. P-index = percent index of increase in population 1955-1962 (1955 = 100).
3. C Tax index = over all local taxes 1962.
4. Dens.-index = degree of population in densely populated areas.
5. SG-index = index of possibilities to be economically active within the commune.

$$SG = \frac{\text{day population}}{\text{night population}} \cdot 100$$

= night population − (commuters out of the commune + commuters into the commune) in percent of total number of economically active persons.

Figure 3: CHOICE OF STRATEGY 2 AMONG PERIPHERAL COMMUNES TRYING FOR STATUS AS CENTRAL TOWN COMMUNE (group 5 have high values for centralization index and index of population increase) essential differences appear in the objectives factor (avoid political change). Within group 5 this split is significant despite a comparatively small number of observations (X^2 = 4.85 after correction for continuity). Since the relation between the proportions in groups 6 and 7 denotes the difference in value (deduced from the model), one can state that the value of becoming a central town commune, is more than doubled when the property of becoming a peripheral commune is with great probability combined with a change of majority. (This provided other things being equal in groups 6 and 7 which a detailed analysis has indicated.)

PRINCIPLES OF THE ANALYSIS

There are, of course, special issues connected with each individual project within the research program. If, for example, one is to study the way in which the press covers local politics and local activities—in order to illustrate the information channels available to the voter—it is clear that the differences between various communes which can thus be demonstrated depend not only on certain characteristics of the communes but also on the structure of the press and on editorial policies (see Birgersson, 1968). At the same time each individual project must contribute toward clarifying the central question of the research program.

Generally speaking, one can say that in the common project we have been working with three kinds of variables: stratification variables, variables measuring the democratic values and efficiency values and a number of intermediate variables (see Figure 4). For the most part the value variables are treated as dependent and the remainder as independent variables.

It is the task of each writer of a dissertation to contribute to the operationalization of a number of democratic values and efficiency values. He must then test and hammer out these variables. When one is seeking an

Independent Variables		Dependent Variables
Stratification variables: Size, density of population etc.	Intervening variables	Democratic and efficiency values

Figure 4: THREE CATEGORIES OF VARIABLES

explanation for variations between various types of communes with regard to these variables, the very sample design points to the stratification variables. If a systematic variation appears in connection with the size of population or population density variables or with the political variable, this suggests that we are on the track of a causal mechanism.

In certain cases stratification variables suffice as causal variables. The fraction of the populations in a commune personally acquainted with their local councillors can be expected to be directly influenced by the size of the commune and its population density. But in the majority of cases one must assume that the size and density variables do not directly influence the dependent variable, but that intermediate variables must be introduced to give a satisfactory explanation.

From many points of view, the intermediate variables present a difficult problem. Since they have not been the basis of our sample design, we cannot be certain that we have covered their variation. Here, however, our impression is that the stratification variables have worked well as "proxy" variables and to a considerable degree guaranteed that a large part of the variation in the intermediate variables has been registered. But it is also clear that there are interdependence problems that cannot be satisfactorily dealt with. There is, moreover, a risk that hypotheses concerning these intermediate variables will be ad hoc hypotheses. It is our intention that the question we started from, concerning the effect of commune apportionment upon the democratic values and efficiency values, should be answered by a study of how local self-government works in various types of communes. The question includes a function-surface problem: what is the connection between the possibility of providing for various functions and the surface? This question then develops naturally into a question of optimization: which surface is the optimum one to provide for those functions that are connected with local self-government?

If the democratic values and efficiency values covary in the same way with type of commune, there should exist an easily identifiable ideal type of commune. It is, however, certainly more realistic to assume that different values are maximally provided for in different kinds of commune. By summing the values, whether one gives them all equal weight or allows them varying weight, one could still theoretically arrive at an optimum type of commune or different types of communes where a majority of the values reach a high level.

What has been planned for the continuation of this investigation is as follows. When the individual projects have been concluded, the results will be reanalyzed. The number of operationalized measures, especially of the democratic values, is very large. It would be suitable at this juncture first to make a factor analysis before taking the optimization question further. Reanalysis will then take place primarily as a simulation process, where one can test the effect of giving different weight to the variables. In order to give realism to the weighting a panel of politicians could be used together with the results of interviews with members of Parliament.

In this way, considerable light should be thrown on the question of provision for the democratic values and efficiency values in various types of communes. Another task for the reanalysis would be to go more systematically into the question of the role of the intermediate variables as causal variables. It is on that level that contributions to a more general political theory can principally be made.

NOTES

1. Another meaning is used, for example, in Jacob (1969).
2. A more detailed presentation of this figure appears in Westerståhl (1970).

REFERENCES

BIRGERSOON, B. (1968) "Municipal politics in the Swedish press." Scandinavian Political Studies 3.

JACOB, P. E. (1969) "Values measured for local leadership." Wharton Quarterly (Summer).

WESTERSTAHL, J. (1970) "The communal research program in Sweden." New Atlantis 2 (Winter).

Chapter 6

Socioeconomic Change and Political Development: Decision-Making in Sixteen Yugoslav Communes

Peter Jambrek

This paper attempts to formulate and test a theory of democratic development in socialist countries. It is a task which has received little attention from social scientists in the West. Indeed, most sociological literature in capitalist countries still views one-party systems, and communist regimes in particular, as being below any threshold of democratic forms. Consequently there is a widespread tendency to view "communist" and "bourgeois" systems of government as basically noncomparable. This has been less true of empirical studies of political development, although even there many of the prevailing assumptions persist.[1]

It is the basic contention of this study that for socialist countries socioeconomic development (modernization) and political development (democratization) must be treated as inseparable processes. Internal socialist revolutions have been successful only in economically backward countries: the Soviet Union, Yugoslavia, China, Vietnam and Cuba. The other East European socialist nations were already relatively modernized when they were drawn into the Soviet orbit. It is no accident that successful internal revolutions occurred in countries where the economy was primarily rural-based, where the population consisted mainly of peasants living in ancestral villages, and where the modern subsectors of the economy were controlled by foreign interests. It was the first task of the revolutionary elite to mobilize the masses and begin the work of

AUTHOR'S NOTE: *I am grateful to both the American-Yugoslav Project in Urban and Regional Studies in Ljubljana and to the Institute of Sociology and Philosophy, University of Ljubljana, who have generously allowed me to use their data. Support for the use of computer facilities and for preparation of the manuscript was made available by the Department of Sociology, University of Chicago.*

modernization. Lipset (1960) has demonstrated the high correlation between economic development and democratic forms of government. His point is well taken, and it is a point understood by socialist leaders in underdeveloped nations. The modernization of the economy and society had to precede the successful introduction of democracy.

The political system which socialist countries have used to undertake the modernization process is well known. It would be useful, however, to remove it from the pejorative context of political dispute and outline its basic features with particular reference to its essential purpose: economic and social development. Those features are as follows:

    (1) The Communist Party is dominant in all sectors and on all levels of society.

    (2) Power is concentrated in the executive branch of government.

    (3) The function of legislative bodies is to legitimize and proclaim the decisions of administration.

    (4) Political organizations serve the purpose of mobilizing the masses for the tasks which are defined by the political center.

    (5) Local political systems are lower-level units of the national bureaucracy.

    (6) All or most economic, educational, and cultural institutions are politically organized on a national basis.

Although this model has been identified by various labels (such as bureaucratic or administrative socialism, the dictatorship of the proletariat, or the totalitarian state), our purpose in presenting it here is to note how each feature is designed to promote economic, political, and social mobilization and modernization. The basic question we are now ready to raise is: To what degree and in what ways does the socialist system promote modernization and consequently democratization? To answer this question we chose to study the relationship between socioeconomic change and political development in one nation, Yugoslavia, by comparing a sample of sixteen local communities.

BASIC PROPOSITIONS

In order to approach so vast a question it was first necessary to formulate some basic propositions. Our propositions are closely linked to two central concepts in the study of modernization and political development. These are

I am also grateful to Andreja Tauber, Janez Jerovšek, and William Kornblum for their help in early stages of the research. Norman Nie has helped me on numerous occasions with suggestions in data processing, and Sidney Verba in general methodology. Robert Buroker provided invaluable editorial assistance. Of course, I owe most to Terry Clark, who has provided excellent guidance and help throughout the course of the research and during my studies at the University of Chicago.

"social mobilization" (Deutsch, 1961) and conditions or "requisites" of democracy (Lipset, 1969).

Social mobilization as initially defined by Karl Deutsch is related to Karl Mannheim's (1940) concept of "fundamental democratization" and denotes a process of change from traditional to modern ways of life. Although an essentially nonvoluntary shift in the life styles is implied, it is not the political force which drafts peasants from their rural inertia towards full citizenship in a modern polity, but a more or less visible hand of environmental inducements such as changes in residence and social setting, occupation, face-to-face associates, institutions, roles, or habits and needs. The problem with this interpretation, however, is that the causal connections among political mobilization, socioeconomic development, and democratization are not clearly spelled out. Indeed, each of the latter two appear to be a condition for the other; as such, they fit into a pattern of circular causation.

Lipset's explanation of the underlying causality is more unidirectional. The concept of "condition" or "requisites" of democracy defines political development as the dependent variable; and changes in that variable are produced by such factors as economic wealth, industrialization, legitimacy, urbanization, education, and the relative strength of the middle classes.

Our theory of modernization and democratic development in socialist countries draws upon and also partly departs from both Deutsch's and Lipset's models. It implies an essentially political mobilization by means of government and party. Social mobilization, as defined by Deutsch, is regarded as the consequence of an effective political mobilization. Both political and social mobilization precede economic development and constitute the latter's "conditions" or "requisites." We postulate that the bureaucratic model of political decision-making precedes and subsequently promotes a self-governing model through encouraging social mobilization and economic development. The bureaucratic model involving powerful administrative actors is considered as instrumental for the take-off stage toward modernization and for accelerated economic growth. After achieving a certain level of economic development, the model ceases to be efficient in terms of its ability to sustain the achieved rate of growth, and becomes increasingly inconsistent with newly created socioeconomic conditions in a more democratic political order. Our two basic propositions may thus be formulated:

(1) The higher the influence of bureaucratic actors, the higher the rate of a commune's socioeconomic growth.

(2) The higher the level of a commune's socioeconomic development, the smaller the influence of bureaucratic actors and the greater the influence of self-governing actors.

METHODOLOGY: A COMPARATIVE APPROACH

The comparative method is an approach which students of community decision-making are finding increasingly useful (Clark, 1968). We decided that the most efficient way to test the above propositions was to adopt this approach. We selected sixteen Yugoslav communes[2] with varying degrees of economic, social, and political development. The assumption was, of course, that each community would pass through essentially the same stages of development and that in each community there were basically the same causal links between socioeconomic and political development. The relatively high degree of central control of local decision-making in Yugoslavia created a problem. The resulting uniformity of local political systems probably tended to reduce the impact of different levels of socioeconomic development. We measured state control of local decision-making by constructing an index of the interdependence of state and local political systems.

DATA

The data bank from which the empirical indicators of our variables were constructed began with the funding by the Assembly of the Socialist Republic of Slovenia of a research project on the communal assembly. It was carried out in the framework of the Law Faculty of the University of Ljubljana during the period from January until May 1968, when the final report was submitted. The main goals of the study were to investigate the role of the communal assembly as the center of local decision-making. A stratified random sample of 20 communes was drawn from the population of 60 Slovene communes. The criteria of stratification were: region, population size of the commune, and G.N.P. per capita. A questionnaire was sent to every third member of the communal assembly[3] in the communes which did, and to each mayor in communes, which did not enter the sample. Nineteen completed questionnaires were returned by the mayors, and 265 by members of communal assemblies from all 20 selected communes.[4]

In May 1968 another project was undertaken which dealt with similar problems. Its focus though was not on the communal assembly alone, but on local decision-making and leadership in general. The study was carried out by the Institute of Sociology and Philosophy of the University of Ljubljana. Data were collected by means of a questionnaire which was administered to 298 respondents in 17 Slovene communes, 16 of which were identical with the previously selected sample of 20 communes. Thus data from both researches are cumulative for those 16 communes. In each commune 16 to 18 local leaders were interviewed, who were treated in the later analysis as generally knowledgeable informants.

The questionnaire contained 24 closed and 9 open-ended questions, most of which dealt with the relative influence of a number of decision-making institutions, organizations and individuals in the following six issue areas:

(1) budget

(2) urban plan

(3) zoning for housing construction

(4) financing of schools

(5) elections of the mayor, and

(6) elections of directors in economic enterprises.

Pieces of data (126 items) on community characteristics were assembled from different sources, but mainly from the Yugoslav census and from the data bank compiled by the American-Yugoslav Project in Regional and Urban Planning Studies in Ljubljana.

All data had to be transformed so that they would fit into the new research design which considers the 16 communes rather than individual respondents as the basic units of analysis. Data from both surveys and the secondary data were collected and transferred in the form of means and percentages to a common deck of IBM cards. Some 433 variables provided the raw data for construction of several indices or theoretical variables. Two considerations were taken into account in this process: the theoretical definition of the common dimension and the degree of correlation among the "indicators."

VARIABLES

To test the basic propositions four sets of variables were operationalized: socioeconomic development, interdependence of state and local political systems, patterns of community decision-making, and types of actors.

(a) Socioeconomic development: We differentiated between the level of development, which simply describes the positions of a given community on a particular dimension at one point in time, and the ratio of socioeconomic growth which measures the change in the "levels of development" that has occurred between two points of time. The years for which data are relevant are presented in brackets following the name of the indicator. Whenever data for two years were available both level of development and ratio of growth were measured.

Urbanization: percentage of population living in towns (legal jurisdictions within communes) with 2,000 or more inhabitants (1961), and percentage of rural from total population (1963, 1966).

Economic wealth: national income per capita (1964), and total resources in economy per capita (1964).

Transportation: passengers on railways per capita (1963, 1966), and motor vehicles per capita (1963, 1966).

Communications: pieces of mail sent and received per capita (1963, 1966), and telephones per capita (1963, 1966).

Mass media: persons per one TV set (1963, 1966), subscriptions to three main newspapers per capita (1963, 1966), and radio sets per capita (1963, 1966).

Standard of living: net income per month of those employed in the socialized sector (September: 1963, 1966), turnover in restaurants per capita (1963, 1966), and passenger cars per capita (1963, 1966).

Mobility of population: immigrants into the commune per capita (1963, 1966), and emigrants from the commune per capita (1963, 1966).

Government and other public resources: consumption of public funds for housing construction per capita (1964), consumption of public funds for education per capita (1964), local budget (in dinars) per capita (1964), and total public resources (budget and funds) per capita (1964).

Economic investments per capita (1964).

Social welfare: doctors per 10,000 persons (1964), and capacity of institutions for child education and child care per capita (1963, 1964).

Education: pupils who completed elementary school per capita (1962/63, 1965/66), students in secondary schools per capita (1963/64, 1966/67), and university students with permanent residence in the commune per capita (1963/64, 1966/67).

Quality of elementary education: number of teachers in elementary schools per 100 pupils (1963/64, 1966/67), pupils who completed elementary school per 100 population (1962/63, 1966/66).

Attendance at cultural events: visitors at cinema performances per capita (1963, 1966), visits to performances of amateur theater groups per capita (1961/62, 1964/65), and enrollment at seminars and courses offered by workers' and peoples' universities (adult education programs) per capita (1963/64, 1966/67).

(b) Interdependence between state and local political system: [5]

Actual influence of state government: This variable was operationalized by the following question—"how much influence has state government on the decisions of your communal assembly: very low, low, high, or very high influence?"

The desired influence of state government was gauged by two measures constructed from two independent sets of data. The first measure is an index, composed of two questions: "How much influence should the state government have on decisions of your communal assembly: very low, low, high, or very high influence?" and "In your opinion, do state and federal laws regulate too few, a proper amount of, or too many issues, which are under jurisdiction of communal assembly?" The second measure was operationalized by the notion of the "desired degree of a commune's autonomy versus dependence upon the state," as measured by the degree to which the respondents would like to see each of 17 issue areas to be made under the jurisdiction of national rather than local decision-making.

The *potential influence of local leadership on national decision-making* ("state policies") was measured by the number of political functions on the state level occupied by leaders of a particular commune.

(c) Patterns of community decision-making:

Influence of local actors: the relative influence of a number of potential actors[6] was scaled from "very high" to "very low." Data for several issue areas are available. An index was constructed for each actor, based upon his influence score in each issue area.

Index of participation consists of the number of actors in a commune who participate with high influence in the seven issue areas (decisions of the communal assembly plus the standard six issue areas). An actor's participation falls in the category of "high influence" if his mean score equaled or surpassed 2.75 points for "decisions of communal assembly," or 3.50 points for any one of the remaining six issue areas. Each actor was counted as many times as he reached the category "high influence."

Index of centralization was obtained in exactly the same manner as the index of participation, except that each actor was counted only once—even if he was attributed "high influence" in more than one issue area. This index is theoretically identical with Clark's index of centralization (Clark, 1968a).

(d) Types of Actors: Bureaucratic and Self-Governing:

By examining both the functions and the attitude among respondents toward the various actors in commune decision-making, we isolated two clusters of actors, bureaucratic and self-governing. The bureaucratic actors exerted their influence through an administrative hierarchy and ranked higher on the actual influence scale than on the desired influence scale. These included the mayor, the communal committee of the League of Communists, and state government. The self-governing actors were democratically organized and ranked higher in terms of desired as opposed to actual influence. The self-governing actors were assembly members and councils, voters' meetings, and neighborhoods. We used these two clusters of actors as indicators of bureaucratic control and trends toward self-government in the sixteen communes.

Table 1 shows the results of interviewing a sample of opinion in the sixteen

TABLE 1
RANK ORDER OF 12 ACTORS ACCORDING TO THEIR (perceived) ACTUAL INFLUENCE AND THEIR DESIRED INFLUENCE ON THE DECISIONS OF THE COMMUNAL ASSEMBLY

Actor	Mean Score of Actual Influence	Mean Score of Desired Influence	Index of Dissatisfaction
1. Voluntary associations	1.54	2.31	+1.77
2. Voters' meetings	1.86	3.49	+1.63
3. Neighborhoods	1.84	2.31	+1.30
4. Members of communal assembly	2.41	3.55	+1.14
5. Committee of the trade unions	2.08	2.72	+0.71
6. Enterprises	2.32	2.91	+0.59
7. Committee of the Socialist Alliance	2.28	2.79	+0.51
8. Councils of the assembly	3.01	3.20	+0.19
9. Committee of the League of Communists	2.66	2.73	+0.07
10. Mayor	3.22	2.41	−0.17
11. Local administration	2.92	2.71	−0.21
12. State government	3.27	2.41	−0.86

communities about the actual and desired influence of these actors. The cluster of actors in both categories (actual and desired influence) seems to confirm our conceptualization of the two types of actors.

The Index of Dissatisfaction was obtained by subtracting the score for actual influence from the score for desired influence. A positive number thus implies that the actor should have more influence than he now possesses, and a negative score indicates that he should have less. The relative influence of each actor was scaled from "very low" (1), and "low" (2), to "high" (3), and "very high" (4) influence (n = 265).

FINDINGS

The data consistently showed that state government is the single most influential actor in Yugoslav local politics. But the amount of state control varies significantly from commune to commune. What are the causes and consequences of such variation? From the general propositions, we derived a series of more specific hypotheses. Although only one correlation (with communications development) proves significant, the pattern of a *negative indicators association* between state influence and all of the level of socioeconomic development is consistent.

(1) The greater the state influence on the commune, the lower its level of socioeconomic development: *accepted*.

TABLE 2
CORRELATIONS AMONG SIX INDICES OF THE LEVEL OF SOCIOECONOMIC DEVELOPMENT AND STATE INFLUENCE[7]

Level of Development of:	State Influence
1. Communications	−.468
2. Quality of elementary education	−.289
3. Total resources of local government	−.158
4. Mass media	−.128
5. Economic wealth	−.126
6. Social welfare	−.109

(2) The greater the state influence, the higher a commune's rate of economic growth: *accepted.*

Two correlations are significant (growth of transportation and communications). Nevertheless, others are rather high as well. Again, the pattern of a positive association is documented in accordance with our expectations.

It may be argued that association between state influence and rate of growth stems from a high correlation between the level of socioeconomic development and its growth. Relatively poor communes might develop more rapidly, and after they achieve a certain level of development, their growth may slow down. Given also the high correlation between level of development and state influence, the relationship between state influence and growth might thus be considered spurious.

We considered this hypothesis by correlating the level and rate of growth of all available variables. Except for the urbanization dimension (decline of rural population) which exhibits a consistently negative and rather strong correlation between level and rate of growth, all other correlations seem to be random.

(3) The higher the commune's level of socioeconomic development, the lower the desired state influence on the commune—as reported by local leaders: *accepted.*

TABLE 3
CORRELATIONS AMONG SIX INDICES OF THE RATIO OF SOCIOECONOMIC GROWTH AND STATE INFLUENCE

Ratio of Growth of:	State Influence
1. Transportation	.467
2. Communications	.428
3. Quality of elementary education	.307
4. Urbanization	.223
5. Living standard	.199
6. Mass media	.134

TABLE 4

CORRELATIONS AMONG NINE INDICES OF THE LEVEL OF SOCIOECONOMIC
DEVELOPMENT AND DESIRED STATE INFLUENCE

Level of Development of:	Desired State Influence	
	Measure I	Measure II
1. Mass media	−.666	−.340
2. Total resources of local government	−.657	−.247
3. Living standard	−.616	−.299
4. Transportation	−.587	−.138
5. Economic wealth	−.583	−.308
6. Social welfare	−.579	−.227
7. Urbanization	−.531	−.407
8. Quality of elementary education	−.365	−.249
9. Communications	−.308	−.398

Several development variables were significantly correlated with our first
measure, although not with the second measure.

(4) The greater the actual and desired state influence, the greater the influence of
bureaucratic local actors and the lower the influence of self-governing local actors:
accepted.

Again the findings are consistent with our proposition. Correlation between
the actual influence of the state and of the "bureaucratic" local actors are
positive, although not significant. There are strong correlations between the
desired degree of a commune's dependence upon the state and both the mayor
and the League of Communists. From the whole set of correlations, only the
relationship between the influence of local administration and "dependence
upon state" was proven rather insignificantly positive. Furthermore, the negative

TABLE 5

CORRELATIONS AMONG THE DEGREE OF ACTUAL AND DESIRED STATE
INFLUENCE, THE INFLUENCE OF SIX LOCAL DECISION MAKERS, AND THE
COMBINED INDICES OF PARTICIPATION AND (de)CENTRALIZATION

Local Actors, Participation, and (de)Centralization	State Influence (actual)	Desired Degree of Dependence Upon the State
Mayor	.217	.442
Local administration	.150	.285
Committee of the League of Communists	.229	.602
Members of communal assembly	−.409	−.482
Councils of communal assembly	−.556	−.235
Neighborhoods	−.289	−.027
Participation	−.417	−
Centralization-decentralization	−.127	−

TABLE 6
CORRELATIONS AMONG NINE INDICES OF THE LEVEL OF SOCIOECONOMIC
DEVELOPMENT AND THE POTENTIAL INFLUENCE OF A COMMUNE
ON THE STATE GOVERNMENT

Level of Development of:	Potential Influence of a Commune on the State Government
1. Social welfare	.496
2. Economic wealth	.453
3. Communications	.424
4. Education	.394
5. Quality of elementary education	.379
6. Standard of living	.356
7. Cultural activities	.348
8. Mass media	.342
9. Urbanization	.302

association between the influence of the state and "self-governing" local actors appears even more clearly confirmed. The same holds true also for the index of participation and to a lesser degree for the measure of decentralization.

(5) The higher a commune's socioeconomic development, the greater the potential influence of its leadership on national decision-making: *accepted*.

All the correlations confirm that the more developed a commune, the more opportunities its leaders have for participation in state decision-making.

(6) The higher the socioeconomic development of a commune, the less the influence of bureaucratic decision makers: *accepted*.

TABLE 7
CORRELATIONS AMONG NINE INDICES OF THE LEVEL OF SOCIOECONOMIC
DEVELOPMENT AND THE INFLUENCE OF MAYOR, LOCAL ADMINISTRATION
AND COMMUNAL COMMITTEE OF THE LEAGUE OF COMMUNISTS

	Actual Influence of:		
Level of Development of:	Mayor	Administration	League of Communists
Mass media	−.490	−.489	−.601
Economic wealth	−.447	−.401	−.586
Living standard	−.443	−.347	−.640
Urbanization	−.428	−.348	−.443
Government resources	−.404	−.229	−.654
Cultural activity	−.394	−.505	−.419
Transportation	−.319	−.677	−.430
Economic investments	−.278	−.344	−.292
Population mobility	−.264	−.152	−.573

TABLE 8

CORRELATIONS AMONG EIGHT INDICES OF THE RATE OF SOCIOECONOMIC
GROWTH AND THE INFLUENCE OF MAYOR, LOCAL ADMINISTRATION,
AND COMMUNAL COMMITTEE OF THE LEAGUE OF COMMUNISTS

Rate of Growth of:	Mayor	Administration	League of Communists
Mass media	.292	−.044	.102
Living standard	.287	.196	.242
Urbanization	.276	.424	.365
Cultural activity	.168	−.357	.305
Population mobility	.153	.353	.211
Transportation	−.276	.070	−.146
Quality of elementary education	−.422	.118	−.434
Communication	−.571	−.381	−.213

The relationships are quite strong. Taken as a whole, they confirm our proposition about the relation between the level of socioeconomic development and the role of actors which fit into a bureaucratic model of decision-making.

(7) The more influential bureaucratic decision makers in a commune, the higher the rate of a commune's socioeconomic growth: *rejected.*

In the above case, the relationships appear somewhat erratic, and our proposition has to be rejected. It may be suggested that—at least under present conditions—neither of the three local decision makers contribute much to the variation of most indicators of socioeconomic growth, or more precisely, they do not contribute to the variation in a consistent way.

(8) The more socioeconomically developed a commune, the greater the influence of self-governing decision makers: *accepted.*

TABLE 9

CORRELATIONS AMONG NINE INDICES OF THE LEVEL OF SOCIOECONOMIC
DEVELOPMENT AND THE INFLUENCE OF MEMBERS OF COMMUNAL
ASSEMBLY, COUNCILS, AND NEIGHBORHOODS

Level of Development of:	Members of Assembly	Councils	Neighborhoods
Urbanization	.770	.730	.495
Mass media	.558	.714	.335
Communications	.473	.646	.403
Cultural activities	.449	.611	.471
Economic wealth	.382	.675	.228
Population mobility	.377	.673	.387
Government resources	.354	.659	.320
Economic investments	.351	.225	.012
Living standard	.299	.665	.184

TABLE 10
CORRELATIONS AMONG EIGHT INDICES OF THE RATIO OF SOCIOECONOMIC
GROWTH AND THE INFLUENCE OF MEMBERS OF COMMUNAL ASSEMBLY,
COUNCILS, AND NEIGHBORHOODS

Rate of Growth of:	Assembly Members	Councils	Neighborhoods
Transportation	−.211	−.242	−.154
Cultural activity	.191	−.006	−.048
Population mobility	.154	−.224	.140
Living standard	.047	.024	.141
Mass media	.007	.355	.278
Quality of elementary education	−.084	−.167	.166
Communication	−.259	−.267	−.388
Urbanization	−.518	−.543	−.611

The hypothesis is clearly confirmed. It thus seems reasonable to say that a certain level of socioeconomic development must be reached before various self-governing bodies of local decision-making are activated.

(9) The higher a commune's rate of socioeconomic growth, the smaller the influence of self-governing decision makers: *rejected:*

The relationships are erratic. There is no negative relationship between various indicators of socioeconomic growth and the influence of "self-governing" decision makers. The hypothesis cannot be accepted.

(10) The greater the centralization of a commune's decision-making structure, the higher the level and rate of its socioeconomic growth: for level, *accepted;* for rate, *rejected.*

Decentralization is positively associated across all dimensions of the level of socioeconomic growth, although only one correlation is significant. The correlations between the rate of socioeconomic growth and decentralization, on the other hand, cannot be interpreted one way or the other. Nevertheless, centralized decision-making seems to be a condition of the growth of cultural

TABLE 11
CORRELATIONS AMONG NINE INDICES OF THE LEVEL OF SOCIOECONOMIC
DEVELOPMENT AND DECENTRALIZATION OF COMMUNITY DECISION-MAKING

Level of Development of:	Decentralization
Cultural activity	.564
Urbanization	.387
Economic investments	.307
Mass media	.296
Economic wealth	.290
Population mobility	.287
Communications	.255
Living standard	.188

TABLE 12
CORRELATIONS AMONG EIGHT INDICES OF THE RATE OF SOCIOECONOMIC GROWTH AND DECENTRALIZATION OF COMMUNITY DECISION-MAKING

Rate of Growth of:	Decentralization
Cultural activity	.564
Transportation	.335
Communications	.203
Mass media	.026
Urbanization	−.013
Quality of elementary education	−.123
Population mobility	−.183
Living standard	−.442

activities (and adult education) and transportation; and decentralized decision-making appears to be a "requisite" associated with the rate of growth of the living standard.

CONCLUSIONS FROM FINDINGS

What do these findings tell us about the validity of our two basic propositions; and, more generally, what do they imply about the general theory of socioeconomic and political development in socialist countries? The two propositions (the higher the influence of bureaucratic actors, the higher the rate of a commune's socioeconomic development; and the higher the level of a commune's socioeconomic development, the smaller the influence of bureaucratic actors and the greater the influence of self-governing actors) were generally confirmed. There remain, however, a number of important unresolved problems for theories of modernization and democratization in socialist countries. When we tried to correlate rates of socioeconomic growth with bureaucratic and democratic forms of decision-making, the results were inconclusive. While centralization correlated consistently and highly positively with the level of growth, there was no corresponding correlation with the rate of growth. What this implies is that the ways in which socialist countries modernize and democratize still need to be located and explained. The Deutsch and Lipset models are still consistent with our findings as well as with our own alternative theory of development in socialist nations. But we must leave to future research the task of spelling out more clearly the precise relationships among forms and types of decision-making, modernization of the society and the economy, and democratization.

NOTES

1. See, for example, Schramm and Ruggers (1967); Olsen (1968); Marsh and Parish (1965); Cutright (1963); Lipset (1960); Fitzgibbon (1961); Shannon (1957); Neubauer (1967); McCrone and Cnudde (1967); Cutright (1965); Lerner (1958); Nie et al. (1969); Smith (1969); Almond and Verba (1963); Russett et al. (1964); Deutsch (1961); Banks and Textor (1963).

2. The terms "commune" (komuna) and "community" (občina) are used interchangeably in Yugoslav terminology. Nevertheless, "commune" is regarded as a normative or ideological term while "community" refers to a legal-administration entity. For further information on this distinction and also basic information on organization and political process in the Yugoslav commune in English, see Fisher (1966: 145-183; 1964: 418-441); Djordjević and Pasić (1961: 390); Jambrek (1969); Hunnius (1969).

3. The number of members of communal assemblies ranges from 132 (Maribor) to 36 (Dravograd).

4. The number of returned questionnaires for each commune ranged from 6 or 50 percent return (Dravograd) to 26 or 59 percent return (Maribor).

5. We use interchangeably the terms "state" and "nation." In the Yugoslav context a nation as an ethnic unit (e.g., Slovenia) is identical with a state, or one of the six federal units of Yugoslavia.

6. Mayor, local administration, secretary of the communal committee of the League of Communists, members of communal assembly, councils of communal assembly, and neighborhoods.

7. Here and in all subsequent tables we report Pearson zero-order correlation. $N = 16$. Correlations at or above 0.4259 are significant with $p = 0.1$, and correlations at or above 0.4973 with $p = 0.05$ (see R. A. Fisher, "Statistical Methods for Research Workers," Table VA). Variables are listed according to the size of their correlations coefficients. Only the six highest correlations are reported.

REFERENCES

ALMOND, G. A. and S. VERBA (1963) The Civic Culture. Princeton: Princeton Univ. Press.

BANKS, A. and R. TEXTOR (1963) Cross Polity Survey. Cambridge, Mass.: MIT Press.

CLARK, T. N. (1968a) "Community structure, decision-making, budget expenditures, and urban renewal in 51 American communities." American Sociological Review 33, 4.

––– (1968b) Community Structure and Decision-Making. San Francisco: Chandler.

CUTRIGHT, P. (1965) "Political structure, economic development, and national social security programs." American Journal of Sociology 70 (March): 537-551.

––– (1963) "National political development: measurement and analysis." American Sociological Review 28 (April): 253-264.

DEUTSCH, K. M. (1961) "Social mobilization and political development." American Political Science Review 55 (September): 475-495.

DJORDJEVIC, J. and N. PASIC (1961) "The communal self-government system in Yugoslavia." International Social Science Journal 13, 3.

FISHER, J. (1966) Yugoslavia–A Multinational State. San Francisco: Chandler.

––– (1964) "The Yugoslav commune." World Politics (April): 418-441.

FITZGIBBON, R. and K. JOHNSON (1961) "Measurement of Latin American political change." American Political Science Review 55 (September): 515-526.

HUNNIUS, G. (1969) Notes on the Yugoslav System of Decentralization and Self-Management. Boston: Information Exchange on Community Economic Development.

JAMBREK, P. (1969) Interrelationships Between Social Conflict and Political System in Yugoslav Communities. Boston: Information Exchange on Community Economic Development.

JEROVSEK, J. (1970) "The structure of influence in the Yugoslav commune." New Atlantis (Winter): 31-47.

KOLAKOWSKI, L. (1969) Toward a Marxist Humanism. New York: Grove.

LERNER, D. (1958) The Passing of Traditional Society. New York: Free Press.

LIPSET, S. M. (1960) Political Man. Garden City, N.Y.: Doubleday.

McCRONE, D. J. and C. F. CNUDDE (1967) "Toward a communications theory of democratic political development." American Political Science Review 61 (March): 72-79.

MANNHEIM, K. (1940) Man and Society in an Age of Reconstruction. Garden City, N.Y.: Doubleday.

MARSH, R. M. and W. L. PARISH (1965) "Modernization and communism: a re-test of Lipset's hypotheses." American Sociological Review (December): 934-942.

NEUBAUER, D. E. (1967) "Some conditions of democracy." American Political Science Review 61 (December): 1002-1009.

NIE, N. M. et al. (1969) "Social structure and political participation: developmental relationships. "American Political Science Review 63 (June, September).

OLSEN, M. E. (1968) "Multivariate analysis of national political development." American Sociological Review (December): 934-942.

RUSSETT, B. (1964) World Handbook of Political and Social Indicators. New Haven: Yale Univ. Press.

SCHERMERHORN, R. A. (1961) Society and Power. New York: Random House.

SCHRAMM, W. and W. L. RUGGERS (1967) "How mass media systems grow," in D. Lerner and W. Schramm (eds.) Communication and Change in the Developing Countries. Honolulu: East-West Center Press.

SHANNON, L. W. (1957) "Is level of development related to capacity for self-government." American Journal of Economics and Sociology (July): 367-381.

SMITH, A. (1969) "Socioeconomic development and political democracy—a causal analysis." Midwest Journal of Political Science 13 (February).

Chapter 7

The Power Structure of
Israeli Development Towns

Erik Cohen

THE PROBLEM

This paper presents a study of the informal power structure of the new towns in Israel, generally called "development towns," as it crystallized during the process of their growth.[1] It is based on empirical research conducted by the author in four development towns between late 1963 and early 1964.

At the time this study was conceived, the discussion between the "elitist" and "pluralist" schools of community power in the United States was at its height;[2] it appeared then to many students and critics that the type of findings depended largely on the method used—reputational or decisional.[3] This, again, led some analysts to assume a relationship between the scientific discipline a researcher belongs to and the findings he will turn up with.[4]

The assumed relationship between discipline, method, and substantive findings has in the meantime been shown as empirically wrong (see Clark et al., 1968b); the whole discussion is also theoretically fruitless, since it does not lead us to a better understanding of community power structure. Hence, an alternative approach to the problem looks more promising: the comparative method. Instead of asking which concept of community power, the "elitist" or

AUTHOR'S NOTE: *This paper is based on the author's Ph.D. dissertation "The Power Structure of Development Towns," presented to the Hebrew University of Jerusalem in 1968 (unpublished). The thesis was prepared under the guidance of Professor J. Ben-David. The research project was partly financed by the Public Council for Community Development. The author wishes to thank Professor Ben-David, Professor S. N. Eisenstadt, and Dr. E. Guttman for their assistance in the preparation of the thesis, and Phillip Bloom, who translated this manuscript from the Hebrew.*

the "pluralist" is the right one, one conceives of all possible community power structures as being arrayed on a continuum, ranging from an elitist (or monolithic, or centralized) pole to a pluralistic (or decentralized) pole.[5] One then asks: How do general structural conditions in the community influence the local power structure toward one or the other of these poles? One also uses a combination of several possible methods so as to avoid dependency on the too limited perspective yielded by any single method.[6]

The study here reported has been conceived in terms of such a comparative approach. Since the inception of this study, several comparative studies have been carried out, most of them in the United States.[7] Comparative studies between the United States and other countries,[8] between other countries,[9] or within them,[10] are still relatively rare. It is in this context that a power structure study in the development towns of Israel has something to contribute at both the theoretical and the empirical level.

DEVELOPMENT TOWNS AND ISRAELI SOCIETY

For various historical and sociological reasons, the Israeli city has developed neither in the way cities developed in Western countries nor in the way they developed in developing countries. Two general characteristics of the city in Israel are pertinent to this discussion: historically, the cities occupied a secondary position relative to rural forms of settlement, such as kibbutzim or moshavim (see Cohen, 1970a); this characteristic stems from the strong preference given to agricultural over urban settlement in the mandatory period and in the early years of statehood; and, secondly, the absence of a tradition of localism, which gave to the national institutions a greater degree of control and influence over municipal affairs than has been the case in many democratic Western nations.[11] The central national institutions—both governmental offices and party headquarters—keep a tight control over local affairs in most Israeli cities, and particularly the smaller and newer ones. The chief instruments of control are the municipal budget, much of which is derived from national funds, and the party-political apparatus—a local leader's career depends largely upon his ability and willingness to carry out the directives of his superiors.

The general characteristics of the Israeli city stand out particularly in the development towns. These towns were founded neither on the basis of visionary ideas nor did they develop in a slow process of growth, conditioned by local ecological factors. Rather, they are new and "planted" towns, established by central national institutions in completely new or underdeveloped areas, so as to provide centers for services, industry and the exploitation of natural resources in the surrounding areas (see Cohen, 1970b). They were mostly settled by new immigrants. However, in many areas established agricultural settlements already existed; these settlements maintained their dominance over the area. Various groups of new immigrants, generally Jews of Oriental origin, were brought directly to the towns upon arrival in Israel. The number of Jewish immigrants of European and American origin brought to development towns was small to begin with, and the rate at which they left those towns was far higher than that characteristic for immigrants of Oriental origin.[12] Thus, the more backward elements inhabit most of these towns. This situation made it difficult for the towns to consolidate a stable and active population.[13] As a result, the population of the development towns had no independent resources of its own to rely on in the event of disagreement or clash of interests with the central institutions. These institutions thus had a free hand in their activities in the towns, and could easily override local opposition to their demands and policies.

Within the development towns the central institutions are generally represented by a group of veterans, who stand out above the mass of new immigrants. This group is composed either of Israeli-born persons, of people who immigrated before the establishment of the State, or of "veteran immigrants" who immigrated after the establishment of the State but moved to a development town only after they had lived for some years in other types of settlements. Many of these veterans were originally members of agricultural settlements; younger individuals often form a significant proportion among them. This group may number from a few up to several hundred families in the various towns. The social significance of the veterans is very great. They mostly constitute a diffuse elite; they fill the central offices in the municipal, party, public and other institutions; they occupy managerial positions and perform the skilled and professional roles in the economic enterprises, in the branches of banks, and in the main business establishments in the towns. They enjoy positions of high prestige in the community. They constitute the link between Israeli society and the inhabitants of the town.

The political parties play an interesting role in the social and political crystallization of the new towns. At an early stage after the establishment of the town, the local inhabitants are completely without influence over the decisions of the institutions through which their lives are managed. The political parties soon start activities in the town in search of the one resource which the local inhabitants have—the franchise. In order to gain the votes of the immigrants, the political parties cannot rely only on political-ideological propaganda, for the local inhabitants are neither interested nor do they understand this propaganda. The only way for the parties to succeed is to provide the inhabitants with real and immediate benefits, by ensuring that their problems of housing, employment, arrangements for children and so on, are taken care of. Thus the parties come to function as intermediaries between the institutions and the inhabitants, handling the immigrants' problems in relation to the institutions in exchange for their support during elections.[14]

DIFFERENCES BETWEEN THE DEVELOPMENT TOWNS

Beyond the generally similar social position of the various development towns, there are some significant differences between them; in fact, the main emphasis in this study was on the structural factors which differentiate between the towns and which lead to differences in their respective power structures.

Many factors may influence the emerging power structure in the new towns, e.g., the size of the town, the functions it performs in relation to the surrounding society, its distance from metropolitan centers, and so on. In this study, emphasis was placed on two characteristics of special importance in the development towns, namely the level of economic and institutional development, and the composition of their population, in terms of origin and length of stay in the country of the various immigrant groups.

(1) Economic and Institutional Development—refers to the extent to which the town enjoys an independent economic basis, as well as a well-developed, diversified institutional system. This variable was measured primarily by the extent of industrialization, the level of commercial services, the extent of development of municipal institutions, the availability of various kinds of education and the existence of local voluntary organizations.[15] The rate of development of the towns varies widely: some of the towns developed rapidly, whereas others lagged behind or remained stagnant. Some towns are modern, dynamic communities, whereas others remained small and underdeveloped, utterly dependent upon the central national institutions.

(2) Population Composition. The development towns were established to absorb new immigrants, that is, immigrants who came since the establishment of the State and mainly since the latter half of the fifties.

In spite of the fact that the development towns are immigrant towns, their composition by country of origin and to some extent also by length of stay in the country, is surprisingly diversified. On the one hand there are the almost completely homogeneous towns, in which almost all the inhabitants come from the same country or broad geographical area; almost all such homogeneous communities are composed of immigrants from North Africa. On the other hand there are the more heterogeneous towns whose inhabitants come from different continents, and from different countries in each continent, embracing Jews of both European as well as Oriental origin.

The development towns are less diversified in terms of length of stay in Israel of the inhabitants than in terms of their country of origin. The majority of the inhabitants of the towns immigrated after the establishment of the State. However, it is still possible to distinguish between those towns in which the majority of the population immigrated during one single short period, and towns whose inhabitants immigrated during various periods, since and even before the establishment of the State.

AIMS OF THE STUDY

The main aim of this study was to investigate the "diffusion," or distribution and differentiation, of power in development towns which accompanies the processes of their economic and institutional development and diversification of their population. The general hypothesis advanced was that the more economically and institutionally developed the town, and the more heterogeneous its population, the more its power structure would tend to be pluralistic. This hypothesis is derived from a broad theoretical consideration, in particular the assumption that economic and institutional development and diversification of the population create new bases for power in the community and this facilitates the emergence of new, local elites; these new elites are then in a position to challenge the "external" political elite controlling the undifferentiated power structure of the development town and thus to bring about a broader diffusion of power in the community.

In order to test this broad hypothesis, changes in several more specific aspects of the power structure were studied in relation to changes in the basic structural characteristics of the towns. The specific aspects of the power structure studied were:

1. Concentration vs. Diffusion of Power. This variable relates to the size of the group of power-bearers in the community. It was expected that the more developed economically and institutionally the community, and the more heterogeneous its population, the more diffused power would be in the community.

2. Differentiation of the Power Structure. It was expected that the power structure would be more differentiated in more developed and more heterogeneous towns, and less differentiated in less developed and more homogeneous towns. The variable of differentiation is a compound one, and hence was studied in two principal ways:

(a) The Extent of Differentiation of the Power-Bearers Among the Various Spheres of Power

Power bearers are those persons who wield influence over basic decisions in the various spheres of social life of the community. The greater the variety of power bearers between the spheres, the more differentiation there will be in this respect. Conversely, the greater the overlap between the power bearers in the various spheres, the less differentiated will power be between the spheres.

(b) The Extent of Differentiation Between the Power Bearers Themselves

The lack of such differentiation will be reflected in the uniformity of the composition and social structure of the group of power bearers. Conversely, differentiation will be reflected in a heterogeneous composition and in the splitting up of the power bearers into subgroups.

There are many possible indexes for this type of differentiation. In accordance with other research in this field, three types of indexes were employed.

Institutional Differentiation—that is, the extent to which the group of power bearers is composed of members of only one institutional elite (lack of differentiation) or of members of various such elites (differentiation).

Socioeconomic Differentiation—that is, the extent to which the power bearers in the community differ from each other in their socioeconomic characteristics (length of stay in the country, ethnic origin, income, occupation and education). Insofar as all or at least the more prominent of these power bearers are similar in this respect, it can be inferred that they belong to the same social stratum, and thus that differentiation between them is relatively low. In so far as the power bearers, particularly the most prominent, differ in their socioeconomic characteristics, it can be inferred that they belong to different social strata, and thus that differentiation between them is high.

Differentiation in Social Relationships ("Sociometric" Differentiation)—Here we refer to the extent of social cohesion characteristic of community power bearers: whether they constitute a socially unified whole or are subdivided into separate and even opposed subgroups. From a different point of view, the question here is whether the power bearers maintain social relationships primarily with one another and not with the other members of the community who do not have power; or conversely whether the power bearers maintain social relationships primarily with those other inhabitants of the community, who do not possess power and not with each other, so that they are actually integrated in the social network of the broader community and are not differentiated from it as a separate group. Insofar as the power bearers constitute a cohesive and unified social group, and insofar as they are separated socially from the other members of the community, it will be said that there is lack of differentiation in the social relationships of the group of power bearers in that community. Conversely, insofar as the power bearers are split among a number of separate groups and insofar as they maintain primarily relationships with the other members of the community who are not power bearers, it will be said that there is a tendency for differentiation of social relationships among the group of power bearers in that community.

3. The Rate of Representation of Various Institutional Elites Among the Power Bearers. The main problem investigated here was the extent to which the various types of development towns differed in the degree to which they are dominated by the political elite. Since a rise in the economic and institutional level of development implies the emergence of new institutional elites, it also implies limitation of control of the dominant elite and differentiation of institutional membership of the power bearers. Thus it can be hypothesized that in the less developed towns political elites will be most dominant, and that this dominance would weaken the more developed the towns.

THE RESEARCH METHOD

In order to test separately the relationship between each one of the two independent variables and the power structure it was necessary to hold the other variable constant. Thus a sample of at least four development towns was required, as shown in the matrix below.

		Level of Institutional and Economic Development	
		Developed	Undeveloped
Composition of Population	Heterogeneous	Developed and Heterogeneous Town	Undeveloped and Heterogeneous Town
	Homogeneous	Developed and Homogeneous Town	Undeveloped and Homogeneous Town

Four towns were therefore selected out of the twenty-two towns existent at the time of the 1961 census. The town of Dimona in the Negev desert was selected as the developed, homogeneous town. Although the majority of Dimona's population was of Oriental origin, there was a larger minority of European and South American immigrants in this town than in the one selected as undeveloped and homogeneous, Netivot (in the Western Negev), where almost all the immigrant population is of North African origin. It should be noted, however, that most of the Europeans and South Americans in Dimona were new immigrants at the time of this study, had only lived in the town a short time by then, and had not yet become involved in local social life. The town of Or Akiva on the Mediterranean Coast was selected as the undeveloped, heterogeneous town. Although Or Akiva is about 3-5 years older than the other towns in the sample, and is closer than the others to an established urban center (Hadera), no other, more suitable town of this type could be found. The town of Kiryat Gat in the Northern Negev was selected as the heterogeneous and developed town. The approximate size of the towns at the time of the study (1963) was as follows (Manpower Planning Authority, 1964):

Dimona	15,250 inhabitants
Kiryat Gat	14,500 inhabitants
Netivot	3,900 inhabitants
Or Akiva	4,800 inhabitants

The two developed towns selected were much larger than the two undeveloped ones; I would have preferred to keep the variable of size constant, but since no small and developed—or large and undeveloped—towns could be found, I had no choice but to include settlements of different sizes in the sample.

In each of the towns, the "potential leadership pool" was determined through a census of the institutional elites in the following spheres:

(1) The Political Sphere—leading role bearers in the principal political institutions in the town: (a) the elected municipal authority—the head and members of the local council; (b) heads of departments in the local council; (c) heads of the various local public institutions such as the Jewish Agency, the General Federation of Labour (Histadrut), the governmental housing company; (d) leaders of public and political groups, such as party leaders and secretaries, important leaders of immigrants' associations, and important informal public-opinion leaders.

(2) The Economic Sphere—leading role bearers in the principal economic institutions in the town: (a) leading figures in large industrial enterprises, such as owners and general managers; (b) representatives of businesses and services, such as owners of large shops and bank managers; (c) labor leaders such as heads of important workers' committees in industrial enterprises.

(3) The Religious Sphere—important role bearers in religious institutions: (a) rabbis and other important religious functionaries; (b) individuals active in the religious sphere—such as the head of the local religious council and the chairman of the religious committee of the General Federation of Labour.

(4) The Educational Sphere—important role bearers in the educational system of the town: (a) most important individuals active in this sphere, such as members of the central parents committee and the chairman of the education

committee of the municipal council; (b) headmasters of schools and other educational institutions; (c) youth movement leaders.

(5) The Social Sphere—people filling important "social roles," which enjoy high social status and prestige: (a) professionals—doctors and engineers; (b) socially active individuals, such as heads of voluntary organizations, and persons socially active in an informal way; (c) prestigious members of ethnic groups.

Though care was taken to include the same type of people into the potential leadership pools in all towns, completely similar representation was obviously not possible; elitism is a continuous variable and the cutting-off point is always arbitrary. It is almost impossible to ensure that the continuum, in each sphere, be cut at precisely the same point in each town. In addition, we also had some difficulties in identifying and reaching all members of the leadership pools as here defined, in the various towns.

The members of leadership pools identified in each town varied between 76 (in Kiryat Gat) and 35 (in Or Akiva). In the large and more developed towns, the leadership pools have been relatively larger, but the differences are not necessarily proportional to the sizes of the towns.

The members of the leadership pools were interviewed thoroughly on questions relating to their influence in seven major spheres of life in town. Most of these spheres were known from a pilot survey to involve disagreements and conflicts between the inhabitants of the towns. The following spheres were studied: (1) economic development; (2) employment; (3) business licenses; (4) welfare funds; (5) education; (6) religion; (7) absorption of immigrants.

For each of these power spheres three questions were formulated, each one referring to a specific aspect of the sphere. Subjects were asked if they did have or had had influence on: (1) the quantitative aspect—such as the amount to be invested in economic development or distributed as welfare; (2) the qualitative aspect—that is, in what to invest or the types of welfare to be allocated; (3) the personal aspect—who will invest or who will receive welfare.

The combination of the aspects "how much," "in what" and "who" was common to all of the "power spheres" except for two, religion and the absorption of immigrants, in which one of the aspects had been differently formulated. This approach systematized to some degree the measurement of power in each sphere and provided a common denominator for the material studied. Since 7 power spheres were investigated, each subject was asked 21 questions of this type.

Responses relating to the various aspects of each sphere were weighted as follows:

Number of aspects in which subject had influence	Weight
No influence	0
Influence in one aspect	1
Influence in two aspects	2
Influence in three aspects	3

The sum of the weights of subjects' responses in all spheres was used as a measure of their overall amount of power in the community. This measure thus could take values between 0 (no influence at all) and 21 points (when the subject gained 3 points in each of the 7 power spheres studied).

This overall measure of the amount of power is based on the assumption that each sphere studied had equal weight. Some attempt was made in the selection of spheres to ensure some unity of "level of importance," but there is no certainty that the spheres really are of equal importance in each of the towns. Some care is therefore required in the interpretation of this measure. Although precise comparisons cannot be based on the measure, it can be used to distinguish several broad types of power bearers. In this way, the following typology of six types of power bearers was formulated.

Type	Points on the index of power
0	0
1	1
2	2-3
3	4-6
4	7-9
5	10-15

(Note: not one subject gained more than 15 out of the 21 possible points)

For comparative purposes, this typology was collapsed to an even more general one, including only three types:

Lacking power	—type 0
Bearers of limited power	—types 1-2
Bearers of considerable power	—types 3-5

DISPERSION VS. CONCENTRATION OF POWER

The types of power bearers, by types of towns, are shown in Table 1. The table indicates some interesting differences in the distribution of power between the developed and the undeveloped towns. In undeveloped towns there are large numbers of individuals with either no power at all, or with very limited power

TABLE 1
TYPES OF POWER BEARERS IN POTENTIAL LEADERSHIP POOLS

Types of Power Bearers/ Types of Towns	0	1	2	3	4	5	Total
Developed towns	18.9	14.7	26.6	23.1	11.2	5.6	100.1
Undeveloped towns	24.0	15.6	32.3	15.6	6.2	6.2	99.9
Heterogeneous towns	17.1	18.9	27.9	18.0	10.8	7.2	99.9
Homogeneous towns	24.2	11.7	29.7	21.9	7.8	4.7	99.9

(types 1-2); they contain very few intermediate power bearers with some, but still limited, power (types 3-4). At the same time there are almost equal percentages of people with very considerable power (type 5) in both developed and undeveloped towns. In contrast, there are only few people who wholly lack power or have only limited power (types 1-2) in the developed towns, whereas there are many more intermediate power bearers (types 3-4). These findings indicate that in the developed towns, the distribution of power is more diffuse; there exist "intermediate elites" between those with considerable power and those lacking power. In contrast, in the undeveloped towns power is more concentrated: there exists a gap in the power structure between the few with very considerable power on the one hand, and the many with only marginal power, on the other hand; between these extremes there exist only few intermediate elites.

It is of interest to note that in the results of Table 1, and of almost all other aspects dealt with in this study, no significant differences were found between the homogeneous and heterogeneous towns.

THE INSTITUTIONAL ORIGINS OF POWER BEARERS

The question posed here was: To which of the above mentioned institutional elites do power bearers belong in the towns studied? To answer this question, the composition of the bearers of considerable power (types 3-5) was studied from two points of view: (a) how are these power bearers distributed among the various types of institutional elites? (b) what is the percentage representation of each institutional elite in this group of power bearers? The comparison between the developed and the undeveloped towns on these lines is presented in Table 2.

The political elite is dominant in both types of towns, and includes about two-thirds of all bearers of considerable power (Column "a" in the table). Cosiderable power characterizes more than half the members of the political elite in the developed towns, but only a third in the undeveloped towns, (Column "b" in the table). In neither type of town does the power of any other institutional elite approach that of the political elite. The economic elite

TABLE 2

BEARERS OF CONSIDERABLE POWER (types 3-5) BY INSTITUTIONAL ELITES

	(a) As a Percentage of All Bearers of Considerable Power	*(b) As a Percentage of the Members of the Institutional Elites in the Town*
Developed Towns		
Political Elite	68.4	56.4
Economic Elite	12.3	23.3
Religious Elite	3.5	40.0
Educational Elite	1.8	6.3
Social Elite	14.0	34.8
Undeveloped Towns		
Political Elite	66.7	36.0
Economic Elite	11.1	20.0
Religious Elite	14.8	50.0
Educational Elite	7.4	20.0
Social Elite	—	—

comprises only about 10-12 percent of bearers of considerable power in both types of towns; the percentage of its members represented in the group of bearers of considerable power embraces in both types of town around 20 percent. The religious elite is a small one, but enjoys relatively high proportional representation among bearers of considerable power. This is particularly true in the undeveloped towns where this elite ranks second with about 15 percent of all bearers of considerable power, and where about half its members are bearers of considerable power. In contrast, in developed towns, the religious elite is less powerful, comprising only 3.5 percent of all bearers of considerable power; at the same time, however, its relative power is once again quite high—about 40 percent of its members enjoy considerable power. The most significant difference between developed and undeveloped towns, however, was found in respect to the educational and social elites. Whilst the educational elite is quite highly represented in the undeveloped towns among bearers of considerable power, it has only very little power in the developed towns. In contrast, the social elite is relatively powerful in the developed towns and is not represented at all among the bearers of considerable power in the undeveloped towns.

It may be concluded, then, that in both types of towns the most powerful elite is the political one. However, while in developed towns the "modern" social elite (mainly professionals and leaders of voluntary organizations) is also prominent, in undeveloped towns the more "traditional" elites, religious and educational, are relatively more prominent. The economic elite is third in rank in both types of towns.

In general, the composition of the group of bearers of considerable power (types 3-5), points to a lack of institutional differentiation, both in developed and undeveloped towns; in fact, great differences between the towns were only found in the analysis of the composition of the group of bearers of limited power (types 1-2), which we shall not present here in full: it was found that while in the undeveloped towns the political elite is clearly dominant even among the bearers of limited power, this dominance is reduced in the developed towns where other elites, in particular the economic, start to be of increased importance.

DIFFERENTIATION BETWEEN SPHERES OF POWER

The question posed here relates to the extent to which the towns differ in the scope of spheres in which the various power bearers have influence. The power spheres will be said to be differentiated from each other insofar as different individuals have influence in each of them, and undifferentiated in so far as the same individuals exercise power in all or most spheres.

The main finding in this context was that in the centralized power structure of undeveloped towns, two distinct types of distribution between the various spheres of power tend to develop. On the one hand there were individuals with a great deal of power in most of the power spheres in the town. On the other hand, there were individuals with only limited power in one or another sphere. When the centralized power structure is broken, and power "thaws," as is common in developed towns, a further type of distribution of power becomes frequent: there appear people who are power bearers in several but not in all spheres. The power monopoly of those with the greatest power has seemingly been broken in some of the spheres. These spheres are usually those in which the balance of power in decision-making has gradually shifted from external national institutions to the town itself, as, for example, happened in the sphere of employment. This finding implies that power thaws in specific ways in the development towns. In those spheres in which few people have influence (generally those spheres where the basis of power is controlled by institutions external to the town, such as is the case in the sphere of absorption of immigrants), power is concentrated in the hands of the central power elite. In spheres in which a certain amount of thawing has taken place, the circle of power bearers widens, and specific elites acquire power; these, consequently, exercise considerable influence in a limited number of spheres. However, a situation of complete decentralization of power in which there would exist a specific power elite in each sphere, which would have no power at all in any other sphere, has not yet been reached in the development towns.

SOCIOECONOMIC DIFFERENTIATION AMONG THE POWER BEARERS

The socioeconomic (or stratificational) structure of the power bearers was studied through five socioeconomic characteristics which have stratificational significance in Israel as a whole, and in the development towns in particular.

These characteristics and their corresponding categories of classification, were defined as follows:

(1) Country of Origin—Europeans (a stratificationally high group) were distinguished from those of Oriental origin (a stratificationally low group).

(2) Length of Stay in Israel—Veterans (immigrated in the period up to the end of mass immigration in 1952) were distinguished from new immigrants (who immigrated since 1953). There were few native-born Israelis among the power bearers—they were classified with the veterans.

(3) Income—People with high income (above I£501 per month) were distinguished from those with low income (less than I£500 per month).

(4) Occupation—High occupational level (professionals and those with important positions in the administration and the local economy) was distinguished from low occupational level (all other occupations).

(5) Education—Those with a high level of education (secondary schooling, Yeshiva, teachers' college and university) were distinguished from those with a low level of education (primary, vocational and uncompleted secondary education).

Table 3 presents the percentage of members of the leadership pools who are high on each of these characteristics. Members of all the leadership pools share some common features: they are generally high in all socioeconomic characteristics—in fact between three-quarters and two-fifths of them were classified in the high categories on each of the characteristics measured. This feature is to some extent an artifact of the method by which the pools were selected, especially in respect of occupational level and to some extent also in respect of income and education. However, this explanation does not hold for all the characteristics, in particular not for origin and length of stay in Israel, since the members of the pools were not selected by these two criteria.

A comparison of developed and undeveloped towns shows that the percentage of those with high socioeconomic characteristics is throughout higher in the former than in the latter. The number of those with a long stay in Israel and with a high income in the developed towns is especially high.

TABLE 3

PERCENTAGE OF MEMBERS OF LEADERSHIP POOLS BELONGING TO THE "HIGH" CATEGORIES OF THE SOCIOECONOMIC CHARACTERISTICS

	Developed Towns	Undeveloped Towns
Origin: European	55.4	43.7
Length of Stay in Israel		
Long (immigrated up to 1952)	73.4	54.8
Income High (I£500+)	76.4	41.5
Occupation: High Level[a]	58.6	44.6
Education High (secondary and above)	66.4	61.5

a. See explanation in text.

In a more detailed analysis significant differences in socioeconomic level between bearers of considerable power and the rest of the members of the leadership pools were found in undeveloped towns; bearers of considerable power in these towns are longer in the country and enjoy a larger income and a higher occupation level than the other members of the pools. No such difference has been detected in the developed towns.

This finding indicates, therefore, that in the less developed towns, the power elite (bearers of considerable power) tends also to be the general stratificational elite in the town. This conclusion has been strengthened by the results of a detailed examination of the intercorrelations among the various socioeconomic characteristics, as well as of the correlations between these characteristics and the variable of power. In the undeveloped towns these correlations were systematically higher than in the developed towns. In particular it should be noted that while correlations between the various socioeconomic characteristics and power were discovered in the undeveloped towns, no such correlations were discovered in the developed towns. Although power bearers in developed towns enjoy high socioeconomic positions relative to the rest of the towns' inhabitants, they do not enjoy higher positions than the rest of the institutional elites included in the leadership pools. This finding strongly supports our hypothesis that undeveloped towns have a monolithic power structure in which the power elite is almost identical with the stratificational elite. On the other hand, the developed towns exhibit a degree of pluralism, in the form of separation between the power elite and the other social elites of the towns.

SOCIOMETRIC DIFFERENTIATION BETWEEN MEMBERS OF THE LEADERSHIP POOLS

We studied the networks of primary relationship of all the members of the leadership pools—i.e., relationships with friends, colleagues at work, neighbors and relatives. The first question we asked was whether these relationships were predominantly confined to other members of the pools, or were also maintained with people outside them (see Table 4).

The results showed that in all the towns studied, the majority of the primary relationships of the members were with people outside the pools. On the average, one-third of the relationships were maintained within the pool and about two-thirds with people outside it.

At first sight this finding seems to indicate that the members of the leadership pools have strong connections with the other inhabitants of the town, since they maintain the majority of their relationships with such people. However, further analysis shows this conclusion to be an oversimplification. While members of the leadership pool of the town number only a few tens of people out of a total population of a few thousand, they all the same maintain one-third of their relationships between themselves, and only the remaining two-thirds with all the

TABLE 4
DISTRIBUTION OF THE SOCIAL RELATIONSHIPS OF MEMBERS OF THE
LEADERSHIP POOLS WITHIN AND OUTSIDE OF THOSE "POOLS" (in percentages)

	Towns				
	Developed	*Undeveloped*	*Heterogeneous*	*Homogeneous*	*Total*
Friends					
Within the "Pool"	40.2	54.3	37.9	50.8	44.9
Outside the "Pool"	59.8	45.7	62.1	49.2	55.1
Total	100.0	100.0	100.0	100.0	100.0
Associates					
Within the "Pool"	33.0	43.6	41.3	32.7	36.1
Outside the "Pool"	67.0	56.4	58.7	67.3	63.9
Total	100.0	100.0	100.0	100.0	100.0
Neighbors					
Within the "Pool"	33.3	38.0	28.9	40.5	34.9
Outside the "Pool"	66.7	62.0	71.1	59.5	65.1
Total	100.0	100.0	100.0	100.0	100.0
Relatives					
Within the "Pool"	9.8	6.8	1.9	14.6	8.9
Outside the "Pool"	90.2	93.2	98.1	85.4	91.1
Total	100.0	100.0	100.0	100.0	100.0
Total					
Within the "Pool"	32.1	39.2	30.2	37.8	34.4
Outside the "Pool"	67.9	60.8	69.8	62.2	65.6
Total	100.0	100.0	100.0	100.0	100.0

other inhabitants of the town. Moreover, in the most selective of the four types of primary relationships, that of friendship, members of the leadership pools demonstrate a particularly strong tendency to establish friendships with each other, so that nearly one-half their friendship ties are of this type. In contrast, almost all of the least selective and most ascribed type of primary relationships—those between relatives—are with people outside the pools. Relations with neighbors and associates fall between these two extremes.

Members of the leadership pools in developed or in heterogeneous towns, maintain more relationships with people outside of the pools, than those in undeveloped or in homogeneous towns. The results thus show that the extent to which members of the leadership pools are distinguished socially from the remaining inhabitants of the town, is greater in undeveloped and in homogeneous towns, than in developed and in heterogeneous towns, where members of the leadership pools maintain stronger relations with the rest of the community.

The networks of primary relationships among the members of the leadership pools were studied in detail. The most important finding was that the majority of members of the leadership pools are related to each other within one central sociometric network. This network includes more than two-thirds of all members of the leadership pools in all the towns, and apart from this central one, the subjects studied had no other sociometric networks. In some towns, a few isolated pairs of relationships were found. The majority of subjects not related to the central network were isolated socially from the other members of the leadership pools; such isolates constitute between one-fifth and one-quarter of the pool in each town studied (apart from Dimona in which they are only one-tenth of the leadership pool).

The fact that the majority of the members of the pools are included in the central sociometric networks demonstrates the generally high degree of social cohesiveness of the leadership pools. The main representatives of the various institutional elites in the towns constitute, then, not only an analytical category, but tend to constitute in every town a real social group. In this respect there are no significant differences between the various types of towns.

In spite of the considerable overall social cohesiveness of the leadership pools in all the towns, some differences in the degree of cohesiveness have been discovered. Detailed analysis revealed that in the two more homogeneous towns the internal cohesiveness of the leadership pools was greater than in the two heterogeneous towns. This was the only case in this study where the composition of the population had a greater influence on the findings than the level of institutional and economic development.

In all the towns a number of "sociometric stars" were found; that is, individuals chosen by a relatively large number of others. It is these sociometric stars which give the network the high degree of cohesiveness discussed above. It appears that the head of the local council is an important sociometric star in most cases, for in two towns he was chosen most often and in another he was chosen second most often. However, the heads of local councils did not reciprocate the choices. They themselves tended either to chose only a small number or even none at all of the other members of the leadership pools.

Apart from heads of local councils, other bearers of central roles were also chosen as stars, such as the secretary and treasurer of the local council, the director of the regional settlement scheme, and the secretary of the Mapai party.

Most sociometric stars are members of the political elite. In fact in three towns (Kiryat Gat, Dimona and Or Akiva) all the important stars were members of this elite. Only in one town (Netivot) was the institutional affiliation of the stars different—in this town they included members of the religious elite and others related indirectly to the religious sphere, such as the manager of the "Hapoel Hamizrachi" Bank (affiliated with the religious sector in Israeli society) or the headmaster of the secondary Yeshiva school (i.e., a governmental school combining secondary education with traditional religious learning).

CONCLUSION

In this study, various aspects of the power structure of Israeli development towns have been investigated. The findings will now be analyzed in the light of the wider problems raised at the beginning of this paper. From all of the tests conducted here, general support was found for only one of the two aspects of our hypothesis: A close relationship was found between the type of power structure and the level of economic and institutional development. In contrast, the factor of composition of population was found to have hardly any effect on the results.

Our findings, then, further confirm the existence of a close relationship between general social differentiation and pluralization of the local power structure. Though this relationship has been reported for other contexts, the fact that it was discovered even under the rather special conditions of the Israeli development towns reconfirms its universality.

The conclusion drawn so far relates, however, only to the most general and "static" finding of this study. Although this study was carried out simultaneously in four towns, some inferences can be drawn relating to the dynamic processes and the mechanisms operating in the transition from the "monolithic" to the "pluralistic" poles of the continuum of community power structures. In the monolithic situation, one central elite holds a monopoly of power in all spheres, apart from which there are only marginal bearers of limited power. This central group of power bearers is in the development towns composed mostly of members of the political elite, who are typically "external" to the town in that they draw their power from their positions in the national political system, which gives them a monopolistic position in the town itself; they are mostly old-timers, sent by the national political institutions to fill some of the more important formal roles in local institutions. We shall refer to them in the following as the external leadership.

Thus in the monopolistic situation there is a gap, or lack of continuity, in the power structure. On the one hand there is a small group of bearers of considerable and diffuse power, and on the other a periphery of bearers of little and limited power.

As the power structure becomes more pluralistic, the gap between those with considerable and diffuse power and those with little and limited power gradually narrows; it is filled by what we called "intermediate elites." Thus a graduated continuum is created from those with considerable power, through intermediate elites, to those with little power.

Even among the intermediate elites a large number of representatives of the political elite can be found, but there also begin to appear representatives of the economic and cultural elites.

The process of pluralization begins when the monopoly of the central group of power bearers is broken in certain spheres, in which power passes gradually to "specific" elites. The spheres in which power has thawed have generally been those freed from external control, i.e., those in which the focus of decision-making has been gradually shifted from national institutions into the community itself. In contrast, the spheres in which the monopoly of the central power bearers is maintained are also the spheres in which the focus of decision-making is still external to the town.

This study concentrated on towns in various stages of the process of change from the monolithic pole to the pluralistic pole, but none of the towns reached the latter pole. In fact, all the towns studied seem to have been closer to the monolithic than to the pluralistic pole; the differences found between them were mostly only in the nature of variations on a theme.

Our findings on the process of pluralization of the power structure in development towns, can now be set against the background of social change in this type of towns (Cohen, 1970b) to show how the findings on the power structure fit the general analysis of the social dynamics in these towns.

As mentioned before, the development towns are "planted" towns, that is, towns planned, erected and developed by national, mostly governmental institutions. The major part of their population are new immigrants, as yet not socially integrated, and lacking much understanding or influence in matters relating to the development of their community.

This initial situation has implications which heavily influence the power structure of the development town. All the resources for the development of the town, and even those for its regular management, are controlled by external factors—the national institutions. The independent organization of the town's inhabitants at this stage is usually weak, and their access to resources extremely limited. The inhabitants in fact do not constitute a counter-weight to the national institutions and their representatives.

Clearly, then, under these conditions the basis of the power of any potential power bearer in the town has of necessity to be external to it—in the national institutions which establish and develop the town. And since these are public, most often governmental, and not private institutions, power bearers in the town rely, in the final analysis, on the power of the central government or of its branches.

In the early stages of the establishment of the town no effective local opposition to the controlling group in fact exists. There is no independent local social or institutional leadership able to resist the power of the external political elite. Only the traditional leadership of the settlers is able to maintain its influence for any length of time, but it is composed mainly of elderly people whose traditional roles do not equip them well to deal with current problems in the new situation they face in Israel. As a result, their intervention is ineffective and their influence progressively decreases. In this study only one town, Netivot, was found where this traditional leadership was seemingly of some significance;

though even this exception is undoubtedly due to the fact that there are large religious institutions in this town, whose population is homogeneously Oriental, mostly religious and generally of a low socioeconomic status.

This initial state of affairs changes with the gradual economic and institutional consolidation and development of the town. After the initial transitional period accompanying immigration, group interests develop along with new local demands. The various groups of people of different ethnic origins organize around the new leadership formed out of the process of change and adaptation. This leadership represents either the particularistic interests of the various groups of origin or the wider interests of the whole population which are often at odds with the policy of the external institutions and their local representatives.

In the early stages of the establishment of the town the external leaders, controlling all the important resources, can afford to ignore almost completely the demands of the new inhabitants and of their leaders. However, they find it increasingly difficult to do so the more these inhabitants overcome their difficulties of absorption and the more the town itself develops. One reason for this is that with the development of the municipal, economic, educational and other systems, representatives of the immigrants steadily take on new roles, although at first only at the lower levels of the institutional systems. These new role bearers form an important pressure group as the representatives of the inhabitants in the towns' institutions, and with time gain control of some spheres of community life and so create for themselves a power basis independent of that of the external leadership.

The most common method of restraining and directing the rising power of immigrant groups employed by the external leadership, is the gradual cooptation of the immigrant leaders into the various political frameworks—such as the local government, the General Federation of Labour, the public institutions and particularly the political parties. These leaders thus gain a certain amount of power, e.g., as intermediate or specific elites, although the key positions continue to be held by the external leadership.

More changes take place as economic and institutional development of the town advances: new social groups then begin to emerge which cut across the ascriptive early social structure, based predominantly on affiliation with groups of ethnic origin. Specific institutional groups and elites than develop, representing new economic, professional, cultural and other interests. These new elites gradually infiltrate the local power structure. Nevertheless, in the towns we studied, their power, too, was still fairly limited. These new elites are no longer dependent on the external political leadership and have the capacity to counter-balance the influence of that leadership in the town. The co-optation of these elites is no longer as easy as was the co-optation of the leaders of the ethnic groups. Thus the owner of a local factory, for example, may make more demands on the official political leadership the more established and successful his factory. These demands have influence on that leadership insofar as the owner employs a large number of local inhabitants. Thus the development of such elites constitutes an important source of pluralization of the local power structure.

The foregoing leads to an almost paradoxical conclusion: to the extent that the external political leadership succeeds in developing the town, new bases of power will be created which will later support new kinds of power bearers in the town; these, in turn, will gradually free themselves of the controlling influence of the original elite. The towns, although created at first by the national institutions which established them out of overall social considerations, thus seem to be gradually gaining independence and freeing themselves from the guardianship of those institutions. Pluralization of the power structure and independence of the town from national institutions seem, then, to go hand in hand in the development towns.

This conclusion points out an important difference between new towns in Israel and other Western countries, and particularly the United States, in respect of the process of the dispersion and differentiation of urban power structures. Whereas in the United States the local economic elite is typically dominant in the monolithic situation, in Israeli new towns it is the political elite which seems to be dominant in this situation. During the process of differentiation in the United States, the basis of power of the established local economic elite is being steadily weakened,[16] and new elites are appearing, mainly political and professional, whose basis of power is often external to the community. In contrast, the process in Israeli new towns is moving in the opposite direction. With the increasing independence of the local community, nonpolitical elites are arising with new, localized bases of power. The process of pluralization of local power structures is thus characteristic of both the United States and Israel. However, while in the former the process is accompanied by a degree of loss of local autonomy, in the latter it is accompanied by the gain of such autonomy.

Clearly, it could be asked whether such differences obtain only between Israeli development towns and American cities, or whether they could be generalized to all types of Israeli and modern Western communities. A fuller picture of the similarities and differences in the process of the crystallization of local power in Israel and elsewhere would require a more comprehensive study of other types of towns in Israel and in other countries.

NOTES

1. On the new towns in Israel, see E. Spiegel (1966) and Cohen (1970b).

2. The elitist position is generally associated with F. Hunter; see his *Community Power Structure* (1953). The pluralist position is most clearly stated in Dahl (1961).

3. See particularly Polsby (1963), whose position has been sharply criticized by Rosenbaum (1967).

4. See Anton (1963); and particularly Walton (1966a, 1966b) and Rosenbaum (1967).

5. This idea underlies the volume of essays by T. N. Clark (1968a: see esp. ch. 5).

6. On the necessity to combine methods, see Bonjean and Olsen (1964: 289).

7. For a general comparative analysis of previously done research on American communities, see Gilbert (1968) and Friedmann (1970); for a list of comparative studies, see T. N. Clark (1968c: 464-467).

8. See, for example, D'Antonio and Form (1965).

9. I understand that a major effort in this respect is being undertaken by the International Studies of Values in Politics project; see Clark (1968c: 465).

10. For one of the few comparative studies within a country outside the United States, see Kornblum (1970), whose study runs on very similar lines to that presented in this essay.

11. See Weingrod (1964) and the comments on his assertions in *Amot* 11.

12. Of the 21 development towns which the Manpower Planning Authority included in its survey, 80 percent of family heads were in 1961 of Afro-Asian origin, and only 18 percent were of European and American origin; the remaining 2 percent were native-born (see Manpower Planning Authority, 1964: 16, table 3).

13. The population of the town of Beit Shean, for example, in the 10 years between 1956 and 1965, grew by 4,800 inhabitants (from 7,900 to 12,700). However, during that period, 9,035 new immigrants were directed to this town; 11,284 residents from other settlements in the country moved there; and the natural population growth added a further 4,833 souls. This represents a total of 25,152 additional inhabitants in the town's population. These figures show that, for every person added to the population of the town in that period, about four others left Beit Shean (based on the data presented in Manpower Planning Authority, 1967).

14. This description of the social and political situation in the development towns is based on Cohen (1970b).

15. My definition of "economic and institutional development" approximates closely the concept of "stages (or levels) of economic and social development" used by Kornblum as the independent variable of his study of two Slovenian communes; see Kornblum (1970: 19 ff). Owing to lack of space, I cannot present here in full detail the specific indicators which I used to measure the level of economic and institutional development. These are given in the thesis on which this paper is based; see Cohen (1970a: ch. 3).

16. A similar trend has been recently reported for British cities; see Morris and Newton (1970) and the studies quoted therein.

REFERENCES

ANTON, T. J. (1963) "Power, pluralism and the study of power." Administrative Science Quarterly 7, 4: 424-457.

BONJEAN, M. and K. OLSEN (1964) "Community leadership: directions of research." Administrative Science Quarterly 9, 3.

CLARK, T. N. [ed.] (1968a) Community Structure and Decision-Making: Comparative Analyses. San Francisco: Chandler.

––– et al. (1968b) "Discipline, method, community structure, and decision-making: the role and limitations of the sociology of knowledge." American Sociologist 3, (August).

––– (1968c) "Present and future research in community decision-making: the problem of comparability," in T. N. Clark (ed.) Community Structure and Decision-Making: Comparative Analyses. San Francisco: Chandler.

COHEN, E. (1970a) "The city in Zionist ideology." Jerusalem: Jerusalem Urban Studies, No. 1.

––– (1970b) "Development towns–the social dynamics of 'planted' urban communities in Israel," in S. N. Eisenstadt, R. Bar-Yosef, and C. Adler (eds.) Integration and Development in Israel. Jerusalem: Israel Univ. Press.

––– (1968) "The power structure of development towns." Ph.D. dissertation. Hebrew University of Jerusalem.

DAHL, R. A. (1961) Who Governs? New Haven and London: Yale Univ. Press.

D'ANTONIO, W. V. and W. H. FORM (1965) Influentials in Two Border Cities: A Study in Decision-Making. Notre Dame, Ind.: Univ. of Notre Dame Press.

FRIEDMANN, P. (1970) "Community decision-making in the U.S.: a review of recent research." New Atlantis 2 (Winter): 133-143.

GILBERT, C. W. (1968) "Community power and decision-making: a quantitative examination of previous research," pp. 139-156 in T. N. Clark (ed.) Community Structure and Decision-Making: Comparative Analyses. San Francisco: Chandler.

HUNTER, F. (1953) Community Power Structure. Chapel Hill: Univ. of North Carolina Press.

KORNBLUM, W. (1970) "The Yugoslav communal system: decision-making in housing and urban development." New Atlantis 2: 12-30.

Manpower Planning Authority (1967) "Manpower research–Beit Shean." Israel: Ministry of Labor. (mimeo) (in Hebrew)

––– (1964) "Manpower in the development towns." Israel: Ministry of Labor. (mimeo) (in Hebrew)

MORRIS, D. S. and K. NEWTON (1970) "Profile of a local political elite: businessmen as community decision-makers in Birmingham, 1838-1966." New Atlantis 2: 111-123.

POLSBY, N. W. (1963) Community Power and Political Theory. New Haven: Yale Univ. Press.

ROSENBAUM, A. (1967) "Community power and political theory: a case of misperception." Berkeley Journal of Sociology 12: 91-116.

SPIEGEL, E. (1966) Neue Staedte/New Towns in Israel. Stuttgart: K. Kraemer.

WALTON, J. (1966a) "Substance and artifact: the current status of research in community power structure." American Journal of Sociology 71, 4: 430-438.

––– (1966b) "Discipline, method and community power: a note on the sociology of knowledge." American Sociological Review 31, 5: 684-689.

WEINGROD, A. (1964) "Immigrants, localism and political government." Amot 10: 15-22. (in Hebrew)

Chapter 8

The Chaos of the Living City

Charles Tilly

As life is disorderly, so is the city. But is the city itself the source of disorder? Since the rise of the industrial metropolis, generations of western men have proclaimed it so. The nineteenth-century sociologists who argued that the mobility, complexity and scale of the modern city were bound to strip men of social ties, disorient them, and thus to push them toward individual and collective derangement were simply articulating a well-established tradition. The tradition has not yet died.

We find the precise tone in Baudelaire:

Swarming city, city of dreams
Where ghosts grab strollers in broad daylight . . .

How admirable it is, he tells us elsewhere, to join the few who are free of the spectral grasp:

And so you go your way, stoic, uncomplaining
Through the chaos of the living city . . .

"Through the chaos of the living city! " A great motto for the study of urban disorder.

"Under the aegis of the city," declares Lewis Mumford (1961: 43) "violence . . . became normalized, and spread far beyond the centers where the

AUTHOR'S NOTE: *This paper is a top-to-bottom revision of "A travers le chaos des vivantes cités," presented to the Sixth World Congress of Sociology (Evian-les-Bains, France), 1966. The original version was published in Meadows and Mizruchi 1969 (citations in this form refer to the list of references at the end of the paper). The research reported in the paper received support from the Center of International Studies (Princeton University), the Social Science Research Council, Harvard University, the MIT-Harvard Joint Center for* great collective manhunts and sacrificial orgies were first instituted." Again we encounter the image of the city as destroyer, of urban life as the solvent of social bonds, of violence as the price paid for living on the large scale. While peasant revolts leave faded souvenirs here and there, the word "revolution" recalls city streets. As deprived millions limp hopefully into the cities of Africa or Latin America, political observers hold their breaths. When will the cities explode? Urbanization, it seems to go without saying, means social disorder.

It does, in a way. Huge wars and devastating revolutions only came into man's life with the flowering of cities. But whether urbanization and collective violence have a necessary or a contingent connection—or, indeed, any genuine causal connection at all—is far from clear.

Some small observations on the nature of that connection form the substance of this essay. I want to comment on the ways urbanization might incite or transform collective violence, raise some questions about the relationship between violent and nonviolent forms of political participation, sketch some means for investigating the political consequences of urbanization, and review some relevant findings from a study of the evolution of political disturbances in France since 1830.

Why and how does urbanization affect collective violence? Sociologists have some well-frozen ideas on the subject. After stressing the disruptive personal effects of migration and the "frictions" produced by the rubbing together of urban and preurban value systems in expanding cities, Philip Hauser (1963: 212) tells us that:

> Another group of serious problems created or augmented by rapid rates of urbanization are those of internal disorder, political unrest, and governmental instability fed by mass misery and frustration in the urban setting. The facts that the differences between the "have" and "have not" nations, and between the "have" and "have not" peoples within nations, have become "felt differences," and that we are experiencing a "revolution in expectations," have given huge urban population agglomerations an especially incendiary and explosive character.

In Hauser's view, the breaking of traditional bonds and the conflict of values feed disorder, while the swelling city's combination of misery and heightened hopes nearly guarantees it. Change produces tension, tension breaks out in collective explosions, and a form of action more frenzied than that of stable, developed countries erupts into life.

Urban Studies, the Canada Council and the National Science Foundation. The Institute for Advanced Study gave me much-prized leisure to complete the revision. I am especially grateful for research assistance to Karen Ambush, Lutz Berkner, Judy Carter, Priscilla Cheever, James Doty, Ronald Florence, Judy Kammins, Lynn Less, A.Q. Lodhi, Ted Margadant, Virginia Perkins, Sue Richardson, James Rule, Ann Shorter, Edward Shorter, Gerald Soliday, Cyrus Stewart, and Sandra Winston. © 1973 by Charles Tilly.

Hauser's analysis, I believe, sums up the predominant sociological position. Seen from the outside, the set of ideas looks solid and chinkless. From inside, it seems much less likely to withstand pressure. For one thing, it contains a notion of the equivalence of different types of disorder. Personal malaise, moral deviation, crime and political upheaval are supposed to flow into each other.

Almost mystically, Louis Chevalier (1958: 552-553) announces that essential unity: outside the major outbursts, he says,

> The political and social violence which has been studied so often and so minutely is replaced by other forms of violence—more continuous, more complex, harsher, involving greater numbers, taking from the rise and the bulk of the masses their progress, their unity and their force. Here is another form of connection among crises: Private dramas, daily ones, add their weight to the public ones, developing outside them, but accumulating and culminating in them.

Chevalier does not hesitate to call nineteenth-century Paris a sick city, or to consider misery, crime, suicide, street violence, and popular rebellion so many expressions of the same pervasive pathology. That is one side of the standard sociological formulation.

Turn this set of ideas over. On the other side is stamped a complementary set: that there is a sharp disjunction between healthy and pathological social states, between the normal and abnormal, between order and disorder, which justifies treating different specimens of disapproved collective behavior as manifestations of the same general phenomenon—"deviance." The responses which other people give to the disapproved behavior win another general label—"social control."

Collective violence almost automatically receives both the complementary treatments. It is easy to treat as the final expression of a fundamental pathology which also shows up as a crime, delinquency, family instability, or mental illness. It is even easier to treat as radically discontinuous from orderly political life. Long before Taine and Le Bon had dismissed the mass actions of the French Revolution as the work of demonic guttersnipes, Plato had shuddered over the outbreaks of man's "lawless wild-beast nature, which peers out in sleep," and James Madison had warned of "an unhappy species of the population . . . who, during the calm of regular government, are sunk below the level of men; but who, in the tempestuous scenes of civil violence, may emerge into the human character, and give a superiority of strength to any party with which they may associate themselves."

More recently, Hannah Arendt (1963: 9-10) has argued that "violence is a marginal phenomenon in the political realm" that "political theory has little to say about the phenomenon of violence and must leave its discussion to the technicians," that "insofar as violence plays a predominant role in wars and revolutions, both occur outside the political realm." And the political realm, to Miss Arendt's mind, contains normal social life.

Here two ideas intertwine. One is that violence appeals to the beast in man and to the beasts among men. The other is that men in becoming violent step over an abyss which then separates them from coherent rationality.

Despite their devotion to death-dealing automobiles, aggressive detectives, and murderous wars, it is true that men ring round most forms of interpersonal violence with extraordinary tabus and anxieties. Yet collective violence is one of the commonest forms of political participation. Why begin an inquiry into the effects of urbanization with the presumption that violent politics appear only as a disruption, a deviation or a last resort? Rather than treating collective violence as an unwholesome deviation from normality, we might do better to ask under what conditions (if any) violence disappears from ordinary political life.

That is, however, a mischievous question. The treatment of collective behavior in terms of change: tension: tension-release and the assumption of drastic discontinuity between routine politics and collective violence cling to each other. Most students of large-scale social change cling to both. Challenging either the fit between the two notions or their independent validity therefore smacks of rabble-rousing. Yet there are some alternatives we simply cannot ignore.

First, collective violence often succeeds. Revolutionaries do come to power, machine-breakers do slow the introduction of labor-saving devices, rioters do get public officials removed. The local grain riot, so widespread in Western Europe from the seventeenth through the nineteenth centuries, often produced a temporary reduction of prices, forced stored grain into the market, and stimulated local officials to new efforts at assuring the grain supply (L. Tilly, 1971). I do not mean that, by some universal calculus, violence is more efficient than nonviolence. I simply mean that it works often enough in the short run, by the standards of the participants, not to be automatically dismissed as a flight from rational calculation.

Second, whether or not it succeeds in the short run and by the standards of the participants, collective protest is often a very effective means of entering or remaining in political life, of gaining or retaining an identity as a force to be reckoned with. Eugene Debs boasted that "no strike has ever been lost" and American advocates of Black Power consider their appeal the only means of mobilizing Negroes as an effective political force. Although there are always Revisionists to argue that the dispossessed will gain power more cheaply by circumventing revolution—even though the Revisionists are often right—collective violence does frequently establish the claim to be heard, and feared. In that sense, too, it can be a rational extension of peaceful political action.

Third, acts of collective violence often follow a well-defined internal order. The order goes beyond the Freudian logic of dreams or that symbolic correspondence Neil Smelser finds between the beliefs embodied in collective movements and the strains which produce them. In many cases it is sufficiently conscious, explicit and repetitive to deserve the name normative. Many western countries on the eve of intensive industrialization, for example, have seen a recurrent sort of redressing action against what the people of a locality consider to be violations of justice: mythical avenging figures like Rebecca or Ned Ludd, threats posted in their names, outlandish costumes (women and Indians being favorite masquerades), routine, focused, roughly appropriate punishments inflicted on the presumed violators of popular rights (see Hobsbawm and Rudé, 1968; Hobsbawm, 1969; C. Tilly, 1969). Disorder displays a normative order.

Fourth, the participants in collective violence are frequently rather ordinary people. Recent studies of popular disturbances in France, England and elsewhere have shifted the burden of proof to those who wish to claim that mass actions recruit from the lunatic fringe (e.g., Belvèze, 1959; Bezucha, 1968; Cobb, 1961-1963, 1964, 1970; Cornelius, 1970; Davies, 1969; Fogelson and Hill, 1968; Furet et al., 1963; Godechot, 1970; Gossez, 1967; Hofstadter, 1970; Kirkham et al., 1970; Masotti and Bowen, 1968; Mazauric, 1970; Nelson, 1970; Peacock, 1965; Rudé, 1970; Rule and Tilly, 1971; Sewell, 1971; Skolnick, 1969; Saboul, 1958; C. Tilly, 1964; L. Tilly, 1971; R. Tilly, 1971; Tønnesson, 1959; Vidalou, 1959; Vovelle, 1965; Williams, 1968). Not that these studies portray the recruitment as a kind of random sampling: real grievances, local economic conditions, established paths of communication, the character of local politics all help determine who takes part. But the rioters and local machine-breakers commonly turn out to be fairly ordinary people acting on important but commonplace grievances. The "dangerous classes" stay out of sight.

Finally, the large-scale structural changes of societies which transform everyday politics through their effects on the organization, communication and common consciousness of different segments of the population also transform the character and loci of collective violence. As the scale at which men organize their peaceful political actions expands, so does the scale at which they organize their violence. As workers in mechanized industries become a coherent political force, they also become a source of disorder. The correlations are obviously complex and imperfect; that is precisely why they are interesting. But they are correlations rather than antitheses.

So there are five reasons for hesitating to assume that collective violence is a sort of witless release of tension divorced from workaday politics: its frequent success as a tactic, its effectiveness in establishing or maintaining a group's political identity, its normative order, its frequent recruitment of ordinary people, and its tendency to evolve in cadence with peaceful political action. The five points are debatable and worthy of debate . . . not to mention empirical investigation. To the extent that they are valid, they lead to somewhat different expectations from the usual ones concerning the development of political disturbances in the course of urbanization.

Urbanization could affect collective violence in three main ways: by disrupting existing social ties and controls, by exposing more individuals and groups to urban institutions and living conditions, and by changing relations between city and country. In fact, an abundant (if largely theoretical and anecdotal) literature asserts the disturbing effects of each of these changes. The disruption of ties and controls is commonly supposed to incite disorder either by removing restraints to impulses which would under normal circumstances be muffled or by inducing anxiety in individuals detached from stable, orderly surroundings. (Mass migration to cities is the standard example.) Exposure to urban institutions and living conditions is usually considered to promote collective violence in two respects: (1) by imposing intolerable privations in the form of material misery and unfamiliar disciplines, or (2) by communicating new goals via heightened communication within large groups sharing common fates and interests, and via the diffusion of higher standards of comfort and welfare from the existing urban population to the newcomers. Thus rapid urban growth is said to exacerbate the "revolution of rising expectations." The changing relations between city and country are often thought to engender disturbance in the country itself as cities expand their claims for goods, men, taxes, and subordination, while rural communities resist those claims. Thus regions of distinct tribal character presumably become ripe for rebellion.

If the disruption of existing ties and controls, the exposure of individuals and groups to urban institutions and living conditions, and the changing relations between city and country all uniformly encourage collective violence, then matters are delightfully simple: the pace and location of upheaval should be closely correlated with the pace and location of urban growth. That hypothesis easily lends itself to testing. The surprising thing is that it has not yet been truly tested.

Even in the absence of good data on either side of the relationship, however, we may legally doubt whether it is so splendidly straightforward. In no western European country have the peak years of urban growth since 1800 also been the peak years of political upheaval. Such quantitative international studies as we have of the twentieth century give relatively little weight to the sheer pace of change in the explanation of the frequency of protest and violence; instead, they tend to substantiate the importance of political structure and of short-term deprivation. So a global connection of upheaval to urban growth seems unlikely.

Happily, the various components of urbanization also lend themselves to separate analysis. We can, to some extent, isolate the political correlates of rapid migration from rural areas to large cities, of miserable urban living conditions, or of the expansion of central control into the rural backland. Rather than the amassing of case studies of violence or the statistical manipulation of general indices drawn from samples of whole countries, two strategies getting at differentials within countries seem particularly suitable. The first is to compare segments of the country—communities, regions, classes, as well as periods—in terms of the frequency and intensity of collective violence, of the forms violence takes, of the participants in it. Whereas international comparisons ordinarily make it tough to disentangle the correlates of urban poverty from those of rapid migration to cities, and case studies usually hide the significance of negative instances, systematic comparisons within countries promise the opportunity to examine the differences between turbulent and placid periods or settings in meaningful detail, with reasonable controls.

The second strategy is to separate—and, where possible, to index—the appearance of different forms of collective violence. This means eschewing summary indices of "turbulence" or "instability." It also means paying as much attention to variations in the form of collective outbursts as to shifts from calm to fury and back again. Here the illuminating work of George Rudé or Eric Hobsbawm, who have depicted the characteristic preindustrial disturbances and stressed their replacement by other kinds of disturbances with the advent of industrialization, offers questions and hypotheses galore.

The power to close in on such hypotheses gives these two strategies their attraction. The ideas about urbanization and collective violence I earlier characterized as the standard sociological treatment immediately suggest predictions: those periods and regions in which the intensest urban growth goes on should be the richest in disturbances; misery, mobility and cultural diversity will have separate and roughly additive effects; while collective violence and other forms of deviance will be positively correlated in gross and will recruit in the same parts of the population, at a given level of urban concentration or a given pace of urbanization they will be negatively correlated, since they are alternative expressions of the same tensions; collective violence will recede as new groups become formally organized, integrated into the nation's political life.

There is surely something to all these hypotheses. They deserve checking. But the second thoughts on the nature of collective violence we encountered earlier suggest some different predictions: a weak connection of political disturbances with crime, misery or personal disorder, a corresponding rarity of the criminal, miserable or deranged in their ranks, a strong connection with more peaceful forms of political contention, a significant continuity and internal order to collective violence where it does occur, a long lag between urban growth and collective outbursts due to the time required for socialization, organization and formation of a common consciousness on the part of the newcomers, a tendency for disturbances to cluster where there is a conflict between the principal holders of power in a locality and more or less organized groups moving into or out of a modus vivendi with those holders of power, a marked variation of the form of the disturbance with the social organization of its setting. On the whole these hunches are harder to verify than those deducible from the standard sociological treatment. Still they can be tested, and should be.

For some years now, a group of sociologists and historians at several different universities in Europe and North America has been working on the relevant comparisons for Germany, France, Italy and a few other European countries since around 1830. The work on France is at present further along than the studies of the other countries, so we are not yet in a good position to make systematic comparisons among the countries. But we do have over a century of French experience well documented, and enough information about the other countries to give some sense which features of France's experience are peculiar, and which commonplace. This paper deals exclusively with the French evidence.

France of the last century and a half is a good starting point. Its territory is fairly constant, the general lines of its political history well known, its violent incidents abundant. The period 1830 to 1960—the main one under examination here—contains several important surges of industrial expansion and urban growth. And the records are remarkably rich—often richer, contrary to our sociological prejudices, for the earlier years than for the later ones.

The raw materials come from French archives, newspapers, political year-books, government reports, and statistical publications, occasional memoirs, and specialized historical works. For information on collective violence, our basic procedures are (1) to enumerate as many as possible of the violent conflicts above a certain scale occurring in France each year and code them all in a summary, standard way; (2) to select a systematic sample of them for intensive analysis, gathering as much additional information about them as possible from the archival sources and historical works, coding them in a very detailed fashion according to a regular scheme; (3) to organize special studies of especially informative periods or conflicts.

The basic unit in the analysis of collective violence is the "disturbance"—any event occurring within the country in which at least one group of fifty or more persons took part, and which some person or property was seized or damaged over resistance. The disturbances in the general sample are all such events trained readers encountered in scanning two national newspapers from 1830 to 1860 and 1930 to 1960, plus three randomly selected months per year from 1861 to 1929. There are about 2,000 disturbances in the general sample, 500-odd in the intensive one, and a dozen disturbances singled out for special analysis.

A good deal of general information about the social settings of disturbances, of course, enters the analysis in the form of observations on the disturbances themselves. But that way of accumulating information slights the settings with few disturbances, or none. We have tried to get around that difficulty by assembling comparable information on major social changes—for example, urban population, net migration, labor force shifts—year by year for France as a whole, for its eighty to ninety departments, and for the larger cities.

We have also begun to deal with other forms of collective conflict by putting together roughly comparable information on most of the strikes (some 100,000 of them) reported in France from 1830 to 1960. The two sets of conflicts overlap usefully, since a small proportion of the strikes turned into violent encounters. Despite this extensive standardization of the sources, however, the sorts of questions this research raises often drive us back to other materials in order to account for contrasts in violent propensities between different years, areas and segments of the French population. In short, the data collected offer the possibility of moderately firm tests of existing hunches concerning differentials in collective violence, plus some good leads for further investigation; they cannot conceivably provide a total explanation of France's turbulent political history.

Figure 1 presents our count of the number of disturbances per year in France from 1830 to 1960, smoothed to five-year moving averages.[1] Despite the considerable smoothing, the curve reveals the tremendous bunching of violent events in time. That bunching in itself rules out many of the similar interpretations of collective violence as a response to structural change, which lead us to expect more gradual crescendoes and decrescendoes of violence. Collective violence is unlike crime, suicide, fertility, marriage, or migration, all of which the pace of industrialization or urban growth does affect directly, and all of which display large but very gradual long-run swings. It resembles strike activity more closely, since strikes come in sudden surges superimposed on massive long-run trends. That is more or less what we should expect of a form of action clearly dependent on slow processes like unionization, industrialization of the labor force and changes in the organization of firms, but also responsive to short-run economic and political crises affecting the position of organized labor (see Shorter and Tilly, 1971). But the fluctuations of collective violence correspond most directly with the ebb and flow of political conflict at the national level. The periods of the Revolution of 1848 and of the Popular Front—both times of massive popular mobilization—dominate the curve.

The swings of collective violence, on the other hand, do not correspond to the pace of urban growth, which was most rapid in the 1850s, the 1920s, and the 1950s. If anything, the correlation runs the other way: rapid urban growth, less collective violence. I expect, in fact, that more detailed studies will reveal a general tendency for collective violence to decline when and where urbanization is most rapid, because rapid urbanization means both that many people are leaving the countryside where they are embedded in communities which are organized for collective action and that many people are arriving in cities where it takes a long time for them to acquire the means of collective action, or to be drawn into the ones which already exist. My premise, obviously, is that violence flows directly from organized collective action instead of being an alternative to it.

Let us close in on the first thirty years of the period, from 1830 to 1860. The three decades lead us through several major upheavals and changes of regime in France: from the Restoration to the July Monarchy via the Revolution of 1830,

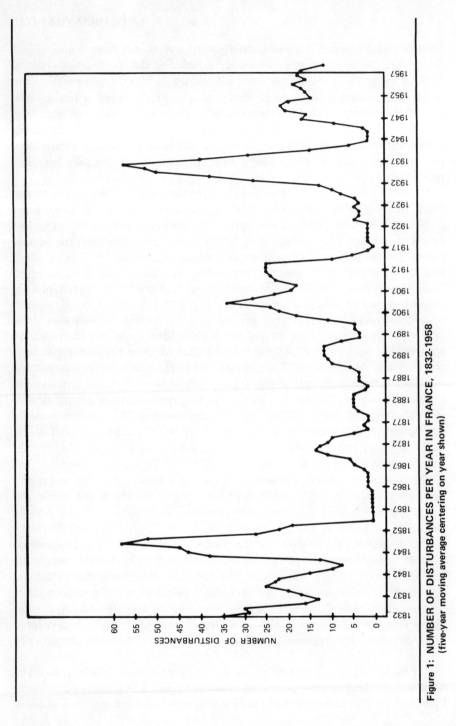

Figure 1: NUMBER OF DISTURBANCES PER YEAR IN FRANCE, 1832-1958
(five-year moving average centering on year shown)

through the Monarchy with its insurrections in Lyon and Paris, from the July Monarchy into the Second Republic via the Revolution of 1848 and its turbulent aftermath, to the Second Empire through Louis Napoleon's coup d'état.

The thirty years also bracket an unprecedented push of economic expansion and urban growth. The expansion was slow in the 1830s, punctuated by depression in the 1840s, and extraordinarily vigorous in the 1850s. During that third decade the railroads proliferated and modern industry got underway. Correspondingly the growth of big cities accelerated from moderate in the 1830s and 1840s to fast in the 1850s. While at the beginning of the period the leaders were mainly the old regional capitals—Toulouse, Strasbourg, Marseilles, Lyon, Paris, with St. Etienne and Roubaix-Tourcoing starting to represent the newer industrial centers—by the 1850s the entire region of Paris and all the industrializing Northeast were full of spurting cities.

On this smaller stage, we still do not see collective violence dancing to the rhythm of urban growth. The turbulent years of this period, even leaving the major revolutions aside, were 1830, 1832, 1848, and 1851. Roughly two-thirds of all the disturbances we have enumerated in the entire three decades from 1830 to 1860 occurred in the seven years from 1830 through 1832 and 1848 through 1851. The later 1850s, those peak years for urban growth, were practically empty of violent disturbances; so were most of the 1860s. Again the correlation over time is inverse: rapid growth, little disturbance.

This does not mean, however, that the cities were calm and the countryside turbulent. The pattern was much more complicated than that. It is true that short-lived disturbances flourished in the smaller towns and rural areas of France in the 1830s and 1840s. Three types of events recur again and again: food riots, violent resistance to taxation, and collective invasions of forests, fields, and other rural property. (A fourth frequent form of collective violence of the mid-nineteenth century—the smashing of machines by unemployed or fearful workers—did not reach its stride in France until the Revolution of 1848.) Here we have the recurrent, and somehow coherent, "preindustrial" forms of disturbance described by Edward Thompson or Eric Hobsbawm. The food riot, with its regular combination of grumbling against price rises, massing in markets, seizure of grains being shipped or held in storage, and forced public sale at a price locally determined to be just, sums up their character.

Even in the 1830s, however, the larger conflicts and the ones which most seriously affected the distribution of power in France clustered in and around the great cities. Paris usually led the way; Lille, Lyon, Rouen, Marseilles, and Nantes rarely stayed out of the action. During any substantial block of time, therefore, we see three broad classes of disturbance: major conflicts centered on the great cities; ramifications of those major conflicts in smaller cities and in the hinterlands of the great cities; smaller-scale events, only indirectly linked to nationwide conflicts, spread through the rest of the country.

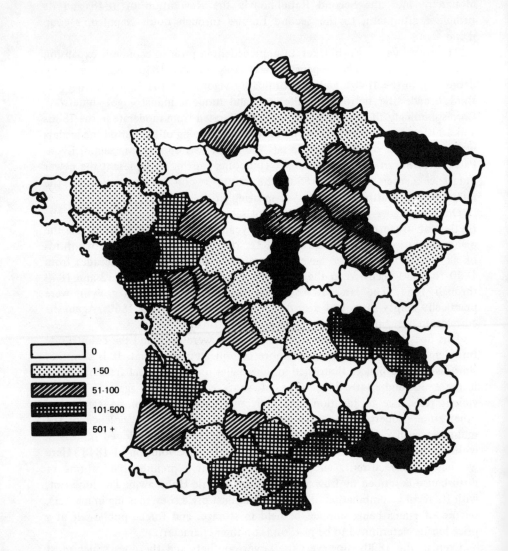

Figure 2: PARTICIPANTS IN COLLECTIVE VIOLENCE PER 100,000 POPULATION, 1830-1832 (corrected to annual rate)

The Revolution of 1830 and its aftermath display this pattern clearly. The central events were no doubt Paris' Three Glorious Days of July, 1830; with large demonstrations and extensive street-fighting across barricades, a coalition of workers and bourgeois brought down the Bourbon monarchy of Charles X and installed the house of Orleans, with Louis Philippe as king. Yet much happened outside of Paris. Almost immediately, struggles for power broke into violence in Dijon, Nantes, Amiens, Bordeaux, Lille, and Toulouse and went on without public confrontation in most other big cities. As the new government attempted to reestablish its control over the provinces, resistance to taxation and to other actions from the center produced clashes through large regions of France. The struggles continued into 1831 and 1832, most notably in the great Lyon insurrection of November 1831, the counter-revolutionary guerrilla of the Vendée and other parts of the West in 1832, and the incessant conflict among segments of the revolutionary coalition in Paris itself.

A map of participation in disturbances during the years 1830, 1831, and 1832 (Figure 2) reveals the considerable spread of involvement in violent conflict. The map, which shows estimated participants in each department per 100,000 population, singles out Paris as a small spot of intense participation in the midst of a region where conflict was under control. It also shows the high involvement in collective violence of the Rhône (which is essentially that of Lyon), the influence of several major conflicts over taxes in Bourges and elsewhere in the Cher, a long series of food riots in Moselle, the repeated conflicts in the West, and the widespread resistance to central power in a whole band of departments running across southern France from Bordeaux to Marseilles.

Let us sum up the pattern statistically. Suppose we calculate rates of participation per 100,000 population for the revolutionary months of July and August, 1830, for the period of consolidation during the remainder of 1830, and for the period 1830-1832 as a whole. The breakdown by urbanity of department is this:

Percentage of population in cities of 10,000 or more	Revolution	Postrevolution	1830 to 1832
0.0	19	54	20
0.1-5.0	42	84	34
5.1-10.0	92	218	66
10.1-15.0	720	136	135
15.1+	2,904	412	727
Total	573	175	158

In general, the more urban the department, the heavier its involvement in collective violence. Yet even the rural departments produced significant numbers of participants—especially during the critical period of reimposition of central control during the last months of 1830.

Collective violence, then, clustered around the cities, but not exclusively in them. Big cities like Lyon and Marseilles stand out, as do their surrounding areas. Paris and its department, the Seine, tower over all the rest. Yet very rural departments like Ariège remain in their company. Furthermore, despite the example of Paris, there is no obvious tendency for the fastest-growing cities or the most rapidly urbanizing departments to produce more collective violence than the rest.

To make that fact clearer, we may turn to a correlational analysis of the same data concerning 1830-1832. Table 1 presents correlations of various indicators of crime, malaise and collective violence with three different measures of urbanism and urbanization: (a) the population in cities of 10,000 or more in 1831, (b) the change in that population from 1821 to 1831, (c) the net migration into the department from 1826 to 1831. In general, the measures of crime, malaise and collective violence are most highly correlated with urban

TABLE 1

CORRELATIONS BETWEEN INDICATORS OF URBANIZATION AND INDICATORS OF CRIME, INDIVIDUAL MALAISE AND COLLECTIVE VIOLENCE, PARTIALED FOR TOTAL POPULATION, FOR DEPARTMENTS OF FRANCE, 1830 TO 1832

	Indicators of Urbanization		
	Population in Cities of 10,000 or More	Increase in Urban Population 1821-1831	Net Migration into Department 1826-1831
1831: Number of Persons Charged with:			
Rebellion	.837	.613	.255
Crimes Against Persons	.246	.122	.236
Crimes Against Property	.823	.626	.259
Vagrancy	.771	.581	.265
Number of Reported			
Illegitimate Births	.771	.502	.290
Suicides	.839	.693	.425
Collective Violence 1830-1832			
Number of			
Disturbances	.671	.673	.328
Participants	.913	.878	.526
Killed and Wounded	.925	.840	.406

NOTE: Partial correlations of absolute numbers in each category, total population partialed out.
SOURCES: Compte de l'administration de la justice criminelle en France, 1831; Censuses of 1821, 1826, 1831; general sample of disturbances; partial correlations among indicators of urbanization: urban population x urban increase .777; urban population x net migration .465; urban increase x net migration .511.

population and least highly correlated with net migration; urban increase regularly occupies the middle position. All the correlations are positive, and some are substantial. As a consequence, a first reading of the table may well produce the impression that crime, individual malaise and collective violence do, after all, spring from urban growth, and in similar ways. That would be hasty.

The problem, of course, is that urban population, urban increase and net migration are sufficiently correlated with one another (even when the relationships are partialed for the total population of the department, as they are here) that their separate effects are hard to distinguish. A multiple regression of the same data separates them more sharply. Within a multiple regression incorporating the number of persons in the department charged with "rebellion" (which covered all sorts of resistance to the law) in 1831, the number of suicides, the total population, population in cities of 10,000 or more, increase in urban population 1821-1831 and net migration 1826-1831, the multiple correlation coefficients and standardized regression coefficients for four different indicators of the magnitude of collective violence came out as follows:

| | | Standardized regression coefficient | | |
Dependent variable	Multiple Correlation	Urban Population	Urban Increase	Net Migration
Number of disturbances	.785	.757	.440	−.075
Participants	.960	.714	.420	.042
Killed and wounded	.959	.677	.333	−.093
Arrested	.928	.665	.307	−.141

The pattern is the same as we saw with the correlation coefficients, but the differences among the three urbanization variables are now far greater. It now appears there was no relationship at all between the volume of recent migration into a department and the extent of collective violence. Whatever the effect of urban increase on collective violence, therefore, it does not operate through the unsettling arrival of uprooted migrants. What is more, the effect of urban population as such appears to be about twice as great as the effect of urban increase. The presence of cities made the big difference; their expansion mattered much less.

When looked at more concretely, the distinction is perfectly plausible, and easy to grasp. The segments of the population with sufficient organization to carry on collective action at a scale large enough to bother the authorities—and therefore to lead to violent encounters with troops, police and others—were concentrated in the larger cities and their vicinities. This is emphatically true of organized workers, and one of the chief reasons for two features of the strike activity of the 1830s and 1840s which our analyses confirm: (a) the considerable correspondence between the geography of strikes and the geography of collective violence; (b) the tendency of strike activity to come disproportionately from the older, established trades rather than from the expanding factory-based industries. In Aguet's careful enumeration the most strike-prone departments are (in descending order) Seine, Rhône, Seine-Inférieure, Loire and Bouches-du-Rhône—which is to say the departments of Paris, Lyon, Rouen, St. Etienne, and Marseilles. These same departments ordinarily rank high in tallies of disturbances. In short, strikes and collective violence went together.

Not that they were the same thing. I have already pointed out how many of this period's smaller disturbances were food riots, conflicts with tax collectors, and forcible invasions of rural property. Practically none of them began as strikes. But a significant number of the minor disturbances were simply the violent parts of series of actions putting workers against employers: demonstrations, political agitation, threats, property damage, strikes as well. They grew from the same basic conflicts. And some of the great outbursts (the insurrections of Lyon being the best-known examples) flashed in direct response to strikes.

George Rudé considers the working-class disturbances of the 1830s to start a great new phase. "For the first time," he concludes, "we find the same workers being engaged in successive political demonstrations, wage demands being put forward at a time of economic depression, and wage earners participating as readily in political as in economic movements" (Rudé, 1964: 165). He might have added that the wage-earners still came from the older crafts and established industries rather than the swelling modern factories. To return to Aguet's enumeration of French strikes, the number of strikes reported by industry for five-year intervals are shown in Table 2. The figures drastically underestimate the total number of strikes and give far too much weight to Paris, but they are the best we have so far.

By sheer bulk, the textile industry dominated both the industrial labor force and the strike scene. For their size, however, construction, mining and, especially, printing seem to have produced exceptional numbers of strikes. As the century wore on, textiles and construction held their own, the mines grew in importance as sources of strikes, the printers lost their force, and the metal-working industries with their factory production came into prominence. The great Parisian series of strikes in 1840 brought out the tailors, papermakers, nailmakers, carters, wainwrights, masons, stonecutters, locksmiths, turners, carpenters, shoemakers, spinners, bookbinders, and bakers—mostly men from the skilled, established crafts.

The same occupations and industries led the Parisian working class political activity, and fed the city's violent confrontations. The city's prefects of police were aware enough of the connection to always have their spies circulating through the workmen's cafes and hiring areas around the Place de Grève and the Place du Châtelet. A prefect's report from July, 1831 read like this:

TABLE 2
NUMBER OF STRIKES IN FRANCE BY INDUSTRY 1830-1944

Industry	Years			Estimated Labor Force in 1840-1845 (in thousands)
	1830-1834	1835-1839	1840-1844	
Agriculture, forestry fishing	0	0	1	7,000
Mining and extraction	3	3	8	108
Food products	3	1	3	256
Chemical products	1	0	1	20
Paper and printing	9	2	12	47
Leather products	2	3	3	235
Textiles	32	26	30	1,560
Wood products	10	6	8	502
Metal products	8	2	6	305
Construction	13	6	21	474
Services and professions	0	0	2	3,000
Total	81	49	95	13,507

SOURCES: Toutain, 1963; Aguet, 1954.

The painters who gathered yesterday at Châtelet said that since the authorities were tolerating recruitment of Legitimist forces for the Vendée, they would take justice into their own hands; and they stated their intention to break into the houses of the Swiss living in the area around Paris and to wreck them.

Those gathered at the Place de Grève started to grumble yesterday; they complained about their poverty, praised the reign of Napoleon and said that in his day there was no shortage of jobs, but since then the working class had always been in bad shape [Archives Nationales $F^{1c}I33$, 22 July 1831].

Now, the workers of Grève and Châtelet talked more than they acted politically, and acted peacefully more than they rebelled. But the spies were in the right place, listening to the right things. For the working-class neighborhoods behind those squares were the breeding grounds of rebellion after rebellion. And the men who took part were, by and large, politically alert, organized, integrated into the life of the city. Not, that is, the uprooted, outcast, dangerous classes.

The studies which have been done of participants in diverse outbreaks of collective violence in Paris between 1830 and 1860 point in the same direction. For the Revolution of 1830, Adeline Daumard observes that "artisans on the border between the common people and the bourgeoisie were at the core of the insurgents" (Daumard, 1963: 578); David Pinkney's (1964) careful enumerations agree. The violent days of April 1834 brought into the action such men as:

36-year-old Louis Bertembois, a shoemaker born in St. Frambourg (Oise);

Francois Soubrebois, 29, a typographer, originally from Perpignan;

TABLE 3

PERSONS ARRESTED FOR TAKING PART IN JUNE DAYS OF 1848 BY INDUSTRY AND BIRTHPLACE

Industry	Birthplace					Number of Workmen Reported in 1848 Survey	Arrests per 10,000 Workers
	Seine	Other France	Foreign	Unknown	Total		
Food	53	348	21	42	464	10,428	445
Construction	363	1,511	70	133	2,077	41,603	499
Furniture	214	352	70	44	680	36,184	188
Clothing	160	724	87	74	1,045	90,064	116
Textiles	71	246	11	18	346	36,685	94
Leather	36	113	9	11	169	4,573	370
Carriagemaking, saddlery, etc.	39	135	12	9	195	13,754	142
Chemicals and ceramics	44	76	11	17	148	9,737	152
Ordinary metals	323	886	45	80	1,334	24,894	536
Fine metals	99	109	8	23	239	16,819	142
Basketry	32	93	4	6	135	5,405	250
Novelties, toys etc.	67	126	12	9	214	35,679	60
Printing	167	217	21	42	447	16,705	268
Transpotation	132	336	25	41	534	–	–
Services	67	321	30	43	461	–	–
Retail trade	168	518	36	69	791	–	–
Military	111	272	15	103	501	–	–
Liberal professions	81	193	17	37	328	–	–
Other	264	770	60	96	1,190	–	–
Not reported	65	169	15	197	446	–	–
Total	2,556	7,515	579	1,094	11,744	–	–

SOURCES: Archieves Nationales F⁷2586, Liste générale en ordre alphabétique des inculpés de juin 1848; Chambre de Commerce de Paris, statistique de l'industrie à Paris résultant de l'enquête faite par la Chambre de Commerce pour les années 1847-1848 (Paris, 1851).

the wagon-painter J. P. Etienne, 17 years old, a Parisian;

caterer Jean Pouchin, 32, from a small town in Calvados, reputed to be a member of the Society of the Rights of Man;

22-year-old Jean Hallot, a cabinet-maker from Paris, labeled in the police reports as an "instigator" [Archives de la Préfecture de Police, Paris, Aa 422].

In the revolution of February, 1848, George Rudé points out, the city's wage earners "left their workshops with their masters and, with them, jointly manned the barricades; radical journalists, students, polytechnicians, and National Guards had also played their part; and on the lists of those decorated for their part in the February events the names of wage earners appear alongside those of shopkeepers, master craftsmen, and members of the liberal professions" (Rudé, 1964: 168-169).

There is one more Parisian case of special interest: the June Days of 1848. That bloody disturbance deserves our attention both because it had the most proletarian appearance of any up to its time, and because it left remarkably detailed evidence concerning who took part. Table 3 summarizes the available information on the origins and occupation of more than 11,000 persons of the probably 15,000 arrested for participation in the June Days. (In order to give a general sense of their relation to the labor force of the time, it also presents the number of workers in each group of industrial establishments reported by employers to the Chamber of Commerce in 1847 and 1848, and relates the arrests to the industries as a series of rates per 10,000 workers.) While comparisons within the sample display a slight tendency for construction workers to have been arrested on suspicion, then released, and a significantly greater tendency for arrested soldiers and persons born in Paris to finally be convicted, this tabulation represents the men and women actually implicated in the rebellion fairly faithfully.[2]

It does not show a simple cross-section of the Parisian population, but it does show a wide spread across its various categories. The largest single occupational group were the 699 day-laborers, who were in the company of 575 stonemasons, 485 cabinet-makers and 447 shoemakers. Construction, metal-working and the clothing trades had the largest shares in absolute numbers. Compared with their parts in the working population of the time, men from construction, food production and metal-working industries seem to have played an exceptional role. Their arrests run around five percent of all the men reported in each industry. Mechanics (especially from the railroads), leatherworkers, and printers also appear to have contributed more than their share to the rebellion. Textile workers, it seems fair to say, were underrepresented.

George Duveau's sketch of the June Days has as its principal characters a mechanic of La Chapelle, a hosier of the Faubourg Saint-Dénis and an ébéniste from the Faubourg Saint-Antoine (Duveau, 1950). If he had added a stonemason from the Hôtel de Ville, a day-laborer from Popincourt, and a tanner from Saint-Marcel, his cast would have been representative.

The distribution we find is remarkably like the strike activity of the time: an amalgam of the old, politically active trades with a few sections of modern industry. By comparison with previous disturbances, the center of gravity was shifting toward the mass-production industries, gradually, in step with other forms of contention and political activity, not in such a way as to call the miserable outsiders into the streets.

The bulk of the rebels had originally come from outside of Paris. That is most true of construction (as one might expect), and least true of printing. Just under a quarter of those arrested and a little less than a third of those convicted were natives of the Seine. But as it happens, Louis Chevalier's data indicate that about 40 percent of Paris' population of the time, including children, were natives (Chevalier, 1950: 45). The adult working population was surely well below that proportion. So there is no clear sign that outsiders were overrepresented. Furthermore, the distribution of departments of origin follows Chevalier's estimates for the Paris of 1833 quite faithfully. In addition to the 2,556 born in the Seine, we find 516 from Seine-et-Oise, 335 from Seine-et-Marne, 362 from Moselle, 276 from Nord, 236 from Creuse, 222 from Somme, 220 from Aisne, and so on through the list of regular suppliers of migrants to Paris. While these data do not make the point, Rémi Gossez (1956: 449), who knows the histories of the individual rebels of June far better than anyone else, remarks:

> The typical insurgent was an individual who, if a native of the provinces, came to Paris to settle or at least to complete his training and who in general was moving up in the world, a move blocked by economic change and crisis.

Again the violent masses turn out to be those integrated into the setting rather than those at the margins of society.

The findings therefore cast doubt on theories which trace a main link between cities and protest through a process of disorganization. On the contrary, the whole array of evidence we have been examining suggests a positive connection between organization and conflict. The moderate relationship discovered earlier between collective violence in 1830-1832 and urban growth from 1821 to 1831, for instance, probably represents the appearance of new contenders for power in the largest industrial centers over the whole decade rather than individual disorientation or malaise at exposure to the modern city.

We are not, in any case, dealing with a constant pattern. Over the long run of the nineteenth and twentieth centuries, collective violence in France drifted away from the countryside and toward the cities faster than the population itself did, as the power and resources which mattered most politically concentrated in the great cities. Politics nationalized and urbanized simultaneously. In the short run, the extent of urban concentration of collective violence depended on the nature of the unresolved political issues at hand. Food riots formed a more dispersed pattern than violent strikes; strikes were more scattered than major struggles for control of the national political apparatus. Since food riots, strikes, and major struggles for control followed different rhythms, the geographic pattern fluctuated. Perhaps the largest alternation went from battles for power at the center (which produced a high urban concentration of collective violence) and resistance to pressures from the center (which produced more disturbances at the periphery). In the period we are examining here, the revolutionary years 1830 and 1848 concentrated their violence in cities, while years of consolidation of central power like 1832 and 1851—both very turbulent times—spread their violence farther and more evenly.

Some of this alternation comes out in Table 4, which chops up the entire period from 1830 to 1860 into five-year blocks. The table shows the striking contrast in overall participation between a revolutionary period like 1830-1834 and a nonrevolutionary one like 1835-1839. It also shows how much steeper the gradient of collective violence from rural to urban departments was in years of fundamental struggle for control of the state than in years of consolidation of state power; a comparison of 1845-1849 (which includes, of course, the revolution of 1848) with 1850-1854 (whose biggest violent conflict was the resistance to Louis Napoleon's 1851 coup, which eventually permitted him to move from elected president to emperor) makes that point dramatically.

The long trend and the short-term fluctuations both followed the same principle: nationalization of political conflict produces urbanization of collective violence. The principle has nothing to do with the disorganizing effects of urban life. It has a great deal to do with the location of groups of people mobilized to join different kinds of struggles for power. Explaining the actions of the participants in collective violence as responses to the chaos of the city discounts the reality of their struggle.

TABLE 4

PARTICIPANTS IN COLLECTIVE VIOLENCE PER 100,000 POPULATION
BY URBANITY OF DEPARTMENT, 1830-1859, CORRECTED TO ANNUAL RATES

Percentage of Population in Cities of 10,000 or More	1830-1834	1835-1839	1840-1844	1845-1849	1850-1854	1855-1859
0.0	17	4	40	25	152	0
0.1-5.0	23	22	16	70	70	0
5.1-10.0	54	22	48	68	43	9
10.1-15.0	104	19	10	81	15	2
15.1+	731	57	64	689	86	0
Total	147	22	37	210	56	3
Total participants (thousands)	240	41	64	371	101	5

That is the general conclusion toward which all our explorations point. The absence of the uprooted, the continuity of different forms of conflict, their gradual change in response to shifts in the collective conditions of work and community life, the sheer lack of correlation between rapid urban growth or extensive inmigration and mass violence all challenge the cataclysmic theories of urbanization. And yet our evidence confirms that the distinctive social organization of cities—their hospitality to formal associations, the complexity of their communication systems, their widespread external relations, their gross patterns of segregation—strongly affects the character of the collective conflicts which occur within them. In that sense, urbanization, over the long run, transforms collective violence.

Through the chaos of living cities, what do we see? Certainly not the lawless disorder a romantic notion of urbanization has advertised. Not bucolic bliss, either. We see men held to their routines by commitments and controls, often dismayed by their routines, sometimes articulating and acting on their dismay, mostly singly, mostly in nonviolent ways, but occasionally being trained in another way of understanding and combatting the evils of their present situation, and joining with other men to strike out against the situation itself. There is a kind of order to the city's collective disorders, if not the one the forces of order would like to see prevailing.

It takes another poet, Christopher Fry, to state the theme properly: "There's no loosening, since men with men are like the knotted sea. Lift him down from the stone to the grass again, and, even so free, yet he will find the angry cities hold him." Angry cities, but not mad. Violent cities, but not pathological. Living cities, and in the last analysis not nearly so chaotic as widespread sociological ideas imply.

NOTES

1. The estimates for 1861 to 1929 are based on a 25 percent sample of the months in that interval, and have not been verified as carefully as those for 1830-1860 and 1930-1960; they are, therefore, subject to considerably greater error. Both general knowledge of the government's treatment of the press and close study of our own data lead me to conclude that censorship probably reduced the number of disturbances reported in the newspapers on which we relied during the post-war periods of 1870-1874, 1918-1921, and 1944-1954. On the other hand, such detailed comparisons as we have been able to make with other full sources (e.g., with all disturbances mentioned in the inventories of the major national series of police reports in Archives Nationales BB 18 and BB 30) indicate that the sharp drops in disturbances during the two world wars and after Louis Napoleon's assumption of power in 1851 are real. For control of the press, see Bellanger et al. (1969); Collins (1959); Hatin (1859-1861); Kayser (1958, 1963); Manévy (1955); Mottin (1949); Weill (1934).

2. The source of quantitative data is a huge register (Archives Nationales $F^7 2586$) containing uniform descriptions of about 12,000 persons arrested for taking part in the June Days; a duplicate of the register resides in the Archives historiques de l'Armeé, as do the individual dossiers of the arrestees. Lynn Lees and I have examined a 1 percent sample of the individual dossiers, which establishes that the registers accurately represent the general characteristics of those apprehended for taking part in the insurrection, but omit a large part of the information actually available concerning the average individual. The register has been drawn on before, by Rémi Gossez (1956), George Rudé (1964), and very likely Georges Duveau (1948); see also Gossez (1967) for background. However, no one has so far reported the sorts of detailed counts and comparisons presented here.

REFERENCES

ARENDT, H. (1970) On Violence. New York: Harcourt Brace.
––– (1963) On Revolution. London: Faber and Faber.
AGUET, J.-P. (1954) Contribution à l'histoire du mouvement ouvrier français: les grèves sous la Monarchie de Juillet (1830-1847). Geneva: Droz.
BELLANGER, C., J. GODECHOT, P. GUIRAL, and F. TERROU (eds.) (1969) Histoire générale de la presse périodique. II. De 1815 à 1871. Paris: Presses Universitaires de France.
BELVEZE, C. (1959) "L'Insurrection des 5 et 6 juin 1832." Diplôme d'Etudes Supérieures, History, Paris. (unpublished)
BEZUCHA, R. J. (1968) "Association and insurrection: the Republican party and the worker movement in Lyon, 1831-1835." Ph.D. dissertation. University of Michigan.
BIENEN, H. (1968) Violence and Social Change: A Review of Current Literature. Chicago: Univ. of Chicago Press.
BOUVIER, J. (1964) "Mouvement ouvrier et conjonctures économiques." Mouvement social 48: 3-28.
BRODE, J. (1969) The Process of Modernization: An Annotated Bibliography on the Sociocultural Aspects of Development. Cambridge: Harvard Univ. Press.
CHEVALIER, L. (1958) Classes laborieuses et classes dangéreuses. Paris: Plon.
––– (1950) La formation de la population parisienne. Paris: Presses Universitaires de France.
COBB, R. (1970) The Police and the People. Oxford: Clarendon Press.
––– (1964) Terreur et subsistances, 1793-1795. Paris: Clavreuil.
––– (1961-1963) Les Armeés revolutionnaires, instrument de la Terreur dans les départments. Paris: Mouton.
COLLINS, I. (1959) The Government and the Newspaper Press in France. Oxford: Oxford Univ. Press.
CONANT, R. W. and M. A. LEVIN [eds.] (1969) Problems in Research on Community Violence. New York: Praeger.
CONNERY, D. [ed.] (1968) "Urban riots: violence and social change." Proceedings of the Academy of Political Science 29.
CORNELIUS, W. A., Jr. (1970) "The political sociology of cityward migration in Latin America: toward empirical theory," in F. F. Rabinowitz and F. M. Trueblood (eds.) Latin American Urban Annual. Beverly Hills: Sage Publications.
DAUMARD, A. (1963) La bourgeoisie parisienne de 1815 à 1848. Paris: SEVPEN.

DAVIES, C.S.L. (1969) "Révoltes populaires en Angleterre (1500-1700)." Annales; Economies, Sociétés, Civilisations 24: 24-60.

DUVEAU, G. (1965) 1848. Paris: Gallimard.

——— (1948) "L'ouvrier de 1848." Revue socialiste n.s. nos. 17-18: 73-79.

FISCHER, W. (1966) "Social tensions at early stages of industrialization." Comparative Studies in Society and History 9: 64-83.

FOGELSON, R. M. and R. B. HILL (1968) "Who riots? a study of participation in the 1967 riots." Supplemental Studies for the National Advisory Commission on Civil Disorders. Washington, D.C.: Government Printing Office.

FURET, F., C. MAZAURIC, and L. BERGERON (1963) "Les sans-culottes et la Révolution française." Annales; Economies, Sociétés, Civilisations 18: 1098-1127.

GODECHOT, J. (1970) The Taking of the Bastille. New York: Charles Scribner.

GOSSEZ, R. (1967) Les Ouvriers de Paris. I. L'Organisation, 1848-1851. La Roche-sur-Yon: Imprimerie Centrale de l'Ouest.

——— (1956) "Diversité des antagonismes sociaux vers le milieu du XIXe siècle." Revue économique: 439-457.

GRAHAM, H. D. and T. R. GURR (1969) [eds.] Violence in America: Historical and Comparative Perspectives. Washington, D.C.: Government Printing Office.

GURR, T. R. (1969) Why Men Rebel. Princeton: Princeton Univ. Press.

HATIN, E. (1859-1861) Histoire politique et littéraire de la presse en France. Paris: Poulet-Malassis and de Broise.

HAUSER, P. (1963) "The social, economic and technological problems of rapid urbanization," in B. Hoselitz and W. Moore (eds.) Industrialization and Society. The Hague: Mouton.

HOBSBAWM, E. J. (1969) Bandits. New York: Delacorte.

——— and G. RUDE (1968) Captain Swing: A Social History of the Great Agrarian Uprising of 1830. New York: Pantheon.

HOFSTADTER, R. (1970) "Reflections on violence in the United States," in R. Hofstadter and M. Wallace (eds.) American Violence: A Documentary History. New York: Alfred A. Knopf.

HUNTINGTON, S. P. (1968) Political Order in Changing Societies. New Haven: Yale Univ. Press.

KAYSER, J. (1963) Le quotidien français. Paris: Armand Colin and Cahiers de la Fondation Nationale des Science Politiques, 122.

——— (1958) La presse de province sous la Troisième République. Paris: Armand Colin and Cahiers de la Fondation Nationale des Sciences Politiques, 92.

KIRKHAM, J. F., S. G. LEVY, and W. J. CROTTY (1970) Assassination and Political Violence. Washington, D.C.: Government Printing Office.

MANEVY, R. (1955) La presse de la IIIe République. Paris: Foret.

MASOTTI, L. H. and D. R. BOWEN [eds.] (1968) Civil Violence in the Urban Community. Beverly Hills: Sage Publications.

MAZAURIC, C. (1970) Sur la Révolution française. Paris: Editions Sociales.

MEADOWS, P. and E. MAZRUCHI [eds.] (1969) Urbanism, Urbanization and Change. Reading, Mass.: Addison-Wesley.

MOTTIN, J. (1949) Histoire politique de la presse, 1944-49. Paris: Bilans Hebdomadaires.

MUMFORD, L. (1961) The City in History. New York: Harcourt, Brace and World.

NELSON, J. (1970) "The urban poor: disruption or political integration in Third World cities?" World Politics 22: 393-414.

PEACOCK, A. J. (1965) Bread or Blood: The Agrarian Riots in East Anglia: 1816. London: Gollancz.

PINKNEY, D. (1964) "The crowd in the French Revolution of 1830." American Historical Review 70: 1-17.

RUDE, G. (1970) Paris and London in the 18th Century. London: Collins.

——— (1964) The Crowd in History. New York: John Wiley.

——— (1958) The Crowd in the French Revolution. Oxford: Oxford Univ. Press.

RULE, J. and C. TILLY (1971) "1830 and the unnatural history of revolution." Journal of Social Issues.

SEWELL, W. (1971) "The working class of Marseilles under the Second Republic: social structure and political behavior." Mouvement social.

SHORTER, E. and C. TILLY (1971) "The shape of strikes in France, 1930-1960." Comparative Studies in Society and History.

SKOLNICK, J. H. (1969) The Politics of Protest. Washington, D.C.: Government Printing Office.

SMELSER, N. J. (1963) Theory of Collective Behavior. New York: Free Press.

SOBOUL, A. (1958) Les sans-culottes parisiens en l'an II. La Roche-sur-Yon: Potier.

THOMPSON, E. P. (1963) The Making of the English Working Class. London: Gollancz.

TILLY, C. (1969) "Collective violence in European perspective," in H. D. Graham and T. R. Gurr, Violence in America. Washington, D.C.: Government Printing Office.

——— (1964) "Reflections on the revolutions of Paris." Social Problems 12: 99-121.

TILLY, L. (1971) "The food riot as a form of political conflict in France." Journal of Interdisciplinary History and (in translation) Annales; Economies, Sociétés, Civilisations.

TILLY, R. (1971) "Popular disorders in nineteenth century Germany: a preliminary survey." Journal of Social History.

TONNESSON, K. (1959) La défaite des sans-culottes. Oslo: University Press and Paris: Calvreuil.

TOUTAIN, J.-C. (1963) La population de la France de 1700 à 1959. Paris: Institut de Science Economique Appliquee; Cahiers de l'ISEA, AF 3.

VIDALOU, H. (1959) "Les mouvements revolutionnaires d'avril 1834 à Paris." (unpublished)

VOVELLE, M. (1965) "From beggary to brigandage: the wanderers in the Beauce during the French Revolution," in J. Kaplow (ed.) New Perspectives on the French Revolution. New York: John Wiley.

WEILL, G. (1934) Le journal. Origines, evolution et rôle de la presse périodique. Paris: Albin Michel.

WILLIAMS, G. (1968) Artisans and Sans-Culottes. Oxford: Oxford Univ. Press.

Part III

Variations in Public Policy

Chapter 9

Community Structure and Innovation:
Public Housing, Urban Renewal, and
The War on Poverty

Michael Aiken and Robert R. Alford

Research on urban politics, community power structure, and local decision-making exhibits a diverse and checkered pattern of development in the literature in political science and sociology in the United States in the past two decades. Starting with the publication in 1953 of Floyd Hunter's *Community Power Structure,* sociologists and political scientists have conducted research about politics and decision-making in numerous American communities.

In retrospect, these studies of community power constituted a sterile debate over the appropriate methodology (reputational, decision-making, positional) and the correct generalizations about the decision-making process in American communities—elitist or pluralistic—and they produced little real understanding of systematic variations in the decision-making capability, and the consequences of varying power and decision-making arrangements for local citizens. In addition, most studies of community power were case studies of single communities, although there were some occasional comparative studies of either community power (Barth, 1961; Agger et al., 1964; D'Antonio et al., 1961; D'Antonio and Form, 1965; Miller, 1958a, 1958b), community performance

AUTHORS' NOTE: *This is a revision and extension of three articles: "Comparative Urban Research and Community Decision-Making,"* New Atlantis *1 (Winter 1970), pp. 85-110; and Aiken and Alford (1970a, 1970b). Certain methodological and theoretical points included in those articles are omitted here because of reasons of space. A few errors found in the tables of the earlier articles have been corrected, which accounts for slight discrepancies.*

This research was supported in part by funds granted to the Institute for Research on Poverty, University of Wisconsin, pursuant to provisions of the Economic Opportunity Act

(Williams and Adrian, 1963), or the formal political structure (Krammerer et al., 1963) that included from two to eight communities. But the unrepresentativeness of these studies in terms of such factors as city size and regional location (most were done within a single state or geographical region) limited the possible insights into the regularities of patterns of community decision-processes and performances.

There are at least two critical questions from this literature on community politics and decision-making that remain to be answered. The first concerns the consequences of decision-making in the local community. That is, what difference does it make for community outputs if there are many or only a few actors or whether only business elites or multiple elites are involved in the formulation of policies for local government? Second, what is the nature of the intervening process that affects these decision outcomes. The dominant values of the community, the degree to which power is concentrated, the centralization and efficiency of the formal structure of government, the degree of community integration, and the degree of community differentiation and continuity have each been proposed as explanations of variations in performances by local communities. Given the state of knowledge about these topics as of the late 1960s, there are at least three ways that one could attempt to address these questions.

First, one could take the studies on community power, conduct a content analysis of them in order to categorize the type of decision-making structure, and then relate the resulting typology both to structural attributes of communities (cf. Walton, 1966a, 1966b, 1970; Gilbert, 1967, 1968a, 1968b; Clark et al., 1968; Aiken, 1970) and to community performance or outputs (cf. Aiken, 1970). While such studies may be helpful and suggestive of alternative approaches, they are plagued by a sufficient number of methodological problems to vitiate the possibility of any definitive conclusions. Chief among these are the problem of taking studies that employed a variety of methodologies and research approaches at face value (cf. Polsby, 1969) and classifying them into a set of decision-making categories, the problem of grouping together studies spanning as many as forty years, and the problem of representativeness of these case studies.

A second approach is to gather data on community performance in a variety of decision-areas for all American communities, relate these to various structural

---

of 1964. We were aided greatly in this research, particularly on the data about public housing, by Louis S. Katz, Chief, Statistics Branch, and Robert S. Kenison, Attorney Adviser, both of the Housing Assistance Administration, Department of Housing and Urban Development. Neither is responsible for errors of fact or interpretation, however. We are also grateful to the Institute for Research on Poverty for its research and administrative support, and to Elizabeth Balcer Fix, Janet Jensen, and Ann Wallace for their very vital and competent assistance.

attributes of communities, and conceive of the intervening process as a "black box" which can be inferred from the results. As an example, Hawley (1963) found that the MPO Ratio was negatively related to high performance in urban renewal, and he inferred that the intervening process was one in which derivate power was too dispersed. While this comparative approach has the advantage of avoiding the problems of sampling inherent in the case-study approach, it is plagued by its own problems. Chief among these is the meaning of the indicators, which may be quite distant from the realities of the intervening process in the black box. But also there is the question, although not unique to this approach, of comparability among various decision outputs. The decision dynamics are likely to be different for various types of policy outputs (cf. Salisbury, 1968; Jacob and Lipsky, 1968; Lowi, 1964).

The third approach is to take a sizeable sample of communities and to use comparable techniques to study the intervening decision-making process in each community, using data from the second approach to define a sampling frame. Ultimately, the understanding of urban politics and decision-making will advance only with studies of this kind (cf. Clark, 1968). Aside from the problems of the enormous number of resources that are required to do such a study, there are two additional problems: the question of what sampling frame to use to maximize knowledge about decision-making and community performance in different subsets of communities and the question of the theoretical concepts and constructs to be tested by the research design. Derivation of the theoretical strategy and concepts from the previous literature on community power runs the danger of too early a closure on the most appropriate theoretical perspective.

Concerned with a desire to increase our understanding of urban politics and decision-making and constrained by some of the dilemmas and problems inherent in the third approach, we opted, at least as a beginning step, for the second strategy outlined above. We have gathered a considerable amount of data on each of the 1,654 incorporated urban places of size 10,000 or more in the United States in 1960, although most of our analysis has been limited to the subset of 676 cities that had a population size of 25,000 or more in 1960. We also have data on SMSAs, counties, and states regarded as possibly important elements of the environment within which cities function. None of these data are reported in this paper, however.

In this paper we shall summarize our findings about three types of policy outputs: public housing, urban renewal, and the War on Poverty, the first two of which are reported in greater detail elsewhere (cf. Aiken and Alford, 1970a, 1970b). In these discussions we have characterized policy outputs as various aspects of community innovation. We define innovation as " . . . the generation, acceptance, and implementation of new ideas, processes, products, or services" (Thompson, 1965; Mohr, 1969; Walker, 1969). Innovation does not mean the first use ever of something new (i.e., an invention) nor the first use by one among a set of actors, but rather the adoption for the first time of a new idea, process, service, product, or program by a given actor. In the present context American municipalities of size 25,000 or more are the actors and the innovations are the successful implementation of federally financed programs in public housing, urban renewal, and the War on Poverty. Our analysis is focused neither on the process of diffusion of these innovations nor on the internal stages of the adoption process, but rather on a search for those community characteristics that are associated with innovations of these kinds as well as an attempt to identify the most appropriate theoretical explanation for the observed regularities.

We examine three aspects of community innovation: (1) the presence or absence of innovations in public housing, urban renewal, and the War on Poverty, that is, whether a given community has adopted these innovations regardless of when that innovation took place or the degree of subsequent involvement in these programs; (2) the speed of innovation, that is, how long after the development of each of these three federal programs before a community entered the program; and (3) the level of output or performance, that is, the intensity of participation in these programs as reflected in dollars received per capita or, in the case of public housing, number of housing units constructed per capita. The strategy employed here has also been used by a number of researchers in sociology and political science to study such community decision outcomes as fluoridation (Crain et al., 1969; Pinard, 1963), urban renewal (Hawley, 1963; Straits, 1965; Wolfinger and Field, 1966; Crain and Rosenthal, 1967), desegregation (Crain and Rosenthal, 1967; Dye, 1968), municipal expenditures (Lineberry and Fowler, 1967) and other referenda (Wilson and Banfield, 1964). In each case the researchers used some community attribute, or set of attributes, to infer the intervening process. Nowhere have these various explanations of community decision-making dynamics been brought together and critically compared with respect to a common body of data. These five theories explaining innovation are:

(1) Political Culture: Cities dominated by majorities holding "public regarding values" are hypothesized to be more innovative with respect to policies benefiting the community as a whole than cities dominated by groups with "private-regarding values" (Banfield and Wilson, 1963; Wilson and Banfield, 1964).

(2) Concentration or Diffusion of Community Power: There are three aspects of this argument: concentration of systemic power (Hawley, 1963), diffusion of power through mass citizen participation (Crain and Rosenthal, 1967), and centralization of elite power (Clark, 1968a). In each case the hypothesis is the same, namely, the greater the concentration of power, the greater the degree of innovation. Conversely, the greater the diffusion of power, the lower the degree of innovation.

(3) Centralization of Formal Political Structure: Cities with centralized administrative arrangements and a strong mayor, that is, cities with city manager or partisan mayor-council governmental structures are hypothesized to be more innovative (Crain et al., 1968).

(4) Community Differentiation and Continuity: Older and larger cities have been hypothesized to be more bureaucratic and consequently less receptive to policy innovations, suggesting that younger and smaller cities should exhibit higher policy innovation (Dye, 1968).

(5) Community Integration: Cities in which community integration breaks down or is extremely low have a lower probability of innovation or other collective actions. Consequently, community innovation should be highest in integrated communities (Coleman, 1957; Pinard, 1963).

We have listed these five explanations separately and shall discuss them in greater detail below because it is possible to conceive of them as five independent theories of community innovation and policy outputs. We turn now to a description of the three output measures, some discussion of sources of data used in this paper, and a description of the methodology employed here.

DATA AND METHODS

An understanding of our findings presumes some knowledge about the various policy outputs included in this study: public housing, urban renewal, and the War on Poverty. Each will be briefly discussed, and the output measure for each will be described. The policy outputs included here share certain characteristics. First, each requires some degree of initiative by the local community. In the federal system of the United States, local communities have a high degree of local autonomy relative to some European nations such as, for example, France or Spain. Unless some local agency takes some initiative and a favorable decision is rendered locally, a community cannot enter these programs. Only two of the programs discussed here—public housing and urban renewal— required approval by the local governing body, however. A second characteristic of these policy outputs is that there is an organization in the local community—a "community decision organization" (Warren, 1967a, 1967b)—that has been specifically created to coordinate and oversee the program. Third, most funds involved come from outside the community, from the federal government, although in each case some local money has to be provided. Fourth, none of these decisions typically involved mass participation by citizens. The decisions are made, in almost all cases, by representative organizations—the community decisions organization, the municipal government, and the city council— although community citizens and groups may be utilized at critical junctures to support or perhaps oppose a decision.

It may well be that the observations and findings of this paper are relevant only to policy outcomes that have these characteristics, and that community decisions not fitting these criteria, such as fluoridation or perhaps school desegregation, may involve different types of community dynamics and, hence, require different explanations.

A. *Public Housing.* The first public housing program in the United States was established in 1933 under the National Industrial Recovery Act (NIRA), one of the early programs of the New Deal of the Roosevelt Administration. In 1937 the U.S. Housing Act (USHA) was passed, and a significant number of public housing units were created in the next few years. In 1949, the U.S. Congress amended USHA with the Housing Act of 1949 (Public Law 171) and this legislation had a greater effect on the construction of low-rent public housing than any previous piece of housing legislation.[1]

From 1933 until June 30, 1966, 393 cities (or 61 percent) of the 646 cities of size 25,000 or more in 1960 had participated in a public housing program of the federal government (30 cities that did not exist in 1930 have been excluded from this part of the analysis). Thirty-three cities first started a federally financed housing project under NIRA, another 151 entered the program from 1937 to 1949, and 209 additional cities started such a program between 1949 and June 30, 1966, the cutoff date of this study. The remaining 253 cities had not initiated a public housing program as of June 30, 1966.

The speed of innovation is measured by the number of years after 1933 before a community began construction on its first housing project. But since a local community could not enter the federal public housing program unless the state in which it is located had first enacted appropriate enabling legislation, it seems appropriate to take such variations into account in constructing a speed of innovation measure. For example, by 1940 there were 39 states with appropriate legislation, but the remaining eleven states were slow to enact legislation required by this program. In June 30, 1966, only the states of Utah and Wyoming were without such legislation. As observed here, there are great differences in the dates of the enactment of state enabling legislation, so we constructed a second speed of innovation measure that takes this variation into account: the number of years it took a city to begin construction in its first public housing project after state enabling legislation was enacted.

The mean of the first speed of innovation measure is 23.2 years and the standard deviation was 12.0 years: the second speed measure has a mean of 18.6 years and a standard deviation of 12.2.

The level of output or performance measure is the number of public housing units constructed per 100,000 population since 1933. The mean of this distribution was 668 (less than 1 per 1,000 population) with a standard deviation of 782.[2]

We analyzed these data not only for the 646 cities reported here, but also for the 472 cities in the 30 states which had enabling legislation by the end of 1937, but since those results were quite similar to the results reported here, we decided to report the findings for the 646 cities of size 25,000 or more in 1960 that were in existence in 1930.

B. Urban Renewal. The urban renewal program was established by the Housing Act of 1949 to contribute to the renewal of urban areas through federally provided funds for slum clearance and urban redevelopment. While there has been debate about utilization of this program (Anderson, 1964; Gans, 1962; Sogg and Wertheimer, 1967; Bellush and Hausknecht, 1967) in terms of who ultimately benefits, we shall not enter into those polemics here.[3]

We measure the presence or absence of innovation in urban renewal by whether or not a community had ever participated in the urban renewal program. Among the 582 cities for this measure of innovation, 372 (or 64 percent) had entered the urban renewal program although 32 of these later dropped out. Among the remaining 340 cities, 187 had completed at least one urban renewal project, 130 others had reached the execution stage, and another 23 were still in planning. There were 210 cities (36 percent) that had never innovated an urban renewal program.

The speed of innovation was measured by the number of years after 1949 before a city embarked on its first urban renewal program. This measure is similar to that of Straits (1965) in his critique of Hawley (1963). As in the case of public housing, we constructed a second speed of innovation measure which took into account the year in which state enabling legislation was enacted: the number of years it took a city to enter the urban renewal program for the first time, after state enabling legislation was enacted.

The level of output or performance in urban renewal was measured by the per capita number of urban renewal dollars. This measure is closely similar to that used by Wolfinger and Field (1966) and Clark (1968). Our measure was constructed by taking the total number of dollars reserved for all urban renewal projects as of June 30, 1966, and then standardizing this figure by the population size in 1960. The mean of this distribution was $53.76 with a standard deviation of $83.54. As in the case of public housing, the measure was highly skewed toward the upper end of the distribution (New Haven, Connecticut, had a mean of $790.25 per capita), so it too was transformed into its natural logarithm (after multiplying by 100 and adding a constant of one cent). Unless otherwise indicated, this transformed distribution was used in the statistical analyses presented below.

C. The War on Poverty. The War on Poverty was started under the Economic Opportunity Act which was signed into law on August 30, 1964, although the first money for projects was not announced until November 24, 1964. This program provided funds to local groups to combat poverty through a variety of programs such as the Neighborhood Youth Corps (designed to give jobs to needy teenagers among the poor), Headstart (designed to provide preschool education to children of the poor), Community Action Programs (designed to provide an opportunity for the poor to participate in decisions affecting their welfare), Job Corps (designed to give vocational training to young adults), and others. At the outset, most of these programs did not require the active concurrence of the local government.

We have eliminated Job Corps programs from our analysis here because they were largely initiated and organized by federal officials. Other types of poverty programs may have also been encouraged by federal officials, but a certain degree of independent initiative was required by local community groups before any program could begin. This is particularly true during the first two years of the existence of the Office of Economic Opportunity (OEO), before a network of officials and agencies were fully established in most communities, thus making the job of applying for money much easier.

The first indicator of innovation in the War on Poverty is whether or not a poverty program was specifically assigned to a city during the first two years of the program. County-wide programs have been excluded here. Of the 676 cities included in this part of our study, 489 (or 72.3 percent) had participated in this program. There were 187 cities that did not have their own poverty programs as of that date.

The speed of innovation in the War on Poverty is measured by the number of months after the first poverty funds were awarded before a city received its first poverty funds. For example, if a city received one of the first grants in November, 1964, it was coded 6483 (the first two digits represent the year; the second two digits represent the proportion of the year for which the first money was received; in this case, the second two digits represent the month of November). The mean of this distribution was 6575 (meaning October, 1965), and the standard deviation was .56.

The level of output or performance measure is the number of poverty dollars per capita allocated to each community. City scores ranged from zero for the 187 cities that had not entered the War on Poverty to $48.02 per citizen in Kansas City, Missouri. The mean of this distribution was $3.67, and the standard deviation $5.74.[4]

D. Measures of Other City Characteristics. The various independent variables were taken from sources such as the *Municipal Year Books* of 1963 and 1964, the 1950 Census of Housing, the 1960 Census of Population, the *1967 City-County Data Book,* and from a survey conducted by Eugene C. Lee, Director of the Institute of Governmental Studies, University of California at Berkeley (Alford and Lee, 1968).

E. Other Methodological Considerations. We employ Pearsonian correlation coefficients to express relationships between variables and statistical tests of significance to establish strength of association. Since the cities included in this study constitute the universe of all the incorporated urban places of size 25,000 or more eligible to participate in these programs, one may question the appropriateness of using statistical tests of significance. We use them for two reasons: first, even given that we have exhausted all units in the universe, statistical tests are still appropriate since there is the possibility that the observations were produced by errors of measurement. Second, in the absence of any other systematic criterion to establish the strength of a relationship, statistical tests of significance can be used (Winch and Campbell, 1969; see Morrison and Henkel, 1969, for an opposing point of view).

We included in our analysis cities which both have innovated in these programs and those which have not because we were concerned with conditions under which innovations take place, not primarily with conditions affecting the intensity and scope of outputs after innovation of a new program has occured. If the cities without any of these programs are excluded, the relationships between the independent variables and the measures of innovation are attenuated, but they remain in the same direction or most are significant in the same manner as the data presented.

F. Relationships Among the Measures of Innovation. In Table 1 are displayed 55 Pearsonian correlation coefficients showing the relationship between each pair of the eleven measures of innovation. Several observations can be made about this table. First, each of the correlation coefficients is sufficiently high ($r = -.30$ is the smallest correlation) to be significant at the .001 level of significance. Second, all the relationships are in the expected direction. That is, each measure of the presence of the three outputs and the level of performance measures are positively related to each other and each of these is negatively related to each speed of innovation measure, meaning that the more that cities participate in these three federal programs and the higher the level of performance, the less time it took to enter each program. Similarly, each measure of speed of innovation is positively related to each other measure of speed of innovation, and each of these speed measures is negatively related to the presence of these three programs and the three level of performance measures. Third, the size of the correlations among indicators of innovation within each type of program (e.g., the measures of innovation in public housing) is consistently higher than the size of the correlations among indicators between types of program (e.g., between measures of innovation in public housing and innovation in urban renewal). The lowest correlation between indicators of innovation within a given program is $-.62$ and the highest is .98. The highest correlation between indicators from different programs is .55. Undoubtedly, the

TABLE 1
INTERRELATIONSHIPS AMONG MEASURES OF COMMUNITY INNOVATION[a]

	Public Housing				Urban Renewal				War on Poverty		
	(1) Presence	(2) Speed 1	(3) Speed 2	(4) Level of Output	(5) Presence	(6) Speed 1	(7) Speed 2	(8) Level of Output	(9) Presence	(10) Speed	(11) Level of Output
Public Housing											
1. Presence of participation in the public housing program since 1933		-.73 (646)	-.60 (646)	.98 (646)	.53 (570)	-.53 (570)	-.50 (570)	.52 (570)	.34 (646)	-.38 (646)	.40 (646)
2. Speed of innovation: number of years before city entered the public housing program			.88 (646)	-.77 (646)	-.39 (570)	.54 (570)	.53 (570)	-.38 (570)	-.30 (646)	.36 (646)	-.38 (646)
3. Speed of innovation: number of years before city entered the public housing program after state enabling legislation				-.64 (646)	-.36 (570)	.50 (570)	.59 (570)	-.37 (570)	-.34 (646)	.38 (646)	-.40 (646)
4. Level of output: number of housing units constructed per 100,000 population (natural logarithm)					.53 (570)	-.56 (570)	-.53 (570)	.53 (570)	.34 (646)	-.38 (646)	.41 (646)
Urban Renewal											
5. Presence of participation in the urban renewal program						-.69 (582)	-.62 (582)	.86 (582)	.34 (582)	-.39 (582)	.39 (582)
6. Speed of innovation: number years before city entered the urban renewal program							.88 (582)	-.80 (582)	-.36 (582)	.45 (582)	-.45 (582)

TABLE 1 (Continued)

	Public Housing				Urban Renewal				War on Poverty		
	(1) Presence	(2) Speed 1	(3) Speed 2	(4) Level of Output	(5) Presence	(6) Speed 1	(7) Speed 2	(8) Level of Output	(9) Presence	(10) Speed	(11) Level of Output
Urban Renewal (Continued)											
7. Speed of innovation: number of years before the city entered the urban renewal program after enabling legislation								−.71 (582)	−.41 (582)	.48 (582)	−.49 (582)
8. Level of output: number of dollars reserved per capita (natural logarithm)									.36 (582)	−.41 (582)	.41 (582)
War on Poverty											
9. Presence of participation in the War on Poverty										−.83 (676)	.92 (676)
10. Speed of innovation: date city was awarded poverty funds											−.85 (676)
11. Level of output: number of dollars per capita (natural logarithm)											

a. Every correlation coefficient shown in this table is significant at the .001 level of significance, based on a two-tail test. The numbers in parentheses refer to the number of cases upon which the correlations are based.

[241]

TABLE 2
THE INCIDENCE OF INNOVATION, SPEED OF INNOVATION, AND LEVEL OF OUTPUT IN PUBLIC HOUSING, URBAN RENEWAL, AND THE WAR ON POVERTY WITHIN REGIONS

Measures of Innovation	North-east	South	Region[a] Midwest	Far West	All Cities
Public Housing					
Presence of participation in the public housing program since 1933	80%	75%	44%	36%	61%
Speed of innovation: average number of years before the city entered the public housing program	21.3	18.1	27.2	27.6	23.2
Speed of innovation: average number of years before the city entered the public housing program after state enabling legislation	18.1	13.2	22.2	22.2	18.6
Level of output: average number of housing units constructed per 100,000 population	888	1,016	351	282	668
Level of output: average number of housing units constructed per 100,000 population (natural logarithm transformation)	5.42	5.25	2.84	2.32	4.11
Number of cities	163	185	209	89	646
Urban Renewal					
Presence of participation in the urban renewal program	85%	71%	53%	40%	64%
Speed of innovation: average number of years before the city entered the urban renewal program	9.1	11.5	13.5	13.9	11.9
Speed of innovation: average number of years before the city entered the urban renewal program after enabling legislation	8.9	8.0	12.7	13.0	10.6
Level of output: average number of dollars reserved per capita	$99.16	$50.85	$29.96	$30.02	$53.76
Level of output: average number of dollars reserved per capita (natural logarithm transformation)	7.27	5.18	3.86	3.10	4.98
Number of cities	159	136	193	94	582

TABLE 2 (Continued)

Measures of Innovation	North-east	South	Region[a] Midwest	Far West	All Cities
War on Poverty					
Presence of participation in the War on Poverty	86%	76%	71%	46%	72%
Speed of innovation: average date city was awarded first poverty funds	6,554	6,570	6,582	6,601	6,575
Level of output: average number of poverty dollars per capita	$5.88	$3.81	$2.51	$2.38	$3.67
Level of output: average number of poverty dollars per capita (natural logarithm transformation)	5.03	4.30	3.70	2.58	4.02
Number of cities	164	191	219	102	676

a. The states included in each region are as follows: *Northeast:* Maine, New Hampshire, Vermont, Massachusetts, Connecticut, Rhode Island, New York, New Jersey, Pennsylvania, Maryland, Delaware, and District of Columbia. *South:* Texas, Oklahoma, Kansas, Missouri, Arkansas, Louisiana, Alabama, Mississippi, Florida, Georgia, North Carolina, South Carolina, Virginia, West Virginia, Kentucky, and Tennessee. *Midwest:* Ohio, Indiana, Illinois, Michigan, Wisconsin, Minnesota, Iowa, North Dakota, South Dakota, Nebraska, Montana, Idaho, Colorado, Utah, Wyoming, Arizona, New Mexico. *Far West:* California, Oregon, Washington, Nevada, Alaska, Hawaii.

experience and expertise developed in participating in one of these programs is used when a new program comes along.

G. *Regional Variations in Innovations in the Three Policy Areas.* The incidence, speed of entry, and level of output in public housing, urban renewal, and the War on Poverty are not uniform among cities in all regions, as shown in Table 2. Cities in the Northeast are highest on all eleven measures of innovation with only one exception. Southern cities tend to be next highest, followed by cities located in the Midwestern states. Cities located in the Far West have in general the lowest scores on these innovation measures. For example, while 80 percent of the cities located in the Northeast have had a federal public housing program, less than 40 percent of the cities in the Far West had ever entered this program. Similarly, 84 percent and 86 percent of the cities in the Northeast have received funds under the urban renewal or War on Poverty programs, respectively, but less than one-half the cities located in the Far West had entered these programs. These findings, together with the fact that there are regional variations in some independent variables such as the percentage nonwhite, the form of government, poverty and deprivation levels, means that we have also examined relationships between the various community characteristics and innovation measures within each region. But just because there are rather dramatic differences in innovation rates by region does not necessarily mean that the relationships based on all cities will not hold up within regions. Logically they may or may not. As we shall report below, we find general support for the major findings of this paper even within regions, although some of the relationships within regions are attenuated, and a few disappear, although some actually increase.

FINDINGS

The data testing the various theories we have considered are shown in Table 3. As we discuss below, a given indicator is sometimes used as an indicator of more than one concept, but we only show each indicator once, usually the first time it is discussed.

First, political culture: There is some question about the authorship of this theory. Wilson (1966b) argues that he and Banfield (Banfield and Wilson, 1963; Wilson and Banfield, 1964) did not develop the political culture thesis that Wolfinger and Field (1966) attribute to them. Regardless of the question of authorship, we include this hypothesis about policy outputs as one of the explanations for variations in community innovation. The thesis is that voters holding "public-regarding values" will be more supportive of policies which benefit the community as a whole than voters who hold "private-regarding values." Banfield and Wilson used voting behavior in local bond and other expenditure referenda in several cities to reflect policy decisions. Ethnicity, Protestantism, and income levels are used as indicators of the degree to which there are "public-regarding values." Their argument is that voters holding public-regarding values would favor metropolitan reorganization, "reform" governmental structures, regional planning, or fluoridation. Those with "private-regarding values" would be less inclined to favor policy choices such as these. While their study was based on comparisons of voting behavior in wards of cities, Wolfinger and Field (1966) supposedly tested their theory in a study of issue outcomes such as urban renewal and city planning expenditures in American cities of size 50,000 or more in 1960, and they strongly criticized the alleged Banfield and Wilson thesis on both theoretical and methodological grounds. While the question of authorship of the hypothesis is unresolved, it is still an important and provocative hypothesis which should be tested with other types of policy outcomes.

Our expectation is that cities having a low proportion of foreign stock, a small proportion of Catholics (we use here the proportion of elementary school children in private schools on the assumption that most private schools in the United States are Catholic), and a high proportion of the population that has high income (as measured by median family income) should be more characterized by public-regarding values, and hence have higher levels of innovation in public housing, urban renewal, and the War on Poverty.

We also argue that the degree of voting for the Democratic party can be construed as a measure of private-regarding values, which means that we conceive of the Republican vote as an additional indicator of public-regarding values. We use the percent of Democratic voting in 1964 in the county in which the city is located to measure Democratic voting. Among the 676 cities over 25,000 in 1960, this measure of Democratic voting was positively related to the degree of ethnicity (r = .34), the extent of Catholicism (r = .24), and the proportion of blue-collar workers in the labor force (r = .21), although there was no relationship with median family income (r = .03). Democratic dominance of a city is seemingly a more direct measure of political culture than any of these demographic characteristics. Thus, in this test of the political culture hypothesis, we should find that Democratic cities also have lower levels of participation in public housing, urban renewal, and the War on Poverty.

In Table 3 are displayed the 44 relationships between the four indicators of public-regarding values and the eleven measures of innovation. In the case of public housing, the political culture thesis is weakly supported by two measures—foreign stock and the Catholic measure—and in the case of urban renewal there is support for the ethnicity measure, but this is not true for the War on Poverty. When these results are controlled for region, however, we find a very mixed set of findings. The expected results between ethnicity and the three policy outputs hold up only in the Midwest and between ethnicity and urban renewal in the Northeast; other relationships between ethnicity and the policy outputs are either not significant or reversed. The expected relationships between the measure of Catholicism and innovation are found only in the Far West for housing and the Midwest for the War on Poverty. For the 100 or so regional relationships between these two measures of private-regarding values and the measures of innovation, no more than one in five of the within region relationships is both in the expected direction and significant.

In the case of the two remaining indicators of political culture—median family income and percent voting Democratic—the findings are in the opposite direction of the public-regarding hypothesis. High median income is associated with less participation in public housing, urban renewal, and the War on Poverty. These very strong relationships are also found to be significant within regions with only a few exceptions, and these occur in the South, but they are in the opposite direction from the prediction of the political culture thesis. In only two instances—urban renewal in the Northeast and the War on Poverty in the Midwest—do we find Democratic vote related to innovation as hypothesized.

While some scattered relationships support the political culture thesis, barely ten percent of the possible relationships between the measures of political

TABLE 3

RELATIONSHIPS BETWEEN INDICATORS OF INNOVATION IN PUBLIC HOUSING, URBAN RENEWAL, AND THE WAR ON POVERTY AND VARIOUS MEASURES OF COMMUNITY STRUCTURE

Theoretical Categories and Empirical Indicators	Public Housing[g]				Urban Renewal[g]				War on Poverty[g]		
	(1) Presence (n=646)	(2) Speed 1 (n=646)	(3) Speed 2 (n=646)	(4) Level of Output (n=646)	(5) Presence (n=582)	(6) Speed 1 (n=582)	(7) Speed 2 (n=582)	(8) Level of Output (n=582)	(9) Presence (n=676)	(10) Speed (n=676)	(11) Level of Output (n=676)
Political Culture											
Percentage of native population of foreign or mixed parentage[a]	-.05	.12**	.17†	-.08*	-.01	-.04	.10*	.02	-.05	.01	-.02
Percentage of elementary school children in private schools[a]	-.04	.06	.12**	-.05	.06	-.08	.05	.08	-.01	.00	.02
Median family income[a]	-.43†	.43†	.44†	-.47†	-.33†	.26†	.37†	-.29†	-.36†	.32†	-.39†
Percentage voting democratic, 1964[b]	.21†	-.20†	-.13**	.22†	.09*	-.13†	-.12**	.08	-.01	-.04	.07
Concentration and Diffusion of Community Power											
MPO Ratio[a]	-.28†	.22†	.16†	-.30†	-.30†	.29†	.21†	-.32†	-.21†	.23†	-.24†
Percentage of adult population with four years of high school education[a]	-.47†	.43†	.31†	-.51†	-.38†	.36†	.32†	-.38†	-.21†	.23†	-.23†
Percentage of registrants voting[d]	.17†	-.12*	-.06	.17†	.14**	-.19†	-.08	.16**	.14**	-.18†	.20†
Political Structure											
Presence of a city-manager form of government[c]	-.18†	.14†	.11**	-.18†	-.16†	.14†	.05	-.14†	-.11**	.14†	-.12**
Presence of nonpartisan elections[c]	-.18†	.10*	.03	-.18†	-.14†	.13†	.04	-.18†	-.09**	.14**	-.12**

TABLE 3 (Continued)

	(1)	(2)	(3)	(4)	(5)	(6)	(7)	(8)	(9)	(10)	(11)
Political Structure (Continued)											
Percentage of city council elected at large[c]	−.03	−.03	−.05	−.01	−.04	−.04	−.10*	−.02	−.04	.04	−.05
Index of Reformism[e]	−.17†	.09*	.04	−.16†	−.15†	.10*	−.01	−.15†	−.11**	.14†	−.13†
Number of members of the city council[c]	.11**	−.09*	−.01	.09*	.16†	−.13†	−.04	.14†	.14†	−.18†	.19†
Community Differentiation and Continuity											
Age of the city (census year city reached 10,000 population)	−.38†	.43†	.39†	−.40†	−.48†	.54†	.46†	−.48†	−.41†	.46†	−.48†
Size of the city (natural logarithm)	.30†	−.46†	−.44†	.30†	.33†	−.50†	−.49†	.33	.28†	−.45†	.38†
Community Integration											
Percentage unemployed	.34†	−.31†	−.25†	.36†	.23†	−.25†	−.24†	.25†	.21†	−.21†	.24†
Percentage migrant	−.23†	.20†	.08*	−.24†	−.23†	.25†	.12†	−.24†	−.04	.06	−.08*
Poverty											
Percentage of housing dilapidated, 1950	.31†	−.36†	−.34†	.36†	.20†	−.14†	−.28†	.13†	.15†	−.15†	.19†
Percentage of families with less than $3,000 income per year, 1959	.40†	−.46†	−.44†	.45†	.27†	−.22†	−.34†	.22†	.26†	−.24†	.30†
Percentage adults with less than five years education (natural logarithm)	.52†	−.52†	−.40†	.55†	.36†	−.36†	−.40†	.34†	.26†	−.29†	.33†
Percentage 14-17 year olds in school	−.40†	.41†	.36†	−.44†	−.33†	.29†	.35†	−.31†	−.26†	.30†	−.31†
Index of deprivation[f]	.46†	−.51†	−.45†	.51†	.31†	−.28†	−.39†	.26†	.26†	−.26†	.31†
Percentage of population this is nonwhite (natural logarithm)	.43†	−.49†	−.44†	.48†	.37†	−.44†	−.46†	.39†	.30†	−.35†	.35†

* p < .05   ** p < .01   † p < .001

Notes on page 248

[247]

culture and innovation in the four regions and the total set of cities are as predicted, and most are for the measure of ethnicity. The overall results appear sufficiently weak and inconsistent to suggest rejection of the political culture hypothesis.

Second, concentration or diffusion of community power: We refer here to three related but different theories about how the concentration or diffusion of community power affects community decision-making: (1) the ecological or systematic theory which sees power as a property of the community as a system, (2) a mass participation theory which argues that those structural features which reduce mass participation will have the consequence of concentrating power, and (3) an elite participation theory which argues that the smaller the number of

---

NOTES TO TABLE 3
a. U.S. Census of Population, 1960. b. COUNTY AND CITY DATA BOOK, 1967. The Democratic vote is the county presidential vote in 1964. The two cities for which data were not available (Washington, D.C., and New York) were assigned to the mean category.
c. THE MUNICIPAL YEAR BOOK, 1963 (International City Managers' Association, 1963). Four to five cities with missing data on one or more of the measures of political structure were assigned to the mean category. The categories for the number of members of the city council were collapsed as follows: 3-4, 5, 6, 7, 8, 9, 10-19, 20-29, 30-50. Means for this table were based on the full distribution.
d. Data are from a survey taken by Eugene C. Lee, Director, Institute of Governmental Studies, University of California at Berkeley. For further details and analysis of the voting data, see Alford and Lee (1968). These correlations are based on 411 cities for the measures of public housing, 370 cities for urban renewal, and 428 cities for the War on Poverty because of missing data.
e. The Index of Reformism was constructed by giving one point if the city had a city manager form of government, one point if the city had a nonpartisan form of election, and one point if 100 percent of the city council was elected at-large.
f. The Index of Deprivation was constructed by multiplying 1,000 times the standard score (the deviation of each city from the mean of the distribution divided by the standard deviation of the distribution) for the four variables: percentage of housing dilapidated in 1950; percentage of families with less than $3,000 income per year in 1959; natural logarithm of the percentage of adults with less than five years education; and percentage 14-17 year olds in school (reversed). These scores were summed and added to 10,000. A high number means high deprivation.
g. The measures of innovation are as follows:
PUBLIC HOUSING
  1. Presence of Innovation in Any Public Housing Program Since 1933
  2. Number of years After 1933 Before Construction Began on the First Housing Project
  3. Number of Years it Took After State Enabling Legislation Was Present
  4. Number of Public Housing Units Constructed per 100,000 Population (natural logarithm)
URBAN RENEWAL
  5. Presence of Urban Renewal Program
  6. Number of Years After 1949 Before Entering the Urban Renewal Program
  7. Number of Years It Took After State Enabling Legislation Was Present
  8. Number of Dollars Reserved Per Capita (natural logarithm)
WAR ON POVERTY
  9. Presence of Participation in the War On Poverty
  10. Date of Entry into the War On Poverty
  11. Number of Dollars Per Capita (natural logarithm)

elite participants and the more homogeneous their interests, the more concentrated the power structure. These theories vary in terms of the aspect of community structure that is most important, but they share a common assumption that the greater the degree to which power is concentrated, the greater the degree of innovation. This inference is not always explicitly stated, but it seems to be an appropriate extension of these theories. We shall test the first two theories directly with quantitative data similar to those already presented, but we shall have to use some indirect evidence as well as data from other studies to test the third hypothesis. Since our discussion of these issues will be both complicated and inferential, we shall examine each of these three aspects of the argument one at a time.

Hawley (1963) developed an ecological or systemic theory in which he reasoned that communities in which power is highly concentrated will have a higher probability of success in any collective action affecting the welfare of the whole. He defined two types of power: functional power required to execute functions and derivative power which "spills over" into external relationships and is involved in the regulation of interactions between parts or units of the system. For relatively routine decisions, power is exercised through established and well-worn channels. But, for nonroutine decisions affecting the entire system, such as urban renewal (and supposedly public housing and the War on Poverty), the manner in which derivative power is distributed is critical. If it is concentrated, the community will more likely be able to act as a unit in almost any emergency; if power is widely dispersed, successful collective action may be less certain. Under conditions of dispersion of power, the probability of a level of coordination sufficiently high to achieve positive community action is quite low; when power is concentrated, adequate coordination should be achieved with less difficulty.

Hawley used participation in the urban renewal program as his measure of a collective action and the MPO Ratio (the proportion of the employed civilian labor force that is managers, proprietors, or officials) as a measure of the concentration of community power. He hypothesized that the higher the MPO Ratio, the greater would be the dispersion of community power and the less likely the community would be successful in urban renewal; conversely, the lower the MPO Ratio, the greater the concentration of community power and the more likely the community would be successful in urban renewal.

Table 3 would seem to confirm Hawley's hypothesis for innovation in each of the three policy areas. The higher the MPO Ratio (low concentration of power for Hawley), the less likely a community participated in the public housing program ($r = -.28$), the urban renewal program ($r = -.30$), and the War on Poverty ($r = -.21$). In addition, the higher the MPO Ratio, the longer it took communities to enter these programs, and the lower the levels of output in each of these three programs, as Hawley's theory would predict. Cities with high MPO

Ratios are therefore less likely to be innovative, consistent with Hawley's thesis. When correlation coefficients are computed for cities within each of the four regions, we find that these relationships remain strong among Northeastern, Midwestern, and Southern cities, but are generally weak among cities located in the Far West. Other than this exception, our findings support those of Hawley, and we conclude that cities with high MPO Ratios are less likely to innovate than cities with low MPO Ratios.

Other information drawn from case studies of community power and from Clark's (1968) study of decentralization question the interpretation that the MPO Ratio measures the dispersion of community power, however. Aiken (1970) classified 31 case studies of community power (which are from the 676 cities in this analysis) on a four-point scale reflecting diffusion of power. This scale ranged from pyramidal to dispersed arrangements using qualitative judgments of the number of groups involved in major issues in the community. The results show, first, that communities with diffused power have higher levels of innovation and outputs, and, second, that cities having high MPO Ratios have more concentrated power arrangements, not less concentrated as Hawley reasoned.

Further confirmation of this reinterpretation of the MPO Ratio is provided by examining Clark's (1970) measures of decentralization. Clark measured the degree of decentralization of community power in 51 communities by determining the number of persons involved in decision-making in four issues: urban renewal, air pollution, poverty programs, and the selection of the mayor. We related Clark's measure of decentralization to the MPO Ratio and found a correlation coefficient of $-.46$, which means that cities having a high MPO Ratio are more centralized, a finding that is again just the opposite of Hawley's interpretation.

We thus conclude that Hawley's empirical prediction that cities with high MPO Ratios will be less innovative in collective decisions affecting the welfare of the whole is verified in the case of public housing, urban renewal, and the War on Poverty. On the other hand, the interpretation that the MPO Ratio is measuring dispersion of community power is seriously challenged by two separate studies; these studies suggest that power is more concentrated in cities with high MPO Ratios. It should be remembered, however, that Hawley was concerned with the dispersion of systemic power, while the studies cited here refer to the degree of elite participation. It is logically possible that systemic power could be highly dispersed, yet there would be only a few actors or power centers in a community. Still, these studies do raise serious questions about the meaning of the MPO Ratio and suggest caution in using it as a measure of power dispersion.

The second aspect of the hypothesis maintaining that the concentration of community power is associated with greater innovation is primarily concerned with citizen participation. Crain and Rosenthal (1967) have argued that communities that have high levels of education are more likely to have higher levels of political participation, which is likely to have the effect of greater conflict, stalemate, and immobilization of the political system. The consequence of this in our terms is likely to be less innovation. Their theory therefore argues that higher levels of education result in less innovation through the intervening processes of heightened political participation, community conflict, and blockage of collective action. We use here the percentage of the adult population that has four years of education as the measure of community educational levels. As shown in Table 3, we find that the educational level does indeed have strong negative relationships with the three measures of the incidence of innovation in public housing, urban renewal and the War on Poverty, strong positive relationships with the various speed of innovation measures, and strong negative relationships with the level of output measures. When correlations are computed separately for cities in the four regions, the relationships remain in the same direction in all cases and most are statistically significant, with the exception of the measures of innovation in the War on Poverty in the South and Far West.

Even if we were to grant that the predicted empirical relationships work sufficiently well, there remains the nagging question about the meaning of this educational variable and the intervening process it allegedly represents. Does a high level of educational attainment in a community reflect the presence of many well-educated, relatively affluent persons? Or does it reflect merely the absence of a poor and needy population? Among the 676 cities, the correlation coefficients between the proportion of adults with a high school education and the upper portions on the educational and income distributions—the percent of adults who have completed college and the percent of families with incomes of $10,000 or more per year—are .71 and .63 respectively. The correlation coefficients between the proportion of adults with four years of high school education and the lower extremes on the education and income distributions—the percentage of adults who have completed less than five years of education and the percentage of families with incomes of less than $3,000 per year—are −.76 and −.45, respectively. Since these correlation coefficients are relatively strong in each case, the interpretation of a variable such as this depends to a great extent on which end of the scale one wants to emphasize, for it is clear that the educational level of a community can be used to measure either the level of poverty and dependency or the probability of having an articulate and active middle class.

In the analysis of 31 case studies discussed earlier (Aiken, 1970), cities having higher educational levels were found to have more concentrated power structures than those with lower educational levels, although the relationship was not strong. Among the 51 American cities in the Clark (1970) study, his measure of decentralization has a correlation coefficient of −.35 with the measure of percent of adults with four years of education, meaning that cities with higher educational levels have more centralized decision-making structures. This provides some additional confirmation for the assertion that cities having higher educational levels are likely to have more concentrated elite configurations.

We could thus make the same argument about the meaning of this educational measure as we did for the MPO Ratio, especially since these two variables are quite highly related to each other ($r = .66$), and both the educational variable and the MPO Ratio are strongly related to the percentage of white-collar ($r = .87$ and $.78$, respectively). Both of these variables clearly seem to be measures of the degree of middle-class domination of a city, and in each case we find that middle-class cities have more centralized power arrangements (less elite participation). It is still possible that the Crain and Rosenthal thesis of greater citizen participation in such cities is correct, however.

But there is a serious problem with the Crain and Rosenthal interpretation. As we noted above, they assume, without providing evidence, that a highly educated population participates more in local politics, which produces conflict, and thus blockage and stalemate on issues such as urban renewal. They lack data, however, on the key intervening variable of citizen participation. Although decent data on political participation do not exist for a large sample of cities, if voting turnout can be regarded as a crude indicator, a recent study has shown that better-educated cities have lower voting turnout than less well-educated cities (Alford and Lee, 1968). We find, as shown in Table 3, that, among the 428 cities in our study for which data on voting turnout are available, higher voting turnout is associated with innovations in public housing, urban renewal, and the War on Poverty (correlation coefficients vary between $.16$ and $.17$), rapid entry into these programs (the two speed measures that take enabling legislation into consideration are in the correct direction but are not statistically significant, although the other three measures are), and higher levels of output (correlations vary between $.16$ and $.20$). Thus, higher levels of citizen participation, as reflected in the degree of voting turnout, are associated with higher rates of innovation, which is just the opposite of their argument about the effect of higher levels of citizen participation. However, the regional controls complicate this generalization. When these correlations are computed within regions, we find significant relationships only in the Far West, although each of the eleven relationships is significant in that region. None of the relationships in the other regions is sufficiently strong to be statistically significant.

Our empirical relationships between level of education and innovation are thus comparable to Crain and Rosenthal's findings, but we have questioned the meaning of the educational level, and we have offered some evidence that questions their theoretical interpretation of this variable. At the same time we do not have evidence sufficiently strong to demonstrate that their thesis is incorrect, but for us we feel that there may be other and better explanations of innovations in public policies, a topic we shall explore in greater detail later in this paper.

The third aspect of the concentration of power thesis is elite participation. The hypothesis here is that the fewer the influential persons in a community (and, by definition, the more concentrated power is in the political system), the easier it is to innovate. Although the community power literature has not dealt directly and systematically with innovation or policy outputs, the implied hypothesis by defenders of both the pluralist and the reputational schools is that the more centralized the political system, the greater its capacity to act. While Hunter (1953) stressed the role of a few heads of large corporations and banks as the source of coordinating leadership, and Dahl (1961) stressed the role of a few political and public leaders as the moving force within an "executive-centered order"—without systematic data and without presenting this general hypothesis except indirectly—both assume that a centralized community system will be more able to make decisions and to make them faster.

We must not make too much of the relevance of the community power literature for our present argument. Both Hunter and Dahl stress the limitations on possible actions created by existing commitments to institutional arrangements, divisions of powers, and allocations of resources. But they, as well as we, essentially restricted their discussion of community decisions to those which are well within the range of the politically feasible at any given time. Federal programs such as those we report on in this paper challenge few established economic or political interests, if any, and thus do not constitute radical innovations.

Both Hunter's and Dahl's studies focused upon single cities. Few systematic comparative studies have been done of the concentration of community power which examined the number of actors in different issues and the consequences for community innovation. But, Clark's (1968) study of 51 cities found that the greater the decentralization of community power as measured by the number of persons involved in decision-making in four issues (urban renewal, air pollution, poverty programs, and the selection of the mayor), the greater the number of urban renewal dollars per capita secured from the federal government. Clark concluded, contrary to his original hypothesis, that more decentralized communities had higher policy outputs, and advanced the new hypothesis that "fragile" decisions were more susceptible to blockage. The point that is relevant here is that decentralization led to higher outputs. As already discussed, Aiken's (1970) coding of 31 case studies of community power into four levels of diffusion of power came to the same conclusion about the relationship between the diffusion of power and policy outputs. To further substantiate this generalization, we related Clark's measure of decentralization to each of our measures of innovation, as shown in Table 4. Cities which are decentralized have

TABLE 4
CORRELATION COEFFICIENT BETWEEN INDICATORS OF INNOVATION IN
PUBLIC HOUSING, URBAN RENEWAL, AND THE WAR ON POVERTY AND
CLARK'S MEASURE OF DECENTRALIZATION OF DECISION-MAKING

	Clark's Measure of Decentralization of Decision-Making	(n)
Public Housing		
1. Presence of participation in the public housing program since 1933	.39**	(50)
2. Speed of innovation: number of years before the city entered the public housing program	−.38**	(50)
3. Speed of innovation: number of years before the city entered the public housing program after state enabling legislation	−.37**	(50)
4. Level of output: number of housing units constructed per 100,000 population (natural logarithm)	.40**	(50)
Urban Renewal		
5. Presence of participation in the urban renewal program	.23	(46)
6. Speed of innovation: number of years before the city entered the urban renewal program	−.32*	(46)
7. Speed of innovation: number of years before the city entered the urban renewal program after state enabling legislation	−.20	(46)
8. Level of output: number of dollars reserved per capita (natural logarithm)	.27	(46)
War on Poverty		
9. Presence of participation in the War on Poverty	.33*	(51)
10. Speed of innovation: date city was first awarded poverty funds	−.42**	(51)
11. Level of output: number of dollars per capita (natural logarithm)	.49†	(51)

* $p < .05$
** $p < .01$
† $p < .001$

SOURCE: Terry N. Clark, "Structure Communautaire, Prise de Décision, et Rénovation Urbaine Dans 51 Communautés Américaines," Amenagment du territoire et développement régional, III (Grenoble: Institut d'Etudes Politiques, 1970), pp. 179-219.

higher incidence of participation in public housing, urban renewal, and the War on Poverty, took less time to enter these programs, and have higher levels of performance in each of these three programs. Only in the case of urban renewal are the relationships not statistically significant. We show slightly lower correlation coefficients between the decentralization measure and the level of performance in urban renewal than Clark (.27 as opposed to .35). This could occur for two reasons. First, the measures were calculated in slightly different ways and, second, we have excluded five cities in calculating our correlation coefficient. Four cities in Florida were excluded because of that state's problematic enabling legislation, and Bloomington, Minnesota, was excluded because it did not exist in 1950. In spite of these technicalities, the generalization drawn from these results is the same; namely, centralized cities have lower levels of innovation in their policy areas while decentralized cities have higher levels of innovation.

In summary, we have questioned the interpretations of both Hawley as well as Crain and Rosenthal. There appears to be the greatest evidence for the conclusion that cities in which power is decentralized—whether from the systemic, citizen participation, or elite participation perspective—have a greater incidence of innovation, more rapid entry and higher levels of performance in public housing, urban renewal, and the War on Poverty. We shall return to this conclusion in a later section.

Third, centralization of formal political structure: This argument has two aspects—one based on centralization of formal power and the second related to the political culture argument. In the first case, the thesis in the literature is that the more centralized the formal political structure, the more capable it is of producing high policy outputs. There is some disagreement on what should be the indicators of centralization, since the usual conception of "reform" government is that its structural devices—the city manager form, nonpartisan elections, at-large elections, small city councils—were intended to centralize power in the hands of a small executive and a professional manager at the same time that potential power in the hands of citizen groups was fragmented and dispersed by removing the instruments of the political party and the ward organization. On the other hand, some have argued that strong political parties were the most effective device for centralizing power. But in either case, there was agreement that administrative or political centralization, regardless of its form, should lead to greater policy outputs (Crain et al., 1969; Greenstone and Peterson, 1968).

The second aspect of political structure is related to the political culture argument, because it has been argued that reform political institutions were part of the array of policies favored by groups with public-regarding values, and presumably the political instruments of such values should produce consequences similar to those of sheer demographic composition.

In most respects, predictions made by either the administrative centralization or political cultural interpretation would be the same. That is, the presence of a city manager, nonpartisan elections, at-large elections, and a small council, should lead to greater policy outputs. The prediction is ambiguous only in the case of the form of election. If nonpartisan elections are regarded as decentralized, then, according to this line of reasoning, they should be associated with low outputs. But, if they are regarded as instruments of groups with public-regarding values, then nonpartisan elections should be associated with high innovation and output.

The centralization argument is supported by none of these findings unless one accepts the argument that partisan elections lead to administrative centralization and therefore to higher levels of policy outputs. The data do support the latter proposition, but only that one. Manager cities, nonpartisan cities, and cities with small city councils either have a lower incidence of participation in these federal programs, took longer to enter them, and have lower levels of outputs, or there is no relationship. In the case of at-large elections, only one relationship is in the expected direction (the second speed measure for urban renewal), but the others are little different from zero. The Index of Reformism, of course, has results similar to those for the city-manager and nonpartisan measures, since these are two of its components.

When correlation coefficients are computed within the four regions, most relationships do not differ significantly from zero, and the ones that do (mainly in the Far West, and to some extent the South) are still inconsistent with the hypothesized relationship with only a few exceptions, mainly between the measures of nonpartisan cities, at-large elections, and the Index of Reformism and the speed measures in urban renewal in Northeast and Midwest. But, of the 220 possible relationships between these aspects of political structure and the measures of innovation only five within the four regions are both statistically significant and in the hypothesized direction. These results hardly support the hypothesis.

As a corollary to this observation, the political culture argument fails again to the extent that it regards structural variation in form of government as indicators of the operation of dominant values. Reform governments are not more innovative than nonreform governments.

These data do not adequately address the hypotheses about community innovation presented by Crain et al. (1969). They suggest that there are two dimensions of community structure that are important determinants of community innovation: the degree of citizen participation in decision-making as well as the degree of centralization of administrative authority. Using the form of government as an indicator of the degree of administrative centralization (council-manager is the most centralized, mayor-council next, and commission the least centralized) and the form of election as an indicator of the degree of citizen participation (presuming nonpartisanship to be associated with higher levels of participation), they posit four city types (and five combinations) and the degree of community innovation. They argue that cities having low political participation and high executive centralization should have the highest rates of innovation. They found that administrative adoption of fluoridation was highest in cities with city-manager government, followed by those with partisan mayor-council, nonpartisan mayor-council, and lowest in those with the commission form of government.

In Table 5 we show the means for the innovation measures in the three policy areas. Cities having the commission form of government have the highest incidence of innovation in public housing, urban renewal, and the War on Poverty; were most rapid in entering these programs (with the exception of the War on Poverty); and had the highest level of output measures for the transformed distributions, although the mean is little different from that of the latter category. Two categories of cities, partisan mayor-council for outputs in urban renewal and this category as well as partisan council-manager for the outputs in the War on Poverty, come out higher for the untransformed distributions, but in each instance this is because of extreme skewness in these distributions. Cities having commission form of government had the lowest rate of innovation in fluoridation (i.e., administrative adoption), however. Like their findings for fluoridation, innovation in public housing, urban renewal, and the War on Poverty was higher and more rapid in partisan mayor-council cities than in nonpartisan mayor-council ones. But, unlike their finding about the degree of innovation in nonpartisan council-manager cities, this category had the highest rate of administrative adoption of fluoridation. We find that nonpartisan council-manager cities had the lowest incidence of innovation, were slowest to innovate, and had the lowest levels of outputs in the three policy decisions considered here.

We conclude that although our findings support some of the predictions of Crain, Katz, and Rosenthal (1969), others are not supported. The inconsistencies in findings as well as the low zero-order correlations between measures of political structure and innovation lead us to the conclusion that such a theory is perhaps not the most appropriate for an explanation of innovation such as those considered here.

Fourth, community differentiation and continuity: Cities that are large and which have been in existence for long periods of time are likely to be more differentiated and have a greater degree of continuity. The question here is whether size and age lead to higher or lower levels of innovation. In the literature on community decision-making, there are arguments for both points of view. For example, Thomas Dye (1968) studied integration in 55 Northern and Southern cities and found that larger and older cities tended to have more innovation than smaller or younger cities. He reasoned that larger cities were

TABLE 5
THE INCIDENCE OF INNOVATION, SPEED OF INNOVATION, AND LEVEL OF
OUTPUT IN PUBLIC HOUSING, URBAN RENEWAL, AND THE WAR ON
POVERTY BY FORM OF GOVERNMENT

| | | Form of Government | | | | |
| | | Partisan | | Nonpartisan | | |
Measures of Innovation	Commis-sion	Mayor-Council	Council Manager	Mayor-Council	Council Manager	All Cities
Public Housing						
Presence of participation in the public housing program since 1933	76%	73%	71%	61%	49%	61%
Speed of innovation: average number of years before the city entered the public housing program	19.2	21.1	24.2	23.6	24.9	23.2
Speed of innovation: average number of years before the city entered the public housing program after state enabling legislation	12.4	17.9	21.2	19.7	19.8	18.6
Level of output: average number of housing units constructed per 100,000 population	1,080	751	684	645	520	668
Level of output: average number of housing units constructed per 100,000 population (natural logarithm transformation)	5.36	4.94	4.68	4.07	3.30	4.11
Number of cities	78	127	41	126	274	646
Urban Renewal						
Presence of participation in the urban renewal program	76%	72%	71%	68%	54%	64%
Speed of innovation: average number of years before the city entered the urban renewal program	9.3	11.0	11.7	12.3	12.9	11.9
Speed of innovation: average number of years before the city entered the urban renewal program after enabling legislation	7.8	10.6	10.7	11.4	10.9	10.6
Level of output: average number of dollars reserved per capita	$72.74	$85.43	$69.70	$44.02	$36.42	$53.76

TABLE 5 (Continued)

		Form of Government				
Measures of Innovation	Commis-sion	Partisan		Nonpartisan		All Cities
		Mayor-Council	Council Manager	Mayor-Council	Council Manager	
Urban Renewal (Continued)						
Level of output: average number of dollars re-served per capita (natural logarithm transformation)	6.21	5.98	* 5.81	4.83	4.15	4.98
Number of Cities	62	118	35	117	250	582
War On Poverty						
Presence of participation in the War on Poverty	83%	77%	80%	74%	66%	72%
Speed of innovation: average date the city was awarded its first poverty funds	6,562	6,564	6,558	6,572	6,586	6,575
Level of output: average number of poverty dollars per capita	$4.21	$4.62	$5.00	$4.06	$2.77	$3.67
Level of output: average number of poverty dollars per capita (nat-ural logarithm transformation)	4.69	4.44	4.67	4.08	3.55	4.02
Number of cities	78	129	41	130	298	676

SOURCE: *The Municipal Year Book,* 1963. (International City Managers' Association, 1963.) The four or five cities with missing data on one or more of the measures of political structure were assigned to the category with the highest frequency.

likely to be more bureaucratic and that " ... large bureaucracies have many built-in mechanisms to resist policy innovations." He argued that older cities would more likely be immobilized because " ... over time persons and organizations adjust themselves to circumstances as they find them." This would lead us to expect older cities to have lower levels of innovation in public housing, urban renewal, and the War on Poverty. Among his findings, he found that older and larger cities were more segregated, at least in the North.

But there is other evidence to support the opposite conclusion. In a study of public health organizations in 93 cities located in four Midwestern states and Ontario, Lawrence Mohr (1969) found that public health organizations of larger cities were more innovative. We would expect these larger cities also to be older cities since the relationship between these two variables among the 219 midwestern cities, as well as among all 676 cities in our study, is .54. His rationale for this finding was that community decision organizations such as public health organizations would be larger in big cities, would have more resources available, and, therefore, would be more innovative. In addition, a number of studies on innovation in complex organizations support the finding that larger organizations are likely to be more innovative (Mansfield, 1963; Hage and Aiken, 1967; Mytinger, 1968).

Table 3 shows that older and larger cities have a higher incidence of innovation in public housing, urban renewal, and the War on Poverty, took less time to enter these programs, and have higher levels of outputs in these policy decisions. Each of the correlation coefficients is strong, in the predicted direction, and statistically significant. When correlation coefficients are computed for cities within each of the four regions, there is not one exception to these findings. Each of the 88 correlation coefficients is statistically significant and in the expected direction. For no other cluster of variables do we find such consistency and only in the case of the percentage nonwhite variable do we find such consistency. We reject the hypothesis that older and larger cities are less innovative. Quite the contrary, they are more innovative in the policy choices considered here than younger and smaller cities.

Fifth, community integration: Cities that are more highly integrated, i.e. those in which citizens and subgroups are linked together, linked to their leaders, and more closely knit, should suffer less from paralyzing conflict in the case of a new issue requiring solution and should more likely have positive outcomes to such problems. Under such circumstances, channels of communications to work out compromises exist, and isolated factions standing fast on their own position would less likely be present (Pinard, 1963; Coleman, 1957). In our terms, integrated communities should have higher rates of innovation, while those with lower rates of integration should experience more conflict, more stalemate, and thus be less innovative.

The indicators of community integration used by Pinard are quite diverse. He hypothesized that there would be more positive outcomes of fluoridation in cities with higher levels of integration, and he included middle-class status, low voting turnout, small population size, low ethnicity, low unemployment, and low inmigration as his indicators of community integration. As we have already seen, middle-class composition, low voting turnout, and small population size are either unrelated to or associated with less innovation in the three federal programs considered here, not more as would be predicted by the integration theory. Seven of eleven relationships between ethnicity and the measures of innovation were not statistically significant, although the other four were in the direction predicted by the integration theory, but most of these did not hold consistently under regional controls and even these are reversed when other factors are controlled in multiple regression analysis. In the case of unemployment and inmigration, the thesis is that high unemployment levels will produce low levels of community integration by reducing citizen attachments to community institutions which will in turn raise the level of conflict, and result in lower levels of community innovation while high levels of inmigration should reduce integration by disrupting long-standing networks of communication and interchange among groups and organizations in a community.

Contrary to expectation, low unemployment is associated with lower rates of innovation in the three policy areas, not more. These relationships hold up when correlations are computed within regions with the exception of innovation in urban renewal and poverty programs in the South where the relationships do not differ from zero. But in each case, both these relationships are in the opposite direction of that predicted by the integration hypothesis.

Other than ethnicity, the only indicator among these six that works in the predicted direction is the degree of inmigration. When the correlations are calculated within regions, we find that only one-third of the 44 correlations for this variable are both statistically significant and in the predicted direction, and these occur primarily for the housing variable. For only two of the six indicators of community integration are any of the relationships as predicted; when correlations are calculated within regions, a few scattered correlations between innovation and ethnicity, voting turnout, and inmigration support the hypothesis, but the overriding majority of relationships do not. We conclude that most of the findings reported here do not support the integration hypothesis.

To summarize our analysis thus far, we have found little support for the hypotheses drawn from the literature, and we have raised questions about the theoretical interpretations of most of those that were as predicted. Innovations in public housing, urban renewal, and the War on Poverty are greatest in older and larger cities, those with low levels of education and income, those having fewer managers and officials, those having higher levels of voting turnout and Democratic voting, and those having a lower degree of inmigration and higher unemployment levels. The question which these results raise is whether or not innovation in these three federal programs is simply a response to higher levels of need and deprivation in these cities. Does the level of deprivation and need in a community—as measured by unemployment, poverty, low education, and poor housing—account for most of the statistical variation in the various innovation measures? If so, this would be an important finding since it would mean that the innovation was a function of the level of deprivation and need in the community, whether manifest in political demands by the needy or in autonomous responses to innovations in these three federal programs, regardless of the values of key groups, the nature of power dispersion in the community, or its level of integration.

Table 3 includes certain measures of poverty and housing conditions and their relationships with the innovation measures. Cities having more dilapidated housing in 1950, many poor families, many poorly educated adults, more high school dropouts, and many nonwhites were indeed more likely to have a higher incidence of innovation in the three programs, to enter them sooner, and have higher levels of output. We also include there an Index of Deprivation constructed by taking the average of the standard scores for the percentage of dilapidated housing in 1950, percentage of families with incomes less than $3,000, percentage of adults with less than five years education (after natural logarithm transformation), and percentage of 14 to 17 year olds in schools (reversed). These averages were multiplied by 1,000 and added to 10,000. The correlation coefficients between the components and the overall index were .89, .92, .87, and .60, respectively. We constructed this index in order to reduce the number of variables that we use later in the multiple regression analyses. As shown in Table 2, correlation coefficients between this index and the various measures of innovation are similar in magnitude and direction to its components (other than the percentage of dropouts which we have not reversed in Table 3). Within regions, each of the relationships for percentage nonwhite is in the predicted direction and significant, and over 80 percent of the other correlations are in the predicted direction and statistically significant. Cities that have high deprivation levels and many blacks have the highest incidence of innovations in public housing, urban renewal, and the War on Poverty, entered these programs sooner, and have higher levels of outputs in these programs, and this is generally true within most regions with the exception of urban renewal and the War on Poverty in the South.

Multivariate Analysis. Given the strong and consistent relationships between these measures of community deprivation and innovation, we may ask whether or not many of the previously discussed variables, regardless of the concepts they were alleged to represent, are not simply functions of a high degree of community need for these various programs. To answer this question we performed regression analyses for each of the five speed of innovation measures and the three level of output measures, and we include most of the variables shown in Table 3. Because of so many cases of missing data, we excluded the measure of voting turnout, and we also included the index of reformism and the index of deprivation instead of the components of these two indices. In all we include fourteen independent variables. We considered the use of path analysis, but we felt that there were too many questions about time ordering of most variables to justify use of that technique. We utilize the traditional criterion that a regression coefficient is at least twice its standard error in establishing its level of significance.

Table 6 shows the results of three regression analyses for measures of innovation in public housing. Five variables are independently related to the first innovation measure: ethnicity, age of city, city size, index of deprivation, and percentage nonwhite. It should be noted that when these other factors are controlled, ethnicity has a negative relationship with the speed of innovation measure, the opposite of its zero-order relationship. Thus, what little support the ethnicity variable gave to both the political culture thesis as well as the community integration thesis is contradicted when the net effect of ethnicity is established. This observation is also consistent with the other findings in Table 6 as well as those in Tables 7 and 8. Age and size of city also make independent contributions to the explanation of the speed of innovation in public housing, and, as we shall see, they make independent contributions to the explanation of most of the measures of innovation. Finally, the deprivation index and percentage of nonwhites are determinants of whether or not a community was quick to innovate in public housing, and once again we shall see that this latter variable makes an independent contribution to the explanation of each of the measures of innovation.

When the speed of innovation measure taking enabling legislation into consideration is regressed on the same characteristics, three variables—age of city, city size, and percentage nonwhite—remain as predictors of speed of innovation. However, the ethnicity and deprivation measures no longer make independent contributions, and in their place are the measures of median family income and size of the city council. Finally, for the level of output measure, we find four city characteristics with significant regression coefficients: age of city, percentage nonwhite, ethnicity, and the percentage voting Democratic. To summarize Table 6, two factors—age of city and percentage nonwhite—make independent contributions to the explanation of all three innovation measures. Two other factors—city size and ethnicity—are strongly related to two of the innovation measures. Finally, four other measures are related to only one: median family income, Democratic voting, city council size, and the level of deprivation. In each regression, between 40 and 47 percent of the variance is explained.

In Table 7 we show three additional multiple regressions of innovation in urban renewal on these same city characteristics. These fourteen variables explain between 34 and 46 percent of the variance in these three innovation measures. Here we find three factors making independent contributions to the explanation of the three innovation measures—ethnicity, age of city, and percentage of nonwhites. Size of the city council and city size are independently related to the two speed of innovation measures, but not the level of output measure. Finally, the measure of median family income has an independent effect on the second speed of innovation measure.

Finally, we show the regressions for two measures of innovation in the War on Poverty in Table 8. Here we explain 36 and 37 percent of the variance in these two measures. Eight factors make independent contributions to explanation of the speed of entry in the War on Poverty, five of which—ethnicity, median family income, age of city, city size, and percentage nonwhite—were

TABLE 6
MULTIPLE REGRESSION OF PARTICIPATION IN THE PUBLIC HOUSING PROGRAM ON SELECTED COMMUNITY CHARACTERISTICS AMONG 646 AMERICAN CITIES

	Speed of Innovation		Speed of Innovation (after enabling legislation)		Number of Housing Units Constructed per 100,000 Population (natural logarithm)	
	Standardized Regression Coefficients	t-value	Standardized Regression Coefficients	t-value	Standardized Regression Coefficients	t-value
Political Culture						
Percentage of native population of foreign or mixed parentage[a]	−.0939	2.07	−.0736	1.53	.1472	3.15
Percentage of elementary school children in private schools[a]	.0474	1.08	.0743	1.59	−.0740	1.63
Percentage voting democratic, 1964[b]	−.0644	1.85	−.0697	1.88	.0859	2.39
Median family income[a]	.0472	.72	.2500	3.61	−.0964	1.44
Concentration and Diffusion of Community Power						
MPO ratio[a]	−.0572	1.23	−.0865	1.76	.0094	.20
Percentage of adult population with 4 years of high school education[a]	.1170	1.71	−.0003	.01	−.1328	1.89
Political Structure						
Index of reformism in local government[c]	.0188	.52	.0590	1.53	−.0728	1.94
Number of members of city council[c]	.0186	.50	.1208	3.07	−.0200	.52

TABLE 6 (Continued)

	Speed of Innovation		Speed of Innovation (after enabling legislation)		Number of Housing Units Constructed per 100,000 Population (natural logarithm)	
	Standardized Regression Coefficients	t-value	Standardized Regression Coefficients	t-value	Standardized Regression Coefficients	t-value
Community Differentiation and Continuity						
Age of city (census year city reached 10,000 population)[a]	.1342	2.89	.2013	4.09	−.1623	3.39
Size of city (natural logarithm)[a]	−.2904	7.56	−.2975	7.29	.0653	1.65
Community Integration						
Percentage unemployed[a]	−.0233	.65	−.0010	.03	.0611	1.64
Percentage migrant[a]	−.0134	.30	−.0502	1.05	.0057	.12
Poverty						
Index of deprivation[a]	−.2357	3.34	−.0833	1.12	.1381	1.92
Percentage of the population that is nonwhite (natural logarithm)[a]	−.1861	4.10	−.1376	2.86	.2767	5.92
	$R^2 = .4716$ $R = .6867$		$R^2 = .4044$ $R = .6359$		$R^2 = .4931$ $R = .6627$	

NOTE: The referents of a, b, and c, in this table as well as Tables 7, 8, and 9, are the same as in Table 3.

TABLE 7

MULTIPLE REGRESSION OF PARTICIPATION IN THE URBAN RENEWAL PROGRAM ON SELECTED COMMUNITY CHARACTERISTICS

	Speed of Innovation		Speed of Innovation (after enabling legislation)		Number of Dollars Per Capita (natural logarithm)	
	Standardized Regression Coefficients	t-value	Standardized Regression Coefficients	t-value	Standardized Regression Coefficients	t-value
Political Culture						
Percentage of native population of foreign or mixed parentage[a]	-.1845	3.84	-.1377	2.78	.1399	2.64
Percentage of elementary school children in private schools[a]	.0460	.97	.0273	.56	-.0245	.47
Median family income[a]	-.0858	1.16	.1555	2.03	.0412	.50
Percentage voting democratic, 1964[b]	.0041	.11	-.0318	.80	-.0340	.80
Concentration and Diffusion of Community Power						
MPO ratio[a]	.0677	1.27	-.0577	1.04	-.0935	1.58
Percentage of adult population with 4 years of high school education[a]	.0787	1.03	.0602	.76	-.0934	1.11
Political Structure						
Index of reformism in local government[c]	-.0168	.42	-.0440	1.06	-.0236	.53
Number of members of city council[c]	.1050	2.61	.1249	3.00	-.0632	1.42

TABLE 7 (Continued)

	Speed of Innovation		Speed of Innovation (after enabling legislation)		Number of Dollars Per Capita (natural logarithm)	
	Standardized Regression Coefficients	t-value	Standardized Regression Coefficients	t-value	Standardized Regression Coefficients	t-value
Community Differentiation and Continuity						
Age of city (census year city reached 10,000 population)[a]	.3671	7.16	.2610	4.93	-.3556	6.28
Size of city (natural logarithm)[a]	-.2058	4.94	-.2786	6.48	.0245	.53
Community Integration						
Percentage unemployed[a]	-.0456	1.15	.0092	.22	.0681	1.56
Percentage migrant[a]	-.0351	.75	-.0841	1.74	.0487	.94
Poverty						
Index of deprivation[a]	.0266	.34	-.0070	.09	-.0611	.71
Percentage of the population that is nonwhite (natural logarithm)[2]	-.3429	7.21	-.2732	5.56	.3335	6.35
	$R^2 = .4629$ $R = .6804$		$R^2 = .4272$ $R = .6536$		$R^2 = .3446$ $R = .5870$	

TABLE 8
MULTIPLE REGRESSION OF PARTICIPATION IN THE WAR ON POVERTY ON COMMUNITY CHARACTERISTICS

	Speed of Innovation		Number of Poverty Dollars	
	Standardized Regression Coefficients	t-value	Standardized Regression Coefficients	Per Capita (natural logarithm) t-value
Political Culture				
Percentage of native population of foreign or mixed parentage[a]	−.2293	4.75	.2236	4.67
Percentage of elmeentary school children in private schools[a]	.0630	1.33	−.1048	.32
Median family income[a]	.2515	3.63	−.3746	5.46
Percentage voting democratic, 1964[b]	.0170	.46	.0140	.38
Concentration and Diffusion of Community Power				
MPO ratio[a]	.0542	1.09	−.0603	1.22
Percentage of adult population with 4 years of high school education[a]	−.1454	1.98	.2684	3.69
Political Structure				
Index of reformism in local government[c]	.0796	2.04	−.0352	−.91
Number of members of the city council[c]	.0181	.45	.0266	.67
Community Differentiation and Continuity				
Age of city[a] (census year city reached 10,000 population)	.2821	5.58	−.3161	6.31
Size of city[a] (natural logarithm)	−.2250	5.50	.1108	2.74
Community Integration				
Percentage unemployed[a]	−.0569	1.45	.0795	2.05
Percentage migrant[a]	−.1389	2.96	.0840	1.81
Poverty				
Index of deprivation[a]	.0670	.89	−.0400	.53
Percentage of the population that is nonwhite[a] (natural logarithm)	−.2432	4.98	.2424	5.01
	R^2 = .3644 R = .6037		R^2 = .3757 R = .6129	

independently related to other innovation measures, but three of which—percentage of adults with four years of high school, the index of reformism, and the percentage migrant—were not. It should be noted, however, that when the effects of these other thirteen factors are controlled, the direction of the relationship between the education variable and this measure of innovation is opposite from the zero-order relationship both for this measure and the poverty output measure shown in the next column. This again questions the validity of the Crain, Katz, and Rosenthal (1969) contention about citizen participation. The regression coefficient for the inmigration measure is also reversed, thus the opposite of that predicted by the integration theory. The level of output measure for the War on Poverty has a similar configuration with the exception that the reformism and inmigrant measures do not predict to this dependent variable, but the unemployment variable does.

How do we summarize these results? One way is to look for consistencies. Only two factors—percentage nonwhite and age of the city—make independent contributions to the explanation of each of these eight measures of innovation. In each case older cities and cities with many nonwhites have higher levels of innovation. But, the net effect of the ethnicity measure is statistically significant in seven of the eight cases, and ethnicity consistently contributes to higher innovation. City size makes an independent contribution in six of the eight regressions, significant except for public housing and urban renewal. Median family income makes independent contributions to the explanation of innovation in four cases, and in each case the direction of the standardized regression coefficients are the same as for the zero-order ones. Cities having high median family income were slower to innovate and had lower levels of output in the poverty program. Results for other variables are less consistent, and do not show such clear results. These results clearly show the relationships of age, size, and other variables with innovation are not simply a function of the deprivation level of the community.

There is a second way in which we can attempt to summarize these data, and that is to examine the amount of variance that is explained by each cluster of factors operating alone and the amount of variance explained by each cluster after the other five clusters of variables have explained as much of the variance in the dependent variable as they can. The first of these might be referred to as the gross effect of each cluster of variables; the second is the net effect of the eight measures of innovation included in Tables 6, 7, and 8 are displayed in Table 9.

To explain briefly the nature of the data in Table 9, we note first that the fourteen variables in the six clusters of variables can explain 47.16 percent of the variance in the first measure of speed of innovation in public housing. The four indicators of political culture operating alone explain 22.61 percent of the variance in this variable. Similarly, the two measures of concentration of

TABLE 9

GROSS AND NET EFFECTS OF SIX CLUSTERS OF COMMUNITY CHARACTERISTICS IN EXPLAINING EIGHT MEASURES OF COMMUNITY INTEGRATION

Measures of Innovation	Political Culture		Concentration of Community Power		Political Structure		Community Differentiation and Continuity		Community Integration		Poverty	
	Gross Effect	Net Effect	Gross Effect	Net Effect	Gross Effect	Net Effect	Gross Effect	Net Effect	Gross Effect	Net Effect	Gross Effect	Net Effect
Public Housing												
Speed of innovation: number of years before the city entered the public housing program	22.61	.89	19.20	.26	1.10	.03	25.97	9.16	11.42	.04	30.44	3.97
Speed of innovation: number of years before the city entered the public housing program after enabling legislation was enacted	20.73	1.74	10.07	.39	.17	.89	22.65	11.74	6.32	.10	23.81	1.36
Level of output: number of housing units constructed per 100,000 population (natural logarithm)	26.53	1.89	25.61	.38	2.59	.35	17.26	2.20	16.13	.24	29.98	5.12
Urban Renewal												
Speed of innovation: number of years before the city entered the urban renewal program	10.19	2.23	13.45	.54	1.81	.97	35.35	13.62	10.11	.18	19.47	5.74

TABLE 9 (Continued)

Measures of Innovation	Political Culture		Concentration of Community Power		Political Structure		Community Differentiation and Continuity		Community Integration		Poverty	
	Gross Effect	Net Effect	Gross Effect	Net Effect	Gross Effect	Net Effect	Gross Effect	Net Effect	Gross Effect	Net Effect	Gross Effect	Net Effect
Urban Renewal (Continued)												
Speed of innovation: number of years before the city entered the urban renewal program after enabling legislation was enacted	14.96	1.15	10.11	.12	.24	1.71	29.41	12.85	6.28	.31	23.38	3.83
Level of output: number of dollars reserved per capita (natural logarithm)	10.93	1.04	15.35	.91	2.65	.23	23.85	6.48	9.83	.38	15.15	5.18
War on Poverty												
Speed of innovation: date city first awarded poverty funds	11.75	2.82	6.20	.38	3.42	.42	26.62	10.94	4.25	1.07	12.45	2.57
Level of output: number of dollars per capita (natural logarithm)	17.44	4.09	7.40	1.37	3.71	.22	25.06	7.58	5.88	.74	13.34	2.68

community power—MPO Ratio and percentage of adults with a high school education—can alone explain 19.20 percent of the variance in this variable. The two measures of formal political structure can explain only 1.10 percent of the variance when operating alone. The measures of community integration not included in other clusters can alone explain 11.42 percent of the variance in this variable, while the cluster of need and dependency—the index of deprivation and percent of the population that is nonwhite—can alone explain 30.44 percent of the variance in this innovation measure. Since the sum of these amounts of variance explained by each cluster operating alone is much greater than the total amount of 47.16 percent that they can explain jointly, it means that, as we have already noted, these independent variables are not independent of each other. Another kind of question we may ask is how much additional variance a given cluster of variables can explain after the variables in the other five clusters have entered the regression analysis, or, said otherwise, the net effect of each cluster of variables. As also shown in Table 9, the four variables in the political culture cluster explain less than 1.0 percent of additional variance in the first speed of innovation in public housing measure. The clusters of concentration of community power, community integration, and formal political structure can explain even less, i.e., .26, .04, and .03 percent, respectively. But, the two measures of community differentiation and continuity—age and size of city—explain 9.16 additional variance in this measure after the other variables have entered the regression analysis. The two deprivation variables explain an additional 3.97 percent of variance in this measure.

If we examine for each of the eight innovation measures shown in Table 9 the amount of variance explained alone and the amount of variance uniquely explained by each of the six clusters of variables, this same story is generally true for other clusters of variables. The two variables assigned to the community integration cluster have the least explanatory power. Similarly, in no instance can the formal political structure cluster or the concentration of community power cluster explain as much as 2.0 percent of additional variance. The variables in the political culture cluster can add from .89 percent to 4.07 percent of additionally explained variance. The poverty cluster can explain between 1.36 and 5.74 percent of additional variance, and in each instance this is primarily contributed by the nonwhite variable. In five of the eight instances shown in Table 9 the unique effect of the poverty cluster is greater than the political culture cluster. Finally, the cluster that makes the greatest unique contribution is the community differentiation and historical continuity cluster, i.e., the age and size of the city. The amount of additional variance explained ranges from 2.16 percent to 13.62 percent. Only for urban renewal does any other cluster—the poverty cluster—have a greater unique effect. The conclusion that one reaches from these data is that city size and especially age are very strong predictors of these various innovation measures.

If we may return for a moment to the various theories we have discussed, we see that there is once again little support here for the theories of political culture, concentration of community power, community integration, and formal political power. In the case of the political culture hypothesis, the variables that do have significant regression coefficients in Tables 6, 7, and 8—ethnicity, median family income, and Democratic vote—are each in the direction opposite of the prediction. Similarly, in the case of the concentration of community power hypothesis, we note that in no instance does the MPO ratio have an independent effect on innovation once the other city characteristics are controlled. And in the case of the education measure we note that only for the poverty measures does it have an independent relationship with innovation, and here the direction of the standardized regression coefficients is the opposite of that predicted direction, i.e., higher education is associated with innovation. In the case of the community integration thesis, the ethnicity measure is inconsistent with this hypothesis once the other variables are controlled; similarly there is nothing in the regression analysis for city size or middle-class composition that supports this hypothesis. In the case of the unemployment variable, in only one instance is a regression coefficient twice its standard error, and the direction of that relationship is still in the wrong direction. Also in only one instance does inmigration have a regression coefficient twice its standard error, and the direction of that relationship is opposite the prediction. Thus, what fragmentary evidence there was for the community integration thesis is removed in the regression analyses. Finally, for the hypothesis about formal political power we note only one regression coefficient that is twice its standard error, and the direction is opposite of that predicted. In three instances the size of the city council has regression coefficients that are twice its standard error, and the direction of these relationships is not reversed, meaning that in the instance of one speed of innovation measure in public housing and both speed of innovation measures in urban renewal, they are now as hypothesized.

This is the only evidence in support of any of these hypotheses after the regression analyses, but it should be remembered that relationships for city council size were not consistent across all regions. Therefore, there is not sufficient evidence here to accept this hypothesis.

From the analysis of these data, we have found that the same city characteristics—age of city, city size, percentage foreign stock, and nonwhite composition—are most consistently related to the incidence of innovation, speed of entry, and level of output in public housing, urban renewal, and the War on Poverty.

Thus, none of the theories discussed above seems to be appropriate for explaining community innovation in various federal self-help programs. We do not intend to imply that these theories are incorrect for all types of community outputs. It may well be that the nature of community decision-making dynamics and hence the types of community attributes that are related to high community performance in other decision-areas are indeed different. The important point here, however, is that these theories do not appear to be the most appropriate for the range of decisions considered here. But if none of these are, what explanation can be offered for these results? We turn now to an alternative explanation of these data.

An Alternative Explanation. If we review the rejected explanations, we see that global properties of cities such as political culture or ethos, centralization, and integration fared poorly. That is, characteristics of the city as a whole, those which cannot be reduced to properties of groups, organizations, or other subsystems, use concepts most distant from the available data and are not supported by these data. If anything, the findings seem to point in the direction of cities with high outputs having characteristics exactly opposite of centralization, integration, and a public-regarding ethos, at least as indicated by the variables of ethnicity, nonwhite composition, city size, and age as well as the qualitative data on centralization from the works of Aiken (1970) and Clark (1970). For example, Clark's decentralization measure has a correlation coefficient of .30 with ethnicity, .27 with city size, and −.46 with age of city (a high number means a young city). An alternative theory of community innovation—at least for such programs as public housing, urban renewal, and the War on Poverty—must begin with the proposition that the most successful performance in such programs is more frequently attained in decentralized, heterogeneous, differentiated, and fragmented community systems.

Some additional data buttress the conclusion that heterogeneous, differentiated, and decentralized cities with historically continuous populations are more innovative, at least for such programs as these. The demographic and other data just described offer some support for this proposition. The size of a city is only a crude indicator of the degree of structural differentiation and organizational complexity of a community. A more direct way of measuring organizational complexity would be to count the number of organizations of various types that play some role in community life—i.e., the "richness" of organizational life (Stinchcombe, 1965).

We have data on the extensiveness of three types of organizations—manufacturing firms, banks, and trade unions—although for only a subsample of cities in each case.[5]

The sheer number of organizations of various kinds in a community is important, but perhaps more critical is the number of organizations that have sufficient resources at their disposal to have a real impact on community decision-making and hence innovation. For this reason we limited our analysis to the number of manufacturing establishments that have 100 or more employees, and the number of independent banks with assets of $10,000,000 or more.

Finally, we include a measure of the extent of unionization in the community which is the approximate percentage of all plant workers employed in manufacturing establishments in which a union contract covered a majority of workers during the period July 1964 to June 1966. Because of different rates of unionization in the North and South, we show the results separately for 77 Northern and 35 Southern cities.

As shown in Table 10, cities having more manufacturing firms and with more independent banks have a higher incidence of innovation in public housing, urban renewal, and the War on Poverty, entered these programs sooner, and have higher levels of outputs in these programs. Because of so few cases in the North and South, most of the correlations for the unionization data are not statistically significant, but they are all in the predicted direction.

If the number of larger manufacturing firms and independent banks, and the extent of unionization are acceptable as measures of community differentiation, then it is clear that more differentiated communities have higher rates of innovation. That is, cities with more autonomous power centers and in which power is more dispersed are somehow able to have higher rates of innovation in these federal programs. But what is it about such fragmented, decentralized, and differentiated community systems that enable them to enter such programs? The complete answer to this question is beyond the scope of the data included here. Such city characteristics as city size, age, ethnicity, and nonwhite composition may be efficient predictors of innovation, but they belie the kinds of internal community processes that account for higher levels of innovation in such cities. In attempting to answer this question, we can only suggest the kind of concepts and processes that appear to us to be most relevant.

Two kinds of processes seem to be involved. The first concerns the characteristics of community systems that explain how community decision organizations that are critical for the initiation, implementation, and institutionalization of innovations of the kinds that are considered here are created, nurtured, and maintained. We have in mind here the discussion of community decision organizations by Warren (1967a, 1967b) as well as Mohr's (1969) study of public health organizations. The second aspect concerns the internal characteristics of such organizations as well as their relationships with other organizations in their environment—i.e., the "organization set" (Evan, 1966) or task environment (James Thompson, 1967). Certain internal characteristics are more conducive to the effectiveness of such community decision organizations than others. Certainly, the nature of the interrelationships between the community decision organization and other organizations in its environment is of critical importance.

There are three key concepts that seem most relevant for understanding how community decision organizations are created, nurtured, and maintained: the quality and stability of interorganizational linkages, the accumulation of experience and information in a community system (continuity), and structural differentiation.

TABLE 10
DIFFERENTIATION OF ECONOMIC STRUCTURE AND INNOVATION IN
THREE POLICY AREAS

Measures of Innovation	Manufacturing[a]	Banking[b]	Unionization[c]	
			North	South
Public Housing				
Presence of participation in the public housing program since 1933	.19**	.19**	.04	.42*
Speed of Innovation: number of years before the city entered the public housing program	−.40†	−.33†	−.15	−.08
Speed of innovation: number of years before the city entered the public housing program after state enabling legislation	−.34†	−.29†	−.17	−.22
Level of output: number of housing units constructed per 100,000 population (natural logarithm)	.23†	.20**	.05	.43**
Number of cities	212	212	76	35
Urban Renewal				
Presence of participation in the urban renewal program	.28†	.30†	.14	.42*
Speed of innovation: number of years before the city entered the urban renewal program	−.41†	−.39†	−.08	−.42*
Speed of innovation: number of years before the city entered the urban renewal program after enabling legislation was enacted	−.33†	−.31†	−.11	−.20
Level of output: number of dollars reserved per capita (natural logarithm)	.31†	.31†	.18	.35
Number of cities	210	210	74	29
War on Poverty				
Presence of participation in the War on Poverty	.21**	.23**	.19	.16
Speed of innovation: date city was first awarded poverty funds	−.35†	−.35†	−.16	−.17
Level of output: number of dollars per capita (natural logarithm)	.37†	.35†	.13	.18
Number of cities	217	217	77	35

* p < .05   ** p < .01   † p < .001

Interorganizational linkages involve the degree of connectedness between the parts of community systems, and the parts we have in mind here are organizational units, although under some circumstances individuals may also be key actors. By "connectedness" we mean such dimensions as the frequency, scope, and continuity of these linkages or exchanges between organizational actors in a system. These linkages are developed historically through the experience of organizational units, their leaders, and staffs with one another. In some communities the interorganizational linkages will be frequent, broad-ranging, and continuous while in others they will be infrequent, limited in scope, and intermittent. The stability of the population of a community as well as the stability in the existence of organizational actors themselves are likely to be conditions which enhance the extensiveness of those interorganizational link-ages, and hence the potential for community decision organizations to increase their capacity for coordination. Under conditions of instability, however, this capacity is likely to be reduced. Keep in mind here that we are not suggesting that every unit be linked with every other unit; that would really be a return to the community integration thesis. On the contrary, what is important is that there are issue arenas or subsystems in which these linkages occur and that the key organizational actors in these issue arenas are linked to other key organizational actors, in particular city government. It is also important to emphasize that we refer to linkages between autonomous organizational units, since we assume that involvement in interorganizational networks does not necessarily imply any great loss of autonomy. The role of those specialized bureaucracies, i.e., community decision organizations, is likely to be critical for selection of the appropriate organization units, the avoidance of others, and the like. In other words these specialized organizations are likely to carry on continual surveillance and monitoring of their environment, and in a highly

---

NOTES TO TABLE 10
SOURCE: Manufacturing and banking data are for the 217 nonsuburban cities in the size range 25,000 to 250,000 population which had 20 percent or more of their labor force in manufacturing in 1960. See Michael Aiken, "Economic Concentration and Community Innovation," unpublished manuscript, 1969, for details on the construction of measures. The banking data were taken from *Polk's Bank Directory* (Nashville: R. L. Polk and Co., March 1966). The unionization of manufacturing establishments is available for 84 metropolitan areas, which provide an estimate of the trade union level of 112 cities within them. These were taken from Bulletin No. 1465-86, Bureau of Labor Statistics, U.S. Department of Labor, Washington, D.C., October 1966, titled *Wages and Related Benefits: Part I, 84 Metropolitan Areas,* 1965-1966. The measure is the approximate percentage of all plant workers employed in manufacturing establishments in which a union contract covered a majority of workers during the period July 1964 to June 1966. We have assigned the degree of unionization in the SMSA to the urban place, as the best estimate we have of the unionization of the city itself.
a. Number of eastablishments of 100 or more.
b. Number of independent banks with assets of $10,000,000 or more.
c. Percentage of plant workers unionized among all industries.

fragmented community this intelligence can be of profound importance for the selection, activation, and coordination of the appropriate organizations for the establishment of these critical coalitions. If we may return for a moment to the theory of Hawley, what we are suggesting is that if we shift Hawley's unit of analysis from the total community to a given subsystem, albeit a loosely defined subsystem, then perhaps his ideas about concentration of power and coordination are more appropriate, although the MPO Ratio would be of no help in testing this idea. We have therefore suggested some ways in which highly differentiated cities with a wide variety not only of specialized community decision organizations, but also a great diversity of other types of organizations, are likely to be more innovative, at least for the kinds of "sponsored" decisions considered here.

We therefore have argued that three community properties—structural differentiation, the accumulation of experience and information (continuity), and the stability and extensiveness of interorganizational networks—are important factors that affect a community's capacity to generate and sustain innovations. Unfortunately, we do not have direct measures of these concepts, and the argument here is only inferential, but such a thesis does appear to be consistent with our findings about innovation in public housing, urban renewal, and the War on Poverty.

Of course, two additional factors may affect these dynamics, although neither is necessarily inconsistent with the imagery developed here. First, there are the kinds of demand units in a community system. To the extent that a city is characterized by various subgroups which are able to apply pressure on the various community decision organizations—and it does not take much imagination in the beginning of the 1970s to conceive of various dissident citizens battering down the doors of some agencies of city government—or even to the extent that the highly specialized staffs of these various community decisions are able to respond to or even anticipate such needs, there is likely to be a higher rate of attempted as well as successful innovations of the kinds considered here.

But more importantly, American cities are creations of state governments, and some state governments take greater interest in the welfare of their offspring than others. For example, several state governments, particularly in the Northeast, have created development agencies that assist cities in the preparation of applications for federal funds, provide technical and other information that is important in reaching such decisions, and generally encourage and abet cities in efforts such as we have considered in this paper. The link here is likely to be between the specialized agency of state government and the specialized local community decision organization such as the housing authority, the community action agency, or the urban renewal authority. In other words, such a specialized agency of state government is a part of the task environment of the local community decision organization. Dill (1958) calls such organizations "regulators." The fact that such specialized agencies of state government exist to a greater extent in the Northeastern states than elsewhere may account for the very high innovation rates in that region that we observed in Table 2. In any event, these qualifications in no way are inconsistent with the model developed above; quite the contrary, they provide us with examples of how units in the local community other than community decision organizations may be key organizational actors as well as examples of how extra-local units may play key roles in the innovation process.

The degree of historical continuity in a community structure is especially important because of its effect on the state of these interorganizational networks, which in turn is likely to have a profound effect on the potential for innovation and subsequent performance of innovated activities. We presume that in cities that have been in existence for long periods of time existing organizations are more likely to have worked out patterns of accommodation and established alliances, factions, and coalitions with other organizations. In such community systems, the state of knowledge that each organizational actor has about other organizational actors, their orientations, needs, and probable reactions to a given proposal for action is likely to be quite high. Under such circumstances a higher proportion of the potential connections between organizations are likely to have been tested, and there will either be ongoing exchanges between such organizational units or an awareness that the interests, orientations, and needs of the other are often incompatible with their own and, therefore, that these units are not potential partners for a new enterprise. This is often the case when given organizational actors have identical goals or activities (Guetzkow, 1966). That is, the more similar given organizational units are, the less likely they will be able to sustain cooperative actions and the higher the potential for conflict between them. In summary, we conclude that the degree of historical continuity in a community system has important effects on the state of interorganizational linkages and, therefore, the potential for coordination and innovation in community systems.

Finally, the degree of structural differentiation and sheer organizational complexity of a community also has important effects on the potential for innovation. First, large cities are richer in organizational resources, not only economic, political, or similar such organizations, but they also are more likely to have more community decision organizations with specific responsibilities for given areas of interest. Larger cities are more likely to have a redevelopment agency, a housing agency, a community action agency, a city development agency for model cities, welfare councils, a planning agency, municipal health and welfare departments, boards of education, and similar organizations (cf. Warren, 1967a, 1967b). Such organizations often have specific mandates concerning various problem areas. To the extent that the city is sufficiently large to have many of these specialized community decision organizations, it is likely to be more innovative. But there is a second aspect to city size. Such organizations are likely to have larger, more specialized, and more professionalized staffs that have more technical, administrative and political knowledge as well as greater resources, qualities that are important not only for innovation within these organizations (cf. Hage and Aiken, 1968; Victor Thompson, 1965; Kahn et al., 1964) but also for innovations in the community sponsored by these organizations, especially innovations that require the activation or exploitation of interorganizational linkages and the creation of critical coalitions. Still another implication of differentiation is that it is precisely in larger, more heterogeneous, and more fragmented cities that it will be easiest to establish these critical coalitions. We make the very important assumption here that it is probably not necessary to mobilize all the key organizational units in a city in order to push through an innovation in a decision like urban renewal, but rather that a coalition that includes a limited number of organizational units can often suffice to bring about a successful innovation. This means that in large, highly differentiated cities there will be a lower proportion of existing key organizations that actually participate in such decisions and that there will be a considerable degree of latitude in the selection of organizations for these coalitions.

Let us now turn briefly to the concepts that are most appropriate for understanding the second perspective, that of characteristics of organizational structures and their interorganizational field. Community systems can be viewed as interorganizational fields (Turk, 1970) in which the basic interacting units are centers of power, although as we indicated above demand units such as citizens' groups may also be centers of power in communities. A center of power can be defined as an organization or unit which possesses a high degree of autonomy, resources, and cohesion. We call the linking mechanisms among centers of power in a community interfaces (cf. Wren, 1967), and, as we indicated above, interfaces can be distinguished in terms of their frequency, scope, and continuity. Interfaces, however, are more than the current set of linkages among organizations in a community; they also include the historical accumulation of knowledge and experience. An issue arena is defined as the participating units (usually centers of power) in the organization set; if we use a community decision organization as the center of gravity of an issue arena, then an issue arena is the same idea as a task environment (Dill, 1958; J. Thompson, 1967). As we indicated above, it is not necessary to activate all organizations for a given decision; in many instances a delimited set of organizations will suffice to insure the successful implementation of an innovation. We do not imply that this process always occurs smoothly or without conflict; conflict and controversy may often surround such decisions. What this would mean is that the issue arena has been enlarged, but not at the initiation of the community decision organization. Obviously, in such instances the state of interfaces in the now enlarged issue arena may not be sufficiently extensive to insure a positive outcome, and the proposed innovation may never come about. But, we would argue, for the range of decision considered here, this is probably not the typical course of events, in spite of the great degree of controversy that has surrounded a program like urban renewal in some cities.

To be more specific, we hypothesize that the greater the number of centers of power in a community and the more pervasive, encompassing, and continuous are the interfaces, the higher the probability that a proposed community innovation will be successful. The reasoning for this hypothesis has already been discussed. The more centers of power there are in a community, the more there are specialized community decision organizations, and the more extensive. There are linkages within and between issue arenas, the higher the probability that there will be a coalition of actors sufficient to make a positive decision and initiate, implement, and institutionalize a given community innovation. Of course, this is explicitly a statement about innovation in a comparative study of communities, and it is not intended to apply to individual cases. It may also not be applicable for the largest American cities such as New York or Chicago. Whether cities of over 500,000 are included or excluded in our study had little effect on our findings. This is not to suggest that the dynamics of decision-making in such cities is unimportant, but rather that our hypothesis does not necessarily apply to the largest American cities, perhaps those with populations of 500,000 or more. In such cities there are likely to be emergent properties, meaning that additional theoretical elements may be necessary to understand fully these more complex, differentiated systems.

Another important theoretical implication is that the dependent variable must be disaggregated as well as the independent variables. That is, the concept of "community innovation" contains the implication that innovation is a property of the community as a whole, like "power structure" and "community ethos." But just as there seems to be reason to hypothesize that such concepts as differentiation and heterogeneity, which refer to the multiplicity of "demand units" in a city, more appropriately describe the independent variables, so we must find some way of characterizing the dependent variable in a way which does not assume global properties. Our procedure, inevitably, has aggregated the numbers of programs and the amount of funds into overall measures of "innovation" for the city as a whole. This procedure should not conceal our belief that these programs are a mosaic of diverse and uncoordinated programs which have been established sequentially, in response to the availability of federal funds, and have no necessary relationship to the welfare of the community as a whole or that of any specific client group.

More specifically, the incentives for the professional staff members of the various organizations to develop grant proposals, demonstration projects, and programs of many kinds should not be assumed to be that of bringing innovations to the community at large. It is entirely possible that these projects are established to maintain and extend the professional prestige, financial resources, and local influence of the organizations and groups which apply for the funds.

And we do not wish to imply that the consequences of the establishing of these programs are for the benefit of the community as a whole. The competition for external resources which leads to a proliferation of such programs may also result in duplicate, overlapping, expensive programs which bring few benefits to their alleged clients.

But such programs must be presented as benefiting the community at large. The rhetoric and symbolism of all three of these programs—public housing, urban renewal, poverty—has been loaded with the aura of the public interest. However, if public housing has largely benefited the construction and banking industries and exacerbated the problems of crowding in the ghettos, if urban renewal has largely torn down housing for the poor without replacing it, and if the poverty programs have been superficial in their approach to the basic problems of jobs, education, and community participation in decision-making, these programs can hardly be regarded as innovations in the sense that they have improved the conditions of life of the people affected by them.

We raise this point here obviously not to settle this issue, but only to indicate that the complex question of the consequences of these programs is a vital one, and connected in a subtle way to the concept of innovation. It may be that innovations which challenge the powers, resources, and functions of established institutions are throttled by the same interorganizational mechanisms which function well to bring in programs which feed the prestige, power, and income of existing interest groups. Investigation of such questions should be high on the agenda of future community research.

Finally, a word about cross-national comparative studies of community decision-making innovation, and performance. It is our suspicion that the sort of imagery we have developed here may be appropriate only under the conditions of a high degree of autonomy, not only for local governments, but for other actors in community systems. If we were able to develop a continuum which measured the degree of autonomy not only of local governmental units, but also of other actors in such community systems, the United States and perhaps Switzerland would probably come out on one extreme of that continuum. In Western Europe, Spain would perhaps come out on the other end of that continuum, with France and Italy nearby (cf. Humes and Martin, 1969). Countries like Belgium, The Netherlands, or the United Kingdom would be somewhere between these two extremes. What this means is that the context of both national government and the prevailing historical, cultural, political, and social traditions are likely to be important contingencies that any cross-national comparative perspective must consider. In the present study this means that while we are of the opinion that a conscious recognition of the great fragmentation, diversity, and differentiation of American cities is necessary for any theoretical framework that pretends to explain policy outputs, such a theoretical approach may not be appropriate if one changes the assumptions about the national political system or the prevailing cultural and social traditions. The state of knowledge about innovation in and performance of community systems in other national contexts is just too limited to pursue this line of reasoning in greater detail at this time. In conclusion, we specifically acknowledge the limitations on the model we have suggested here.

NOTES

1. Information about participation of communites in the public housing program is taken from Report S-11A, Consolidated Development Directory, U.S. Department of Housing and Urban Development, Washington, D.C., 1967, and from the files of the Housing Assistance Administration.

2. Because this distribution was so skewed toward the upper end of the distribution, the natural logarithm transformation of this distribution was computed (after adding a constant of 1 per 100,000 since there is no natural logarithm transformation of zero). The mean of the transformed distribution was 4.11 with a standard deviation 3.35. Unless otherwise indicated, the transformed distribution was used in all the statistical analyses.

3. We have included in this part of the analysis the 582 cities in states that permitted cities to enter the urban renewal programs previous to 1958 and those cities in existence in 1950. Seventy-four of the 676 cities were omitted because they were located in eleven states without enabling legislation until 1958 or later (Idaho, Montana, New Mexico, Utah, and Wyoming), or which had highly restrictive enabling legislation, reversals of decision, or no enabling legislation at all as of June 30, 1966, or had a combination of these (Florida, Louisiana, Maryland, Mississippi, Oklahoma, and South Carolina). Twenty additional cities that did not exist in 1950 were also excluded. Information about participation in the urban renewal program was taken from the Urban Renewal Directory, June 30, 1966 (U.S. Department of Housing and Urban Development, Washington, D.C.).

4. Since this measure was so skewed toward the upper end of the distribution, it was also transformed into its natural logarithm (after multiplying by 100 and adding a constant of one cent), yielding a distribution slightly skewed toward the lower end of the scale. This transformed distribution had a mean of 4.02 and a standard deviaion of 2.71. Unless otherwise stated, the natural logarithm transformation of this variable is used in all subsequent analyses.

5. Manufacturing and banking data are available for the 217 nonsuburban cities in the size range 25,000 to 250,000 population which had 20 percent or more of their labor force in manufacturing in 1960. The unionization of manufacturing establishments is available for 84 metropolitan areas, which provides an estimate of the unionization of the 112 cities within them. Unfortunately, we do not have comparable information for other, more critical, types of organizations such as political parties, community decision organizations, voluntary associations, or the like.

REFERENCES

AGGER, R., D. GOLDRICH, and B. E. SWANSON (1964) The Rulers and the Ruled. New York: John Wiley.

AIKEN, M. (1970) "The distribution of community power: structural bases and social consequences," in M. Aiken and P. E. Mott (eds.) The Structure of Community Power: Readings. New York: Random House.

——— and R. R. ALFORD (1970a) "Community structure and innovation: the case of urban renewal." American Sociological Review 35 (August): 650-665.

——— (1970b) "Community structure and innovation: the case of public housing." American Political Science Review 64 (September): 843-864.

AIKEN, M. and J. HAGE (1968) "Organizational interdependence and intraorganizational structure." American Sociological Review 33 (December): 912-930.

ALFORD, R. R. and E. C. LEE (1968) "Voting turnout in American cities." American Political Science Review 62 (September): 796-813.

ANDERSON, M. (1964) The Federal Bulldozer: A Critical Analysis of Urban Renewal. Cambridge, Mass.: MIT Press.

BANFIELD, E. C. and J. Q. WILSON (1963) City Politics. Cambridge, Mass.: Harvard Univ. Press.

BARTH, E.A.T. (1961) "Community influence systems: structure and change." Social Forces 40 (October): 58-63.

BELLUSH, J. and M. HAUSKNECHT (1967) Urban Renewal: People, Politics, and Planning. Garden City, N.Y.: Doubleday Anchor.

CLARK, T. N. (1970) "Structure communautaire, prise de decision, depenses budgetaires, et renovation urbaine dans 51 communautes amercaines." Amonagement du territoire du developpement regional, III. Grenoble: Institut d'etudes politiques: 179-219.

——— (1968) "Community structure, decision-making, budget expenditures, and urban renewal in 51 American communities." American Sociological Review 33 (August): 576-593.

——— et al. (1968) "Discipline, method, community structure, and decision-making: the role and limitation of the sociology of knowledge." American Sociologist 3 (August): 214-217.

COLEMAN, J. A. (1957) Community Conflict. New York: Free Press.

CRAIN, R. L. and D. B. ROSENTHAL (1967) "Community status as a dimension of local decision-making." American Sociological Review 32 (December): 970-984.

——— E. KATZ, and D. B. ROSENTHAL (1969) The Politics of Community Conflict: The Fluoridation Decision. Indianapolis: Bobbs-Merrill.

DAHL, R. A. (1961) Who Governs? Power and Democracy in an American City. New Haven: Yale Univ. Press.

D'ANTONIO, W. V. and W. H. FORM (1965) Influentials in Two Broder Cities: A Study in Community Decision-making. South Bend, Ind.: Univ. of Notre Dame Press.

——— C. P. LOOMIS, and E. C. ERICKSON (1961) "Institutional and occupational representation in eleven community influence systems." American Sociological Review 26 (June): 440-446.

DILL, W. M. (1958) "Environment as an influence on magerial autonomy." Administrative Science Quarterly 2 (March): 409-443.

DYE, T. R. (1968) "Urban school segregation: a comparative analysis." Urban Affairs Quarterly 4 (December): 141-165.

EVAN, W. M. (1966) "The organization-set: toward a theory of inter-organizational relations," in J. D. Thompson (ed.) Approaches to Organizational Design. Pittsburgh: Univ. of Pittsburgh Press.

——— and G. BLACK (1967) "Innovation in business organizations: some factors associated with success or failure of staff proposals." Journal of Business 40 (October): 519-530.

GANS, H. (1962) The Urban Villagers. New York: Free Press.

GILBERT, C. W. (1968a) "The study of community power: a summary and a test," in S. Greer et al. (eds.) The New Urbanization. New York: St. Martin's Press.

——— (1968b) "Community power and decision-making: a quantitative examination of previous research," in T. N. Clark (ed.) Community Structure and Decision-Making: Comparative Analysis. San Francisco: Chandler.

——— (1967) "Some trends in community politics: a secondary analysis of power structure data from 166 communities." Southwestern Social Science Quarterly 48 (December): 373-381.

GREENSTONE, J. D. and P. E. PETERSON (1968) "Reformers, machines, and the war on poverty," in J. Q. Wilson (ed.) City Politics and Public Policy. New York: John Wiley.

GUETZKNOW, H. (1966) "Relations among organizations," pp. 13-44 in R. V. Bowers (ed.) Studies on Behavior in Organizations. Athens: Univ. of Georgia Press.

HAGE, J. and M. AIKEN (1967) "Program change and organizational properties: a comparative analysis." American Journal of Sociology 72 (March): 503-519.

HAWLEY, A. H. (1963) "Community power structure and urban renewal success." American Journal of Sociology 68 (January): 422-431.

HUMES, S. and E. MARTIN (1969) The Structure of Local Government. The Hague: International Union of Local Authorities.

HUNTER, F. (1953) Community Power Structure. Chapel Hill: Univ. of North Carolina Press.

JACOB, H. and M. LIPSKY (1968) "Outputs, structure, and power: an assessment of the changes in the study of state and local politics." Journal of Politics 30 (May): 510-538.

KAHN, R. L., D. L. WOLFE, R. P. QUINN, and J. D. SNOEK (1964) Organizational Stress: Studies in Role Conflict and Ambiguity. New York: John Wiley.

KAMMERER, G. M., C. D. FARRIS, J. M. DeGROVE, and A. B. CLUBOK (1963) The Urban Political Community: Profiles in Town Politics. Boston: Houghton Mifflin.

LINEBERRY, R. L. and E. P. FOWLER (1967) "Reformism and public policies in American cities." American Political Science Review 61 (September): 701-716.

LOWI, T. J. (1964) "American business, public policy, case studies, and political theory." World Politics 16 (July): 677-715.

MANSFIELD, E. (1963) "The speed of response of firms to new techniques." Quarterly Journal of Economics 22 (May): 290-311.

MILLER, D. C. (1958a) "Industry and community power structure: a comparative study of an American and English city." American Sociological Review 23 (February): 9-15.

——— (1958b) "Decision-making cliques in community power structures: a comparative study of an American and an English city." American Journal of Sociology 64 (November): 299-309.

MOHR, L. B. (1969) "Determinants of innovation in organization." American Political Science Review 63 (March): 111-126.

MORRISON, D. E. and R. E. HENKEL (1969) "Significance tests reconsidered." American Sociologist 4 (May): 131-139.

MYTINGER, R. L. (1968) Innovations in Local Health Services. Arlington, Va.: U.S. Department of Health, Education and Welfare Public Health Service.

Office of Economic Opportunity (1966) Information Book as of June 30, 1966. Washington, D.C.

PINARD, M. (1963) "Structural attachments and political support in urban politics: a case of a fluoridation referendum." American Journal of Sociology 68 (March): 513-526.

POLSBY, N. W. (1969) "Pluralism in the study of community power, or erklarung before verklarung in wissenssoziologie." American Sociologist 4 (May): 118-122.

PERRUCCI, R. and M. PILISUK (1970) "Leaders and ruling elites: the interorganizational bases of community power." American Sociological Review 35 (December): 1040-1057.

SALISBURY, R. H. (1968) "The analysis of public policy: a search for theories and roles," pp. 151-175 in A. Ranney (ed.) Political Science and Public Policy. Chicago: Markham.

SOGG, W. S. and W. WERTHEIMER (1967) "Legal and governmental issues in urban renewal," in J. Q. Wilson (ed.) Urban Renewal: The Record and Controversy. Cambridge, Mass.: MIT Press.

STINCHCOMBE, A. L. (1968) Constructing Social Theories. New York: Harcourt, Brace and World.

––– (1965) "Social structure and organizations," in J. G. March (ed.) Handbook of Organizations. Chicago: Rand McNally.

STRAITS, B. C. (1965) "Community adoption and implementation of urban renewal." American Journal of Sociology 71 (July): 77-82.

TERREBERRY, S. (1968) "The evolution of organizational environments." Administrative Science Quarterly 12 (March): 590-613.

THOMPSON, J. (1967) Organizations in Action. New York: McGraw-Hill.

THOMPSON, V. A. (1965) "Bureaucracy and innovation." Administrative Science Quarterly 10 (June): 1-20.

TURK, H. (1970) "Interorganizational networks in urban society: initial perspectives and comparative research." American Sociological Review 35 (February): 1-19.

U.S. Department of Housing and Urban Development (1967) Report S-11A. Consolidated Development Directory. Washington, D.C.: Statistical Branch, Housing Assistance Administration.

––– (1966) Urban Renewal Directory: June 30, 1966. Washington, D.C.

WALKER, J. (1969) "The adoption of innovations by the American states." American Political Science Review 63 (September): 880-899.

WALTON, J. (1970) "A systematic survey of community power research," in M. Aiken and P. Mott (eds.) The Structure of Community Power: Readings. New York: Random House.

––– (1966a) "Substance and artifact: the current status of research on community power structure." American Journal of Sociology 71 (January): 430-438.

––– (1966b) "Discipline, method, and community power: a note on the sociology of knowledge." American Sociological Review 31 (October): 684-689.

WARREN, R. L. (1967a) "Interaction of community decision organizations: some basic concepts and needed research." Social Service Review 41 (September): 261-270.

––– (1967b) "The interorganizational field as a focus for investigation." Administrative Science Quarterly 12 (December): 396-419.

WILLIAMS, O. P. and C. R. ADRIAN (1963) Four Cities: A Study in Comparative Policy Making. Philadelphia: Univ. of Pennsylvania Press.

WILSON, J. Q. (1966a) "Innovation in organization: notes toward a theory," in J. D. Thompson (ed.) Approaches to Organizational Design. Pittsburgh: Univ. of Pittsburgh Press.

––– (1966b) Communication to the editor. American Political Science Review 60 (December): 998-999.

——— (1964) "Public-regardingness as a value premise in voting behavior." American Political Science Review 58 (December): 876-887.

WINCH, R. F. and D. T. CAMPBELL (1969) "The significance of tests of significance." American Sociologist 4 (May): 140-143.

WOLFINGER, R. E. and J. O. FIELD (1966) "Political ethos and the structure of city government." American Political Science Review 60 (June): 308-326.

WREN, D. A. (1967) "Interface and interorganizational coordination." Academy of Management Journal 10 (March): 69-81.

Chapter 10

Diversity and Integration in the Yugoslav Commune

Eugen Pusić

Local government on the continent of Europe is a many-layered product of social development. Many historical tendencies come together in its institutions, leaving their recognizable deposits, many goals and purposes, successively and simultaneously, have shaped and are shaping its structure, determining its profile.

The memories of feudal estates, of city liberties, of primary local isolation and of self-sufficiency in poverty are alive in many places just as the hopes of a better society through local pluralism and self-government are exercising their pull from the future. The present expects local government to provide services of growing variety and complexity for an urbanizing society, to function as local outposts of central administrations, to be a platform for participation, a link between the individual and the increasingly alienated and alienating organizational behemoths populating our world.

Local government in Europe, generally, is much more of a social crossroads than in America, where the different functions have remained to a greater extent distinct from each other, embodied in special districts, in local branch offices of federal departments, in privately or corporately owned and operated service networks, in national political parties.

One of the consequences is the different position of local government research in Europe and the United States. In America local government is one among many arenas in which the answer to the question "who governs?" must be sought. The problem is to get the interaction of different structures into proper focus. In Europe local government is, to a greater extent, the focus of many ideas, expectations, forces, activities. The problem is to disentangle the various functions of the same structure.

I

In the case of Yugoslavia the interplay of past, present and future in the shaping of local government is particularly vivid.

As in most parts of Eastern Europe, the feudal past as a system persists in Yugoslavia deep into the nineteenth century while its consequences, in ideas as well as actual structure, are felt in the political and economic upheavals of the twentieth century. The eastern half of Yugoslavia was for centuries part of the Ottoman empire, with its exploitative, military feudalism, its sharp cleavage between the Moslem rulers and their non-Moslem subjects, its mentality of a foreign, though permanent, occupying force, its basically nomadic and rustic lack of sympathy with the city and urban development. The role of the local units, a territorial expression of the traditional clan, and tribal structures as well as the family cooperatives of the Slavic herdsmen and peasants, was in a sense complementary to the attitude of the Ottoman invaders and occupiers. Organizations for self-help and self-defense, the local units were, for a long time, semi-legal or illegal from the point of view of the Ottoman administration. Centuries of this ambivalent relationship where "normal" local functions such as road building or arbitration in local disputes went together with armed resistance qualified as banditry by the Turkish authorities bred in the population an opposition to and a mistrust of central government which did not disappear when the national state came to replace the hated foreign conqueror.

At the same time the North West of present-day Yugoslavia was a part of feudal Europe embodied in the Habsburg monarchy ruling from Austria over Slovenia, Croatia, Hungary, Bohemia, and other countries. The local unit, the village, as elsewhere, was caught in the perpetual dilemma between allegiance to its feudal lord and resistance to his oppression and exploitation. In the bleak world of the serf, the city, free from its immediate feudal environment and subject to the distant king and emperor, was a haven of liberty exercising attraction long before industrial development added its economic inducements.

In the south, on the shores of the Adriatic, the old Greek and Roman settlements had developed, after Mediterranean fashion, into city-republics ruled by councils of their citizen-families and maintaining, sometimes, by all the stratagems of statecraft, a more or less precarious independence against much stronger political and military forces in their neighborhood.

This manifold heritage was then exposed, first, to the influence of industrial and administrative urbanization and to the doctrine and practice of local self-government in the classical sense where local units had to embody simultaneously the roles, to an extent contradictory, of disciplined parts in central administrative networks and autonomous defenders of individual local liberties against central might. Lately the opposition became even more pronounced. On the one hand is Marx's ideal of the commune, the free association of producers, self-governed, preferably by methods of direct democracy, and only loosely federated with other similarly sovereign communes into progressively more encompassing associations.

On the other hand, however, are attempts at a centrally planned and administered economy, where all local independence must be subordinated to central law and directive. All this is present in local government in Yugoslavia today, but not everywhere to the same extent; every single feature is changing but not always at the same rate.

II

In spite of existing actual variety the formal development of local government in Yugoslavia after World War II went in the direction of growing uniformity. From four main types of local unit—commune, city, district, region—today only one is left, the commune. Its organization has standard features fixed in the federal Constitution. A bicameral communal assembly, one chamber—the Commune Council—elected by general franchise, the other—the Council of Working Organizations—by all voters employed in any enterprise, institution or agency. A president elected by the assembly among its members for the same four-year term as the assembly itself. A number of executive councils, corresponding to the main departments of local government, composed of members of the assembly, citizens co-opted by the assembly, into an executive council, and citizens delegated to it by enterprises, institutions and nongovernmental organizations. A secretary appointed by the assembly from candidates participating in a public competition for the post, coordinating a number of administrative units and associated agencies.[1]

The other basic trend in the development of local government in Yugoslavia during the last 25 years was the consistent growth in size of the basic unit. The same territory was divided in 1945 into nearly 12,000 local People's Committees—as the basic local units were then called—and encompassed in 1970 only 500 communes. The communes had to establish auxiliary structures and territorial subdivisions, such as Local Communities or Local Offices, but it is understood that these are only forms of implementing direct self-government or assisting in tasks of communal administration; they are not units of local government. Table 1 illustrates both trends.

The third main feature in the development of Yugoslav local government, finally, is the growing autonomy of institutions and service-agencies within the commune from communal administration. After practically the whole non-agricultural economy was nationalized by two federal laws—in 1946 and 1948—all enterprises up to a certain size were managed and coordinated by local government. Local administration was then directly responsible for the

TABLE 1
TRENDS IN DEVELOPMENT OF LOCAL GOVERNMENT IN YUGOSLAVIA

Year	Region	Districts	Cities	Communes	Local People's Committees
1946	2	407	81	–	11,556
1947	2	338	85	–	7,886
1948	1	339	88	–	7,967
1949	23	344	198	–	7,782
1950	20	360	236	–	7,101
1951	–	360	236	–	7,104
1952	–	327	265	3,811	–
1953	–	327	264	3,904	–
1954	–	329	268	3,912	–
1955	–	107	–	1,479	–
1956	–	107	–	1,479	–
1957	–	106	–	1,441	–
1958	–	95	–	1,193	–
1959	–	91	–	1,103	–
1960	–	75	–	839	–
1961	–	75	–	782	–
1962	–	75	–	759	–
1963	–	40	–	581	–
1964	–	40	–	577	–
1965	–	40	–	577	–
1966	–	23	–	516	–
1967	–	17	–	510	–
1968	–	–	–	501	–

SOURCE: *Statistical Yearbook of the Socialist Federal Republic of Yugoslavia*, 1968, p. 62.

supervision, direction, organization, staffing and budgeting of all enterprises, institutions and agencies in its territory except those that were, because of their importance, attached directly to state or federal departments.

After 1950, when worker self-management was introduced in enterprises, government lost its role of manager and its functions in the economy were gradually reduced to general regulation, framework planning, and financing investment or initiating new enterprises that were, however, from the moment of their establishment managed by their employees. The same system was then extended to all institutions and agencies, so that public services—such as health, education, public utilities, local transportation, social welfare, libraries, museums, theatres, etc.—based on networks of institutions, or enterprises (designated collectively as "working organizations") one after the other became to a large extent independent of local or central administration. They are managed by councils elected for two years by their employees among themselves and by directors appointed by the councils for four-year periods. Local government has general competence to regulate their activities through local by-laws, to approve their rates, and to intervene directly only in case of a breach of law. The services are financed by dues charged to the users or by special funds, fed by earmarked taxes, independent from the local budget.

The assumption is that the self-managed institutions and enterprises should have, in local government, a higher-level self-management platform where they coordinate their activities and adjust their mutual interests and those of their clients and users through their own delegates in the respective executive councils and in the council of working organizations.

III

Research on Yugoslav local government is oriented towards the three points indicated as dominating its recent development: to explore existing variety among local units and its consequences, to test the assumptions underlying their constant expansion in size, and to investigate the difference between local government and the self-management of institutions and enterprises.

The span of variety among Yugoslav communes is visible from general statistical data[2] as illustrated in Table 2. The first question is: how do existing differences combine into patterns and what types of communes emerge from this combination? For an answer to this question, a principal component analysis of 25 basic variables for all 516 Yugoslav communes as well as a principal component analysis and a factor analysis of 50 basic variables for 111 communes in one federated republic, Croatia, was undertaken.[3] The list of basic variables is attached as Appendix I. The subsequent discussion refers primarily to the analysis of the 111 communes of Croatia.

Factor I emerging from the analysis is clearly related to the dimension of industrialization and urbanization. The factor loadings, before and after rotation are presented in Table 3. The factor accounts for 24 percent of the total variance. Among the 25 communes ranking highest on this factor 18 are cities and large industrial centers, 6 are important seaside resorts, and 1 is a mining town. The process of rotation according to the Varimax criterion (7 iteration cycles) tends to emphasize the economic indicators of industrialization. There is, however, reason to keep in mind the following remark: "The nature of the Varimax criterion is such that general factors, if originally present in the principal component solution, tend to be 'destroyed' during rotation." (W. W. Colley and P. R. Lohnes: Multivariate Procedures for the Behavioural Sciences. New York: John Wiley & Sons, 1962, p. 172)

Of the remaining 9 factors that were subject to rotation and account together for another 41 percent of the total variance, 4 are related to the kind of urban or industrial character displayed and 4 to rural areas under the influence of beginning industrial transformation or the attraction exercized by large cities in

TABLE 2
GENERAL STATISTICAL DATA ON VARIETY AMONG YUGOSLAV COMMUNES

Indicators	Span of Difference
1. Area	11 communes under 50 sq km/18 over 1,200 sq km
2. Rural population	28 communes under 10%/66 over 80%
3. Industrial employment	57 communes under 10%/8 over 70%
4. Fixed assets (except agricultural land)	21 communes under 10 mill./19 over 2,000 mill. dinars
5. National income, per capita	20 communes under 1,000 din./25 over 10,000 dinars
6. Retail trade—shops	2 communes under 10/66 over 200
7. Retail trade—turnover per capita	3 communes under 220 din./48 over 3,660 dinars
8. Commune budget	13 communes under 2,5 mill./18 over 50 mill. dinars
9. Expenditures for schools	2 communes under 500,000/47 over 13 mill. dinars
10. Expenditure for health services	37 communes under 500,000/12 over 40 mill. dinars
11. No. of schools	11 communes under 4/62 over 50 mill. dinars
12. No. of doctors	234 communes under 10/5 over 500 mill. dinars
13. No. of hospital beds	137 communes under 50/66 over 500 mill. dinars
14. No. of TV subscribers	17 communes under 100/17 over 16,000 mill. dinars

SOURCE: *Statistical Yearbook of Yugoslavia, 1970, pp. 503-509.*

their vicinity, or, finally, by the general climate of change prevailing in the country, while one is composed of rural and urban communes. The factor loadings (after rotation), on basic variables, of 0.25 and larger, for each factor are listed in Appendix II.

The types of communes that emerge can eventually all be understood as stages of development together with an aggregate of specific circumstances for each. The poor rural commune with strong demographic pressures foreshadowing migratory movements if economic development within the commune should not provide, in the near future, increased employment, education and interests to the growing young generation (Factor V). Of the top-ranking 10 communes on that component, 5 are so near to large cities that they will be eventually swallowed by the urban agglomeration.

The large rural commune in which the attraction of the nearby large city is felt already in various ways, e.g., the drain of trained and educated manpower. If any are left in the commune they are not employed in local government (Factor

II). Of the 10 top-ranking communes 2 are actually suburbs with a large rural area included and the remaining 8 are in the immediate vicinity of industrial cities.

Places existing around and depending on single industrial developments built in a rural environment, still traditional in their attitudes, exposed to stresses, expressed in intermittent employment, following the ups and downs in their narrow economic base (Factor IV). Two of the top-ranking 10 communes are mining-towns, 2 depend on textile production, 1 on ship-building.

The communes representing areas of tourism and recreation, organized around this industry, with skilled workers in tertiary activities (hotels and catering) and high on the characteristic equipment of their trade (TV) (Factor VII). Three of the top-ranking 4 communes are islands in the Adriatic.

There is a mixed group of rural and urban communes factoring around the characteristics of administrative efficiency (Factor VIII). The rest are all oriented on the dimension of urban development, differing among themselves as to the type of industry dominating their economy, as to wealth, as to the dynamism of their growth. There are traditional cities with older industries, slower in their movement, but with comparatively good administration (Factor II), or places based on labor intensive industries with a semi-skilled work force and low productivity (Factor IX). The typical industrial suburb (Factor VI). The growing town round a dynamic industry (Factor X).

The quality of local government seems little related to any of the main types.[4] Characteristics of administrative efficiency represent a factor in themselves (VIII), and the correlation of these indicators with other important variables of development, size or wealth is, on the whole, insignificant (see Table 4). Only the educational level of the personnel in local administration tends to respond to the level of development and wealth of the commune and to follow the educational pattern existing in the general population.

The assumptions behind the constant trend towards an increasing size of local units in Yugoslavia on the dimensions both of area and population (see Table 1) were those widely shared by lay and professional opinion the world over.[5] Particularly, it is believed that an increase in size results automatically in an improvement of the financial position of the commune, assuring more abundant resources and, in this way, a better quality of local administration and the possibility of greater independence and autonomy in relation to central government. There is, however—so the assumption goes—a price to pay for this increasing affluence of the larger unit, there is less participation in local affairs by the inhabitants of the distant periphery, less interest for local government, less knowledge about it.

This hypothesis was tested first by the factor analysis mentioned in the previous section. In addition, 825 citizens in a predominantly rural commune, chosen for its relatively poor roads and unfavorable communication possibilities between center and periphery, were interviewed on their interests in relation to

TABLE 3
FACTOR LOADINGS

Basic Variable	Before Rotation (only 0.25 and higher)	After Rotation
1. Area	−.28	−.20
3. Employed in agriculture	−.77	−.63
5. Infant mortality	−.35	−.32
6. Employed outside agriculture	.71	.60
7. Employed in mining and industry	.33	.08
8. Fixed assets except agricultural land	.74	.78
9. Gross investment	.81	.90
10. Per capita income in commune	.83	.88
11. Revenues of local government	.50	.70
12. School funds	.43	.52
13. Farm land	−.48	−.33
14. Apartments built	.38	.15
15. Automobiles	.70	.62
16. Retail trade	.80	.83
17. Tax on hotels and restaurants	.53	.55
18. Percentage of population in elementary school	−.54	−.36
19. Movie visits	.79	.83
20. T.V. sets	.64	.48
21. Doctors	.90	.73
22. Population	.80	.72
26. Personnel in local administration with university education −required by job plan	.49	.28
27. −actual	.58	.32
33. Personnel with elementary education− actual	−.56	−.28
35. Local budget material expenditure	−.35	−.21
36. Women employed	.30	.31
37. Highly skilled workers (in population)	.47	.26
38. Skilled workers	.39	.19
40. Unskilled workers	−.53	−.27
41. Population without completed elementary school	−.44	−.29
43. Population with secondary education	.73	.70
45. Population with university education	.78	.59
50. Employed in scientific and research activities	.63	.40

TABLE 4
CORRELATION OF INDICATORS WITH OTHER DEVELOPMENT VARIABLES

	Inhabitants per Employee in Local Government 23	Items Received in Local Adm. per Inhab. 24	Items Transacted in Local Adm. per Employee 25	Employees with University Education 27	Employees with Elementary Education 33	Local Budget-Personnel 34
1. Area	.16	−.05	.19	.10	.13	−.08
8. Capital Assets	−.004	−.04	−.03	.35	−.27	−.04
9. Gross Investment	−.06	−.004	−.08	.37	−.31	.02
10. Per Capita National Income	.04	−.06	−.04	.37	−.34	−.05
11. Per Capita Local Budget	−.07	.08	.02	.25	−.08	.02
12. Per Capita Expenditure Schools	.00	−.008	−.05	.20	−.22	.05
15. Automobiles	−.02	−.10	−.17	.29	−.29	.11
16. Turnover in retail trade	−.08	.04	−.06	.36	−.37	.05
19. Cinema Visits	−.04	.04	−.01	.30	−.34	.03
20. Number of T.V. Sets	.07	−.10	−.07	.50	−.45	.05
21. Number of Doctors	.12	−.10	−.01	.46	−.37	.11
22. Population	.51	−.18	.31	.26	−.29	.04
27. Percentage of Work-force highly skilled	.10	−.11	.03	.24	−.34	−.03
40. Percentage of Work-force unskilled	.06	.08	.09	−.32	.40	.01
41. Percentage of Population Without Completed Elementary Education	.06	−.04	−.07	−.34	.21	−.06
45. Percentage of Population with University Education	.09	−.15	.002	.57	−.47	.07
50. Percentage employed in Scientific Research	14	−.16	.02	.38	−.33	.02

the activities of the commune and on their perception of the influence of various bodies and individual officers on communal affairs.[6]

The correlation between size, expressed in area and in number of inhabitants, with budget revenue and total income of the commune government in absolute terms and per capita is shown in Table 5.

"Total income" includes beside the budget, separate funds for special purposes (such as roads, education, child welfare, public utilities and urban infrastructure, etc.) which are not included in the budget but are subject to the decisions of and control by the communal assembly.

Area is significantly positively related to budget revenue and total income in absolute terms only for the group of nonurban communes,[7] one of the main

TABLE 5
CORRELATION BETWEEN SIZE WITH BUDGET REVENUE AND TOTAL INCOME
OF THE COMMUNE GOVERNMENT

Financial Indicators	Area of Commune (km^2)		n of Inhabitants	
	All Communes	Non-urban Communes	All Communes	Non-urban Communes
Budget: revenue in absolute terms	.217	.562	.852	.854
Budget: revenue per capita	−.190	−.193	.020	−.671
Total income of commune in absolute terms	.179	.522	.907	.929
Total income of commune per capita	−.291	−.382	−.348	−.510

forms of taxation being a land-income tax calculated on the basis of the average return per hectare in the area for the last ten years. That the correlation is not higher is the consequence of the unproductiveness of land in large parts of the country, which are barren limestone. The positive correlation between size and absolute revenue and, even more, income becomes pronounced when size is measured by number of inhabitants. To interpret this finding it is necessary to keep in mind that most of the communes that are nonurban by legal definition have a city or smaller urban settlement as the center of an otherwise predominantly rural territory. This suggests the possibility that the increase in population positively correlated with revenue and income is the consequence of urbanization and not of mere size. We shall see that this suggestion is confirmed by the analysis.

On the other hand, budget revenue as well as total income, when considered on a per capita basis, are negatively correlated with size, and significantly so for nonurban communes when size is measured by number of inhabitants. At the same time the absence of correlation between budget revenue and number of inhabitants when all communes are considered suggests a positive correlation for urban communes alone. Indeed, the factor-loading for the variable "budget revenue per inhabitant" for Factor I (urbanization and industrialization) is .697.

The tentative conclusion is that the dogma about increasing size leading to greater affluence of the local unit should, at least, be critically reexamined. It is very well possible that the link is, partly, a spurious one, the independent variable being urbanization leading both to more inhabitants and more resources. The doubts are substantiated by the negative correlation between size and resources per inhabitant, as at least for some local services, e.g., education, expenditure is proportionate—after initial investments were made—to number of users. The correlation between size and the indicators of quality of local administration is shown in Table 6.

TABLE 6
CORRELATION BETWEEN SIZE AND INDICATORS OF QUALITY OF
LOCAL ADMINISTRATION

	Area (km²)	No. of Inhabitants	Budget: Revenue per Inhabitant
Number of inhabitants per employee in local administration	.160	.507	−.076
Number of items transacted per 1,000 inhabitants	−.048	−.183	.080
Number of items transacted per employee	−.187	.311	.025
Education of employees in local administration (percentages)			
University	−.101	−.003	.257
College	.121	.320	−.037
Middle School	−.190	−.077	−.063
Elementary	−.129	−.050	−.077
Local Budget (percentages)			
Personnel expenditure	−.146	−.074	.053
Material expenditure	.008	.086	−.077

The positive correlation between number of inhabitants and the relation of inhabitants to employee in local administration (.507) as well as between the same indicator of size and the number of administrative items transacted per employee (.311) can be interpreted as meaning that the size of the local administrative establishment does not vary in proportion to the number of inhabitants—in larger communes, there are simply more inhabitants per employee—but the size of the workload, to an extent, does. The individual employee in the larger commune has more items to transact.

The significant fact is the absence of correlation between the income of local government, when measured by inhabitant, and the indicators of quality of local administration. That is, even if increase in size of the commune, by territory or by population, should result in greater affluence, there is no guarantee that this will result in better administration, proportionately to the larger work load.

Finally, let us consider the relation between the first ten factors and the indicators of quality of local administration, as shown in Table 7.

The analysis shows significant positive loadings on budget revenue per inhabitant and expenditure on schools per inhabitant for Factor I ("urbanization and industrialization"—accounting for 24.3 percent of the total variance), but practically no relationship with the indicators of quality of local administration. A particularly surprising detail, for instance, is that the loading on the variable "percentage of active population with university education" is higher (.589) for Factor I than the loading on the corresponding variable "percentage of local administration personnel with university education" (.325).

TABLE 7
ROTATED FACTORS

	I	II	III	IV	V	VI	VII	VIII	IX	X
Budget revenue per inhabitant	**.697**[a]	.107	-.079	-.035	-.023	-.068	-.233	.018	-.125	-.158
Expenditure on schools per inhabitant	**.522**	.019	-.117	-.163	-.307	-.144	-.004	-.067	.079	-.077
Number of inhabitants per employee in local administration	-.040	**-.351**	.251	.122	.243	-.309	.024	**.468**	-.007	.051
Number of items received per 1,000 inhabitants	.041	**.332**	**-.388**	-.130	-.079	.167	-.159	**.591**	.045	-.089
Number of items transacted per employee	-.025	.023	-.023	.007	.083	-.064	-.055	**.894**	-.107	-.014
Education of employees in local administration (percentages)										
– University	**.325**	.256	.041	.071	.022	-.256	.016	.005	-.088	**.582**
– College	.106	-.112	**.338**	-.030	.022	-.023	.148	**.445**	.056	**.389**
– Secondary school	.046	-.076	-.146	.071	-.134	.012	**.831**	-.079	.041	-.184
– Elementary school	-.275	-.016	-.089	-.123	.068	.121	**-.738**	-.059	-.018	**-.363**
Local Budget (percentages)										
– Personnel expenditure	.067	.104	-.256	**-.462**	.038	-.082	.288	-.082	.087	.129
– Material expenditure	-.217	.126	-.066	**-.545**	.174	.059	-.101	.144	-.048	-.051

a. The communality of the ten factors is 65.2 percent. All correlations above 0.32 are bold face.

It is more difficult and less relevant for our present purpose to try to interpret such "freak" items as the high loadings on the variables "employees in local administration with secondary school" (.831) and "with elementary school" (.738) for Factor VI (4 percent of total variance). The significant loadings on the variables "number of inhabitants per employee in local administration" (.468), "number of items received per 1,000 inhabitants" (.591), and, particularly, "number of items transacted per employee" (.894) for Factor VIII (3.75 percent of total variance) seem to indicate a situation where increasing population increases considerably the workload, while the size of the local administrative establishment lags behind. This interpretation is corroborated when considering the top-ranking 10 communes on that factor. Seven of them correspond to the description: traditional old small-town with new industrial or other economic development. The traditional local bureaus are slow to adapt in size to the new requirements. The "slack," however, present in the local system is sufficient to carry the increased workload.

Here again the assumption that economic and social development result ipso facto in improvements in local administration, or at least in an increase of its capacity, merits a close second look.

Finally, the most far-reaching theoretical implications are attached in Yugoslavia to the role of the commune as part of a generalized system of self-management.

Enterprises and institutions are administered by the people working in them who elect a workers' council as the supreme decision-making body in the organization. The workers' council, numbering from 15 to 120 members, depending on the size of the work force, makes the decisions which would, in a corporation, fall into the competence of both the board of directors and the shareholders meeting. It appoints the general manager, allocates the income, decides on investments, determines the individual share of each employee in both profits and losses, legislates on all problems which require general regulation within the organization.

The central question in such a system, where every individual organization enjoys in principle a far-reaching autonomy in decision-making, is how to achieve the necessary integration of many and diverse parts into a whole, to counteract centrifugal tendencies, to build a system. In this respect the commune is assigned, by hypothesis and doctrine, an outstanding role. The commune assembly with its chambers, its executive councils, the voters' meetings, the local communities and their councils and other mechanisms of direct and representative territorial self-government should function as a meeting place of the diverse interests motivating the people who work in enterprises, institutions, and agencies. These same people in their role as consumers as well as in their role of citizens, members of a nation or other territorial group, a professional association, a political movement. The members of the chamber of working organizations of the commune assembly and the largest part of the membership of the executive councils are defined, by constitution and laws, as delegates of the enterprises and institutions of their constituency. They are supposed to be in constant contact with their constituents to report to them periodically on developments in the political bodies of the commune, to act and vote in these bodies according to the guidelines received from their constituents. The relationship between enterprises and institutions on one hand and the commune on the other are seen as a two-tier system of self-management where the commune is the upper tier in the role of meeting-place, coordinator and adjusting mechanism for the diverse interests generated in the lower tier.

In order to test these assumptions ten communes were selected of which four were urban in character, three suburban and three rural (but all in the same region). A questionnaire of 25 questions was administered to 210 members of communal assemblies, councils, officers, and administrators, as well as to members of workers' councils, management boards and employees of service institutions in the same communes. A total of 103 minutes of assemblies, executive council's management boards and workers' meetings over a period of 2 years, with a total of 770 analytical units was content-analyzed.[8]

Table 8 compares the responses to the question "what are, in your opinion, the most important problems facing the commune?" with the items appearing most frequently on the agenda of the political bodies of the commune. All matters were grouped under four headings corresponding to the main roles the commune is assumed to have: the coordinating and adjusting role just mentioned, the role of providing services to the citizens of the local community, the role of functioning as local outputs of the governmental power system, and, finally, business related to the internal administration of the communal mechanism itself.

The coordinating role, by assumption central for the commune, as the second level in the system of workers self-management, takes comparatively little

TABLE 8

COMPARISON OF RESPONSES OF QUESTIONNAIRE WITH FREQUENTLY
APPEARING AGENDA ITEMS OF POLITICAL BODIES OF COMMUNE
(in percentages)

	Urban		Suburban		Rural		Average	
	R	M	R	M	R	M	R	M
Co-ordination	18.8	16.9	5.8	33.7	22.0	21.2	16.2	23.2
Service	47.6	19.1	72.5	14.4	57.5	22.0	57.8	18.7
Power	11.8	50.7	5.0	39.4	9.2	44.8	9.0	45.5
Administration	21.7	13.3	16.7	12.5	11.2	12.0	16.9	12.7
Total	99.9	100.0	100.0	100.0	99.9	100.0	99.9	110.1

R=response to questionnaire; M = minutes of meetings.

time—less than one fourth on the average—in the political bodies of the commune, but even less in the interest of the political decision-makers. The service role is clearly central in the minds of the decision-makers but markedly less frequent on the agenda of assembly and executive councils. For the power role the opposite is true: they are practically no concern of the local politician but take by far the most time in the work schedule of assemblies and councils. Problems of internal administration, finally, are quite a respectable residual quantity for both politicians and political bodies.

Also, the problems of public services are of greatest importance to the members of political bodies and officers in the suburban communes that are in transition from rural to urban character. The place held in these communes by new industrial enterprises is expressed in the comparatively larger share—slightly over one third—of time for agenda items related to the coordinating role of the commune. And the attention decision-makers have to pay to problems of

TABLE 9
COMPARISON OF RESPONSES TO QUESTIONS

Territorial Administration	(% of all cases)		Chi^2
	Communes	Institutions	
Decisions based on formal authority	37	7	
	(129)	(100)[b]	28.12; p <0.001
Technical differences resolved by	27	18	
hierarchical authority	(277)	(277)[a]	27.69; p <0.001
Methods of achieving discipline			
— Authoritative methods used to			
achieve discipline at work	76	61	14.69;[c] p <0.001
— Nonauthoritative methods	19	36	14.69;[c] p <0.001
— Other methods	5	3	14.69;[c] p <0.001
	(217)	(151)	
Number of decisions influencing the	64	34	
work process originating outside	(262)	(274)[a]	48.04;[c] p <0.001
the organization			
Intensity of outside influences	35	17	
	(322)	(289)[a]	26.16;[c] p <0.001
Differences in hierarchical rank are	23	57.9	
not causes of conflict	(105)	(95)[b]	26.17; p <0.001
Domination in resolving conflicts			
— Conflicts resolved by domination	37	7	
— Conflict resolved by compromise	56	70	33.48;[c] p <0.001
— Other methods	7	23	
	(129)	(100)[b]	

a. Number of cases mentioned by respondents in questionnaire.
b. Number of respondents.
c. Degree of freedom in computing Chi^2 equals 2.

internal administration in the more developed urban communal establishment is roughly the double from the corresponding part in rural communes.

Without insisting, for the moment, on differences related to the character of the commune, there is fairly strong evidence for the conclusion that the activities related to the commune as part of the self-management system in the wider sense are less prominent than theory would have us believe. This might be related to the circumstance that the commune is still much more traditional local government than part of an egalitarian and participatory system of self-management.

The relationship between the self-managing service institutions in the commune and the communal organization itself was tested by comparing the responses of officers and employees in both institutions and communes to questions related to the prevailing atmosphere at work to the methods of achieving discipline, to the characteristics of interest relations in the two settings. The results are shown in Table 9. The reliance upon authority, the intensity of outside influences, the prevalence of domination is still markedly larger in communes than in institutions. The suspicion that the communes are still more government than self-management is tentatively confirmed.

IV

Behind these findings on the commune in Yugoslavia, however tentative and exploratory, there emerges the perennial dilemma in social development between subjective planning and objective necessity.

Yugoslavia is on its way towards an industrial society: its per capita national income has increased four times in the course of the last 20 years, the population structure has changed from a ratio of 75 percent rural and 25 percent urban to 40 percent rural and 60 percent urban, at present half of its GNP is derived from industry and less than one fifth from agriculture. Still the differences existing among the various parts of the country are great, the problems of transition serious, economic capacity limited by the present ceiling of $700 per capita of national income. The country has all the characteristics of a developing society.

At this stage, for reasons that cannot be explored within the framework of the present article, an institutional model has been introduced, consciously planned and constructed and applied to all fields of human co-operative endeavor. A system of self-management started in industrial enterprises in 1950 has gradually been extended to all organizations, associations and agencies, to local government, to the machinery of the state and generalized, by the Constitution of 1963, as the basic principle of all political and economic life in Yugoslav society. It is a system, by intention, of a very high degree of openness, equality, participation and, therefore, complexity. Relationships within the system are conceived nonhierarchically with built-in mechanisms for the equalization of interest satisfactions. As a model it is similar to the tendency foreseen for the future in the technologically most developed societies: adaptable systems of co-operating groups without pronounced hierarchies, where interest-coalitions are open and in changing equilibrium.

This purpose has to contend with an environment geared to much lower levels of structural elaboration, where the traditions of domination, by the employer or by the state, are still very much alive, where educational averages as well as incomes are not high enough to make a tendency towards equality in technical contribution possible or a tendency towards equality in interest-satisfaction uncontroversial.

The question is, what can be done with what exists? What kind of compromises with reality are necessary in order to insure the day-to-day functioning of essential cooperative networks in production, the services, general social regulation, without abandoning the egalitarian vision of a society where domination, technologically unnecessary, will gradually become socially obsolete?

In the battery of practical measures and institutions of transition, necessary to bridge the gap between the desirable and the possible, local structures, whatever their nature and their future transformation, have obviously a major role.

NOTES

1. For a more detailed exposition of the machinery of government in a Yugoslav city, see Pusić and Walsh (1967).
2. The source of the statistics on Yugoslav local government, if not otherwise indicated, is the Statistical Yearbook of Yugoslavia, an official publication of the Federal Statistical Agency.
3. The analysis was planned and implemented by a research team of the Institute of Social Research of Zagreb University in 1967 with the assistance of the computing facilities of Resources for the Future, Inc., Washington, D.C., which I wish to thank for help.
4. For discussion of factor analysis in studying political outputs, see Clark (1970).
5. See Köttgen (1956: 228); Alderfer (1956: 14-18); Morris (1960: 107).
6. For a more detailed description, see Pusić (1969a).
7. "Urban communes" are, as defined by the Statistical Yearbook of Yugoslavia, communes consisting of a city and densely populated suburban settlements linked to it by common public utilities and services and by a shared economic and cultural life. Of Yugoslavia's 500 communes, 70 are considered urban by this definition. This means that settlements defined as urban by general statistical criteria (population above 20,000) can exist in communes treated statistically as rural, taking into account their whole territory.
8. For details on the other methods applied and the whole research-project, see Pusić (1969b).

REFERENCES

ALDERFER, H. F. (1956) American Local Government and Administration. New York.

CLARK, T. N. (1970) "Urban typologies and political outputs: causal models using discrete variables and orthogonal factors, or precise distortion versus model muddling." Social Science Information 9 (December): 7-33.

KOTTGEN, A. (1956) "Wesen und Rechtsform der Gemeinden und Gemeindeverbände," in H. Peters (ed.) Handbuch der kommunalen Wissenschaft und Praxis. Berlin.

MORRIS, J. H. (1960) Local Government Areas. London.

PUSIC, E. (1969a) "Area and administration in Yugoslav development." International Social Sciences Journal 21, 1: 68-81.

——— (1969b) "Territorial and functional administration in Yugoslavia." Administrative Science Quarterly No. 1: 62-72.

——— and A. H. WALSH (1967) Urban Government for Zagreb. New York: Frederick A. Praeger.

APPENDIX 1
YUGOSLAV PROJECT: DESCRIPTION OF VARIABLES USED IN PRINCIPAL ANALYSES

Data Sets				
50	*26*	*25*	*35*	
1	1	1		1. Area of commune in square kilometers, 1965.
–	2	2		2. Number of settlements in commune, 1965.
2	3	3		3. Percentage of the total population classified as economically active (i.e. employed in gainful activity or seeking employment) as of April 3, 1965.
3	4	4		4. Percentage of economically active population employed in Agriculture (including specialists employed by agricultural enterprises but not performing tasks customarily classed as agricultural), 1961.
4	5	5		5. Rate of net natural increase of population (1/1/64-12/31/64).
5	6	6		6. Number of child deaths per 1,000 live births, 1964.
6	7	7		7. Percentage of the employed population working in the socialist sector, 1965. Note: The socialist sector includes all public employees, all employees in enterprises of five or more employees (mandatorily socialized) and employees in smaller enterprises organized under the workers self-management system.
7	8	8		8. Percentage of the employed population engaged in mining and industry, 1965.
–	9	9		9. Percentage of the employed population engaged in social or cultural activities, 1965. Note: "Cultural and social activities" include artistic and cultural activities, social welfare activities, public health, and some educational activities devoted to adult education.
8	–	–		10. Total fixed assets (buildings, materials, and equipment) per capita engaged in productive activities in 1,000 dinars, 1965.
9	–	–		11. Total gross investment in fixed capital, operating capital, inventories, and social funds, 1964.
10	–	–		12. Total communal income per capita in 1,000 dinars, 1964.
–	–	–		13. Total communal income originating in mining and industry per capita, 1964.
11	–	–		14. Total revenues to commune government in 1,000 dinars per capita, 1964.
12	–	–		15. Expenditure per capita of communal social funds for school construction, 1964. Note: Social funds here include all sources of financing available to the communes except private sources and subsidies from federal or republic governments.
–	–	–		16. Expenditure per capita of communal social funds for housing construction, 1964 (see note, item 1).
13	10	10		17. Percentage for the total land area of the commune in farms, 1965.
–	11	11		18. Number of quintals of wheat produced per hectare of land planted in wheat, 1965.

APPENDIX (Continued)

Data Sets				
50	26	25	35	
–	12	12		19. Number of quintals of corn harvested per hectare of land planted in corn, 1965.
14	13	13		20. Number of completed apartments per 1,000 persons, 1965.
–	14	14		21. Completed construction cost per square meter of housing per 1,000 dinars, 1965. Note: The validity of these figures is doubtful. Fisher suggests that they may have "relative validity."
15	15	15		22. Number of individual automobiles registered in the commune per 1,000 people, 1965.
–	16	16		23. Number of post offices in the commune, 1965.
16	17	17		24. Retail trade per persons in 1,000 dinars, 1965.
17	18	18		25. Turnover tax per 1,000 persons paid by hotels, restaurants, and catering services, 1965.
–	19	19		26. Number of public and private schools of all types except higher education, 1965.
18	20	20		27. Number of students in grammer school as percentage of total population, 1965.
–	21	21		28. Number of movie theaters, 1965.
19	22	22		29. Number of paid admissions to movie theaters, 1965.
–	23	23		30. Number of libraries in communes, 1964.
–	24	24		31. Number of registered radios per 1,000 persons, 1965.
20	25	25		32. Number of registered television sets per 1,000 persons, 1965.
–	–	–		33. Number of hospital beds per 1,000 persons, 1965.
21	–	–		34. Number of doctors residing in commune per 10,000 persons, 1965.
22	26	–		35. Estimated population as of June 30, 1965.
23				36. Number of inhabitants per persons employed in local administration.
–				37. Number of local bureaus.
24				38. Number of cases received per 1,000 inhabitants (including net attended cases from earlier years). Note: A "case" consists of all written documents related to the case subject matter.
25				39. Number of cases transacted per employee in administration.
26 27				40-41. Percentage of local administration personnel with university education: 40. Required by job plan; 41. Actual situation.
28 29				42-43. Percentage of local administration personnel with higher education: 42. Required by job plan; 43. Actual situation.
30 31				44-45. Percentage of local administration personnel with secondary education: 44. Required by job plan; 45. Actual situation.

APPENDIX (Continued)

Data Sets				
50	26	25	35	
32				46.-47. Percentage of local administration personnel with lower education:
33				46. Required by job plan; 47. Actual situation.
34				48. Wages and salaries as percentage of local administrative income.
35				49. Outlays for materials as percentage of local administrative income.
36				50. Women as percentage of active population.
37				51. Highly skilled workers as percentage of active population.
38				52. Skilled workers as percentage of active population.
39				53. Semi-skilled workers as percentage of active population.
40				54. Unskilled workers as percentage of active population.
41				55. Percentage of active population that has not completed elementary school.
42				56. Percentage of active population with lower education.
43				57. Percentage of active population with secondary education.
44				58. Percentage of active population with higher education.
45				59. Percentage of active population with university education.
–				60. Percentage of workers working in posts occupied for 1 shift.
46				61. Percentage of workers working in posts occupied for 2 shifts.
47				62. Percentage of workers working in posts occupied for 3 shifts.
48				63. Percentage of workers employed in intermittent work.
49				64. Percentage of workers performing machine work.
50				65. Percentage of workers employed in scientific and research activities.

APPENDIX 2

NUMBER OF FACTORS ROTATED   10
NUMBER OF ITERATION CYCLES   7

ROTATED FACTOR MATRIX

	FACTOR I	II	III	IV	V	VI	VII	VIII	IX	X
Variable: 1	-0.20300	0.02758	0.23488	0.19112	0.48734	0.09135	-0.01422	0.14778	-0.25229	-0.10238
Variable: 2	-0.14775	-0.37009	0.17518	0.00303	-0.59875	-0.13672	-0.06787	0.15243	-0.22901	0.03396
Variable: 3	-0.63429	-0.06845	0.22924	-0.27637	-0.22309	0.10677	-0.12169	0.16153	-0.19236	-0.40084
Variable: 4	-0.02417	-0.21442	0.05857	-0.12673	0.76296	0.16852	-0.13026	0.08814	-0.00809	0.17962
Variable: 5	-0.31656	-0.13976	0.16127	0.16513	0.00376	0.11338	0.10088	0.39191	-0.07567	-0.18349
Variable: 6	0.59851	-0.05956	-0.06156	0.07134	-0.02288	0.07682	0.02398	-0.08925	0.01340	0.53992
Variable: 7	0.07157	-0.11501	-0.11389	0.09935	-0.00238	0.04601	-0.07678	-0.01665	0.06209	0.74065
Variable: 8	0.78095	-0.09703	-0.10973	0.23323	0.15765	0.04650	-0.05247	-0.05174	-0.03832	0.24227
Variable: 9	0.89511	0.04643	-0.02742	0.09084	0.02499	-0.01058	-0.00862	-0.08563	-0.04873	0.09085
Variable: 10	0.87687	-0.07521	0.06139	0.15924	-0.11452	-0.13651	-0.06131	0.02404	-0.02314	0.11440
Variable: 11	0.69703	0.10736	-0.07956	-0.03475	-0.02295	-0.06757	-0.23262	0.01832	-0.12488	-0.15782
Variable: 12	0.52242	-0.01936	-0.11749	0.16272	0.30746	-0.14375	-0.00423	-0.06699	0.07897	-0.07707
Variable: 13	-0.33036	-0.35654	0.14393	-0.16286	0.21057	0.02047	0.16961	0.10345	-0.22251	-0.28672
Variable: 14	0.14676	0.03748	0.02157	0.04503	0.02151	-0.84969	0.01513	-0.01243	0.07993	0.17976
Variable: 15	0.62344	0.04846	0.00450	0.05804	-0.09018	-0.03972	0.09302	-0.15952	0.11473	0.29919
Variable: 16	0.82694	0.12521	0.12241	-0.00535	-0.17212	0.11342	0.18541	0.03352	0.04143	0.14748
Variable: 17	0.54965	0.27759	-0.10412	-0.02435	0.03153	0.07312	0.34438	-0.22699	0.09526	-0.06820
Variable: 18	-0.36056	-0.08703	0.09652	-0.09367	0.68163	0.12426	-0.01909	0.09662	-0.01540	-0.21513
Variable: 19	0.83262	0.14026	0.07764	-0.00493	-0.09054	-0.00448	0.20346	0.00471	0.02588	0.05569
Variable: 20	0.48390	0.17669	-0.17052	-0.02276	-0.29525	-0.11500	9.25542	0.08393	0.13112	0.27311
Variable: 21	0.73041	0.00517	0.03692	0.12269	-0.06259	-0.19501	0.09525	-0.05444	0.04924	0.51052
Variable: 22	0.71604	0.00645	0.07826	0.03347	-0.15081	-0.43838	0.04856	0.05590	0.09638	0.20222
Variable: 23	-0.04041	-0.35147	0.25073	0.12206	0.24252	-0.30882	0.02425	0.46817	-0.00682	0.05139
Variable: 24	0.04131	0.33244	-0.38798	-0.12982	-0.07914	0.16750	-0.15913	0.59062	-0.04568	-0.08900
Variable: 25	-0.02543	0.02260	-0.02338	-0.00730	0.08293	-0.06301	-0.05482	0.89385	-0.10716	-0.01410

ROTATED FACTOR MATRIX

	FACTOR I	II	III	IV	V	VI	VII	VIII	IX	X
Variable: 26	0.28066	0.04127	0.32216	-0.05166	0.05551	-0.12522	0.23554	-0.00478	-0.24216	0.54073
Variable: 27	0.32540	0.25621	0.04145	0.07000	0.02198	-0.25594	0.01628	0.00527	-0.08833	0.38191
Variable: 28	-0.18522	0.19400	0.01843	-0.04433	0.20135	0.23056	-0.06993	0.11440	0.09990	-0.15343
Variable: 29	0.10591	-0.11244	0.33794	-0.3098	0.02165	-0.00294	0.14701	0.44472	0.05649	0.38868
Variable: 30	-0.19731	-0.10932	-0.78477	0.05451	0.03054	0.12150	0.15339	0.06348	0.10774	-0.10383
Variable: 31	0.14609	-0.07632	-0.14643	0.07151	-0.13491	0.01167	0.83090	-0.07606	0.04093	-0.18434
Variable: 32	0.04531	-0.16410	0.16367	-0.03528	-0.24709	-0.29918	-0.37360	-0.21213	-0.02606	-0.14792
Variable: 33	-0.21461	-0.01625	-0.08936	-0.12251	0.06780	0.12165	-0.73845	-0.05868	-0.01841	-0.36303
Variable: 34	0.05714	0.10444	-0.25578	-0.10144	0.03763	-0.08103	0.28794	-0.08225	0.08704	0.12921
Variable: 35	-0.21930	0.12018	-0.00630	-0.54546	0.17427	0.05893	-0.10133	0.14414	-0.04797	-0.05120
Variable: 36	0.31542	-0.14379	-0.05063	-0.33015	-0.06316	-0.16393	0.10363	0.03540	0.56652	0.09037
Variable: 37	0.25718	0.06310	-0.07693	-0.72769	0.18215	0.50402	0.24261	0.05718	0.00203	0.23321
Variable: 38	0.18904	0.19452	-0.15027	0.69314	0.08547	-0.10264	0.30376	-0.10437	-0.09494	0.09178
Variable: 39	-0.11511	0.06230	-0.07524	0.20930	0.01707	0.04703	-0.04998	-0.14837	0.69608	-0.09824
Variable: 40	-0.27272	-0.33437	0.01049	-0.59657	0.10476	0.11662	-0.30788	0.06896	-0.30054	-0.10200
Variable: 41	-0.2 689	-0.61407	-0.24000	-0.17410	0.13244	0.10283	-0.09197	-0.11940	-0.13843	-0.08542
Variable: 42	-0.09113	0.69468	-0.01734	-0.07303	0.13818	0.13043	-0.09831	0.11835	0.35662	-0.11899
Variable: 43	0.70295	0.08972	0.22394	0.12160	-0.27428	0.02519	0.22392	0.16024	-0.05298	0.09219
Variable: 44	0.04293	0.01779	-0.06268	-0.01529	-0.04027	-0.90449	0.02112	0.03312	0.06308	0.02368
Variable: 45	0.58876	0.05932	0.31205	0.03949	-0.29166	-0.23009	0.11775	0.05749	-0.11065	0.44722
Variable: 46	0.05551	0.07914	0.05220	-0.12052	0.02436	-0.13192	0.13174	-0.05770	0.67893	0.01079
Variable: 47	0.00379	-0.69357	-0.15755	0.01209	0.09561	0.06247	-0.00258	0.06143	0.21069	-0.03043
Variable: 48	0.01997	-0.02890	-0.08797	0.60302	-0.03095	0.02051	-0.28001	0.18610	-0.13345	0.04377
Variable: 49	-0.14360	-0.53818	0.00792	-0.07864	-0.08858	0.08140	-0.27717	0.19273	0.48934	0.06643
Variable: 50	0.39918	0.00309	0.05178	0.09257	-0.18705	-0.22983	0.04710	0.03973	-0.01749	0.52639

Chapter 11

Politics, Economics, and Federalism:
Aspects of Urban Government in
Austria, Germany, and Switzerland

Robert C. Fried

An important question raised by recent studies of state and local government in the United States concerns the relative importance of politics, as opposed to economics and other things, in shaping government outputs at subnational levels. Much of the newer research suggests that what are regarded as key traits of state and local political systems, such as the degree of interparty competition and the ostensible orientation of the controlling party, may have little power, statistically at least, when it comes to accounting for the diversities in government policies.[1] The same kind of question is now also being studied in non-American contexts. Traditionally, the study of state and local outputs abroad, just as at home, has been dominated by students of public finance, who have seldom included political variables in their analysis. Even when such studies were carried out by political scientists, little attention was paid to politics. Thus when, in 1940, Arnold Brecht published a comparative analysis of state and local expenditures in Weimar Germany, even he stressed the importance of urbanization and density, but omitted to include any political items as possible independent variables in his analysis.[2]

AUTHOR'S NOTE: *For assistance in the preparation of this paper, I would like to thank the following: the Academic Senate, Campus Computing Network, and Institute of Government and Public Affairs, UCLA; Professors Terry N. Clark, Frederick Engelmann, Carl Hensler, Dwaine Marvick, Francine Rabinovitz, and George Romoser; Ann Hayman and Wayne Swanke; Mr. Heinz C. Naef, Consul General of Switzerland (Los Angeles); Dr. U. Zwingli, City Statistical Office (Zurich); Dr. Hofmann, Federal Statistical Office (Berne); Dr. Krumsiek, German Municipal Association (Cologne): Dr. W. Lanc, Information Center for Local Finance (Vienna); and Mr. Eduard Löser, Municipal Research Institute (Vienna).*

Recent studies of subnational outputs, both in the United States and abroad, have begun to remedy this traditional neglect of politics as a possible explanation of policy, although embarrassingly enough, these efforts to rescue politics from neglect have often resulted only in showing how relatively unimportant politics may be. The traditional neglect of politics is often shown to have been correct in spite of itself, or at least partly correct. What recent studies have shown is that political factors, at least those susceptible to treatment by computers, are often not the most predictive independent variables, though sometimes they are. One of the tasks of emerging middle-range theories of state and local policy-making must accordingly be an attempt to identify as precisely as possible the conditions under which political factors seem to be important and what the consequences of political diversities are likely to be.

This present study of West German, Austrian, and Swiss cities is an attempt in that direction. It follows upon a previous study of policy variations in Italian cities, in which, despite the polarization of Italian party politics, party variables were found to be less important than "ecological" variables in explaining the variance in most of the output variables examined.[3] This was contrary to expectations; for while given the ideological proximity of the two major American parties, Republican and Democratic cities and states might not be expected to vary greatly in their public policies, somewhat greater policy diversity should have been found among cities controlled by Communist, Christian Democratic, and Neo-Fascist administrations. Nonetheless, party was found to be much less important than region (i.e., North-South differences) in accounting for differences and uniformities in the politics adopted by Italian city councils. Communist strength was found to be associated with conservative policies in the North and progressive policies in the South; Christian Democratic power, in contrast, was associated with progressive policies in the North and conservative policies in the South. Exactly what variables or complex of variables make for the regional differences, which hold up even when a number of socioeconomic variables are held constant, is not clear.[4] In any case, the Italian study does point to the relative weakness of party variables in shaping policy and also to the possibility of major discrepancies between the kinds of policies we might expect to be associated with different kinds of political forces and the kinds of policies with which, in practice, they are actually associated.

This study of Swiss, Austrian, and West German cities is concerned with the same kinds of questions: namely, the extent and direction of party impact on municipal policies. The cities of West Germany, Austria, and Switzerland were chosen for several reasons. First of all, comparative data on many aspects of municipal government in those countries are systematically collected. Yearbooks of the German, Austrian, and Swiss municipal associations date back as far as 1890, 1894, and 1931, respectively. The data for comparative studies within each national set of cities exist, even though they have seldom been subjected to systematic analysis. Second, in all three countries, municipal government is competitive, party government so that one can test the relative impact of party on policy, as well as the direction of party impact, if any. Where municipal government is nonpartisan or is dominated by the same party, neither of these two questions can be directly examined. Third, although the emphasis of this study is on variations within national sets of cities, the three countries chosen have enough in common to permit some degree of inter-nation comparison. The dominant political forces in the three countries are parts of European political cultures that transcend and overlap national boundaries. In each country there is a Social Democratic movement, a Christian Democratic movement, and one or more organizations of the secular middle classes.[5] These similar political forces, moreover, contend for power and cope with responsibilities of government in very similar institutional frameworks. All three countries have federal systems of government and strong traditions of municipal autonomy.[6]

On the other hand, there are important differences among the three countries—differences that may make it more fruitful, at least at this early stage, to emphasize intra- rather than international comparison. Germany, Austria, and Switzerland differ vastly in the size and number of cities they offer for study. Switzerland and Austria each have 5 cities with 100,000 or more people, as compared to West Germany's 57. Austria has 47 cities and towns with 10,000 or more people; Switzerland has 75; West Germany has 636.[7] There are also institutional differences to be kept in mind. Although the Swiss Constitution of 1874, the Austrian Constitution of 1920, and the West German Basic Law of 1949 established federal unions, these federations vary a great deal in the degree to which they sanction autonomy and diversity at the state and local level. The Austrian federal system is more unified than the German, and the German is more unified than the Swiss. Characteristically, in Austria, national constitutional law establishes much of the form, powers, and resources of urban governments (Articles 115-120 of the Constitutional Law as amended in 1962); within the terms of these provisions, local government is regulated by Land laws and for the major cities, by city charters. Urban finances are regulated by a national financial equalization law *(Finanzausgleichgesetz)* and a national financial constitutional law *(Finanzvergassungsgesetz)*. The West German federal system is somewhat more decentralized, while the Swiss system is more decentralized still. Thus, there tends to be a good deal of institutional uniformity in Austria, some in West Germany, and very little in Switzerland.

The same differentiating principle applies to the party system of the three countries, with greater uniformity and centralization in Austrian party politics than in West German politics, and greater uniformity and centralization in West German politics than in Swiss politics. The particularism of the Swiss party system or party systems matches the particularism of the Swiss federal system—despite the fact that Switzerland occupies half the space that Austria does and one-sixth the space of the German Federal Republic. West Germany is divided into ten constituent states or *Länder* (not including West Berlin); Austria is divided into nine provinces, also Called Länder; the much smaller Swiss territory is divided into 25 cantons.[8] While the same party systems can be found in all Austrian provinces and communes and in all West German Länder and *Gemeinden,* this is not true for Switzerland, where few parties have nationwide organizations; these are decentralized and composed of highly separatistic units. Thus while all three countries have Social Democratic, Christian, and secular middle-class parties, these parties occupy different positions within their respective party systems. Together, the Social Democrats and Christian Democrats in West Germany win, on an average, over 80 percent of the vote in cities of 100,000 or more. In Austria, the Socialists and Populists (Catholics) account for an average of 84 percent of the municipal vote in cities and towns of 10,000 or more people. The Social Democrats and Catholic Conservatives in Switzerland, however, win an average of only 45 percent of the vote in national, and presumably also municipal, elections; they share power with a variety of other parties, particularly the Radicals, who win, on an average, 26 percent of the vote in towns of 15,000 or more people. The rest of the vote in Switzerland, just under 30 percent, is splintered among a variety of centrist parties, most of them regional, and some even local.

It hardly needs to be added that the particularism of the Swiss institutional and party system corresponds to the particularism of Swiss society. The Austrian cities, again, would appear to be, of the three sets of cities, the most socially homogeneous, at least from the point of view of religion and ethnicity.[9] West German cities are homogeneous from an ethnic point of view, but they are differentiated by religion and this, as we shall see, has some political and policy-making importance. Of the German cities in this study, 20 have Catholic majorities, while 37 have Protestant majorities.

The Swiss cities we are studying are also divided along religious lines: 20 have Protestant majorities; 9 have Catholic majorities. To this religious cleavage is added an ethnic cleavage. The religious and ethnic cleavages among the Swiss cities do not, however, coincide:

	German	French	Italian		
Protestant	13	7	0	=	20
Catholic	6	2	1	=	9
Total	19	9	1		29 *cities*

Greater uniformity and centralization in West Germany and Austria make comparative study of urban government rather easier in those countries than in Switzerland. Vast amounts of information about West German and Austrian cities are centrally collected and published that are simply not available for Swiss cities.[10]

The study involves rather different national groups of cities. For Switzerland, it covers the 29 cities with 15,000 or more people; Basel, which is governed by a joint commune-canton and is therefore not comparable to the other cities, has been excluded. For Austria, the study covers the 47 cities and towns with 10,000 or more people, including Vienna.[11] For West Germany, it covers the 57 Grossstädte—i.e., cities with 100,000 or more people. Thus while all the German cities in this study have at least 100,000 people, only 5 of the 29 Swiss cities and 5 of the 47 Austrian towns have that many inhabitants.

Internation comparisons are made difficult by the fact that very few output indicators are shared by cities in all three countries. We might more easily compare Austrian, Swiss, and German cities if they carried out similar functions and their performances could be measured by some common functional output denominators. Unfortunately, there are very few common output indicators, and functions are differently allocated among levels from country to country. Actually, since all three countries are federal systems, the allocation of functions and resources varies, within each of them, from state to state. This means that comparisons between these countries are even more difficult to justify. Given the political, institutional, demographic, and social differences between national systems of city governments, it may be prudent at this stage to concentrate on within-system rather than between-system comparisons.

For this study, a number of output indicators for Swiss, German, and Austrian cities were intercorrelated with a number of socioeconomic and political variables in order to identify the correlates of performance variations among the cities in each country.[12] The variables were selected partly on the basis of availability and partly on the basis of their presumed relevancy. The political variables measured party shares of the vote and election turnout. The socioeconomic variables were selected from among those items available in municipal yearbooks and national censuses that proved to be important in previous studies of municipal outputs. The output or performance variables were chosen because they were available and also because they were likely to reflect the impact, if any, of party politics on performance. In general, it was expected that leftism in elections would be reflected in the scope of city government, as measured by statistics on taxes, expenditures, city employment, public housing, etc.

In all three countries, however, the coefficients of simple correlation between the socioeconomic variables and the performance variables are higher than they are between the political variables and the performance variables (see Table 1). In almost every case, some socioeconomic variable like rate of population growth, per capita income, population density or age structure is much more highly correlated with performance than any of the political variables. The

TABLE 1A
AUSTRIAN CITIES: INPUT/OUTPUT CORRELATIONS[a]

	Exp.	Own Revs.	Debt	Pub. Housing	Co-op Housing	City Emps.	Tax Costs	Rev. Shares	Fed. Grts.	Prov. Grts.	Grts.	Budgetary Dependence
Soc. Dem. Vote	–	-.29	–	–	–	.39	.39	–	–	–	–	–
Chr. Dem. (OVP) Vote	.40	–	–	–	–	–	–	.28	–	–	.28	.27
"Lib." (FPO) Vote	–	.26	–	–	–	–	–	–	–	–	–	–
Commun. (KLS) Vote	–	-.25	–	.44	–	–	–	-.25	–	–	–	–
Elect. Turnout	.34	-.47	-.31	–	–	–	–	–	–	–	-.25	–
Pop. Size	.34	–	–	.45	–	–	–	.75	–	–	.71	.32
City Area	–	–	–	.36	–	–	–	.63	–	–	.59	–
Pop. Density	–	–	–	.49	–	.24	-.26	.51	.37	–	.51	.26
Pop. Growth	–	–	–	–	-.31	-.50	-.29	-.27	–	.32	–	–
Indust. Empl.	-.30	–	-.53	–	.25	-.34	–	–	-.26	–	–	–
P/C Income	–	.77	–	–	–	–	–	–	–	–	–	-.61
Dw. w. r. Water	.24	.42	–	-.27	–	–	–	–	–	–	–	–

a. Only coefficients at the 95% level of confidence or better are listed.

TABLE 1B
WEST GERMAN CITIES: INPUT/OUTPUT CORRELATIONS

	Pup/ Class	Pup/ Rm	Prop Tax	Tax Revs	Welf Exp	Exp	Lib Exp	Debt	Real Estate	Police Emps	Educ Emps	City Emps	Budget Dependence
Soc. Dem. Vote	–	–	–	–	–	–	–	–	-.31	.30	.31	.27	–
Chr. Dem Vote	.54	.43	-.25	–	–	–	–	–	–	-.41	-.42	-.42	–
Elect. Turnout	–	–	–	–	.48	-.34	–	-.23	-.37	–	.23	–	.23
Cars/Person	–	–	.57	.28	-.35	.71	–	.35	.32	–	–	–	-.65
Prot. Relig.	-.52	-.34	–	–	–	–	–	–	–	–	.32	.33	.24
Refugees in Pop.	-.30	-.24	–	–	–	–	–	–	–	–	–	–	.24
Workers in l.f.	–	–	-.48	–	.23	-.28	–	-.43	.38	–	–	–	.24
Sal. Emps. in l.f.	–	–	.68	.23	–	.52	–	.48	.39	.30	–	-.31	-.40
Civ. Serv. in l.f.	–	–	.33	-.24	–	–	-.28	.26	.38	–	–	–	–
% 65 yrs & Older	-.47	-.37	.48	.29	.24	.30	–	–	–	.55	.45	.60	–
% 15 yrs or Less	.40	.33	-.71	-.46	–	-.56	–	-.26	–	-.50	-.25	-.51	.23
Pop. Growth	.52	.54	–	–	–	–	–	–	–	–	–	-.24	-.39
City Size	–	–	.31	.46	.37	.32	–	–	–	.74	.53	.68	–
City Area	–	–	.27	.27	–	.33	–	–	–	.74	.60	.71	–
Pop. Density	–	–	–	.32	.29	–	.28	–	-.55	–	–	–	–
Indust. Empl.	–	.27	-.55	–	–	-.32	–	-.43	-.46	-.30	-.23	-.32	–
Dw. w. Bath	–	–	.33	.33	–	.29	–	–	–	–	–	–	–
Subst. Housing	–	-.27	–	–	-.23	–	–	–	–	–	–	–	–
P/C Income	–	–	.45	.50	-.23	.67	–	–	–	.23	–	.27	-.70

TABLE 1C
SWISS CITIES: INPUT/OUTPUT CORRELATIONS

	Revs	Exp	Utility Emps	Regul Emps	Grts	Housing Aid	Public Housing	Budgetary Dependence
Soc. Dem. Vote	—	—	—	—	—	—	—	—
Communist Vote	—	—	—	—	—	—	—	—
S.D. + Comm. Vote	—	—	—	—	—	—	—	—
Radical Vote	—	—	.38	—	—	—	—	—
Cath.-Conserv. Vote	—	—	—	—	—	—	—	—
Swiss-Germans	—	—	—	—	—	—	—	—
Swiss-French	—	—	—	—	—	—	—	—
Swiss-Italians	.55	.39	.48	.44	—	—	—	—
Protestants in Pop.	—	—	—	—	—	—	—	—
Foreigners in Pop.	—	—	—	—	—	—	—	—
% Under 19 Years	-.50	-.43	-.38	-.44	—	—	—	—
City Area	.34	—	—	—	—	—	.40	—
Pop. Size	.44	.31	—	—	—	—	.75	—
Pop. Density	—	—	—	—	—	—	—	—
Pop. Growth	-.49	-.42	-.47	-.51	—	—	—	—
Cars/Person	—	—	.39	—	—	—	—	—
Industrial Employmt.	—	—	—	—	—	—	—	—
Persons/Room	—	—	-.38	-.42	-.35	—	—	—
P/C Income	—	—	—	—	—	—	.59	—

[320]

relative weakness of the political variables can be confirmed, using a variety of statistical tests.[13]

However, political factors—or at least those used in this study—are far from negligibly correlated with the outputs. To be sure, the average correlation for the leading political variables is .30; for the leading socioeconomic variables, .53. But if the leading socioeconomic variable is held constant, a political variable is often the independent variable next most highly correlated with the output variable (see Table 2). Political variables are most important in 4 of the 34 outputs examined; next-most-important in 9 more of the outputs; in 8 cases, political factors are the third most highly correlated independent variables, when the first two variables are held constant.[14] Political variables are among the most important, if not *the* most important correlates of diversity in municipal outputs in the three countries of this study.

Political variables are the strongest single independent variables in four cases: pupils/class and CDU vote (West Germany); turnout and p/c welfare expenditure (West Germany); per capita operating expenditure and Populist (OeVP) vote (Austria); tax collection costs and Social Democratic (SPOe) vote (Austria). It is far from clear why political factors should be important for these particular outputs and not for others, or why political factors should be next-strongest (second best) in helping to explain some other outputs. In the introduction to this study, researchers were urged to discover the conditions under which politics was important in shaping outputs. If a pattern had emerged from the correlation tables showing the greater incidence of politics in some types of outputs, we might feel that we were making some progress towards that goal. But such a pattern did not emerge. Certainly one can think of plausible reasons to explain why politics might play a major role in shaping the outputs in which politics seems to play second fiddle, if that. One way of determining whether these results are haphazard artifacts of data and methodology rather than empirical realities is to see whether the decision makers involved can themselves make sense of the results. Statistical studies of decisions will have to be supplemented by statistical surveys of decision makers. Even this route out of our dilemma may be blocked, of course, by the frequent lack of awareness among decision makers of the patterns in their own behavior.[15]

If we are at pains to explain why some outputs are apparently more politicized than others, we will probably find it less difficult to understand why so few outputs are politicized to begin with. Why, after all, should political variables explain the variance in municipal outputs?

(a) Perhaps they do, but this fact is obscured by the nature of the study itself, dealing, as it does, with local outputs, measured in per capita terms. It is just possible that political variables are more powerful at state than at local levels, if only because at the state level, there is less direct dependence on local resources, if any, and consequently, greater scope for interparty differen-

(text continued on page 325)

TABLE 2A
REGRESSION FORMULAE FOR WEST GERMAN CITY OUTPUTS[a]

Dependent Variable	Simple Coeff.	Regr. Coeff.	Stand. Error	Beta Weight	% Cumulative Variance Explained
Per Capita Debt					
% white collar	.48	3.9530	.9323	.610	22.6
% FDP vote	−.13	−2.3493	.9326	−.362	33.9
Constant: −285.4693					
Per Capita City Taxes					
Per capita income	.51	.2809	.0541	.565	25.9
City size	.46	2.8640	.5438	1.222	38.2
City area	.27	−0.0802	.0186	−1.040	52.6
% Protestant	.16	1.4921	.5184	.317	61.1
Industry	.12	12.2196	6.9050	.183	64.4
Constant: −168.3205					
Per Capita City Expenditures					
Cars per person	.71	4.5571	.6472	.855	50.3
City area	.33	.0317	.0133	.247	60.1
% refugees	−.08	5.1274	2.2104	.232	63.4
% dependent workers	−.28	4.9535	2.2162	.271	66.6
% post-1949 housing	.29	4.2716	1.9196	.230	69.1
% over 65 years	.30	16.5701	9.4885	.195	71.7
Constant: −8895.2850					
Pupils Per Class					
% CDU vote	.55	.1618	.0511	.393	29.5
Pop. increase	.52	1.2516	.4812	.336	44.1
Industry	.31	.6864	.3298	.248	49.1
% Refugees	−.30	−.1138	.0682	−.207	52.9
Constant: 258.4605					
Dependency on Grants-in-Aid					
Per capita income	−.70	−.0020	.0013	−.284	48.6
Cars per person	−.65	−.0232	.0088	−.497	53.3
% post-1949 housing	−.43	−.0400	.0192	−.246	56.8
Industry	.11	−.2229	.1331	−.229	60.0
Constant: 100.0195					
Per Capita Library Expenditures					
% post-1949 housing	−.35	−.6898	.2997	−.340	12.0
Pop. density	.28	45.8579	25.2301	.269	19.1
Constant: 496.8744					
Per Capita Policemen					
City area	.74	.0128	.0021	.598	55.3
% over 65 years	.55	5.1328	1.5914	.363	61.6
% CDU vote	−.41	−1.0352	.3093	−.376	65.4
% Protestant	.22	−.4557	.1636	−.349	71.7
Constant: 79.4149					

TABLE 2A (Continued)

Dependent Variable	Simple Coeff.	Regr. Coeff.	Stand. Error	Beta Weight	% Cumulative Variance Explained
Per Capita City Employees					
City area	.713	.0344	.0070	.532	50.8
% over 65	.60	13.2698	4.7345	.310	61.4
% CDU vote	−.42	−1.7851	.8549	−.211	65.6
Constant: 442.3248					
Per Capita Teachers					
City area	.60	.0065	.0015	.543	36.4
% CDU vote	−.39	−.4238	.1958	−.274	43.6
Constant: 192.2151					
Pupils Per Room					
Pop. increase	.54	1.8368	.5480	.454	29.6
% CDU vote	.44	.1356	.0605	.304	38.0
Constant: 297.5575					

TABLE 2B
REGRESSION FORMULAE FOR AUSTRIAN CITY OUTPUTS

Per Capita Federal and Provincial Grants					
City size	.71	85.3876	13.8804	.717	50.1
% OeVP vote	.28	589.4263	228.2120	.301	59.2
Constant: 50,875.3725					
Percentage Public Housing					
Pop. density	.49	.0077	.0019	.523	24.4
% Communist vote	.44	1.8619	.5215	.476	47.0
Constant: −7.5742					
Per Capita Expenditures					
% OeVP vote	.40	43.7050	16.6842	.406	15.7
City size	.34	2.2973	1.0148	.351	28.0
Constant: 2274.3126					
Per Capita Shared Revenues					
City size	.75	.8817	.1241	.760	56.5
% OeVP vote	.28	5.7808	2.0399	.303	65.7
Constant: 457.6318					
Tax Collection Costs					
% SPOe vote	.39	.2081	.0885	.389	15.1
Constant: 27.8261					
Per Capita Revenues (all sources)					
Per capita income	.89	.0073	.0006	.861	78.4
Electoral turnout	−.28	−16.2669	5.6186	−.208	82.8
% Communist vote	−.21	−19.0164	9.1230	−.150	85.1
Constant: 2106.2216					

TABLE 2B (Continued)

	Independent Variables of Decreasing Strength				
Dependent Variable	Simple Coeff.	Regr. Coeff.	Stand. Error	Beta Weight	% Cumulative Variance Explained
Per Capita Own Revenues					
Per capita income	.77	.00833	.0008	.808	58.6
Electoral turnout	−.47	−34.8267	6.8278	−.367	75.4
% OeVP vote	.16	8.5096	2.2934	.273	83.0
Pop. increase	.15	5.2579	2.2304	.1688	85.9
Constant: 3445.8826					

TABLE 2C
REGRESSION FORMULAE FOR SWISS CITY OUTPUTS

Percentage Public Housing					
City size	.75	.0003	.0000	.759	55.8
Per capita income	.59	.4108	.0897	.474	72.4
Pop. increase	−.16	.0382	.0139	.307	79.7
Constant: −52.7261					
Per Capita Expenditures					
% youths	.43	−3.6179	1.5673	−.433	18.8
Constant: 1784.8768					
Per Capita Revenues					
% youths	.50	−3.7844	1.3608	−.501	25.1
Constant: 1729.3015					
Per Capita Municipal Utility Employees					
Pop. increase	−.47	−.0010	.0005	−.337	22.1
% radical vote	.38	.0229	.0093	.4044	33.1
Cars per person	.39	.0066	.0030	.376	45.9
Constant: −.7078					
Per Capita Municipal Employees					
Pop. increase	−.51	−.0013	.0003	−.623	25.9
Per capita income	−.25	−.0060	.0024	−.417	42.0
Constant: 2.4652					

a. These tables give the results of stepwise multiple regression, which selects the independent variables in order of the relative explanatory power. Independent variables below the 95% confidence level have been omitted; this has meant exclusion of the entire regression formulae for some of the dependent budgetary variables, including (for Swiss cities) dependency on grants, % of subsidized housing, and per capita grants-in-aid. The program followed was that of Norman H. Nie et al., *Statistical Package for the Social Sciences* (Nov. 1968 edition).

tiations.[16] It is possible that political variables are more powerful in explaining variations in the kinds of outputs, particularly symbolic outputs, that are less easily quantified. Politics may be least important in explaining just those outputs for which we have comparative statistics. Even in the case of outputs for which we have comparative statistics, the statistics themselves seldom indicate the distribution patterns of goods and services: politics may be important less in determining the absolute or per capita levels of performance than the distribution of outputs as among social groups and intracity districts. These possibilities must be explored in future research before any just assessment can be made of the weight of politics in subnational decision-making.

(b) The apparent weakness of political variables might also derive from the (statistical) intervention of some third variables, particularly those relating to community social and economic characteristics. Leftist or conservative political forces might not appear to produce different policies because of the sheer strength of the socioeconomic differences among the cities they controlled. If this were the case, the correlations between party and outputs would rise if possibly interfering socioeconomic factors were held constant. Partial correlation analysis, examining the relations between party and outputs, holding constant such factors as religion, class structure, city size, age structure, and population growth rate, shows that, instead of raising party/output correlations, holding one or more socioeconomic variables constant tends to maintain those correlations at moderately low levels or even, in one or two important instances, to reduce them close to zero. Thus, for example, the rather interesting and significant correlation between party and pupils per class in West Germany, −.19 for the SPD, .54 for the CDU, is reduced to .03 for the SPD and .34 for the CDU, when religion is held constant. Thus the party/output correlation in this instance is to some extent really an "ecology"/output correlation. Similarly, holding constant housing conditions (percentage of houses with running water) sharply reduced the party/output correlations in Austrian towns, and suggests again that what may appear to be party/output correlations are, in reality, ecology/output correlations.

The strength of socioeconomic as compared to party variables is reaffirmed when ecology/output correlations are examined, holding party variables constant. Holding such variables constant tends in fact to raise, rather than diminish the ecology/output correlations. If anything, party variables tend to blunt or disguise ecology/output correlations, rather than vice versa.

(c) The weakness of the party variables might be merely apparent also because of federalism. Federalism permits many municipal affairs to be determined not by the federal governments or by the municipalities themselves, but by the intermediate level of government—the eleven *Land* governments in West Germany, the nine Austrian Länder, and the 25 cantons in Switzerland. Intercity policy differences based on party might as a result be hidden by

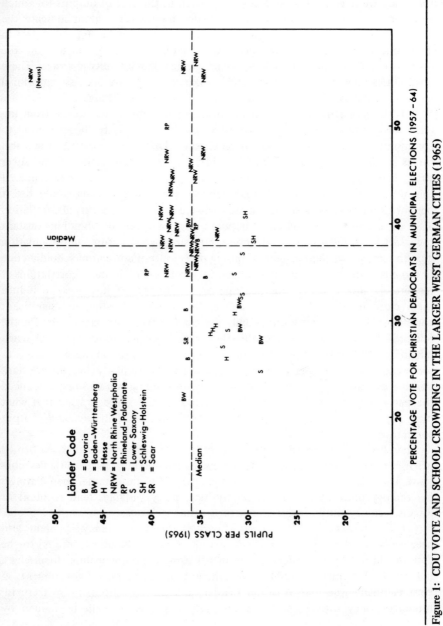

Figure 1: CDU VOTE AND SCHOOL CROWDING IN THE LARGER WEST GERMAN CITIES (1965)

differences among the states; such differences, then, might actually turn up only within the Länder or cantons, rather than between them.

The impact of state policy as a possible intervening third variable can be seen in scatter diagrams that graph the relations between putative inputs and outputs. Thus in Figure 1, which plots the relationships between CDU voting strength and pupils per class—the strongest party/output correlation found for the West German cities—the impact of interstate differences is glaring. Figure 1 shows that, in West German cities as a whole, there is a moderately strong correlation between CDU voting strength and class size, but it also shows that the cities in the high-CDU-strength + high-pupils-per-class quadrant, i.e., the cities responsible for this correlation, are almost all located in a single state of the Federal Republic, namely the state of North-Rhine-Westphalia (NRW). The party/output correlation on the national level would appear to be instead or also a correlation between state policy and educational output. CDU voting strength, at least in German cities, is largely confined to North-Rhine-Westphalia. Since all of the cities of North-Rhine-Westphalia tend to have high pupils/class ratios (i.e., relatively crowded schools), the CDU cities also have high pupils/class ratio. This fact produces the nationwide correlation between CDU strength and crowded classes. Thus what is at once a party/output correlation on the national level, an apparent link between party and educational output, and the major differences between Social Democratic and Christian Democratic cities turns out to be a correlation between state policy and educational output—a difference, that is, between the cities of North-Rhine-Westphalia and the cities of the other West German Länder. This correlation, of course, is equally unfortunate, for it means that the cities of West Germany's richest state, North-Rhine-Westphalia, have its most crowded schools.

If federalism creates basic parameters for intercity policy variations, as sometimes appears to be the case, then perhaps the real impact of the parties is to be seen within the single states, rather than in the nation as a whole. Correlation analysis for the 25 Rhenish Westphalian cities in the study shows no remarkable change in the strength of party/output correlations, as compared to ecology/output correlations. The average SPD/output correlation rises from .17 (West Germany) to .24 (North-Rhine-Westphalia), but the average CDU/output correlation drops from a not very significant .24 (West Germany) to an even less significant .20 (North-Rhine-Westphalia).[17] Correlation analysis suggests that about the same, modest level of partisan differentiation exists among the cities in North-Rhine-Westphalia as among the cities in the Federal Republic as a whole.

When party/output correlations for the NRW cities are calculated, with various ecological variables held constant, for several outputs, interparty differences remain modest, while for some others, party differences remain perceptible and even increase. This implies that while state policy ("federalism")

TABLE 3A
AUSTRIA: OUTPUT/OUTPUT CORRELATIONS

	P/C Rev	P/C Debt	P/C Water	P/C Exp	P/C Fed Gt	P/C Rev Sh	P/C Prov Gt	Public Housing	Budg Dep	Co-op Hous	P/C City Empl	Tax Coll Costs
P/C Auton, Rev	—											
P/C Debt	.31	—										
P/C Water	.26		—									
P/C Expend	.29			—								
P/C Fed. Gt.					—							
P/C Rev. Share				.43		—						
P/C Prov. Gt.							—					
Public Housing	-.27				.49			—				
Dependence	.56					.51	.39	.29	—			
Coop Housing									-.26	—		
P/C City Empl.			.24	.72		.36					—	
Tax Coll. Costs			-.25									—

[328]

may account for some of the weakness of party as a rival type of independent variable, party variables in some cases remain influential, even when state policy and ecology are held constant.

The strongest party/output correlation for the German cities was, as we have seen, that between CDU voting and pupils/class (.54). In North-Rhine-Westphalia, however, the correlation drops to .31 while the SPD/pupils per class correlation "rises" from −.19 to −.27. And if the highly deviant case of the city of Neusz is removed from the correlation analysis, the CDU/pupils-per-class correlation in NRW turns from .31 to −.04, while the SPD correlation changes from −.14 to .08.[18] Thus within North-Rhine-Westphalia, there are no significant interparty differences with regard to this particular and not unimportant output. Figure 1 also shows a clustering of cities by states for the other West German Länder; presumably, state policy is as influential in shaping the particular output in the other states as it appears to be in NRW. When state policy is this influential, nationwide correlations are being formed not by individual cities but by clusterings of cities by state.

It is difficult to tell, however, whether the uniformities or clusterings that appear on scattergrams reflect state policy as such, or rather some other intrastate variable. The clusterings of cities in state groupings might be the product of uniform state policy they might result from a common level of economic development or some common social characteristic. Where there are sharp social, economic, religious, and political diversities, as in the State of North-Rhine-Westphalia, clustering suggests the impact of state policy per se. Where, as in some Austrian provinces, policy uniformities within various provinces are matched by social, economic, and political uniformities, it is difficult to tell whether *Land* policy or "ecology" or both are producing the similarities in policy.[19]

(d) Another reason for the relative weakness of party on municipal policy seems to derive from the nature of the outputs, or rather the intercorrelations among them. Table 3 shows that the various outputs chosen for study are not highly intercorrelated among themselves—that performance in one sphere is not very related to performance in other spheres.[20] This makes it highly unlikely for the few political variables to be highly correlated with many of the outputs.

So far, four possible kinds of reasons have been advanced to account for the weakness of political variables: (a) the nature of the study; (b) the power of ecology; (c) federalism; and (d) the nature of the outputs. To this list must be added: (e) the nature of the parties themselves and of the systems they constitute. The impact of parties on municipal policy-making may, indeed, be considerable, but it may also, at the same time, be self-negating.

(e) The statistical impact of party on municipal policy may, in fact, be blunted by the tendency of different parties to pursue the same policies and the same parties to pursue different policies in order to control a diversified group of

TABLE 3B
WEST GERMANY: OUTPUT/OUTPUT CORRELATIONS

	Pupils/Class	Pupils/Room	P/C Prop Tax	P/C Tax Rev	P/C Welf Exp	P/C Exp	P/C Libr Exp	P/C Debt	P/C Real Est	P/C Pub Safety Emp	P/C City Empl	P/C Educ Empl	Budg Dep
Pupils/Class	–												
Pupils/Room	.60	–											
P/C Prop. Rev. Tax.	–.38	–.33	–										
P/C Tax Revs.	.31		.48	–									
P/C Welf. Expend.				.24	–								
P/C Expend.			.59	.57		–							
P/C Libr. Expend							–						
P/C City Debt			.30			.27		–					
P/C Real. Est. Acreage			.34			.25		.25	–				
P/C Pub Safety Empl.			.36	.39	.26	.44		.47		–			
P/C City Empl.	–.31	–.27	.41	.41	.29	.69		.45		.92	–		
P/C School Empl.					.23			.32		.74	.82	–	
Budgetary Dependency	–.26	–.26			.47	–.58							–

TABLE 3C
SWISS CITIES: OUTPUT/OUTPUT CORRELATIONS

	P/C Revs	P/C Exp	Publicly Assisted Housing	City Housing	P/C Munc Ent Empl	P/C City Emps	P/C Grants	Budgetary Dependency
P/C Revs	–	.88			.59	.83	.40	
P/C Exp		–			.44	.76	.43	
Publicly Assisted Housing			–					
City Housing				–				
P/C Mun Ent Empl					–	.55	.46	.36
P/C City Emps						–	.42	
P/C Grants							–	.96
Budgetary Dependence								–

cities. By means of progressive policies Christian Democrats may seek to extend their natural power base from rural areas to the cities, generally; from Catholic cities to Protestant cities; from middle-class cities to industrial, working-class cities. Through conservative policies Social Democrats may seek to extend their base from the proletarian cities to the increasing number of prosperous, commercial cities.

As Table 4 makes quite clear, in all three countries, the Social Democrats control a wide range of cities, as do the Christian Democrats. The single greatest differentiating factor between Socialist and Christian Democratic cities is, at least in West Germany and Switzerland, religion—a factor that is less immediately related to most urban government outputs than class-connected issues.[21] Sharp differentiations in the kinds of cities controlled by the two kinds of parties can be found only at the subnational level, as for example in North-Rhine-Westphalia; in the latter, there is a clearer demarcation between the poor, industrial, proletarian cities controlled by the SPD and the more prosperous, middle-class cities controlled by the CDU. But in West Germany as a whole the cities that vote for the SPD are not very different from those that deliver a strong vote to the CDU. The SPD tends to be strong in cities with a Protestant majority, while the CDU is strongest in cities with Catholic majorities, but there are important exceptions, such as Catholic Munich with its strong Social Democratic tradition. There is only a slightly greater working class, industrial tendency among SPD cities and a slightly greater middle-class orientation among CDU cities, but the differences in socioeconomic structure and level of economic development are not striking. The SPD controls a number of wealthy, commercial, middle-class cities like Frankfurt, while the CDU is strong in some poor, industrial cities such as Mönchen-Gladbach and Solingen. Party differences alone are not powerful enough to produce output differences.

Differences between Socialist and non-Socialist cities in Austria and Switzerland are even less marked than in West Germany. Socialist towns in Austria are more apt to be industrial and to have bad housing but they do not differ as a group from OeVP towns with regard to income, size, age structure, or density.[22] Swiss towns with strong Social Democratic voting blocs tend to be Protestant, rather than Catholic, but not to differ greatly in other respects from the cities where the SPS is relatively weak. The SPS is strong in both rich and poor cities ("poor" for Switzerland, that is), industrial and nonindustrial cities, French and German cities. The major factor that Swiss cities with strong Communist voting blocs have in common is not that they are rich or poor, industrial or nonindustrial, but that they are French-speaking. Swiss Social Democracy correlates with Protestantism (.68), while Swiss Communism correlates with French predominance (.80) and the absence of German (−.68). Catholic-Conservative strenth, like Social Democratic strength, at least in the cities, follows religion. The strength of the Radical party, earliest and in some ways most typically Swiss of the Swiss parties, has no strong socioeconomic, linguistic, or religious correlates, although its center of gravity would seem to be the smaller, reasonably well-off Catholic towns.[23]

The effort to win and maintain power in several types of cities undoubtedly introduces a measure of incoherence in the way each party approaches municipal problems.

(f) Party impact may also be weakened by country-specific factors. Thus, one might naturally expect little party impact in a country such as Switzerland, where the multiplicity of parties and the collegality of executive government work against any pronounced party impact on policy, whether at the federal, cantonal, or communal level.[24]

(g) It may be thought that the lack of party influence on outputs is a relatively recent development—perhaps the result of *Entideologisierung* or "the end of ideology."[25] Perhaps the noted decline in ideology particularly among the Socialist or Social Democratic parties is what accounts for the lack of any real policy differences between Socialist and non-Socialist city governments. To investigate this possibility, albeit in cursory fashion, the relations between party and municipal outputs under the Weimar Republic were examined. During this period, political parties were seldom accused of lacking ideological commitment. Tables 5 and 6 show the range of performance and party strength among the 45 large German cities now located in the Federal Republic. Table 7 shows the correlations between party strength in municipal elections (circa 1928) and outputs related to public housing and public spending. It shows that, even in Weimar Germany, apparently, ideological polarization among the parties did not result in or from polarization in municipal policy.

A possible reason for the lack of strong party/output correlations for Weimar-German cities may lie in the fact that the two dominant parties in German urban politics in the late twenties, at least in what is now West Germany, seem to have been even more socially heterogeneous in their electoral followings than they became after the Hitler regime. Strictly for suggestive purposes, I have contrasted the social bases of the various political forces in the two periods, using the ecological data of the 1960s. Table 8 shows the apparent shift in the social bases of the SPD and the Center-CDU, particularly the former. SPD urban strength in the sixties correlates only moderately (.45) with SPD urban strength in the late twenties, presumably because the SPD moved after World War II to take over much of the Communist clientele of the twenties. CDU urban strength in the late sixties correlates a good deal more (.77) with Center party strength in the twenties; its social base, apart from religion, remains as heterogeneous as it was in the twenties. Only the Communists were strong in a group of cities with a sharply defined social base.

Even so, their electoral strength was not associated with leftist municipal policies, and this may mean either that the lack of leftist municipal policies

(text continued on page 338)

TABLE 4A
AUSTRIAN CITIES: INPUT/INPUT CORRELATIONS

	Area	Pop	OeVP Vote	SPOe Vote	FPOe Vote	KLS Vote	Density	Pop Growth	Industry	Inc	Turnout	R Water
Area	—	.86					.40	-.29				.56
Population		—					.65					
OeVP Vote			—	-.60		-.46			-.40			-.66
SPOe Vote				—	-.37	.41						.41
FPOe Vote					—	-.27						-.48
KLS Vote						—						
Density							—	-.26	-.28			
Pop Growth								—				
Industry									—		-.50	
P/C Income										—		
Turnout											—	
Running Water												—

[333]

TABLE 4B
WEST GERMAN CITIES: INPUT/INPUT CORRELATIONS

	Soc D Vote	Chr D Vote	FDP Vote	Turnout	Prot	Autos	Refug	Workers	Pop Size
Soc Dem Vote	—								
Chr Dem Vote	-.48	—							
FDP Vote	-.46	.23	—						
Turnout	.31		-.32	—					
Protestants	.42	-.59	.39	-.48	—				
Autos	-.28					—			
Refugees					.36	-.33	—		
Workers	.38		-.28			-.58		—	
Pop size	.35								—
Older pop	.23	-.29			.52				.49
Industry	.35		-.29			-.50		.83	
Civ Serv	-.40		.23			.36		-.78	
White Coll	-.29		.37	-.30		.76		-.79	
Density									.41
Area	.37				.27				.89
P/C Income				-.31		.71		-.25	.23
Youths		.29	-.26		-.26	-.54		.41	-.52
Pop Growth		.29			-.43	.23	-.33		

TABLE 4B (Continued)

	Older Pop	Ind	Civ Serv	White Collar Empl	Density	Area	P/C Income	% Youth	Pop Growth
Soc Dem Vote									
Chr Dem Vote									
FDP Vote									
Turnout									
Protestants									
Autos									
Refugees									
Workers									
Pop Size									
Older Pop									
Industry	–.36	–							
Civ Serv		–.86	–						
White Coll	.28	–.82	.60	–					
Density					–				
Area	.43					–			
P/C Income				.51		.26	–		
Youths	–.74	.47		–.63	–.30	–.39	–.33	–	
Pop Growth	–.40						.32	.23	–

TABLE 4C
SWISS CITIES: INPUT/INPUT CORRELATIONS

	Soc Dem Vote	Soc & Comm (left) Vote	Radical Vote	Cath Conserv Vote	Prot	Germ	French	Italian	Pop Size
Soc Dem Vote	–								
Soc & Comm Vote	.76	–							
Radical Vote			–						
Cath Conserv Vote	–.44	–.40	–.34	–					
Protestantism	.68	.55		–.72	–				
German-Speaking		–.55				–			
French-Speaking		.62		.34		–.91	–		
Ital Speaking					–.43	–.34		–	
Pop Size (1967)									–
Pop Incr (1950-6-)		–.35							–.44
% Under 19		–.49				.48	–.40		–.48
Density				–.38					.49
Area					.34				.69
Industry			–.42						–.35
P/C Income									
P/C Cars						–.47		.55	
Persons/Rm			–.35						
Foreign Residents						–.48		.55	
Communist Vote		.74				–.86	.80		

TABLE 4C (Continued)

	Pop Incr	% Under 19	Density	Area	Ind	Income	P/C Cars	Crowding	Foreigners	Comm Vote
Soc Dem Vote										
Soc & Comm Vote										
Radical Vote										
Cath Conserv Vote										
Protestantism										
German-Speaking										
French-Speaking										
Ital Speaking										
Pop Size (1967)										
Pop Incr (1950-6-)	–									
% Under 19	.83	–								
Density	–.56	–.71	–							
Area				–						
Industry	.55	.48	–.51		–					
P/C Income			.35		–.37	–				
P/C Cars		–.46	.51		–.39	.52	–			
Persons/Rm	.42							–		
Foreign Residents		–.59	.40				.50		–	
Communist Vote		–.62					.56		.44	–

TABLE 5
THE RANGE OF MUNICIPAL PERFORMANCE UNDER THE WEIMAR REPUBLIC

	Minimum	Maximum	Average	Median
% Housing Privately Built (1928)	0 (Munich)	78.5 (Mönchen-Gladbach)	37	38
% Housing Built by the City (1928)	0 (8 cities)	97 (Wiesbaden)	18	12
Per Capita (1928) Operating Expend	RM 9,912 (Braunschweig)	RM 26,294 (Frankfurt)	RM 13,480	RM 15,156

TABLE 6
THE RANGE OF MUNICIPAL VOTING POWER UNDER THE WEIMAR REPUBLIC

	Minimum	Maximum	Average	Median
% Social Dem Vote (city election)	5.7 (Aachen)	41.6 (Darmstadt)	21.7	22.6
Communist Vote in City Elections	1.9 (Würzburg)	34.6 (Gelsenkirchen)	14.3	12.7
Center Party Vote in City Elections	0 (9 cities)	53.1 (Mönchen-Gladbach)	18.18	17.3

TABLE 7
PARTY AND MUNICIPAL OUTPUTS UNDER THE WEIMAR REPUBLIC

	Private Housing	City Housing	Per Capita Spending
Social Dem vote	−.34	.10	.21
Communist vote	.23	−.13	−.11
Zentrum vote	.37	.05	.02

created the bases for strong Communist voting, or that the lack of actual municipal power prevented the Communist from steering municipal policies in a leftward direction.[26] Then, too, the Communists under Weimar may have had some power but used it, as did the Italian Communists twenty years later, to promote conservative policies.[27]

The de facto conservatism of municipal policy-making, under whatever

TABLE 8
WEST GERMAN CITIES: INPUT/INPUT CORRELATIONS FOR WEIMAR AND
BONN COMPARED

Environment Variables (1960s)	SPD Urban Strength, 1920s	SPD Strength 1960s	Center Party Urban Strength 1920s	CDU Strength 1960s	Communist Urban Strength, 1920s
SPD strength 1960s	.45	–	–.41	–.47	–
CDU strength 1960s	–.70	–.47	.77	–	–
Protestantism	.45	.42	–.56	–.59	–
Dependent workers	–	.38	–	–	.69
Manufacturing	–.24	.35	–	–	.79
Civil servants	–	–.40	–	–	–.78
White-collar emps	.37	–.29	–	–	–.62
Miners	–.33	–	.34	–	.47
Per cap income	.34	–	–	–	–.24

political auspices and under whatever political regime, is strongly indicated by the fact that, despite social and political upheavals of historic proportions, one of the most powerful predictors of per capita spending by West German cities in the 1960s is per capita spending by those same cities under the Weimar Republic. Current per capita income correlates with 1963 per capita municipal spending at .67; current automobiles-per-peron correlates with spending at .71; per capita spending in 1928 correlates with per capita spending in 1963 at .64. The budgetary process clearly has a politics of its very own.

If the impact of party is variable, with a marked tendency towards weakness, what is the direction of that impact? Do the leftist cities pursue leftist policies: do they spend more, tax more, build more public housing, employ more people, spend more on public welfare and education, maintain a broad range of municipal enterprise or own vast acreages of real estate? Is the scope of government, that is, vaster under leftist control than under rightist control? We have already partly answered this question in the negative by noting the large number of municipal outputs in each country which are only slightly related, if at all, to party strength. Table 1 shows that in a large number of cases, there simply are no significant interparty differences—no direction of party impact. In others, the direction of party impact is contrary to expectations. Thus while the SPD in West Germany is slightly associated with less crowded schools, higher taxes, and higher public employment levels, it is not associated with higher spending, whether in general, or for welfare or public libraries; SPD strength is negatively correlated, moreover, with per capita city-owned real estate. While CDU strength is correlated with crowded schools and lower public employment levels, it is not associated with lower taxing and spending levels.

Higher pupil/class and pupil/classroom ratios for CDU cities do not derive, as one might think, from the existence of a large, competing parochial school system. There is no parochial school system in West Germany, but rather a mixed system of denominational and secular schools, all publicly controlled and financed.[28] However, as we have seen, the differences between SPD and CDU cities are related in some way to religious differences; for when religion is held constant, the correlation between CDU strength and pupils/class drops from .54 to .31, while the negative correlation between SPD voting and pupils/class changes from −.19 to .03. Even so, interparty differences remain even when religion is held constant. The other major point of interparty difference in West Germany regards public employment levels. City size plays some part in creating this interparty difference, for if it is held constant, the correlations between SPD vote and per capita city employment, per capita public safety employment, and per capita public school employment drop from the .3 to .4 level down to zero. The negative correlations between CDU power and public employment levels, however, remain moderately strong. We may conclude that in West Germany there are some important policy differences between cities apparently deriving from the general orientation of the parties in power; these do not regard taxing and spending, but rather policies towards schools and public employment.

To the south, in Austria, we find Socialist power associated with greater public housing efforts, but, at the same time, also with lower levels of taxing, spending, and public employment. The Austrian Populists, on the other hand, if predictably opposed to public housing, seem less opposed than the Socialists to spending, taxing, and hiring large city staffs. The scope of municipal government in Austria would seem to be broader where the anti-Socialists are in control. These policy differences diminish somewhat if community living standards (measured by the percentage of houses with running water) are held constant. Thus the scope of government in Socialist towns seems to be restricted by poverty of local resources and lack of outside aid. The scope of government in OeVP towns is larger than in SPOe towns because, in addition to an evident willingness to tax and spend, the OeVP towns enjoy both greater local resources and larger per capita shares in provincial and federal revenues.

For some reason, the Socialist towns appear to be less efficient than the OeVP towns: even at comparable levels of income and living standards, the Socialist towns spend more than the OeVP towns to collect their taxes. Curiously, this does not seem to be related to any general tendency in the Socialist towns toward the higher public employment levels.

Turning west, to Switzerland, there are other ironies to be found in the confrontation of ideology with actual policy. To be sure, the scope of government in the most conservative cities, those where the Catholic-Conservatives are strongest, is predictably low—low in taxing, spending, municipalization, budgetary dependence, publicly assisted housing, and public housing.[29] On the other hand, the Radicals, who form a middle-of-the-road party of the secular middle classes, seem to favor a larger scope for government than do the parties of the "proletariat": the Social Democrats and the Communists. With regard to taxing, spending, municipalization, and public employment, the Radicals are more to the left than the Marxists; with regard to public housing, however, the Radicals seem to be further to the right than the Catholic-Conservatives.

Given the low correlations between Social Democratic and Social-Democratic-cum-Communist voting and policy outputs, it is hazardous to speak of any direction whatsoever in the apparent leftist impact on municipal policy in Swiss cities. When community age-structure is held constant, the positive correlations between Leftist strength, on the one hand, and spending and taxing levels on the other, are reduced from .18 and .22 to −.09 and .01, respectively, and the correlations between leftist voting and municipalization and municipal employment drop from .00 and .17 to −.27 and −.06. The association between leftism and government scope seems in these cases to be the product more of demography than of politics. Controlling for various socioeconomic factors does not have the same effect for the Catholic-Conservatives or the Radicals. The Catholics seem to have a consistently conservative impact on policy, irrespective of community social and economic characteristics, while the Radicals, in all types of communities, tend to pursue a progressive or expansionist policy with regard to spending, taxing, municipalization, and employment. "Ecology" does play a role, however, in the apparent Radical and Catholic opposition to public housing: if city size is held constant, Radical opposition drops from −.29 to −.08, while Catholic-Conservative opposition changes sign—from −.10 to .10. The small size of Catholic-Conservative and Radical towns may account for the apparent opposition of these parties to public housing.

The lack of a clearly defined progressive impact on policy of the Swiss Social Democrats is not apparent on the cantonal level—quite the contrary, as Table 9 demonstrates. The lack of Social Democratic impact at the local level may derive from the differences between the kinds of cities in which the Social Democrats are relatively strong—a very heterogeneous collection of localities—and the kinds of cantons in which they are strong—which tend to be large, industrial, Protestant, and wealthy, i.e., much more homogeneous as a group.[30] If one compares the ecology of urban party strength in each of three countries, it would seem, at least on the basis of data from Table 4C, that the ecological base of the Swiss Socialists is by far the most diversified of the three Socialist parties. The center of gravity in the West German Social Democratic cities would seem to be among the poor, industrial cities, as it would also seem to be for the Austrian Socialists. The Swiss Social Democratic cities seem to have nothing in common with each other except religion. Given the power of "ecology," the more diversified base of Swiss socialism, at least at the municipal level, apparently means a diversity of policy orientation and outputs, and this helps to explain the low party-output correlations.

TABLE 9
SWISS CANTONS: PARTY VOTE/CANTONAL OUTPUTS CORRELATED

Canonal Outputs	Soc Dem Vote	Comm Vote	Cath Vote	Rad Vote
P/C expend	–	–	–	–
P/C tax revs	.40	–	−.52	–
P/C adm exp	.60	–	−.41	–
P/C military exp	–	–	.43	–
P/C educ exp	.60	–	−.40	−.40
P/C relig exp	.49	.37	−.66	–
P/C highways exp	−.63	–	.62	–
P/C health exp	.47	–	−.60	–
P/C welf exp	.39	–	−.41	–
P/C unemp exp	.39	–	−.51	–
P/C justice exp	.53	–	−.34	–
P/C soc sec exp	.66	–	−.55	–

This study of German, Austrian, and Swiss cities provides evidence for two basic findings about municipal policy:

(1) Party does not seem to be the most important factor shaping municipal policy, although sometimes it is among the most important.

(2) The direction of party impact, when discernible, is sometimes contrary to expectation based on a party's ideology or location in the political spectrum: location in the policy spectrum does not necessarily coincide with location in the political spectrum.

These two findings for German, Austrian, and Swiss cities accord well with findings of the author regarding Italian cities. They are in accord also with recent findings with regard to British cities.[31]

But these exploratory findings require considerable elaboration, refinement, and substantiation. The extent, direction, and conditions of party impact on subnational government will have to be explored using other techniques and approaches. Given extant municipal data collections dating back for decades or more in several countries, there are rich possibilities for longitudinal studies of subnational decision-making.[32] Such studies may permit us to observe the impact on policy not only of general party orientation but also of (1) major systemic changes, such as regime changes and (2) more informal political variables, such as informal decision rules, changes in leadership and the like. Cross-sectional and longitudinal studies of objective indicators, whether political inputs or program outputs, will require supplementary studies of correlated subjective attitudes and values. Survey data dealing with elite and mass attitudes may, in fact, provide us with "political" variables of greater efficacy in predicting and explaining municipal performance than the objective variables used in this study.

NOTES

1. The unimportance of political factors was originally and most forcefully argued by Dawson and Robinson (1963); Dye (1966); Hofferbert (1966). The unimportance has been challenged by, among others, Sharkansky (1967, 1968, 1970); Lineberry and Fowler (1967); Clark (1968); Fry and Winters (1970).

Economists, for their part, have been similarly concerned by the apparent lack of impact on government outputs of economic system variables (see Pryor, 1968: esp. 284-287); Taira and Kilby (1969).

2. See Brecht (1941).

3. See Fried (1971). Studies of British cities have also tended to stress the relative importance of nonpolitical factors in municipal outputs. For an early study, see Crane (1953); more recently, see Oliver and Stanyer (1969); Boaden and Alford (1969).

4. For a discussion of the impact of regionalism on American state government outputs, see Sharkansky (1970). For the controversy surrounding the concept of political dualism in Italy, see Muller (1970: 800).

5. On Swiss party politics, see Girod (1967); Tschäni (1966: ch. 5); Gruner and Siegenthaler (1963); Siegfried (1948: 157-187); Codding (1961: ch. 8); Gruner (1969).

On Austrian party politics, see the articles by Gehmacher, Shell, and Secher in Shell (1969); Marvick and Stiefbold (1966); Hannak (1963); Powell (1969) Engelmann (1966).

On West German party politics, see the references in Deutsch and Breitling (1963); Collotti (1968); Edinger (1968); Neumann (1966).

On the Socialist Party movement in the three countries, see Langner (1965). For a detailed study of the Swiss Socialists, see Masnata (1963); of the German Socialists, Chalmers (1964); and of the Austrian Socialists, Shell (1962). The Catholic parties in the three countries are treated in Fogarty (1957). See also Henig (1969: 21-67, 282-319, 365-383) for West Germany, Austria, and Switzerland, respectively.

The institutional framework for Swiss local government is described in the citations listed in note 5, above, and in Codding (1967); Rees (1969).

Austrian local institutions are described in Schütz (n.d.); Koja (1967); Oesterreichischer Gemeinebund (1957); Humes and Martin (1961: 268-271). City council politics in Vienna are analyzed in Gerlich and Kramer (1969).

On West German local institutions, see Wells (1932, 1953, 1961). See also Jacob (1963); Wagener (n.d.).

On the role of urban governments in their respective national systems of public finance, see (for Switzerland) Laufenberger (1961); May (1969: 99-106, 1965); Haller (1969); Gangemi (1967); Eidgenössisches Steuerverwaltung (1968, 1969); (for Austria) Schachner-Blazizek (1967); Tautscher (1961); Verbindungsstelle der Bundesländer (n.d.); Oesterreichischer Statistisches Amt (1970); (for West Germany) May (1970: 107-114); Villani (1968); Timm and Giere (n.d.); Gumpel and Böttcher (1963); Zimmerman (1970); Henle (1964).

6. The remarkable strength of municipal autonomy as a German political tradition is shown in the lip service paid to its principles even by the National Socialist regime. See, for example, the essay on changes made in German local institutions under the Nazi regime by Gaertner (1939-1940). On this problem, see a review of the new work by Matzerath (1970) in Der Städtetag (organ of the West German municipal association) for April 1970.

It should be noted that local autonomy, rather than democratic local self-government, was the political tradition involved, and that Nazi practices were as little respectful of the principles of local autonomy as they were of the principles of nationalism and socialism.

7. For statistics on the three systems of cities, see *Statistisches Jahrbuch Deutscher Gemeinden* (1965: xi); *Statistisches Jahrbuch österreichischer Städte* (1968: 7); *Statistik der Schweizer Städte* (1969: 8). In future citations these will be referred to, respectively, as SJDG, SJOeS, and SSS.

Some of the problems involved in using statistics for purposes of intercity comparison within Switzerland are discussed by Zwingli (1969).

8. Actually, for purposes of electing representatives to the upper house of the federal parliament, Switzerland is divided into nineteen cantons and six half-cantons. But for purposes of state government, the full and half-cantons have the same semi-sovereign position. For the sake of brevity, the expression "cantons" is used here when cantons and half-cantons might be more precise.

9. Austria has a small Protestant minority, amounting to about six percent of the total population; it is concentrated in rural areas, however, and thus religion does not serve as a significant form of differentiation among Austrian cities and towns. For the distribution of the Protestant population, see the map in *Kennst du Oesterreich?* (1966: 80-81). There are small pockets of Croats and Magyars in Burgenland and of Slovenes in Carinthia, but these are also predominantly rural and number only about sixty thousand people. For their distribution, see Gabert and Guichonnet (1965: 62-63).

10. Thus, in this study, the data regarding party electoral strength in West Germany and Austria are drawn from the centrally collected statistics of the West German and Austrian municipal associations and these statistics cover city elections. Such statistics are not collected for Swiss cities, except at the cantonal level. As a result, one is forced to derive indicators of party strength in Swiss cities from electoral statistics dealing with federal, rather than city, elections, trusting in the tendency for there to be a rough correspondence between local, cantonal, and federal election results.

The percentages won by the various parties in cantonal elections seem to correspond fairly closely to the percentages they win in federal elections. See the data on cantonal legislature composition and the composition of cantonal delegations to the Federal Parliament in *Annuaire Statistique de la Suisse 1968,* on pages 543, 546-547. Communal electoral results, in turn, seem to resemble the results in cantonal and federal elections, with regard to relative party shares. For example, see the data for Basel-Stadt-canton elections in the *Basler Stadtbuch 1969,* pages 277-278.

11. Inclusion of Vienna, which is also a city-state, did not skew the results for the Austrian intercity comparisons; Vienna was therefore kept in the universe of Austrian cities. Likewise, the city-states of Hamburg, Berlin, and Bremen were also included in most computations involving the German city governments.

12. The output indicators and their sources are as follows: **For Swiss cities,** per capita revenues (total revenues from taxes, grants, shared revenues, business profits, etc.) from SSS (1969: 54); per capita expenditures (operating and capital expenditures) from SSS (1969: 56); city employees per 1,000 residents (includes church employees) from SSS (1969: 26); municipal utility employees from SSS (1969: 28). Percentage of housing built with government aid from SSS (1968: 36); percentage of housing built directly by the city from SSS (1968: 36). Per capita grants (federal and cantonal) is calculated from SSS (1969: 54); percentage of city budget from outside sources ("budgetary dependence") is calculated from SSS (1969). **For Austrian cities,** per capita operating expenditures from SJOeS (1965: 37); per capita revenues (city revenues apart from grants-in-aid and shared revenues) from SJOeS (1965: 40); per capita revenues 1968 from SJOeS (1968: 42); per capita debts from SJOeS (1968: 47; 1961 population); per capita expenditures from SJOeS (1968: 39; 1961 population); per capita water supply (liters/person/day) from SJOeS (1968: 30). Per capita federal grants is calculated from SJOeS (1965: 40); per capita shared revenues is

calculated from the same source, as are the figures for per capita provincial grants. Percentage of new housing built by the city is calculated from SJOeS (1968: 25). Budgetary dependence (shared revenues and grants-in-aid as percentage of total revenues, 1965) from SJOeS (1965: 40). Percentage of new housing built by cooperatives from SJOeS (1968: 25). City employees (including utility employees) per thousand residents from SJOeS (1965: 46). Tax collection costs (expenditures on financial administration, 1968, as percentage of revenues produced by the financial administration) from SJOeS (1968: 40-41). **For West German cities,** pupils per class (Volkschulen only) is taken from SJDG (1965: 240), as is pupils per room; per capita property tax receipts from SJDG (1963: 301-307), as is per capita taxes (all taxes) for the same year, 1962. Information on 1964 is derived from SJDG (1965: 358-366); on 1964 relief expenditures from SJDG (1965: 171-173); on 1963 per capita operating expenditures from SJDG (1965: 303-310); on 1964 per capita library expenditures from SJDG (1965: 248-249); on 1964 per capita city debt from SJDG (1965: 370-371). The ratio of public safety employees per thousand residents in 1963 is calculated from SJDG (1964: 413-415); the ratio of public education employees per thousand residents from SJDG (1964: 413-415); the ratio of total city employees per thousand residents from SJDG (1964: 407-408).

The input variables and their sources are as follows: **For Swiss cities,** area, population density, population increase from SSS (1969: 8); percentage of industrial employment from SSS (1969: 20); motor cars per 1,000 residents from SSS (1969: 40); percentage of taxpayers in lowest bracket (federal income tax) from SSS (1969: 58). Percentage of population fourteen years of age or younger from SSS (1968: 12-13); percentage Protestant from SSS (1968: 20); per capita federal corporate and personal income tax payments from SSS (1968: 66). The party share of the vote is calculated from Eidgenössisches Statistisches Amt (1968: 70-89). Data from Basel-Stadt, including the commune of Riehen, are missing from these returns. Per capita federal personal income tax payments from SSS (1968: 66). The linguistic proportions of the population are calculated from Eidgenössisches Statistisches Amt (1963-1964). **For West German cities,** party vote, 1957-1962 elections, is taken from SJDG (1963: 379-380); percentage Protestant from SJDG (1963: 408-409); private cars per 1,000 residents from SJDG (1963: 105-107); percentage of housing built after 1949 from SJDG (1963: 388-391); percentage of refugees, 1961, from SJDG (1963: 408-409); percentage dependent workers in labor force from SJDG (1963: 441-443); percentage turnout, city elections, 1957-1962, from SJDG (1963: 379-380); 1961 population, percentage of population 65 years old or more and under 15 years of age, from SJDG (1963: 408-409); percentage industrial employment from SJDG (1963: 428-429), as is percentage of civil servants in the labor force (SJDG, 1963: 441-443); percentage of miners in the labor force is taken from SJDG (1965: 162-163); area from SJDG (1963: 2-3); per capita personal income from SJDG (1964: 438-440); data on housing from SJDG (1963: 140-142, 388-391); population increase, 1951-1961, from *Statistisches Jahrbuch für die Bundesrepublik Deutschland 1953* (1951 population), pages 38-39. **For Austrian cities,** area, 1961, is taken from SJOeS (1965: 6); 1961 population from SJOeS (1965: 7); density from SJOeS (1968: 7); 1951 population from SJOeS (1959: 13); industrial employment from SJOeS (1965: 7); infant mortality figures from SJOeS (1968: 9); per capita product from SJOeS (1968: 65); party vote, 1961-1965, from SJOeS (1965: 19); turnout from SJOeS (1965: 18); percentage of houses with running water from SJOeS (1962: 67).

13. These tests included comparisons of the simple correlation coefficients; comparison of the amount of variance explained by the political variables, holding the socioeconomic variables constant, and vice versa, in stepwise and multiple regression; and comparison of the beta weights in multiple regression equations. Considerations of space preclude presentation of the correlation and regression tables, some of which are available in the original form of

this article as presented in paper form to the conference on European bureaucracy at Indiana University in December 1970. That paper also provides tables showing the range of variation of the independent and dependent variables.

14. Some of the regressions calculated have been omitted from Table 2 for reasons of space.

15. Election campaign materials, city public relations materials, and city documents, generally, might also be an important means of identifying these patterns.

16. See Sharkansky (1969: 19).

17. Note that the correlations for North-Rhine-Westphalian cities must be higher than those for all West German cities in order to be of equal significance. Correlations for the NRW cities must be at least .34 to be significant at the .05 level of probability. Note also that the correlations in Table 2 are not directly comparable from country to country, since different numbers of cities are involved in each country. Correlations for the 29 Swiss cities must be somewhat higher to match, in significance, correlations for the 47 Austrian cities and even higher still, to match the correlations for the 57 German cities. To reach the .05 level of significance, correlations for the Swiss cities must be at least .34; correlations for the Austrian cities, at least .24; and correlations for the German cities, at least .23.

18. Neuss is a manufacturing town on the Rhine, opposite Dusseldorf. It is 73 percent Catholic, above-average in per capita income, and votes about 55 percent for the CDU. Why it has such a high pupils/class ratio and why it spends less than half the amount per capita spent by other NRW cities is not clear.

19. In most scattergrams showing party/output or ecology/output relations for Austrian cities, the nine Styrian cities tend to cluster in the quadrant opposite from that occupied by the five Vorarlberg cities. The Styrian towns, in southeastern Austria, are poor, industrial, and Socialist, while the Vorarlberg towns, on the Swiss border, while equally industrial, are prosperous and anti-Socialist. At the provincial government level, however, both Styria and Vorarlberg have been controlled by the Populists of the OeVP, except for the short period (1953-1957) when the SPOe had a relative majority in Styria. While Socialist majorities, at least relative majorities, have been common in Austrian city governments, they are very rare in Austrian provincial governments, except for those of Vienna and Carinthia. Data on Austrian provincial politics can be found in Verbindungsstelle der Bundesländer (1966). Annual reports on policy developments at the provincial level can be found in *Oesterreichisches Jahrbuch* (published by the Bundespressedienst).

The question of state impact must, of course, be directly attacked in comparative studies of state and local policy, rather than merely inferred, as I am doing here. See the measures used by Ira Sharkansky (1970) to determine the impact of region on American state government policy and the general discussion by Teune (1970).

20. Note that the three performance indicators in West German public education (pupils/class, pupils/room, school employees/10,000 residents) are not highly intercorrelated. Pupils per class correlates at .60 with pupils per room, but only at .06 with school employees per 10,000 residents.

21. Compare the importance of Roman Catholicism in Clark (1968).

22. The SPOe is strong in a variety of towns ranging in size from Vienna, with 1.6 million people, to Fohnsdorf in the Mur valley, with 12,000. The SPOe is strongest in percentages in the small mining and manufacturing towns of the Mur valley, and in the province of Styria, the center of Austrian heavy industry. The SPOe is weakest in the equally industrial towns of Western Austria, on the Swiss border, in the province of Vorarlberg. The OeVP, as of 1968, held relative majorities with 14 of the 47 Austrian cities; OeVP towns included Innsbruck, with 100,000 people (57 percent of the vote) and Lienz, also in Tyrol Province, with 11,000 people (58 percent of the vote).

23. In multiple regression, religion, area, motorization, language, growth rate, income, population, percentage of foreigners, industrialization, density, persons per room, and age structure will account for: 99.8 percent of the variance in the Communist vote; 89.0 percent of the variance in the Catholic Party vote; 79.1 percent of the variance in the Social Democratic vote; and 74.5 percent of the variance in the Radical vote.

24. On the unique decision rules of Swiss politics and policy-making, see the sources listed in note 5.

25. The "end of ideology" in Swiss, Austrian, and West German socialism is treated in Langner (1965) and in Lipset (1964).

26. Data on urban performance under Weimar are derived from *Statistisches Jahrbuch deutscher Städte,* 1928, volume 23, pages 63-65, 282-289, 308-311.

27. See Fried (1971).

28. In the 290 largest West German cities (1965), there were only 43 private schools at the elementary level, with 6,369 pupils, out of a total of 5,090 elementary schools, with 1.9 million pupils (SJDG, 1965: 221).

29. The results might be somewhat different if we could differentiate between the impact of the Social Christian factions and the Catholic-Conservative factions in the Swiss Catholic political movement. In this study, the Social Christian electorate has been counted with the Catholic-Conservative electorate in defining the relative strength of political Catholicism in Swiss cities.

30. The Socialist vote at the cantonal level correlates at .58 with industry; .38 with per capita income; .31 with motorization; .46 with canton population; .38 with canton population growth; .40 with percentage of foreigners in the population; and .81 with percentage of Protestants. At the local level, however, Socialist voting strength correlates with industry at .14; with income at −.21; with motorization at −.25; with city size at .00; with population growth at −.22; with foreigners at −.31; and with Protestantism at .68.

Data on Swiss cantons are drawn from *Annuaire Statistique de la Suisse 1967; Statistische Quellenwerke der Schweiz,* 1965, volume 28; Union Bank of Switzerland's publication, "Switzerland in Figures, 1968"; Masnata (1963: 243); Tschäni (1966: 367-368). For another analysis of Swiss cantonal performance data, but without political variables and combining cantonal and local outputs, see Stohler and Frey (1967).

31. See the studies cited in notes 3 and 4.

32. For an early study of European and American municipal statistics, see the chapter on comparative municipal statistics in Fairlie (1908: 275-285).

REFERENCES

BOADEN, N. T. and R. F. ALFORD (1969) "Sources of diversity in English local government." Public Administration (Summer): 203-223.
BRECHT, A. (1941) "Three topics in comparative administration: organization of government departments, government corporations, expenditures in relation to population," pp. 289-318 in C. J. Friedrich and E. S. Mason (eds.) Public Policy, 1941. Cambridge, Mass.: Harvard University Graduate School of Public Administration.
CHALMERS, D. (1964) The German Social Democratic Party. New Haven, Conn.: Yale Univ. Press.
CLARK, T. N. (1968) "Community structure, decision-making, budget expenditures, and urban renewal in 51 American communities." American Sociological Review (August): 576-593.

CODDING, G. A., Jr. (1967) Governing the Commune of Veyrier. Boulder: University of Colorado Bureau of Governmental Research.

––– (1961) The Federal Government of Switzerland. Boston: Houghton Mifflin.

COLLOTTI, E. (1968) Storia delle due Germanie, 1945-1968. Turin: Einaudi.

CRANE, P. (1953) Enterprise in Local Government: A Study of the Way in Which Local Authorities Use Their Permissive Powers. London: Fabian.

DAWSON, R. E. and J. A. ROBINSON (1963) "Interparty competition, economic variables, and welfare politics in American states." Journal of Politics (May): 265-289.

DEUTSCH, K. and R. BREITLING (1963) "The German Federal Republic," in R. Macridis and R. Ward (eds.) Modern Political Systems. Englewood Cliffs, N.J.: Prentice-Hall.

DYE, T. R. (1966) Politics, Economics and the Public: Policy Outcomes in the American States. Chicago: Rand McNally.

EDINGER, L. (1968) Politics in Germany: Attitudes and Processes. Boston: Little, Brown.

Eidgenössenschaft Steuerwaltung (1969) Finanzen und Steuern von Bund, Kantonen, und Gemeinden 1967. Berne: Statistische Quellenwerke der Schweiz.

––– (1968) Steuerbelastung in der Schweiz: Charge fiscale en Suisse 1967. Berne: Statistische Quellenwerke der Schweiz.

ENGELMANN, F. C. (1966) "Austria," in R. A. Dahl (ed.) Political Oppositions in Western Democracies. New Haven, Conn.: Yale Univ. Press.

FAIRLIE, J. A. (1908) Essays in Municipal Administration. New York: Macmillan.

FOGARTY, M. P. (1957) Christian Democracy in Western Europe, 1820-1953. London: Routledge and Kegan Paul.

FRIED, R. (1971) "Communism, urban budgets, and the two Italies: a case study in comparative urban government." Journal of Politics (November).

FRY, B. R. and R. F. WINTERS (1970) "The politics of redistribution." American Political Science Review (June): 508-522.

GABERT, P. and P. GUICHONNET (1965) Les alpes et les états alpins. Paris: Presses universitaires de France.

GAERTNER, E. (1939-1940) "Die Wandel des kommunalen Aufgabenkreises von der Machtübernahme bis zur Jetzzeit," pp. 1-64 in Volume 6-7 of Jahrbuch für Kommunalwissenschaft. Stuttgart: Kohlhammer.

GANGEMI, L. (1967) Sistemi finanziari comparati. Turin: UTET.

GERLICH, P. and H. KRAMER (1969) Abgeordnete in der Parteiendemokratie. Munich: R. Oldenbourg.

GIROD, R. (1967) "Geography of the Swiss party system," pp. 132-161 in E. Allardt and Y. Littunen (eds.) Cleavages, Ideologies, and Party Systems. Helsinki.

GRUNER, E. (1969) Die Parteien in der Schweiz. Berne: Franke Verlag.

––– and J. SIEGENTHALER (1963) "Die Wahlen in die eidgenössischen Räte in Oktober 1963," pp. 113-154 in E. Gruner (ed.) Jahrbuch 1964 der Schweizerischen Vereinigung für Politische Wissenschaft. Lausanne.

GUMPEL, H. J. and C. BOTTCHER (1963) Taxation in the Federal Republic of Germany. Chicago: Commerce Clearing House.

HALLER, H. (1969) "Der finanzausglerch in der Bundesrepublik Deutschland und in der Schweizerischen Eidgenössenschaft." Schweizerische Zeitschrift für Volkswirtschaft und Statistik (June): 121-137.

HANNAK, J. [ed.] (1963) Bestandaufnahme Oesterreich 1945-1963. Vienna: Forum Verlag.

HENIG, S. [ed.] (1969) European Political Parties: A Handbook. New York: Praeger.

HENLE, W. (1964) Die Ordnung der Finanzen in der Bundesrepublik Deutschland. Berlin: Duncken and Humblot.

HOFFERBERT, R. I. (1966) "Some structural and environmental variables in the American states." American Political Science Review (March): 73-82.

HUMES, S. and E. MARTIN (1961) The Structure of Local Governments Throughout the World. The Hague: Martinus Nijhoff.

JACOB, H. (1963) German Administration Since Bismarck. New Haven, Conn.: Yale Univ. Press.

Kennst du Oesterreiches (1966) Vienna: Oesterreichischer Bundesverlag für Unterricht, Wissenschaft und Kunst.

KOJA, F. (1967) Der Verfassungsrecht der österreichischen Bundesländer. Vienna: Springer Verlag.

LANGNER, A. (1965) Katholizismus und freiheitlicher Sozialismus in Europa. Cologne: Bachem.

LAUFENBERGER, H. (1961) Economie des finances suisses. Geneva: Librairie de l'Université.

LINEBERRY, R. L. and E. P. FOWLER (1967) "Reformism and public policies in American cities." American Political Science Review (September): 701-716.

LIPSET, S. M. (1964) "The changing class structure and contemporary European politics." Daedalus (Winter): 271-303.

MARVICK, D. and R. STIEFBOLD (1966) Wahlen and Parteien in Oesterreich. Vienna: Oesterreich Bundesverlag.

MASNATA, F. (1963) Le parti socialiste et la tradition démocratique en Suisse. Neuchâtel: La Baconnière.

MATZERATH, H. (1970) National-sozialismus und kommunale Selbstverwaltung. Stuttgart: Kohlhammer.

MAY, R. J. (1969) Federalism and Fiscal Adjustment. Oxford, Eng.: Oxford Univ. Press.

MULLER, E. N. (1970) "Cross-national dimensions of political competence." American Political Science Review (September): 792-809.

NEUMANN, R. G. (1966) The Government of the German Federal Republic. New York: Harper and Row.

Oesterreiches Statistisches Amt (1970) Gebarungsübersichten 1968 (Bundesländer, Gemeinde-verbände un Gemeinden). Vienna.

OLIVER, F. R. and J. STANYER (1969) "Some aspects of the financial behavior of county boroughs." Public Administration (Summer): 169-184.

Osterreichischer Gemeindebund (1957) Zehn Jahre österreichischen Gemeinden. Vienna.

POWELL, G. B. (1969) Social Fragmentation and Political Hostility. Stanford: Stanford Univ. Press.

PRYOR, F. L. (1968) Public Expenditures in Communist and Capitalist Nations. London: George Allen and Unwin.

REES, I. B. (1969) "Local government in Switzerland." Public Administration (Winter): 420-450.

SCHACHNER-BLAZIZEK, P. (1967) Finanzausgleich in Oesterreich. Graz: Leykam.

SCHUTZ, E. (n.d.) Die Stellung osterreichischen Gemeinden. Vienna: Informationszentrum für kommunale Finanzierungen.

SHARKANSKY, I. (1970) Regionalism in American Politics. Indianapolis: Bobbs-Merrill.

––– (1969) Public Administration. Chicago: Markham.

––– (1968) Spending in the American States. Chicago: Rand McNally.

––– (1967) "Economic and political correlates of state government expenditures: general tendencies and deviant cases." Midwest Journal of Political Science (May): 173-192.

SHELL, K. [ed.] (1969) The Democratic Political Process: A Cross-National Reader. Waltham, Mass.: Ginn, Blaisdell.

––– (1962) The Transformation of Austrian Socialism. New York: State University of New York.
SIEGFRIED, A. (1948) La Suisse: Démocratie-Témoin. Neuchâtel: La Baconnière.
STOHLER, J. and R. L. FREY (1967) "Das verhältnis von regionaler Wirtschaftstruktur und öffentlichen Ausgaben." Revue suisse d'Economie politique et de Statistique (September): 353-386.
TAIRA, K. and P. KILBY (1969) "Differences in social security development in selected countries." International Social Security Review 22, 2: 139-153.
TAUTSCHER, A. [ed.] (1961) Handbuch der österreichischen Wirtschaftspolitik. Vienna: Bastei.
TEUNE, H. (1970) "Cross-level analysis: national and local systems." Presented to the Southwestern Sociological Association, Dallas, March.
TIMM, H. and G. GIERE (n.d.) "Gemeindefinanzen," pp. 299-319 in Volume IV of Handwörterbuch der Sozialwissenschaften.
TSCHANI, H. (1966) Profil der Schweiz: Ein lebendiges Staatsbild. Zurich: Rascher.
Verbindungsstelle der Bundesländer (1966) Die Wahlen in den Bundesländern seit 1945: Nationalrat und Landtage. Vienna.
––– (n.d.) Das Steueraufkommen der Gemeinden im Jahr 1964 and 20 Jahr Wohnbaufinanzierung des Bundes, der Bundesländer und Gemeinden, 1945-1965.
VILLANI, A. (1968) Le strutture amministrative locali. Milan: Franco Angeli.
WAEGENER, F. (n.d.) "Gemeindeverwaltung," pp. 323-328 in Volume IV of Handwörterbuch der Sozialwissenschaften.
WELLS, R. H. (1961) The States in West German Federalism. New York: Bookman.
––– (1953) "Local government," in E. H. Litchfield (ed.) Governing Postwar Germany. Ithaca: Cornel Univ. Press.
––– (1932) German Cities. Princeton: Princeton Univ. Press.
ZIMMERMAN, H. (1970) Oeffentliche Ausgaben und regionale Wirtschaftsenwicklung. Basel: Kylos.
ZWINGLI, U. (1969) "Les villes suisses à la lumière des chiffres." Bulletin d'information de l'Union des villes suisses (November): 4-12.

Part IV

THEORETICAL AND METHODOLOGICAL ISSUES

IN CROSS-NATIONAL RESEARCH

Chapter 12

Research Perspectives in Comparative Local Politics:
Pitfalls, Prospects, and Notes on the French Case

Mark Kesselman

The past several years have witnessed the rapid emergence of comparative local politics as a special field of study (for reviews of literature on local politics outside the United States, see Cazzola, 1971; Daland, 1969; Hanna, 1972-1973; Hanna and Hanna, 1971; Kaufman, 1970; Kesselman and Rosenthal, 1972; Kuroda, 1970; Médard, 1970; Rabinovitz, 1968; Rosenthal, 1968; Zawadski, 1970). Given the extensive literature on American local politics, a temptation exists simply to apply research perspectives from the study of American local politics to non-American settings. The purpose of this article is to oppose such an approach. Indeed, an understanding of the pitfalls in the field of American local politics can improve prospects for clarifying the scope of comparative local politics.

AMERICAN LOCAL POLITICS

The field of American local politics has been dominated since World War II by a methodological and substantive dispute centering on the internal

AUTHOR'S NOTE: *This article incorporates material revised from other papers I have written: "Research Choices in Comparative Local Politics," The New Atlantis, 1 (Winter 1970), 48-64; "Overinstitutionalization and Political Constraint: The Case of France,"* Comparative Politics, *3 (October 1970), 21-44; and "Research Perspectives in Comparative Local Politics: Pitfalls and Prospects,"* Comparative Urban Research, *1 (Spring 1972), 10-30. I am grateful for financial assistance from the Guggenheim Foundation, the National Science Foundation (Grant GS-2537), and the Institute on Western Europe, Columbia University.*

distribution of power in American communities. (Propositions culled from the community power literature are tested by Gilbert, 1972.) Two major errors have resulted from divorcing the study of local politics from larger political issues. The nature of local power was obscured by failing to recognize that cities were not masters of their fate and that not everyone with local influence was a local resident. This failure to recognize that geographically external components were integral elements of the local political process was complemented by a failure to examine the impact of local politics on the broadest aspects of American politics.

The Political Context of Local Politics

Most studies of American local politics have treated cities as self-sufficient and have assumed that attention could appropriately be confined to actors and issues within the city's geographic boundaries. If it has been easier to simplify the conceptual landscape in this way, the consequence has been to confuse the geographic map for the map of effective political influence. There is no logical reason for a "residency requirement" in order to qualify as locally influential. Yet, possibly because it is difficult conceptually to integrate geographically external actors and forces within the scheme of local power, social scientists appear to have imposed such a requirement de facto. The fact that we may not yet have devised sufficiently sensitive research instruments to measure the intermittent influence of officials outside the community does not mean that their influence is negligible. (Nor am I focusing on the problem of nondecisions, raised by Bachrach and Baratz, 1970. The question raised here cuts across the distinction between decisions and nondecisions: influence outside the city may enter into either type of decision.)

An objection might be that a Pandora's box is being opened—to the possible influence exerted on local politics by such external agencies as absentee-owned corporations, and national elected and administrative officials. Yet, if external agencies *are* influential and accepted theories and techniques do not identify their influence, the fault lies with the research, not with the reality the research is intended to illuminate.

One observer notes, "Several of the most basic books have dealt with the local government as a closed system, seemingly removed from the environment to which it is expected to respond" (Sherwood, 1969: 64). The most influential works on American local politics typically stress the importance of the wider political context—and then proceed to ignore it.

Hunter states that "the primary interest here is in discussing the nature of the exercise of power in a selected community and as this community relates to the larger society" (Hunter 1963: 2). But virtually his only other reference to these relationships merely reaffirms that "Regional City cannot be isolated from state, national and international affairs. To understand the community as a metro-politan entity the fact cannot be overemphasized" (Hunter, 1963: 167, 98).

In one of the few passages where Dahl refers to the relationship of New Haven to the larger setting of American politics, he emphasized the importance of the relationship: "It might be said that the political system of New Haven is scarcely autonomous enough to furnish us with adequate explanations of its own stability, for stability may depend much less on the beliefs of the citizens locally than on state and national institutions" (Dahl, 1961: 13). Yet no analysis is provided of how external institutions impinge on the decision-making process in New Haven to promote stability. (Ironically, in *After the Revolution?*, Dahl cautions advocates of community organization and participatory democracy to realize that the local community cannot be separated from the larger society.)

Agger, Goldrich, and Swanson (1964: 1-2) assert that modern local governments "are affected by what takes place in ... other communities, by what takes place in the national and state systems of which they are a part, and by what takes place in foreign countries." But they make only brief allusions (in chs. 2, 5) to these external influences.

There are several exceptions to the general trend. Banfield and Wilson (1965) devote a chapter of *City Politics* to the city in the federal system. In a comment on external political forces in "American Political Science and the Study of Urbanization," Sayre and Polsby (1965) call for research on the representation of cities in the state legislature and links between local officials and higher levels of government. Sayre and Kaufman (1965) discuss officials of other govern-ments in the city's political process. The increased importance of external actors is indicated by Sayre in a subsequent publication (Sayre, 1970), where he suggests that among the New York City mayor's six constituencies, two—the state and national government—lie outside the city. Yet among the myriad studies of local power in America, few focus on the way in which the city is articulated with a wider environment. For example, among recent volumes devoted to the study of local politics (Hawley and Wirt, 1968; Aiken and Mott, 1970; Bonjean et al., 1971; Wirt, 1971; Ricci, 1971), only one article (Walton, 1968) explicitly focuses on the integration of the community with the larger political setting. (Several other exceptions include Altshuler, 1965; Connery and Leach, 1960; Derthick, 1970; Kirkpatrick, 1970; Martin, 1965; Nuttall et al., 1967; Roig, 1967; Vidich and Bensman, 1958; and studies of metropolitan government, e.g., Bollens and Schmandt, 1970. The two best works on this question, Grodzins, 1968, and Warren, 1963, will be analyzed below. Judging from research in progress summarized in Clark, 1971, the future will not be much different from the past.)

The failure to relate local and national politics is especially striking given the stress placed by students of American politics on the localistic nature of those politics. Students of political parties (Grodzins, 1968), legislative behavior

(Miller and Stokes, 1963), and administrative activity (Selznick, 1949) have deftly integrated local influences in these sectors.

Grodzins' study of the complex nature of American federalism has profound implications for local politics. He demonstrates that, because of the intimate linkages of personnel, functions, and power among different levels of government, "It is difficult to find any governmental activity which does not involve all three of the so-called 'levels' of the federal system" (Grodzins, 1968: 9-10). Grodzins examines the subtleties of American federalism through history, case studies of specific functions, and channels of integration, and suggests a more comprehensive view of the local impact of government than is generally found in the literature on local politics. The implication for local politics, which Grodzins did not explore in view of his primary interest in the consequences of federalism for higher levels of government, is that the subject cannot be isolated from contextual factors. Yet Grodzins' work has had little impact on research perspectives in local politics.

Other studies which systematically integrate external influences within the study of local politics are little known: Baker (1971), Martin (1965), and Warren (1963). Warren notes, "Unfortunately, the growing recognition of the importance of extracommunity ties has not been accompanied by a commensurate development of research on the nature of such ties or of conceptual tools for analyzing them. . . . [Most studies make] the implicit assumption that the larger society is somehow extraneous to the community. . . . [Yet] one need not go 'outside' the community to find the larger society. The larger society inheres in the local community . . . " (238, 239, 269). (Also see Adrian and Scoble in Wirt, 1971: 13 and 41 respectively; and Smith and LaNoue, 1971.)

The general trend has thus been either to ignore the wider political context in which American local politics occurs or to consider the problem one of intergovernmental relations.

Systemic Consequences of Local Politics

The second major error resulting from not relating local politics in American cities to the wider context is the converse of the first. As the first error resulted from a failure to appreciate the impact of larger political forces on local politics, so the second results from a failure to appreciate the impact of local politics on larger political forces. Little attention has been given to the consequences of American local politics for questions of political power, conflict, repression, and change in American politics.

The very notoriety and success of the methodological debate within the American community power literature promoted a provincialism in terms of larger questions which the literature left unanswered and, indeed, unformulated. The articulation of local politics with wider political forces was framed in terms of analogy—not causal relationship. Disputes about the distribution of power within communities were also viewed as disputes about the distribution of power within the larger American arena, with a surprisingly facile readiness to generalize from the micro level of a local community to the macro level of a large nation-state. (Scoble points out, "No matter how good, i.e., how valid and reliable, the study of a particular American community may be, it does not permit us to draw inference about the distribution of power in the national polity," [Scoble in Wirt, 1971: 111].) Because the argument about the contours of community power was transposed so readily to the level of whole political systems, a comfortable feeling was conveyed that the debate centered on real-world, large political issues. This feeling, in turn, further discouraged analysis of the actual political consequences of local politics: a problem quite distinct from the internal distribution of community power. Because the controversy seemed so appealing on its own terms, no one bothered to ask if it might not represent a tempest in a teapot.

Given the great emphasis in the United States on local autonomy, it is especially noteworthy that the consequences for American politics of the way local politics is structured have been studied so little. Indeed, Tocqueville was one of the few to speculate on the systemic consequences of American local government. (For an analysis which studies comparable linkages between the structure of state politics and the wider course of American politics, see McConnell, 1966.)

I would suggest that local government in America has performed an important function of political control during periods of rapid social transition and upheaval, when control by the national government was weak. Local government was influential in assimilating immigrant groups and nullifying the radical challenge they might have represented. Local politics was an important channel for mobilizing new groups, functioning precisely as Huntington (1968) counsels institutionalization should proceed: local government incorporated new social forces at minimum disruption to established political arrangements.

The conservative effects of local government upon American politics have rarely been described. Thus, for example, although Dahl (1961) studies the changing pattern of political control in New Haven and traces shifts in power from aristocrats to merchants to ethnic machine politicians, he nowhere points out that no matter who controlled local government, it functioned primarily to dampen and limit change. The important role American local government played in promoting stability cannot be understood without reference to its links to organized labor (see Greenstone, 1969) and the political machine. Classic studies of the machine (whether pro or con) stress its importance in organizing the newly mobilized. But the conclusion is less often drawn that the machine's unique "contribution" was that it derived its strength from lower class ethnic immigrants, while its leaders forged close ties with the established economic elite. What is usually stressed is that the growth of the machine disturbed established political arrangements, yet the machine can also be regarded as an ideal co-optive device for controlling change and limiting a structural redistribution of power.

This interpretation is corroborated by the turmoil surrounding the decline of the machine. And nowhere is the depoliticization of issues by relegating them to the local arena more evident, the conservative consequences of local politics more clear, than in the description of recent revolutionary insurgent discontent (both inchoate and organized) as the "urban crisis."

Similarly, under the guise of enlarging participation, local governments are seeking devices (e.g., local city halls, neighborhood councils) to reestablish stability and control. Although extensive literature on urban riots suggests linkages between what occurs in cities and the turmoil presently confronting American politics, students of local politics often define the question as an urban problem and merely a new phase of local politics. Yet the "urban crisis," with the concomitant response by local government (in cooperation with other levels of government) of force and institutional innovation, is a critical factor in contemporary American politics. (For signs of a new approach, see Katznelson, 1972; Lipsky, 1970; Parenti, 1970.) The broad significance of local politics is obscured (with conservative consequences) if it is viewed as discrete activity occurring within thousands of localities. The broad significance and pattern of local politics can only be ultimately measured by the cumulative impact on the body politic of the local political activity occurring in manifold and diverse locales.

A reciprocal relationship may have sustained the parochialism of the study of American local politics and national politics: some of the largest dramas of American politics were relegated to the field of local politics (ethnic and racial conflict, urban growth, environmental deterioration), with the implication that these were local matters and thus not really of great moment for American politics. But, conversely, the field of American local politics has generally studied politics within cities as if conflicts were isolated and random, without aggregate consequence for the course of American history. While public housing, highway construction, urban renewal, and education affect the structure of conflict in the United States, these issues have been treated, from the perspective of local politics, merely as providing grist for the mill of "who governs"; their larger significance has thus been lost.

Many students of American politics assume that, in contrast to virtually every other political system, the United States is exempt from basic conflicts. A dominant concern of scholars has been to understand (and, frequently, to foster) consensus and stability, with a corresponding neglect of conflict and change.

Comparative politics provides better theoretical guidelines in this regard because it has placed at the center of concern large questions of modernization, political order and decay, institution-building, violence, revolution, and change. The field of comparative politics has not been without shortcomings. Its major aim, buttressed by an implicit trickle-down theory of political power, has been to assist those in power to increase their dominance, not to aid the powerless (see Hopkins, 1972; Kesselman, 1973).

Moreover, students of comparative politics have not come to grips with the converse of the problem regarding local politics raised here. With the notable exceptions of Stein Rokkan (1970), and Fred Riggs (1964), students of comparative politics have not attempted to integrate the study of local government and politics with the study of political change. Despite stress on the importance of political parties, political culture, the military, bureaucracy, education, and other elements, little attention has been given to how mobilization is related to institutionalization at local levels, particularly the growth of local government.

In its concern with macro level processes (most commonly, national matters located at the center), comparative politics has often overlooked local politics, parties, and institutions. (Zolberg, 1966: ch. 5 and "Conclusions" makes a similar point.) Urbanization has been amply studied (e.g., see Hauser and Schnore, 1965) but the relationship between urbanization and local politics or the implications of urbanization for political power at local and higher levels have not.

Urbanization represents a change in the location, quantity, distribution, and quality of political power. In Lowi's terms (1964), urbanization is potentially both distributive and redistributive in its effects. (Horowitz, 1967, recognizes the latter, when he observes that urbanization weakens rural elites, but he does not point out the distributive potential of urbanization.) The precise character of the transformation which urbanization produces, however, is variable, and cannot be understood without reference to the intervening variable of local political structures. (At the micro level, Nie et al., 1969, find a null relationship between urbanization and individual participation. They do not aggregate relationships.)

The failure to appreciate its complexity has led analysts to see urbanization as simply supportive of "modernity" (Lerner, 1958), or simply disruptive (Huntington, 1968). Yet, just as the first view ignored the potentially destabilizing effects of urbanization, so the latter view neglected the extent to which local political structures may exert control. (This is what led Huntington, 1968, to overestimate the political challenge posed by squatters' settlements in Latin America.)

But if comparative politics has overlooked local politics or adopted a manipulative approach, it has at least emphasized the importance of political dynamics, crisis, and historical change. In this respect comparative politics provides elements superior to the traditional approach toward American politics and local politics.

The literature on linkage politics evinces a comparable concern to relate that which was formerly seen as disparate and unrelated (Rosenau, 1969). Rosenau's comment on the relationship of international and national politics is parallel to the point being developed in this article for national-local relationships: "The world may well be passing through a paradoxical stage in which *both* the linkages and the boundaries among polities are becoming more central to their daily lives" (Rosenau, 1969: 47).

Some Reasons

What—in addition to the reasons already analyzed—accounts for the provincialism of American local politics, the failure to integrate the study of local politics with the wider political setting, and the lack of attention to the consequences of local politics for the American political system?

(1) The logic of social inquiry partially explains lacunae in the study of American local politics. The field was defined in recent times by Hunter (1963, first published 1953). If succeeding literature took issue with Hunter's major argument about the distribution of community power and the methods he used, it took for granted the context of the argument, which assumed an insulation of local from national politics. The "dialectics" of the scholarly controversy centered around one important question but ignored others.

(2) The methods used to study local power, including the reputational, positional, and decisional, make it difficult to locate actors outside the city who might be locally powerful. Sociometric questions focus on those actually living within the city. (Questions from various studies are presented by Fox, 1971: 6.) "Decisions" are defined in such a way as to exclude the influence exerted by those outside the city. And the *frequency* with which a given official intervenes is not an adequate indication of his *power*. (For a similar point, see Wright, 1969: 233.)

(3) Two additional reasons for the insularity of the study of American local politics relate to the American tradition of local autonomy. First, stress on the political autonomy of American cities (both a presumed fact and a value) encouraged the study of local politics in isolation from national politics. It is frequently asserted that American political parties are decentralized, with major power located at the base rather than the summit. (When the concept of reciprocal deference was introduced by Eldersveld, 1964, to challenge the theory, only county leaders and—at the limit—state leaders were introduced into the scheme.)

Clark asks, "Precisely *how great* a degree of autonomy must exist before a community or community complex can be classified autonomous?" (Clark, 1968: 85-86, emphasis in original.) But the difficulty goes beyond measuring the relative autonomy of communities or deciding how much autonomy must exist before analyses of community power are appropriate. The point is not that community studies are illegitimate if community autonomy is limited but that, regardless of the relative autonomy, if there are actors external to the community who are intimately involved in the local political game, they should be included in systematic analyses of that game. And, conversely, the ultimate point of that game can only be understood from the perspective of politics—not merely local politics.

The relative degree of autonomy of American cities has varied (and doubtless diminished) through time. But the relationships are not unilinear. (I am grateful to Wallace Sayre for this and other suggestions.) Efforts in the late nineteenth and early twentieth centuries to increase local autonomy (frequently associated with the Progressive movement) include the short ballot, separate election dates for local and national elections, the nonpartisan ballot, and constitutional home rule.

(4) In addition to the political autonomy of American cities, their presumed financial autonomy helps account for the failure to relate the study of American local politics to larger issues. Compared with cities elsewhere, American cities are relatively autonomous financially. One study of budgetary expenditures in forty-five countries found that the United States ranked fourth in terms of the ratio of municipal to national governmental expenditures (Vieira, 1967: 161, cited in Sherwood, 1969: 71). The relative financial autonomy of American cities is illusory, however. American cities face severe financial difficulties and are heavily dependent on state and national governments for financial assistance, particularly during recent decades as new programs in the fields of education, poverty, and welfare have considerably increased state and federal involvement in the local political process. Even if, as Grodzins (1968) and McConnell (1966) persuasively argue in this regard, he who pays the political piper may not call the tune (since localities have other resources which need to be assessed in measuring the flow of influence), nonetheless the financial network of intergovernmental relationships (tax collection, grants-in-aid, fiscal policy) makes the process of local decision-making more complex than community power studies suggest. Again, the historical factor needs to be stressed. Federal grants-in-aid, primarily since the New Deal, have increased local resources but diminished local financial autonomy. Revenue sharing may (but probably will not) reverse the trend.

COMPARATIVE LOCAL POLITICS

Studies of local politics outside the United States converge in pointing to the importance of linking local politics with the wider political setting. In many cases, sophistication has been displayed in studying how local political processes are interwoven with national politics, and, conversely, how local politics affects the articulation of national conflict. In a study of African local politics, William and Judith Hanna observe, "It is not customary to include center actors in an analysis of a 'local' political system, but we have done so here because of the obviously incomplete picture of locally relevant politics that would otherwise result." (Hanna and Hanna, 1969: 191.) The Hannas (1971: ch. 9) also review what they term interlevel bases of political integration. They identify three kinds of linkage: formal (legally prescribed intergovernmental relationships), informal (among influentials at various levels), and mixed (within the political party).

In Latin America, Francine Rabinovitz states, "There is also strong theoretical justification for beginning analysis of local politics with the national sphere. While in countries where urban politics are more autonomous, the overall national level of urbanization may not be an important factor, for Latin

American national processes of all kinds are integrally and perhaps decisively related to urban actions" (Rabinovitz, 1969: 98-99; also see Rabinovitz 1968; and, for a similar point regarding Italy, Balbo, 1969).

And Donald Rosenthal explains that the reason he did not carry out the kind of community study in India he had originally planned was that Indian communities perform functions requiring analysis in different terms than American communities. Rosenthal cites as one of these functions "orientations to the wider arenas" of state and national politics; and he concludes, "Ultimately, of course, decisions are made for the municipality even if they are not made locally. . . . How such decisions for the locality are made at higher levels is a subject requiring additional study. . . . " (Rosenthal, 1968: 299; see also Rosenthal, 1970 and Kuroda, 1970).

The point is applicable for both rural and urban localities. Edward Hassinger notes that "to understand what is happening in rural areas we must take into account the decisions of centralized agencies and their bureaucratic organizations . . . " (Hassinger, 1961: 358). Annmarie Walsh observes that "city and metropolitan organization are inextricably bound up in national systems of government and politics. . . . " (Walsh, 1969: 128).

Rokkan's research on the mobilization of the periphery (Rokkan, 1970) focuses on the timing and manner by which Norwegian localities became mobilized and on the dynamics by which congruent cleavages developed in diverse locales. From his perspective (and ours), there is no rigid separation between local politics and comparative politics.

My suggestion has been that an examination of shortcomings in American politics can clarify the study of comparative local politics. While theory and model building are unwarranted at this time, the following list of questions and concerns (far from exhaustive) is aimed at further refining research perspectives in comparative local politics in order to account for complex realities.

Questions for Research and Theoretical Clarification

(1) The unit of analysis. While primary attention in the study of local politics has usually focused on the municipal level, other levels may also be influential. At the submunicipal level, neighborhoods, linkage associations, street level government, and bureaucracy and private associations warrant close study. At higher levels than the city, there are such units as the county, the metropolitan region, and the megalopolis. Aiken and Alford point out, "The analyst should not prematurely assume, just because his *data* refer to cities, for example, that the theoretical concepts appropriate for an adequate explanation must also be defined in terms of the city as the causal agency. The basic causal forces may be at a larger, more macro level (the state, region, or nation as a whole), or at a more micro level (organizations, individuals), or perhaps at all three levels" (Aiken and Alford, 1970: 862; also see Przeworski and Teune, 1970).

The general problem of the level of analysis is complicated by the relationship of the unit chosen to juridical boundaries: a unit may not have a juridical existence, it may straddle several juridical entities, or it may contain several.

(2) Interlevel interventions. National and state officials commonly intervene in local affairs. In addition to the range of formal state and national regulations regarding tax collection, performance, and requirements which sanction local intervention by officials at higher levels, these officials also intervene informally and draw upon skills, experience, resources, and status in an attempt to influence local decision-making.

The flow of influence is by no means in one direction, however. Intervention by local officials at higher levels, both individually and collectively, is probably a frequent (and little-studied) occurrence.

Local intervention may be particularistic, such as obtaining a bureaucratic position for a constituent or a local improvement for a town; or it may be collective: action by local officials throughout the country on behalf of all localities (e.g., changing national regulations, obtaining larger funds for grants-in-aid). The constant struggle by localities for funds from higher levels of government is probably a critical feature of local politics in all countries. Interest group representation and intervention in national affairs by local officials is an important aspect of the complex of intergovernmental relations. (Scarrow, 1971, observes that it is a frequent practice in Great Britain; see my comments on France below.)

In addition to government officeholders, other power wielders geographically external to the community may directly influence local politics. Two obvious examples are economic influentials (decisions regarding plant location, wage and personnel policy, etc.) and cultural style setters (see Warren, 1963: ch. 8).

(3) Overlap among personnel. Frank Myers (1970) has pointed to what he terms "legislative *pantouflage*" in France: the practice in the Fifth Republic of national administrative officials (cabinet ministers, members of ministerial *cabinets,* prefects, etc.) running for municipal and legislative office. (Also see Médard, 1972 and Kesselman, 1970.) The linkage between political party cadres and local officials has received little attention. (See my article elsewhere in this volume.) More generally, recruitment patterns and overlap of personnel may link diverse sectors, such as the national and regional bureaucracy, party system, legislatures, and local government.

(4) A dimension requiring additional elaboration is centralization-decentralization. Walsh points out, "Decentralization and centralization are treated as opposites in a zero-sum relation, although practical experience suggests that an increase in local roles does not necessarily entail a decrease in central power, and vice versa" (Walsh, 1969: 179, also see Fesler, 1965; Roig, 1966; and Sherwood's [1969] critique of the centralization-decentralization concept as summing up the variability of power relations between local and national officials).

More generally, better conceptual tools and theory are needed to describe the dynamics of the areal organization of power (see Maass, 1959; Heaphey, 1971). As Rosenthal (1970) and Tarrow (1971) have pointed out, one should not assume a unilinear process of urbanization or mobilization of the periphery. Moreover, local government may be articulated with national politics in ways that combine different kinds of linkages at different levels and sectors. Thus, patron-client relations may prevail in rural settings alongside class and interest-based organization in urban areas, while traditional local elites may seek modern local government positions as a way to protect corporate privilege. Describing a complex set of relationships by one concept—interest representation, centralization-decentralization, patron-client relations, corporatism, etc.—may misleadingly designate one component as exclusively influential.

By asserting that the study of local and national politics should be integrated, I do not mean to imply that cleavages in local politics may not cross-cut cleavages salient in other arenas. Indeed, one focus might be on the degree to which cleavages in national and local arenas, or different local arenas, are superimposed (e.g., Great Britain and, to a lesser degree, the United States) or cross-cutting (e.g., France).

(5) Introducing the time dimension also permits study of the dialectical relationship of local and national politics. Yet care should be taken to avoid a teleological bias (as Huntington, 1971, points out). For example, rather than cleavages in diverse localities necessarily becoming more uniform and congruent with national cleavages through time—a nationalization of local politics—the opposite process may occur (which might be considered the localization of national politics). (I noted this development in post-de Gaulle France in Kesselman, 1972: 286.) Or the relationship between national and local cleavages may change in other ways.

(6) A general problem is the very distinction between local politics, subnational politics, local factors in national politics, and national factors in local politics. For example, Swartz distinguishes local-level politics from local politics by asserting that "the latter is not incomplete as local-level politics is" (Swartz, 1968: 1). However, he reduces the value of the distinction—although adhering closer to reality—when he questions whether "there now exists a group or groups sufficiently isolated and self-determined to qualify as having local politics." Swartz' concept of local-level politics comes closest to capturing the nuances I would like to convey. (Also see Daland, 1969; Milbrath, 1970; Przeworski and Teune, 1970; Ostrowski and Teune, 1970. Kesselman and Rosenthal, 1972, question the value of distinguishing local politics from comparative politics and suggest a framework for comparative local politics.) If local politics is an integral part of the study of comparative politics, this should not minimize its importance, suggest that its character is transparent, or preclude the possibility of its having special features. On the contrary, the job of analysis is complicated rather than simplified by the fact that the tailor-made model—available from the study of American local politics—is inappropriate.

FRENCH LOCAL POLITICS

To illustrate how the study of local politics needs to be conceptualized differently from the way American local politics is normally approached, the structure of local politics in France will be examined. With respect to local politics and its study, the French tradition of a unitary state, extreme centralization, and prefectural administration presents a polar contrast to American theory and practice.

Until recently French scholars neglected the study of local politics. (See Kesselman, 1967, and—for evidence of a changing approach—Médard, 1970, and Mabileau, 1972.) A parallel contrast between French and American political practice was a contrast between the approaches used to study local politics in the two countries: the French were so far from considering the study of local government to be political that they termed the field "local administration" and confined attention to administrative law. It was presumed that everything to be learned about local government could be obtained by examination of the *Code Municipal* (given sufficient exegesis). Thus, whereas in the United States it was assumed that local governments were autonomous and local politics could be understood without reference to outside actors, in France it was assumed that local politics did not even exist because of administrative centralization.

Just as local politics is not autonomous in the United States, however, there is a lively field of local politics in France. The following notes are concerned with some of its central features. The first difficulty encountered in studying French local politics is to define the research site itself; several factors complicate the choice of the unit to be studied.

Since the Revolution, France has been divided into communes, the basic territorial unit. Communes vary widely in size—from nearly a million for Marseille (Paris, the largest city in France, has a different legal status from other communes), to communes so small that they are legally uninhabited. Yet there is no distinction in France between rural and urban communes comparable to the American distinction between incorporated and unincorporated areas. All communes have basically the same legal powers, whether they contain 300 inhabitants or 300,000.

Related to the legal definition of the commune is a question concerning the "informal" definition of a city. In the United States, urban areas frequently spill over the boundaries of any one incorporated area. (At the limit, this leads to the "1400 governments" that Wood [1964] describes as governing the New York metropolitan area.) In France, the same problem exists—although the creation of urban districts and urban communities both simplifies and complicates the problem of defining the unit to be studied.

But equally important is that the converse also occurs in France. Whereas in the United States, urban jurisdictions contain exclusively urban populations, in France urban areas may be located within a commune which also contains a large proportion of rural residents. The census definition of a nonagricultural commune is one which contains an agglomeration of 2,000 inhabitants. However, many rural residents may live in a commune but outside the agglomeration. According to the census definition, these inhabitants are urban dwellers. (Jambrek, 1969, alludes to a similar phenomenon in Yugoslavia.)

French communes are less self-sufficient than are American cities. Compared to the latter, French communes raise a far smaller proportion of their own and of total government revenue. The French administrative system is highly centralized. Communes are regulated by a legal code which delegates extensive supervisory powers to the prefect (a national official). Local decisions must be approved (and may be annulled) by the prefect. Thus, a question arises concerning the extent to which the commune is a viable decision-making unit.

Moreover, for these reasons, the territory legally defined as a commune may not constitute a community with a sense of collective self-identity. Laurence Wylie (1967) questions whether Chanzeaux exists for its citizens as a meaningful entity, as does Edgar Morin for Plodèmet (1967)–and they answer the question differently. Indeed, a critical aim of many French mayors is to make salient or heighten communal identity in part to strengthen the commune's bargaining position with the state (Kesselman, 1967).

Related to the question of the commune's existence as a meaningful collectivity is the extent to which it is unified as a political community. Analysis of voting behavior points in opposite directions. MacRae (1967) found that French localities are considerably more split by national elections than are American communities. Multiple regression analysis demonstrates that "group differences in the vote" are greater at the local level in France compared to the United States. On the other hand, communes are far more united when they vote in local elections than when they vote in national elections: the commune remains a more solidary unit for municipal elections. The danger of fragmentation within the commune in response to national cleavages triggers a consensual response regarding local politics. The "rhetoric of apolitisme," prevalent in many French localities, describes an ideal and, to some extent, a reality of local political life. Thus, the commune may be both united as a solidary unit and fragmented regarding national issues (Kesselman, 1967).

Another factor relevant for the definition of the field of local politics in France is the commune's strength vis-à-vis the state; a central assumption has heretofore been that French communes are not autonomous and that decisions are not made *by* the locality but *for* the locality.

Local Dependence

A leading theme in the "folklore" about French local politics is that little exists. France is highly centralized and most decisions are presumed to be made by the national government, either by the Parisian ministries or by the prefect, the government's representative in a locality. Many factors sustain a distorted view of the distribution of power in provincial France. It is not because such factors are not influential but because others also exist that a different picture of local power in France is closer to reality.

Historical and Social Factors. De Tocqueville first enunciated the view that, beginning long before the Revolution, France has been undergoing a process of increasing centralization. Wealth, talent, and power have flowed from the provinces to Paris, leaving the former weak and impoverished. Subsequently, the prefect, the successor of the celebrated intendant as ruler, has maintained and strengthened Parisian dominance. (For an amusing discussion of this theme, bordering on caricature, see Leuthy, 1955.) Hortatory works (by Parisians) urging Frenchmen to decolonize the provinces testify to the continued importance of the theme (Club Jean Moulin, 1969; Mayer, 1968; Brindillac, 1957).

Legal Factor. Generations of students in the Ecole Libre de Science Politique (now Institut d'Etudes Politiques) and France's law schools have studied local government from the perspective of administrative law. (The subfield is named local administration, which implies much about the way the field is regarded.) Administrative law teaches that local governments owe their creation to the unitary state, and such creation does not signify the slightest delegation of sovereignty. The powers local governments exercise derive exclusively from a revocable grant by the state which, through its representative, the prefect, maintains close surveillance—and a potential veto—over local decisions. The *tutelle,* the term used to denote national control over local decisions, is the same term used to describe the relationship between parent and ward. It is an easy step from the position that local governments are *legally* subordinate to the view that they lack *effective* power.

Number of Communes. The large number of communes in France reinforces the assumption that each one is weak. France contains nearly 38,000 communes. And the infamous French rationality has led to a virtually uniform legal system inevitably geared to the limited capacities of small communes. Thus, the large number of communes appears to reduce the autonomy of any one—perhaps not accidentally consistent with the classic principle of divide and rule. (Administrative reforms being carried out in the early 1970s may modify this picture.)

Finances. Linked to the large number of communes is their weak financial base. The taxes communes are allowed to levy do not permit financial autonomy. Many communes are dependent on a national equalization tax fund for the minimum resources needed to administer the commune. All communes are partially dependent on the government for grants-in-aid and loans for public works. Local financial servitude reinforces political servitude as well.

Apathy Toward Politics. It has often been asserted that interest in local government, as measured by voting turnout in local elections, is low. (The situation is more complex but the misunderstanding influences scholarly assessments of local autonomy. See Kessleman, 1967, and Tarrow, 1971, for a rebuttal.) Lack of interest in local government reduces the vitality of local politics—and presumably leaves communes weaker.

Local Autonomy

It would be foolish to deny the extent to which communes rely on the state. But to accept this obvious reality does not require accepting the view that communes are without influence vis-à-vis the state. While strong centralizing factors exist in France, other factors exert a decentralizing influence. Local officials, in fact, are highly skillful at resisting state pressure and achieving their limited goals. One can begin to identify the extent of local power in relation to the national government merely by enumerating the various ways the national government has failed to achieve changes it has sought. (Also see Roig, 1966.)

The national government repeatedly tried to reform local finances without success. In the first months of the Fifth Republic, the government issued a decree fundamentally modifying the local tax system. The reform would normally have required legislative approval but the government was acting at the time under special powers delegated to it by the referendum of October 1958. Indeed, the government probably used the decree procedure because it feared seeking parliamentary approval for the reform. Yet, despite its extraordinary power, the government decided to postpone application of the reform because of widespread opposition from local officials. Six years passed without the issue being revived. And when the government finally presented the plan to parliament in 1964 (which it was forced to do since its special powers had lapsed), more than 150 deputies of the majority threatened to break discipline and vote against the government if it did not compromise: it did (Roig, 1964; *Nord-Matin*—Lille, Dec. 22, 1965).

Similarly, the government has devoted major (but generally unsuccessful) efforts to reforming the communal structure. Various plans have been presented to regroup communes, including intercommunal associations, the fusion of communes, urban districts and industrial development zones (Belorgey, 1967). Most provide for voluntary arrangements and approval by the municipal councils concerned is required. Local governments have taken advantage of plans for the limited pooling of personnel and services. However, despite the government's proffer of financial incentives, local governments have not voluntarily agreed to accept more sweeping proposals, such as urban districts and fusion of communes. Years after the plans were launched only 10 of the 41 cities over 100,000 population had adopted the plan of an urban district; less than one percent of French communes had merged with neighboring communes (Bernard, 1969). In a plan for the compulsory grouping of communes in four metropolitan areas (Bordeaux, Lille, Lyon, and Toulouse), parliamentary approval was slow in coming despite a Gaullist majority. Although provisions for compulsory membership of communes exist in several other plans, the government has not attempted to invoke its power to force recalcitrant communes to join.

Plans for comprehensive local reform have been officially proposed and then not pursued to completion after the government calculated that the political cost of pressing for adoption was too high (Morice, 1968, 1969). In some cases, the government feared even to release the contents of possible reforms. (A leak in *Le Monde* about one such plan was utilized extensively by the opposition in the referendum campaign of April 1969.)

In 1964, the government launched an ambitious regional reform, providing for regional development councils, teams of regional development experts, regional prefects, and conferences among regional administrative officials. The reform was stymied (among other reasons) by the opposition of local office holders (Grémion, 1966; Grémion and Worms, 1968a, 1968b). The most sweeping regional reform plan proposed by the government was defeated in a referendum in 1969 and led to de Gaulle's resignation (see below).

When mayors have resisted the national government, it has occasionally retaliated—but usually in vain. For example, the government attempted to replace the Association of French Mayors, the largest interest group of French mayors—which frequently opposes government policies—with a new organization of its own creation (the Mayors Bureau). Yet mayors refused to be swayed from their original allegiance and the government eventually admitted defeat (Roig, 1964; Kesselman, 1967: ch. 7).

Thus, we can conclude that local governments are not as powerless as the usual view suggests. Measured by their ability to resist changes, they appear to possess substantial power indeed. The minister of the interior was not simply flattering local officeholders when he stated "Everything is possible with the cooperation of local officeholders; nothing is possible without it."

Strangely enough, in a country often cited as a model case of centralization, politics in France is highly localistic. One reason is that institutional factors foster localism: the ratio of deputies to the electorate is four times higher than in the United States. In the United States, the smaller size of election districts for the House of Representatives compared to the Senate encourages a more localistic outlook among representatives than senators. The even smaller size of French legislative districts results in an extremely localistic orientation. The French electoral system encourages legislators to place a high priority on the defense of local interests and officeholders; the French legislature vigilantly defends localities against the government and the bureaucracy.

Two additional institutional features strengthen the French parliament's attachment to localities. The *cumul* makes it possible to hold municipal and legislative office simultaneously; a majority of French deputies are also municipal councilors, mayors, and general councilors. (And the proportion is increasing: see Dogan, 1965, 1967; Médard, 1972.) The power of the *député-maire* or *sénateur-maire* is thus reinforced—as is his concern for his local power base. An extreme case is provided by Jacques Chaban-Delmas, who, when prime minister during 1969-1972, remained mayor of Bordeaux and frequently presided over meetings of the Bordeaux city and metropolitan council. French localities thus have the most direct possible access to the center. Secondly, French senators are elected by an electoral college primarily composed of mayors and municipal councilors. The method of selecting senators ensures that the Senate will act as representative of local officials. The Senate, in fact, is often referred to as the Chamber of Communes. An even higher proportion of senators than deputies hold local office in addition to their legislative position.

More significant as sources of support, however, than their allies in the legislature—and more fascinating to study—are administrative allies of local officials. For the existence of such allies in the state administrative apparatus calls into question a second theme in the "folklore" about French local politics—the opposition between localities and the state.

If the commune does not exist in relative isolation from the national context, neither is it merely an appendage of national agencies or in perpetual combat with these agencies. The factors already discussed create the necessity for close and continued contact between local and national officials. The system of their relationships (as Grémion, 1970: 54 puts it) is complex; its importance places it at the heart of French local politics. To study local politics in France means focusing on the character, relevance, and consequences of relationships between national and local officials. Parliamentary representatives, general councilors, the prefect and prefectural officials, officials in Paris ministries—all of whom live outside the commune and would not be considered part of the local system of power if that system were circumscribed territorially—are among the leading actors in the system of linkages that constitute an integral aspect of local politics in France. Grémion and Worms (1968a, 1968b, 1970) stress the importance of the *relais* which secure the commune's access to the state; Roig (1964, 1966) emphasizes the importance of the *réseaux* of public and private, national and local officials. However named, the linkages are not merely another dimension of French local politics but one of its essential features. Some features appear constant; others are variable.

Linkages: Constant Features

At the center of the game are what Jean-Pierre Worms calls the prefect and "his" notables (Worms, 1966). A number of other actors appear, including senators, deputies, and general councilors, when elites are questioned about key figures (Grémion, 1969, 1970; Longpierre, 1970). However, especially in rural communes, the two dominant figures are the mayor and the prefect, to whom we will confine attention.

Certainly there is opposition between the two. The prefect is charged with administering laws which mayors often resent and resist. The prefect has major responsibility for exercising the *tutelle,* which mayors profess to regard as humiliating evidence of the low regard in which they are held by the state. In addition to his negative powers of control, the prefect is also expected by the government to obtain from mayors political cooperation and support for government policies. The prefect continually seeks to persuade mayors to sponsor government-favored reforms.

From the mayor's viewpoint, he is dependent on state help in order to achieve his own goals. Negatively, he wants to prevent government reforms from endangering his position. Positively, in order to achieve his goals, the mayor needs the state's approval and financial support—which the prefect plays a critical role in obtaining.

In brief, the power of each depends in ample measure on maintaining good relations with the other. *And it is precisely because each needs the other, because there is mutual dependence, that a relationship not of opposition and hostility but of symbiosis develops.*

A study of government in large cities throughout the world notes, "In the most centralized systems, the channels of control are so complex and overlapping that local officials rely heavily on their personal ability to influence and bargain with authorities at the center in order to break logjams. At the same time, central authorities remain largely dependent upon the will and skill of local officials to carry out their policies and to fulfill their targets" (Walsh, 1969: 129-130). Worms suggests that the tacit cooperation between prefect and notables is based upon partial convergence of their interests, what he terms the "profound solidarity of prefect and notables" (Worms, 1966: 261; also see Avril, 1971; Grémion, 1970).

(1) Each has an interest in obtaining the kind of legitimacy that the other has the power to grant. The prefect aims at demonstrating to local interests his representativity and devotion to the département's welfare. His success in this attempt improves both his performance within the département and his standing with his hierarchical superiors. The mayor hopes to demonstrate to his constituents his strategic bargaining position in face of the state and—paradoxically—the special position he occupies as the state's representative in the commune. During interviews I conducted, mayors often introduced me to constituents as having been sent by the prefect, not the less significant because false. Each uses the other to strengthen his bargaining position with the state. The success with which each thereby improves his performance as relay between state and citizenry influences his power position. Thus, in their attempt to achieve legitimacy, which enhances their ability to bargain with the state bureaucracy, mayor and prefect are in a state of mutual dependence.

(2) Each needs the other's support to help maintain the local harmony each one separately points to as evidence of his own leadership skills. The mayor's major aim within the commune appears to be defensive—to prevent political (particularly partisan) struggles from disrupting municipal harmony. In order to foster local unity, he can point to the need for a united front in his dealings with the prefect, who represents the majesty, power, and largesse of the state. And the favorable access he enjoys to the prefect, in turn, strengthens his hand in preventing local conflicts.

The prefect's primary responsibility is to maintain law and order in the department. Mayoral cooperation plays a key role in the prefect's exercise of the police function. And, conversely, mayors can damage local harmony by throwing the weight of their position to the side of disruption (e.g., by siding with strikers against the government, refusing to carry out government decrees, and resigning from office).

(3) Conversely, each needs the other as a scapegoat to explain his *lack* of success—the mayor to justify the slow pace of local improvements, the prefect to justify his meager success in achieving government-favored reform. And each can enhance his power by presenting the other as a formidable opponent, in face of whom a united (and docile) front is necessary.

(4) Each has substantial need of the other's positive cooperation. The prefect is well-situated to reward his friends and punish his enemies. Given the commune's legal and financial dependence on the state, the prefect represents a potential ally in the enemy camp. He can, is expected to, and does act as the representative of local interests in the bureaucratic machine. Mayors need the prefect's help in untangling administrative red-tape for their constituents. Given the lack of expertise in most communes, mayors need the services of the prefecture to help administer the commune. And they expect the prefect to expedite their applications for grants-in-aid.

The prefect also requires the mayor's help in carrying out his positive goals. The prefect can only advise departmental and local governments to sponsor local investments; he is not empowered to sponsor public works under his own authority. The need for the prefect to secure local cooperation is underscored by the fact that most civilian public works in France are carried out by municipalities (although the funds to pay for local improvements frequently derive from national grants-in-aid and loans).

(5) Mayors and the prefect occupy similar roles and are subject to similar kinds of pressures. Both are political executives of a geographic constituency. Both attempt to represent their constituency externally. Both orient decisions on the basis of the "general interest" rather than specialized technical interests. Shared interests are strengthened in face of shared enemies. The alliance of mayors and prefect protects each from other groups, including citizens, field service administrators, the Paris bureaucracy, and interest groups.

(6) More generally, both share an interest in the maintenance of a traditional political game in which they are experienced, skillful, and successful players and from which they derive manifold benefits. Thus both have been found to resist attempted innovations in the French administrative structure which would threaten the traditional equilibrium (see the works of Grémion and Worms). "The resistant capacity of tradition is much greater than generally realized. . . . The search for local influence has led each administration (a ministry's representative in the départe-ment) to organize . . . a group of notables who use access to the administrative apparatus in order to block any local initiative capable of endangering the equilibrium of *situations acquises*" (Club Jean Moulin, 1969: 38). To illustrate the process: it appears that the consequence of regional reforms of 1964 was not to weaken departmental political institutions but rather to strengthen them by heightening departmental loyalties among local notables and national field adminis-trators (Grémion and Worms, 1968a: 111).

A major consequence of the mutual dependence between mayors and the prefect, the partial convergence of their interests, and the potential sanctions each can bring to bear against the other, is close cooperation in opposing reform. That the government recognizes such a situation is attested to by its frequent rotation of prefects. And, as an example of what the government wants to prevent, on the occasion of the departure from one département of an administrative official (not a prefect but a representative of the ministry of agriculture), the president of the general council spoke of the "immense services he has rendered the département. In cooperation with local agricultural organizations, we tried to obtain from the ministry his maintenance in the Tarn but in vain" (Républicain du Tarn, October 8, 1965).

When the ministry of the interior ordered a sudden and extensive shift of prefects in 1967, the decision encountered great opposition from local officials. The député-maire of Metz (an ally of the Gaullists who subsequently became a cabinet minister) complained about the lack of consultation. The mayor of Toulouse protested against the "brutality of an unexpected movement." As a government clears the choice of its ambassador with with foreign government and the American President clears local administrative appointments with the senator from the state concerned, powerful officials in a French département expect to be consulted about the choice of the département's prefect.

The referendum of April 1969 on regional and senatorial reform, whose defeat cost de Gaulle the presidency, represents the most dramatic example where local officials successfully opposed administrative reform. In a survey of local officials throughout France, most general councilors and urban mayors interviewed reported voting "non" in the referendum. Small town mayors were more divided. (For a description of the survey and a presentation of other data, see my other article in this volume.)

The Gaullist regime learned well the lesson of the referendum: after avoiding the question of regional and local reform for more than a year following the referendum's rejection, subsequent proposals completely abandoned comprehensive reforms envisaged earlier. Instead, municipal regrouping arrangements must be approved by local officials; on the regional level, existing départements are loosely linked and traditional general councilors (rather than both general councilors and representatives of functional associations) are designated to represent a département at the regional level. (For an analysis of institutional reforms of 1970-1971, see Mawhood, 1972.)

By way of conclusion, one report observes that "there exists a local society far more rich and lively than Parisians generally imagine. If its capacity to innovate has been extremely weak, its capacity to resist changes remains extremely strong" (Grémion and Worms, 1968b: 59). And the "local society" consists of the dense network of relations between national, departmental, and local officials which is an integral aspect of local politics in France. (In addition to the administrative factor discussed here, which concerns the relationship between prefects and mayors, an additional factor is political opposition between the Gaullist government and many local officials. The subject is explored in Kesselman, 1970, and my other article in this volume.)

TABLE 1
LOCAL OFFICIALS' VOTE IN APRIL 1969 REFERENDUM

	% Yes	% No	Abstention and No Answer	%	(n)
General councilors	24	69	7	100	(110)
Small-town mayors	49	42	9	100	(55)
Urban mayors	25	60	15	100	(48)
Total					(213)

Linkages: Variable Features

Variations occur in addition to the relatively constant features of the political game in provincial France that have been described. The variations relate to differences among localities, differential access to the state, the differential importance of various figures in urban and rural areas, and the impact of reforms. What follows represents an attempt to systematize some of the relationships by suggesting what might be termed "lower middle range" propositions.

1. Differential Behavior in National and Local Politics

   1.1 The larger the commune, the more chance: local politics will diminish in importance as a means of symbolizing local solidarity;

   1.2 the commune will be fragmented by local elections;

   1.3 cleavages in local elections are apt to converge (be congruent, coincide) with cleavages in national politics.

   1.4 the more local political cleavages converge with national cleavages, the more likely: interest in local politics (as measured by voting turnout) will decline;

   1.5 interest in national elections (as measured by voting turnout) will exceed interest in local elections (Kesselman, 1967).

2. Access to Paris

   2.1 The further from Paris the commune is located, the less frequently can local elites travel there;

   2.2 the less frequently they travel to Paris, the less likely they will establish direct links to national official there;

   2.3 the less they establish direct ties, the greater the need for intermediaries.

   2.4 The importance of extra-communal political representatives is correlated with the extent of the commune's distance (isolation) from Paris (Grémion and Worms, 1968a).

3. Role of Individual Actors and Urbanization

   3.1 The prefect's power is greater in rural than urban areas. (Grémion, 1969, found that the prefect had fewer potential competitors for power in rural areas.)

3.2 In rural areas the prefect's role is more likely to be diffuse and to include the functions of integrator, politically prominent figure, and economic expert; in industrial areas, his power is more apt to become specialized in the direction of overall integration rather than either of the other two functions.

3.3 As localities become more urbanized: the prefect's supremacy is apt to be challenged by the député-maire (or sénateur-maire) of a large urban center;

3.4 the prominence of other traditional figures, such as the president of the general council, deputies without a local mandate, and mayors without a national mandate, decline in importance (Grémion, 1969).

3.5 Mayors of communes in the process of economic expansion are more likely to accept conflicts of interest as legitimate (Kesselman, 1967).

4. Political Differences among Localities

4.1 Communist mayors are more likely to lead communes where power is centralized (Roig et al., 1970); and where policy outputs are higher (Roig et al., 1970; Kesselman, 1967).

4.2 Départements which are regional capitals are more likely to: establish direct links with Paris;

4.3 be more receptive to regional reform;

4.4 favor more rational methods of distributing local resources (as compared to equalitarian distribution; Grémion and Worms, 1968a).

5. Functional Differences among Elites

5.1 Political elites are more likely than economic or administrative to be attached to traditional political institutions.

5.2 Political elites are less likely to accept reform proposals than are other elites (Grémion and Worms, 1968a).

6. Economic Variables

6.1 Communes with greater possibilities for self-financing: are more centralized than others;

6.2 have fewer direct links to Paris (Roig et al., 1970).

6.3 Economically disadvantaged regions are more likely to accept reform proposals (Grémion and Worms, 1968a). However, the economically disadvantaged region that Grémion and Worms study, Acquitaine, has the rich resources of a large regional capital and an uncommonly powerful mayor, which facilitate acceptance of regional reform. The plight of a more truly deprived region, such as neighboring Limousin, might suggest that a threshold must be reached before a disadvantaged region is well enough off to try to remedy its disadvantaged status.

These propositions do not begin to form a coherent theory of local power in France. They do direct attention to the central role played in local politics by the network of national-local relationships.

IMPLICATIONS

My aim has been to show that research on American local politics has underestimated the impact of actors and forces outside the city and has exaggerated the isolation and autonomy of American local politics. Although comprehensible in light of American conditions and mythology, the consequence ironically was to diminish the importance of local politics—a fact to which the sterility of traditional work on "state and local politics" in the United States bears witness. When interest in the field of local politics increased in the 1950s and 1960s, the reason was not so much because of findings illuminating the nature of American politics or even local politics, as because of general debates which were provoked centering around the issue of pluralism.

The scattered observations cited above by scholars studying local politics outside the United States suggest the need to grapple with the general theoretical issue discussed here. The study of France can provide help. Given the French system of unitary government, with a strong national bureaucracy and prefectural administration (an administrative system, incidentally, far more widely copied than the American), it has been difficult to dissociate the study of local politics from national influences. Yet, just as American scholars frequently accepted mythology for reality and studied local politics in isolation, French scholars accepted the mythology of administrative law which considered local governments to be legal wards of the national government.

My argument has been that comparative local politics should have as a foremost concern an issue barely studied in the United States and usually studied from a narrowly juridical perspective in France: the complex game of allocating political and economic resources to localities that is carried on by actors from various governmental levels and functional sectors. The game is not primarily one involving "intergovernmental relations" although different levels are involved; nor of interest group pluralism, although there are features in common; nor of administrative law, although legally defined powers are influential. It is also quite different from the field of local politics represented by American community studies.

While it is possible to describe some elements in the game, many others remain unexplored. What are the different types of *réseaux* established in different communes (see Roig, 1969)? What is the articulation between French local governments, political parties, and interest groups? (see Mabileau, 1972; Kesselman, 1970, and my other article in this volume.) What changes have structural reforms wrought, such as the creation of regional planning institutions and urban communities (see Grémion and Worms, 1968; Mawhood, 1972; Bodiguel, 1969)?

Moreover, concomitantly with empirical research, additional theoretical work needs to be done which explores and clarifies the interrelationships among concepts such as local politics, subnational politics, intergovernmental relations, street level politics and bureaucracy, the localistic aspects of national politics and the localistic ingredients of national politics.

It would be premature to generalize from the limited research available. However, although the French case appears distinctive when viewed from an American perspective, it may ultimately appear quite typical when viewed from the perspective of comparative local politics.

REFERENCES

AGGER, R. E., D. GOLDRICH, and B. E. SWANSON (1964) The Rulers and the Ruled: Political Power and Impotence in American Communities. New York: John Wiley.

AIKEN, M. and R. R. ALFORD (1970) "Community structures and innovation: the case of public housing." American Political Science Review 64 (September): 843-864.

AIKEN, M. and P. E. MOTT [eds.] (1970) The Structure of Community Power. New York: Random House.

ALTSHULER, A. (1965) The City Planning Process: A Political Analysis. Ithaca: Cornell Univ. Press.

AVRIL, P. (1971) "Le Système local français et la modernisation politique." Analyse et Prévision 12 (November): 1319-1328.

BACHRACH, P. and M. S. BARATZ (1970) Power and Poverty. New York: Oxford Univ. Press.

BAKER, J. H. (1971) Urban Politics in America. New York: Charles Scribner.

BALBO, L. (1969) "Perception of community issues and political demand: a study of decision-making in a Southern Italian community." Presented to the meetings of the International Conference on Community Decision-Making, Milan, July.

BANFIELD, E. and J. Q. WILSON (1965) City Politics. Cambridge, Mass.: Harvard Univ. Press.

BELORGEY, G. (1967) Le gouvernement et l'administration de la France. Paris: Armand Colin.

BODIGUEL, J. L. (1968) "Les communautés urbaines," pp. 473-479 in Institut d'Etudes Politiques de Grenoble, Aménagement du territoire et développement régionale.

BOLLENS, J. C. and H. J. SCHMANDT (1970) The Metropolis: Its People, Politics and Economic Life. New York: Harper & Row.

BONJEAN, C. M., T. N. CLARK, and R. L. LINEBERRY [eds.] (1971) Community Politics: A Behavioral Approach, New York: Free Press.

BRINDILLAC, C. (1957) "Décoloniser la France." Esprit 25 (December): 862-877.

CAZZOLA, F. (1971) "Bibliografia." Science Sociali 1 (April): 124-144.

CLARK, T. N. [ed.] (1971) "Research in progress on the community." University of Chicago Department of Sociology, Society for the Study of Social Problems, Committee for Community Research, International Sociological Association and the Committee for Community Research and Development.

Club Jean Molin (1969) Le citoyen au pouvoir: 12 regions, 2000 communes. Paris: Seuil.

CONNERY, R. and R. H. LEACH (1960) The Federal Government and Metropolitan Areas. Cambridge, Mass.: Harvard Univ. Press.

DAHL, R. (1970) After the Revolution? Authority in a Good Society. New Haven, Conn.: Yale Univ. Press.

——— (1961) Who Governs? New Haven, Conn.: Yale Univ. Press.
DALAND, R. T. [ed.] (1969) Comparative Urban Research: The Administration and Politics of Cities. Beverly Hills: Sage Publications.
DERTHICK, M. (1970) The Influence of Federal Grants: Public Assistance in Massachusetts. Cambrdige, Mass.: Harvard Univ. Press.
DOGAN, M. (1967) "Les filières de la carrière politique en France." Revue française de sociologie 8 (October): 468-492.
——— (1965) "Le personnel politique et la personnalité charismatique." Revue française de sociologie 6 (July): 305-324.
ELDERSVELD, S. J. (1964) Political Parties: A Behavioral Analysis. Chicago: Rand McNally.
FESLER, J. (1965) "Approaches to the understanding of decentralization." Journal of Politics 27 (August): 536-566.
FOX, D. M. (1971) "Methods within methods: the case of community power studies." Western Political Quarterly 24 (March): 5-11.
GILBERT, C. W. (1972) Community Power Structure: Propositional Inventory, Tests, and Theory. Gainesville: Univ. of Florida Press.
GREENSTONE, D. (1969) Labor in American Politics. New York: Alfred A. Knopf.
GREMION, P. (1970) "Introduction à une étude du système politico-administratif local." Sociologie du travail 12 (January): 51-73.
——— (1969) La Structuration du pouvoir au niveau départemental. Paris: Centre de Sociologie des Organisations.
——— (1966) "Résistance au changement dans l'administration territoriale." Sociologie du travail 3 (July-September): 276-295.
——— and J. P. WORMS (1970) "L'Etat et les collectivités locales." Esprit 38 (January): 20-35.
——— (1968a) Les institutions régionales dans la société locale. Paris: Centre de Sociologie des Organisations.
——— (1968b) "La concertation régionale: innovation ou tradition" in Institut d'Etudes Politiques de Grenoble, Aménagement du territoire et développement régionale, I. Paris: La Documentation française.
GRODZINS, M. (1968) The American System. Chicago: Rand McNally.
HANNA, W. J. [ed.] (1972-1973) Special issues, Journal of Comparative Administration (November; February).
——— and J. L. HANNA (1971) Urban Dynamics in Black Africa: An Interdisciplinary Approach. Chicago: Aldine-Atherton.
——— (1969) "Polyethnicity and political integration in Umuahia and Mbale," pp. 162-202 in R. T. Daland (ed.) Comparative Urban Research: The Administration and Politics of Cities. Beverly Hills: Sage Publications.
HASSINGER, E. (1961) "Social relations between centralized and local social systems." Rural Sociology 26 (September): 354-364.
HAUSER, P. and L. F. SCHNORE [eds.] (1965) The Study of Urbanization. New York: John Wiley.
HAWLEY, W. D. and F. M. WIRT [eds.] (1968) The Search for Community Power. Englewood Cliffs, N.J.: Prentice-Hall.
HEAPHEY, J. J. [ed.] (1971) Spatial Dimensions of Development Administration. Durham, N.C.: Duke University Press.
HOPKINS, R. (1972) "Securing authority: the view from the top." World Politics 24 (January): 271-292.
HOROWITZ, I. L. (1967) "Electoral politics, urbanization, and social development in Latin America." Urban Affairs Quarterly 2 (March): 3-35.

HUNTER, F. (1963) Community Power Structure: A Study of Decision Makers. Garden City, N.Y.: Doubleday Anchor.

HUNTINGTON, S. P. (1971) "The change to change: modernization, development, and politics." Comparative Politics 3 (April): 283-322.

――― (1968) Political Order in Changing Societies. New Haven, Conn.: Yale Univ. Press.

JAMBREK, P. (1969) "Some methodological problems of cross-national comparison of community decision-making: the case of Yugoslavia." Presented to the International Conference on Community Decision-Making, Milan, July.

KAUFMAN, C. (1970) "Latin American urban inquiry: some substantive and methodological commentary." Urban Affairs Quarterly 5 (June): 394-411.

KATZNELSON, I. (1972) "Participation and political buffers in urban America." Presented to the annual meeting of the American Political Science Association, Washington, D.C., September.

KESSELMAN, M. (1973) "Order or movement? The literature of political development as ideology." World Politics 26 (October): 139-154.

――― (1972) "Changes in the French party system." Comparative Politics 4 (January): 281-301.

――― (1970) "Overinstitutionalization and political constraint: the case of France." Comparative Politics 3 (October): 21-44.

――― (1967) The Ambiguous Consensus. New York: Alfred A. Knopf.

――― and D. B. ROSENTHAL (1972) "Local power and comparative politics: notes toward the study of comparative local politics." Presented to the annual meeting of the American Political Science Association, Washington, D.C., September.

KIRKPATRICK, S. J. (1970) "Multidimensional aspects of local political systems: a conceptual approach to public policy." Western Political Quarterly 23 (December): 715-732.

KURODA, Y. (1970) "A comparative study of local politics in Asia: a review and methodological suggestions." Presented to the Congress of the International Political Science Association, Munich.

LERNER, D. (1958) The Passing of Traditional Society. New York: Free Press.

LIPSKY, M. (1970) Protest in City Politics. Chicago: Rand McNally.

LONGPIERRE, M. (1970) "Permanance des conseillers généraux et renouveau des traditions administratives départementales," pp. 3-32 in Institut d'Etudes Politiques de Grenoble, Aménagement du territoire et développement régionale, III. Paris: La Documentation française.

LOWI, T. J. (1964) "American business, public policy, case studies, and political theory." World Politics 16 (July): 677-715.

LUETHY, H. (1955) France Against Herself. New York: Frederick A. Praeger.

MAASS, A. [ed.] (1959) Area and Power: A Theory of Local Government. New York: Free Press.

MABILEAU, A. [ed.] (1972) Les Facteurs locaux de la vie politique nationale. Paris: Pédone.

McCONNELL, G. (1966) Private Power and American Democracy. New York: Alfred A. Knopf.

MacRAE, D. Jr. (1967) Parliament, Parties, and Society in France, 1946-1958. New York: St. Martin's Press.

MARTIN, R. C. (1965) The Cities and the Federal System. Chicago: Aldine-Atherton.

MAWHOOD, P. (1972) "Melting an iceberg: the struggle to reform communal government in France." British Journal of Political Science 2 (October): 501-510.

MAYER, R. (1958) Féodalites ou démocratie? Paris: Arthaud.

MEDARD, J.-F. (1972) "La recherche du cumul des mandats par les candidats aux élections législatives sous la Cinquième République," pp. 139-159 in A. Mabileau (ed.) Les Facteurs locaux de la vie politique nationale. Paris: Pédone.

——— (1970) "La recherche sur la vie politico-administrative locale en France." Presented to the Congress of the International Political Science Association, Munich.

MILBRATH, L. W. (1970) "A paradigm for the comparative study of local politics." Presented to the Congress of the International Political Science Association, Munich.

MILLER, W. E. and D. E. STOKES (1963) "Constituency influence in Congress." American Political Science Review 57 (March): 45-56.

MORICE, B. (1969) "Quelle réforme communale? " Revue politique et parlementaire no. 800 (June): 70-73.

——— (1968) "Les Municipalités à l'heure de choix." Revue politique et parlementaire no. 788 (April): 53-63.

MORIN, E. (1967) Commune en France: La metamorphose de Plodèmet. Paris: Fayard.

MYERS, F. (1970) "Social class and political change in Western industrial systems." Comparative Politics 2 (April): 389-412.

NIE, N. H., G. B. POWELL, Jr., and K. PREWITT (1969) "Social structure and political participation: developmental relationships, I." American Political Science Review 3 (June): 361-378.

NUTTALL, R. L. et al. (1968) "On the structure of influence," in T. N. Clark (ed.) Community Structure and Decision-Making. San Francisco: Chandler.

OSTROWSKI, K. and H. TEUNE (1970) "Local political systems and general social processes." Presented to the Congress of the International Political Science Association, Munich.

PARENTI, M. (1970) "Power and pluralism: a view from the bottom." Journal of Politics 32 (August): 501-530.

PRZEWORSKI, A. and H. TEUNE (1970) The Logic of Comparative Inquiry. New York: John Wiley.

RABINOVITZ, F. F. (1969) "Urban development and political development in Latin America," pp. 88-123 in R. T. Daland (ed.) Comparative Urban Research: The Administration and Politics of Cities. Beverly Hills: Sage Publications.

——— (1968) "Sound and fury signifying nothing? A review of community power research in Latin America." Urban Affairs Quarterly 3 (March): 111-112.

RICCI, D. (1971) Community Power and Democratic Theory: The Logic of Political Analysis. New York: Random House.

RIGGS, F. W. (1964) Administration in Developing Countries: The Theory of Prismatic Society. Boston: Houghton Mifflin.

ROIG, C. (1969) "Structure sociale et structure du pouvoir local en milieu urbain." Presented to the International Conference on Community Decision-Making, Milan, July.

——— (1967-1968) "L'évolution de la planification urbaine aux Etats-Unis." Actualité économique (July-September; October-December; April-June).

——— (1966) "Théorie et réalité de la décentralisation." Revue française de science politique (June): 445-471.

——— (1964) "L'administration locale et les changements sociaux," pp. 13-84 in Institut d'Etudes Politiques de Grenoble, Administration traditionnelle et planification régionale. Paris: Armand Colin.

——— and P. KUKAWKA (1970) "Social structure and local power structure in urban areas: analysis of 17 French townships." New Atlantis 1 (Winter): 65-84.

ROKKAN, S. (1970) Citizens, Elections, Parties. New York: David McKay.

ROSENAU, J. N. (1969) Linkage Politics: Essays on the Convergence of National and International Systems. New York: Free Press.

ROSENTHAL, D. B. (1970) "Deurbanization, elite displacement, and political change in India." Comparative Politics 2 (January): 169-202.

——— (1968) "Functions of urban political systems: comparative analysis and the Indian case," pp. 269-303 in T. N. Clark (ed.) Community Structure and Decision-Making. San Francisco: Chandler.

SAYRE, W. W. (1970) "The mayor," in L. C. Fitch and A. H. Walsh (eds.) Agenda for a City: Issues Confronting New York. Beverly Hills: Sage Publications.

——— and H. KAUFMAN (1965) Governing New York City: Politics in the Metropolis. New York: W. W. Norton.

SAYRE, W. S. and N. W. POLSBY (1965) "American political science and the study of urbanization," pp. 115-156 in P. Hauser and L. F. Schnore (eds.) The Study of Urbanization. New York: John Wiley.

SCARROW, H. A. (1971) "Policy pressures by British local government." Comparative Politics 4 (October): 1-28.

SELZNICK, P. (1949) TVA and the Grass Roots. Berkeley: Univ. of California Press.

SHERWOOD, F. P. (1969) "Devolution as a problem of organization strategy," pp. 60-87 in R. T. Daland (ed.) Comparative Urban Research: The Administration and Politics of Cities. Beverly Hills: Sage Publications.

SMITH, B.L.R. and G. R. LaNOUE [eds.] (1971) "Urban decentralization and community participation." Special issue of the American Behavioral Scientist 15 (September).

SWARTZ, M. J. (1968) "Introduction," in M. Swartz (ed.) Local-Level Politics: Social and Cultural Perspectives. Chicago: Aldine-Atherton.

TARROW, S. (1971) "The urban-rural cleavage in political involvement: the case of France." American Political Science Review 65 (June): 341-357.

VIDICH, A. J. and J. BENSMAN (1958) Small Town in Mass Society. Princeton: Princeton Univ. Press.

VIEIRA, P. R. (1967) "Toward a theory of decentralization: a comparative view of forty-five countries." Ph.d. dissertation. University of Southern California.

WALSH, A. H. (1969) The Urban Challenge to Government: An International Comparison of Thirteen Cities. New York: Frederick A. Praeger.

WALTON, J. (1968) "Differential patterns of community power structure: an explanation based on interdependence," pp. 441-459 in T. N. Clark (ed.) Community Structure and Decision-Making. San Francisco: Chandler.

WARREN, R. L. (1963) The Community in America. Chicago: Rand McNally.

WIRT, F. M. [ed.] (1971) Future Directions in Community Power Research: A Colloquium. Berkeley: Institute of Governmental Studies.

WOOD, R. C. (1964) 1400 Governments. Garden City, N.Y.: Doubleday Anchor.

WORMS, J.-P. (1966) "Le Préfet et ses notables." Sociologie du travail 3 (July-September): 249-275.

WRIGHT, D. S. (1969) "The city manager as a development administrator," pp. 203-248 in R. T. Daland (ed.) Comparative Urban Research: The Administration and Politics of Cities. Beverly Hills: Sage Publications.

ZAWADSKI, S. (1970) "Study of local power in Poland." Presented to the Congress of the International Political Science Association, Munich.

ZOLBERG, A. R. (1966) Creating Political Order: The Party-States of West Africa. Chicago: Rand McNally.

Chapter 13

The Institutional Approach as a Strategy

for Comparative Community Power

Structure Studies

Delbert C. Miller

Comparative community power research reintroduces and intensifies the problem of research design and method with which the researcher is confronted in a single case study. It is axiomatic that comparative research invites a greater expenditure of time, money, and manpower. Once undertaken, the central core of the design must be frozen in order to insure comparability. There are no more methodologies or instruments of measurement available to the researcher simply because he has expanded the number of communities in his research universe. And the problem of determining what knowledge is of most worth to a growing scientific base becomes more important. The social scientist is pledged to a search for those aspects of social structure which are relatively stable and exhibit recurring regularities or patterns. In community power phenomena much of the data are ephemeral: the current issues, the political party in power, the current leaders and interpersonal relations between them, and sometimes even the economic and social composition of the community is in rapid flux. Of what value is this transitory data to a scientific commitment which seeks to build a base of knowledge characterized by persistence in time and wide sceop in social space? The answer is very little unless the collection of data is guided by concepts, models, patterns, or processes that may be compared and related.

The comparative researcher knows that he must have a design which makes comparability possible between his intranational or international communities. If he chooses cross-sectional analysis, then he must ask himself if he or other researchers can use his concepts and methods for future longitudinal study. And more than that, it is important to anticipate whether he and future researchers can utilize the findings in the task of accumulating research knowledge. John Walton and Claire Gilbert who independently have made strenuous efforts to compare large numbers of community power studies can attest to the difficulty of classifying previous work.[1] Such an apparently simple demand as the classification of a community as monolithic or pluralistic through data reported by different observers can bedevil the most careful research compilation. Currently, we have two opposing statements each carefully documented about the influence of the method employed. Walton says the type of method employed (reputational or decisional), influences whether the researcher finds a monolithic or pluralistic community.[2] Clark and his co-workers say no; that the method bears no statistical correlation of significance.[3] Meanwhile, it is reported that an analysis of fourteen comparative studies under way shows that there are at least six major areas in which many of these studies are collecting data: demographic composition, economic structure, political organization, power structure, leadership values, and community public opinion.[4] Three widely used methodologies introduce further variation: the use of the reputational approach, the decisional or issue approach, and the positional approach.

Just to make matters a little worse (if that is possible) community power research introduces a major distinction between power structure as a potential for future action and influence as "social action within the general normative framework of a power structure."[5] These phenomena are different and the failure to distinguish between them has embroiled researchers in many vehement controversies over the best method of studying community power structure. Power as a structure with potential for action and influence as a pattern of social action are equally capable of scientific treatment. But it must be realized that appropriate concepts and designs must be applied. Comparative study is a research adventure committed to a comparison of data not only between the cases studied but with all other relevant research.

The central questions with which the social scientist must deal are: What generalizations may be drawn about power structures and influence systems within different types of social and political structures? What is the significance of the differences within each of the various sociopolitical systems for power structures and influence systems? If community power is to build a systematic body of knowledge, these considerations must be primary.

In this chapter I will discuss what may be called the institutional approach to comparative community power research. This approach is believed to be capable of comparability and to yield findings that are anchored to institutional foundations which have high persistence and stability. It has been utilized by the writer during the past fifteen years in which successive studies have been made of Seattle, Washington; Bristol, England; Cordoba, Argentina; and Lima, Peru. Findings from Lima, Peru will be introduced for illustration of a system model based on institutional analysis. A comparison of the four world cities will indicate the importance of institutional variation in community power analysis.[6]

The essence of the institutional approach is found in the emphasis placed on the national and community institutional power profile as the base from which to view the relationship of other community power phenomena. The determination of the relative distribution of power in the institutional sectors invites careful probing for norms, culture patterns, values, and historic belief systems and ideologies. Subsequent steps include the contemporary social structure with its economic and social base as it relates to the identity of influential organizations and leaders. Finally, interpersonal relationships between influential leaders are examined in the light of prevailing institutional and social structure in the community and nation. I will introduce the major concepts proposed in these areas for comparative analysis and will suggest some requirements for future research.

THE COMMUNITY POWER SYSTEM MODEL

The Community Power Structure is a pattern of five component parts defined as follows:

(1) Institutional power structure of the society refers to the relative distribution of power among societal institutions.

(2) Institutionalized power structure of the community refers to the relative distribution of power among local institutions.

(3) Community power complex is a power arrangement among temporary or permanent organizations, special-interest associations, and informal groups emerging in specific issues and projects.

(4) Top influentials are those persons who are reputed to exert the most influence and power in community decision-making.

(5) Key influentials are acknowledged leaders among the top influentials.[7]

Each part is believed to be interrelated with and to influence the nature of each successive part. This means that the entire structure is greatly influenced by the nature of the institutional power structure of the society. Institutional dominance may vary among such sectors as business and finance, government, labor, military, religion, society and wealth, independent professions, education, mass communications, recreation, social welfare, and cultural and artistic institutions. In general, the power pattern of the society puts its stamp on the institutional power structure within the community. In turn, organizations and leaders draw their power and influence from the institutional power structure of the community.

The validity of the model rests on the following assumptions:

(1) In the institutional power structure of society, influence is derived from dominant values which are exercised by certain social institutions. The power of these institutions is due to their resources, the rate at which they use their resources for political influence, and the efficiency with which they use their resources.

(2) The institutional sectors of the local community reflect the institutional power structure of the society (nation) because of high interrelationships of economy, communication, and transportation.

(3) Organizations composing the community power complex have identifiable interest groupings anchored in institutional sectors.

(4) Top influentials will occur in number and influence proportionate to the power distribution of institutions in the institutionalized power structure of the community.

(5) Key influentials reflect top influentials in attitude and behavior but are selected out more rigorously because of their higher power ranking and their leadership abilities.

Partial breakdowns of these assumptions are known to take place. The study of the four cities was designed to test the model and determine the points of divergence.

APPLICABILITY OF SYSTEM MODEL OF COMMUNITY POWER STRUCTURE

Five Component Parts of the community power structure have been set forth. A summary of relevant data for Lima, Peru is shown in Table 1. The data were gathered in 1965-1966 when Peru was a Democratic Republic under the leadership of Fernando Belaúnde Terry. A three-step reputational method was employed, top leaders making the final judgments as shown in Table 1. An interrelationship is clearly indicated between the institutional power structure of society and the institutionalized power structure of the community with a Spearman rank correlation of .93. This almost perfect correspondence probably results from the fact that Lima is the capital city and is thus clearly tied into the national government and economy. Only two minor differences in rank are noted: business and finance rises from fourth rank nationally to third rank in Lima while the military drops from third rank nationally to fourth rank in Lima, and religion is given slightly more influence in Lima than nationally, moving from eighth to seventh position. From the institutionalized power structure of the community, the theory of successive influence in the parts would predict that the community power complex and the top and key influentials would be dominated by government, political parties, business and finance, and the military.

A correspondence was noted between the community power complex and the institutionalized power structure of the community. Five of the organizations ranked as most influential in getting things done in community life represent

TABLE 1
SUMMARY OF DATA SHOWING INTERRELATIONSHIPS BETWEEN COMPONENT
PARTS OF THE SYSTEM MODEL OF COMMUNITY POWER STRUCTURE
FOR LIMA

Peru		Institutional Identity of					
		14 Most Influential Organizations		33 Top Influentials		14 Key Influentials	
		Lima					
Power Ranking of Institutional Sectors	Power Ranking of Institutional Sectors	(n)	%	(n)	%	(n)	%
1. Government	Government	1	(7)	6	(18)	3	(21)
2. Political parties	Political parties	4	(29)	6	(18)	4	(29)
3. Military	Business and finance	4	(29)	10	(30)	1	(7)
4. Business and finance	Military	–	–	1	(3)	–	–
5. Labor	Labor	1	(7)	1	(3)	–	–
6. Mass Communication	Mass Communication	2	(14)	2	(6)	2	(14)
7. Education	Religion	–	–	2	(6)	1	(7)
8. Religion	Education	1	(7)	4	(12)	3	(21)
9. Society and wealth	Society and wealth	–	–	–	–	–	–
10. Independent professions	Independent professions	1	(7)	1	(3)	–	–
11. Social welfare	Social welfare	–	–	–	–	–	–
12. Culture and art	Culture and art	–	–	–	–	–	–
13. Recreation	Recreation	–	–	–	–	–	–

political parties and government, and four represent business and finance. However, an important slippage occurs in religion and military, where no civic organization is ranked as influential. On the other hand, labor (with an organization ranked as most influential), religion, and mass communication show greater strength than predicted.

Top influentials bear out partially the predicted relationship. Business, political, and governmental leaders are numerous. As expected, the military and labor are also represented, but each of these sectors has only a single representative. Key influentials likewise reproduce partially the predicted patterning of the component parts. A high representation (50 percent) of political and government leaders is found. Business and religion are represented, but by only one key influential each. The military and labor have no representation, while education has three and mass communication two.

The hypothesis stating that the power structure will be dominated by business, military, religious, and political leaders is partially validated. Religious leaders are reported weaker than the operating hypothesis. Educators and mass communication leaders are more important than indicated by the institutional ranking of their sectors.

The system model has revealed a pattern of interrelationships among the five component parts. It breaks down in the case of the military and labor; both were ranked high in institutional influence but no military or labor leaders were revealed as active influentials in the community. It is now clear that the model can approximate a predictable pattern, but that it will break down when community power is exercised by a collective representation that does not rely on highly personalized leadership.

Labor, the military, and the Catholic Church revere their established institutions and consider the needs of the institution more important than individual leaders. In fact, leaders are often rotated. Labor uses election machinery for this purpose; the military and the Church employ planned policies of rotation. Instead of setting up civic organizations and working upon issues and projects in the community life, they use their own collective power—labor, the strike; the military, threat or use of coercive force; the Catholic Church, moral persuasion and sanctions—for their own interests. Or they work through established organizations and institutions—labor has chosen a political party (APRA) to wield political influence; the military supports and pressures governments to follow its dictates; the Church functions through government, its own schools, and other community agencies to establish its influence. Each of these institutional sectors must be studied carefully to understand how it generates collective influence without highly visible leaders. In the Lima of 1965, the military was almost a faceless institution. Many top leaders did not know the men who would command a military junta. The military was isolated from community life. This does not mean that the military lacked communication. On the contrary, three high-ranking military officers sat in the President's cabinet, they had close ties with the joint chiefs of staff, and General Jose Benavides y Benavides, chief of the national intelligence, was attached to the President's personal staff. One expert told me that the military had high concern in three matters: the threat of increased Communist influence and social disorder, the size of the budget for the armed forces, and concern over rapid inflation.[8] Any of these matters could bring military pressure. What was not foreseen was that the nationalization of the International Petroleum Company would loom as a major aspiration of the military. Few if any observers were aware of the growing social and economic consciousness of the military and their ideological aspirations to build a new nationalism in Peru.

INSTITUTIONALIZED POWER STRUCTURES
OF THE FOUR COMMUNITIES

The variety of the Institutionalized Power Structures of Seattle, Bristol, Cordoba, and Lima is apparent from the relative power rankings of major institutions shown in Table 2. There is much similarity in that business, labor, and government are among the top five most powerful institutions. The fact that all the cities are industrialized communities accounts for this similarity. It is the rank order of the institutions which emphasizes the individuality of their community power structures.

Perhaps the most significant similarity in these four cities is their common reliance on private business enterprise. In the midst of great political pressure to nationalize industrial operations, private enterprise has generally survived and flourished. Through the growth of enterprise, each city has grown, has offered more jobs at better rates of pay, and has watched a middle class constantly expand. While most of these cities own and operate many of their own utilities and some house nationalized industries, these public enterprises remain in small minority, not only because of economic or political pressure from the propertied interests, but also because nationalized industry can fall heir to a series of troubles: corruption; lack of efficiency; political appointments to jobs; technical stagnation; lack of worker motivation; waste; tax burdens for investment, maintenance, and expansion; and lack of capable leadership. Each city has experienced these problems in developing city or nationally owned industries and services. People in all social classes are aware of these dangers and so resist or are indifferent to political pressure and threats to throw private enterprise out. For more than ten years all major political parties in Peru have been calling with constant clamor for the nationalization of the oil fields and refineries of Standard Oil. Only naked military coercion finally prevailed in 1968.

A relatively stable power position is also held by labor and the political party it supports. In all four cities, these two elements represent the major countervailing force to economic power. When the labor-supported party is in

TABLE 2
RELATIVE POWER RANKINGS OF THE MOST INFLUENTIAL INSTITUTIONS IN
SEATTLE, BRISTOL, CORDOBA, AND LIMA

Seattle	Bristol	Cordoba	Lima
Business and finance	Local government	Religion	Local government
Local government	Business and finance	Business and finance	Political parties
Mass communication	Labor	Labor	Business and finance
Education	Education	Military	Labor

a. Rankings were determined by the reputational methods with top influentials responding in Cordoba and Lima; judges were used in Seattle and Bristol.

power, the influence of labor is augmented. Usually, this results in a demand for and a provision of increased social services. Whether local governments are weak or strong in these four cities depends partly on the governmental structure (recall the contrast between Seattle's nine-man, elected-at-large council and Bristol's ward system of 112 members) and partly on the achievement of consensus within the party and between parties. Failure of consensus in Cordoba and Lima constantly threatens to lower the influence of the government by throwing it into deadlocks and impotence.

The most significant difference in these four cities is the presence of the military that intervene frequently in Lima and Cordoba as their countries fall under military dictatorships. This is so common in the recent history of these cities that each is constantly aware of military pressure and influence. When problems mount, disorder and political deadlocks appear and the temporary intervention of the military government is expected. In contrast, Seattle and Bristol do not regard a military government as a possibility. It is interesting to note that under all kinds of government, "city hall" must continue to handle city business very much as usual. Even in the absence of a mayor and council, policy decisions must be made to meet the demands of urban life and experienced civilians are needed.

Other differences among the cities occur because they have different resource and stratification patterns. As a result, different political pressures are filtered through traditional patterns and values.

An extended analysis for the four cities has been made comparing their important associations, issues, top and key leaders.[9] Limitations prevent a fuller presentation here. What is most valuable now is to assess the research and evaluate future requirements.

REQUIREMENTS FOR FUTURE RESEARCH

A Broader Conceptualization of Community Power and the Accompanying Structure. No future step is more important than broadening the concept of community power. The concept of community power as political decision-making and its methodology as issue analysis is valuable but very limiting. This concept emphasizes the dynamic and transitory movement of power arrangements as issues are debated in the community. It fails to tap fully the structure of influence and power which molds opinion and exerts a covert as well as an overt manifestation of that structure. Community power may be defined broadly as the network of influences that bear upon all decisions that have a general effect upon the community. Community decisions of general importance occur around general community issues and projects, status and power allocations in voluntary, political, and governmental organizations, in work organizations, and in decisions over land use.

No community power research has yet focused around such a broad concept, and as a result the total base of community power has not yet been found. In that base, positional, reputational, and issue-decisional leaders play independent and overlapping roles. The degree of leadership overlap is no longer important as a test of validity. What is important is the manner in which each category of leadership functions. It is well known that reputational leaders tend to avoid involvement in issues and prefer to associate with noncontroversial projects. It is well known that positional leaders play important roles in the status and power allocations within their own organizations. They can establish personnel and other policies which have a large effect on the community or they can practice an isolation policy which alters role relationships throughout their firms. It is well known that real estate interests are important in land-use decisions but little research has been undertaken since Everett C. Hughes made his study in the 1920s.[10] The leaders influential in the status and power allocations within voluntary, political, and governmental organizations have seldom been studied. The need now is to utilize all methods of leadership, organizational, and institutional identification and relate them to the broader conception of community power. The Miller-Form system model of community power structure points in that direction. The use of the reputational method to examine leaders, organizations, and institutions and establish their relative influence is an example of a search in depth. Similar efforts should be made with the issue and positional techniques. Newspaper, questionnaire, and documentary analysis will serve as directly complementary tools.

The Measurement of Collective Institutional and Organizational Power. Nothing has been made more clear in this study than the great gap that now exists in the understanding of collective institutional and organizational power. There was a tendency in earlier studies to dismiss the power of labor, religion, and the military when no key influentials were identified with these sectors. However, the rating of institutions and organizations for their influence quickly revealed that the collective power of labor, religion, and the military often ranks very high. When it is taken as a given that community power rests on a structure, it is not difficult to accept the importance of collective organizational power. Future community power research will most certainly seek to assess and relate this type of power. It has been demonstrated that the reputational approach can be applied to the rating of institutions and organizations, assessing their relative influence. Additional appraisal might well follow Dahl's suggestion that power potential rests on resources, willingness to use the available resources, and the efficiency of their use.

Leaders may come and go but organizations carry within them resources that must be reckoned with. This is especially true if their potential is high. Good examples are the military with its coercive potential and labor with its political strength and economic weapons such as the strike. The moral legitimization or negative sanctioning of the church can be vital on many issues. The worldwide impact of the Roman Catholic Church on birth control provides a case in point.

The Mapping of Interinstitutional Linkages. Interinstitutional linkages are especially important as two or more institutional sectors find that their interests are drawn together. In modern industrial life business and government have become ever more closely interlocked. Indeed, C. Wright Mills in *The Power Elite* claimed that big business, big government, and big military are a ruling triumvirate in the United States, sharing common interests, intermeshing leadership, and maintaining a common ideology. His ideas invited a hundred critics, but all agreed on the difficulty and importance of identifying the intricate character of the interinstitutional linkages between business, government, and military. In England, the cry of "Establishment" evokes visions of a tight coalition of family, education, government, and business. In Latin America, the cry of "Oligarchy" raises the specter of the Catholic Church, landholders, and the military in a conspiracy to maintain the status quo against all efforts to achieve social change.

Discovering the "truth" in these allegations about coalitions is a giant undertaking in macro-sociology. The mapping of interinstitutional linkages poses on the macro level what the determination of decision-making relationships among top influentials raises on the micro level.

Hunter undertook the task of ascertaining institutional linkages in his study, *Top Leadership, U.S.A.* His book can be used as one model for analysis. He relied heavily on interviews with top leaders in all parts of the United States, and he mapped their interrelations through contacts, participation in national policy interests, and their specific roles in relation to government.

In this research, the study of Lima forced recognition of the alleged coalition of Catholic Church, large landholders, and military leaders. Numerous efforts were made to discover interlinkages. The search was first directed at finding some "key" that would reveal the interrelations. The successive topics chosen for study were the old families, the list of large landholders, the members of the President's cabinet, the political party leaders, the principal government leaders, the economic dominants (such as bankers, investment, and real estate holders), the chief religious leaders, the chief military leaders, the social clubs, the joint chiefs of staff, the homes of key leaders, cocktail parties, and finally father-son chains. While much was learned, no one can recommend a "shotgun" strategy. But no alternative is yet clear. The determination of bases of power for leaders as established by the ratings of top leaders is a promising tool. The study of overlapping economic, government, social, familial, religious, and military identities is important. Such study provides questions for interpretation. Focused interviews with top influentials and informants can provide that interpretation, although it becomes more and more clear that no one in a large city knows even the top of the power structure in its entirety. Any strategy to secure such a total picture must be a planned piecemeal operation in which one informant describes a part that must be fitted to other parts as they are received from other especially vantaged informants.[11]

NOTES

1. See Walton (1966a); Gilbert (1967).
2. See Walton (1966b)
3. See Clark et al. (1968). The differences in findings may be due entirely to differences in sample; Clark et al. included a much larger sample of studies.
4. See Clark (1968: 467-474).
5. See Clark (1968: 54).
6. See Miller (1970: 205-208).
7. See Miller (1970: 12-13). The basic theoretical framework was developed with William H. Form and was first introduced in Form and Miller (1960: 433-452).
8. For a Peruvian account of militarism, see Villanueva (1962).
9. See Miller (1970: 208-227).
10. See mmmm
11. An elaboration of this complete chapter was published in 1973 by D. C. Miller, "Design strategies for comparative international studies of community power," Social Forces 51 (March): 261-274.

REFERENCES

CLARK, T. N. [ed.] (1968) Community Structure and Decision-Making: Comparative Analyses. San Francisco: Chandler.
——— , W. KORNBLUM, H. BLOOM, and S. TOBIAS (1968) "Discipline, method, community structure, and decision-making: the role and limitations of the sociology of knowledge." American Sociologist 3 (August): 214-217.
FORM, W. H. and D. C. MILLER (1960) Industry, Labor and Community. New York: Harper.
GILBERT, C. W. (1967) "Some trends in community politics: a secondary analysis of power structure data from 166 communities." Southwestern Social Sci. Q. 48 (December): 373-383.
HUGHES, E. C. (1928) "A study of secular institution: the Chicago real estate board." Ph.D. dissertation. University of Chicago.
MILLER, D. C. (1970) International Community Power Structures: Comparative Studies of Four World Cities. Bloomington: Indiana Univ. Press.
VILLANEUVA, V. (1962) El Militarismo en el Peru. Lima.
WALTON, J. (1966a) "Substance and artifact: the current status of research on community power structure." American Journal of Sociology 71 (January): 430-438.
——— (1966b) "Discipline, method, and community power: a note on the sociology of knowledge." American Sociological Review 31 (October): 684-699.

Chapter 14

Local Political Systems and General Social Processes

Kryzstoff Ostrowski and Henry Teune

Approaches to the study of local political or social (communities) units can be identified by the constraints on their level and kind of generalization. First there are within unit studies. Some of these are limited to descriptions of specific processes; others attempt to extrapolate to more general local processes occurring throughout a system.[1] Although often limited to one unit, these studies may focus on establishing some modal forms of behavior; indeed, they may be so organized that some kind of generalization across particular types of units is warranted. Second, there are studies which deal with variance across communities in a manner conducive to explaining certain kinds of variance in terms of other kinds of variance, including changes over time.[2] These studies are largely confined to a specific level of local units for which generalization is considered appropriate, in particular units considered "comparable." The level of observation, the local unit, remains coterminous with the level of explanation and analysis. Variance is explained in terms of variance at that level. A third, alternative, way of studying local units involves the interpretation of the variance observed at the local level as a characteristic of a more encompassing system. The variance observed among local units is seen as a decomposition of the processes occurring at other levels. This approach requires demonstration that the variance observed at the local level is greater than or different from the processes occurring at a more general level, or conversely, that the variance among local units is not merely a decomposition of the behavior of a system more general than local systems.

AUTHORS' NOTE: *This paper was prepared for the Eighth World Congress of the International Political Science Association, Munich, August 31-September 5, 1970.*

The latter approach entertains the hypothesis that observations of variance among local units are specific manifestations of more general processes. The conditions under which such an approach is necessary will be elaborated.

SYSTEMS AND COMPONENTS: NATIONAL AND LOCAL POLITICAL SYSTEMS

Although what is intended is a general statement conceptualizing the linkages between systems and their components and a procedure for analyzing these linkages, we will discuss this problem in the context of local and national political systems. The critical question is whether particular groups of elements are aggregations of elements whose properties co-vary without regard to their interaction and as a consequence of social regularities or whether these elements constitute components of a system whose properties co-vary as a result of their interaction. The implication of this question for local political systems is that if some sets of local political units are, and this is almost "true" by definition, a part of some more encompassing system, then their behavior can be explained in terms of their being components of this larger system rather than in terms of the local unit being a member of a defined population of local systems.

The alternative approach can be distinguished from that of "comparing" across communities according to whether the local political units themselves comprise systems—the appropriate level of "comparison" or generalization is the local system. If the local political units are components of a larger system, then the level of generalization must be shifted. These alternatives can be evaluated only if there are criteria, and procedures for applying them, for determining whether the local units are themselves systems or are components of a system. Empirically, the question is whether the local units are free to vary on the dimensions being examined—the critical assumption of "comparative" or cross-community studies.

Whether or not any particular set of local units selected for cross community analysis can be treated as systems (they are free to vary) will depend on the dimensions being examined. Local political units in many countries, for example, were designed as focal points for popular participation in elections or other structures. But most local political units are part of larger economic regions or economic systems and thus are not free to vary on employment or level of wealth. These dimensions are determined at another level, and, consequently, the level of explanation must take place at that level. Employment, located in the space of local political units, will largely be the result of the interactions of components of an economic system of which institutions within local political units may be a part, but in which local political units as such only have a marginal role. Specifically, in correlating industrialization with political participation, it might be possible to treat the local political unit as a participatory system but not as an economic system. The alternative would be to treat all local political units within an economic region as a single system, whose variance on economic dimensions would depend on and be the same as the variance among regions.

DETERMINING THE LEVEL OF ANALYSIS: PHYSICAL SPACE AND BEHAVIOR

The very idea of a local political unit implies something about relationships between space and interaction. Although there has been a tradition of research and speculation about the behavioral influence of topography (mountains versus plains), local political structures, especially as they are rationalized as a part of a national political system, contain some assumptions about how people interact over space or at least how distance influences the opportunities for interaction. These assumptions provide at least a set of hypotheses about the kinds of behavior for which local political units are likely to be local political systems.

Most of these assumptions are quite difficult to evaluate with evidence. They include: the connection between the symbolic presence of immediate authority and the compliance of the population with more remote authority; the ability of people to contact the administration and the administration to contact the people to hear grievances or to collect taxes; the correlation between smallness and the probability that people will form participatory structures (smallness being linked to frequency of contact and the like). In addition there are judgments about "the best" size for viable economic concentration in the United States.

Although the formal structures of local political units are often designed to provide for local variance on policy, such as in schools, revenue, and transportation, in order to reflect local conditions or needs, it is not at all clear whether actual variances among the local units, even on these discretionary matters, can be explained in terms of processes occurring within the local unit. For example, individual electoral behavior may in part reflect the local conditions, circumscribed by the local political system, but regional or national forces may overwhelm what is purely local. Alternatively, although the character of the local public transportation decisions or the decision-making style on hospitals may be accounted for by differences in the terrain or the presence of local political activists, it is still probable that the general factors which contribute to variances in the local scene are in fact some general forces occurring throughout the more general system. The urban problem in the United States, for example, although discussed in terms of New York, Chicago, and Philadelphia, most probably represents certain national shifts in the technology of the economy, making it unnecessary for people to be concentrated either for access to power to run machines or for face-to-face contact to make decisions. What appears to be specific to cities is perhaps a manifestation of general relationships between the economic system, the location of people, and the peculiar urban form of concentration in the United States.

Of the various forms of spacial aggregations of economic, administrative, or political functions, only some may be behaving as systems. The problem is to determine which level of territorial aggregation constitutes a system, which by definition would mean that the variance observed among units within those systems is determined by the variance of that system of which those units are components. One empirical criterion for determining the appropriate level of explanation is the amount of variance explained. That level of spacial aggregation which accounts for the most variance on some specified dimension is the level of system for explanation; and all levels of spacial aggregation "below" or contained within this system should be treated as that system's components whose variance reflects a decomposition of the general variance of that system.

What level of special aggregation indeed constitutes a system can initially be stated as an hypothesis concerning the effects of space on interaction for some particular dimension. A system then becomes defined empirically as that level of aggregation which best explains the variance among the units being aggregated (the units of local government) and that level of aggregation also becomes the "boundaries" of the system and its components. In order to avoid a statistical fallacy, it should be shown that the units being aggregated indeed do or can interact. As interaction is being used to define a system, the statistical expressions of variance explained should reflect some "real" interaction.

If relationships between variables hold across various kinds of aggregation (and it is possible to discount certain "context effects," by holding them constant in analysis, such as size, and to adjust differences in correlations due to differences in the numbers of observations), then we are in a position to make statements about general social processes. There would be little or no system interference, that is, the kinds of interactions taking place are general, not circumscribed by any particular set of components. Thus, the relationship between economic development and political participation may be similar for cities, state governments or nations, and characteristics of political systems, such as size or autonomy, would not have to be taken into account. At this point it would be possible to study certain dimensions without regard to systemic factors. If, however, we know that the units being observed indeed do interact and it is possible to explain the variance at one level by the variance in another, then systemic factors are operating and one level of observations constitute the components of a system at another.[3] At this point it is necessary to incorporate system level factors, hold them constant, and search for the general processes which explain differences among these types of systems. The relationship between conflict and effort across local political units may be positive in one country and negative in another. There are two options for explaining this cross-national difference: either there are other variables at the local political level which need to be introduced, or there is a set of characteristics of the national political system which needs to be incorporated into the analysis.[4]

If a local political unit is taken as a point of departure in examining political participation (the hypothesis is that this unit is a system with regard to political participation), and we have observed variance in participation among those units, there are several alternative levels of explanation. First, we might be able to explain participation with a set of variables of units below the level of the local political unit, say grommadas in Poland or townships in the United States. If so, then we face the alternative that insofar as political participation is concerned, this local political unit does not constitute a system, but rather is a point of aggregation of several smaller participatory systems. Second, we may find that this local unit better accounts for the variance in participation than those units contained within it. At this point the local unit becomes a candidate for the best system. Third, we may know that the local unit interacts with the politics of some higher level unit, such as a state or voivodship. The alternative now is that the local political units are not participatory systems, but rather are components of some higher participatory systems. The analysis of the components of the variance might proceed by examining whether the variance across the local units is better collapsed into variance across some other level. Fourth, there is still the possibility that the nation is the level of system and thus the optimal level of system for explanation. In order to determine this, however, we need cross-national data.

As we move to more general levels of aggregation we are in effect testing a variety of space-behavior hypotheses. The spatial dimension, however, is a name for unspecified factors. At some level of spatial aggregation we would have to entertain a notion of social space across which interactions take place with little regard to physical space constraints, that is, the influence of factors contained in spatial parameters, approaches "O" as a determining factor in the behavior under examination. Thus we could find that for certain kinds of behavior, national organizations and communications networks absorb physical spacial factors and an hypothesis about the local political unit, based on some space-behavioral linkage, is not viable.

Although it happens that for local political units there are given aggregation levels, such as the state governments or republics, and at least in this century an ultimate point of possible or reasonable aggregation—the nation-state—it is not desirable to limit the analysis to these given points of aggregation. Regions, either parts of several local administrative units, may provide the optimal level differentiation. Where one starts the process of inquiry and testing for systemic parameters depends both on hypotheses concerning spatial influences on behavior and knowledge about a particular set of systems, in our case countries.

In applying these two general criteria of a system—that the important interaction takes place within the unit and that the variance among them is better explained at that level than at any other level of aggregation (even if there is some cross-level interaction), it is highly likely that there will be various "mixes" of levels in any comprehensive type of explanation. For example, if it turns out that the local political units are systems for political participation, but regional systems are more appropriate for economic behavior, then an examination of the impact of economic forces on political participation would have to include observations of local units, and observations of several regions. The regional "scores" for the local units then are defined by membership in particular regions, and there will be a mixture of levels in explanatory analysis.

DEFINING A SYSTEM

The first step in the analysis is to test whether a particular level of local political units constitute a system or components of other systems. Let us take a powiat or a middle-sized American city as candidates for a system—its political behavior is determined by the behavior of the components within it and it is more than a point of aggregation of the elements within it. Let us hypothesize that these units are systems with respect to political dimensions but not economic dimensions. The powiats and cities are thus political systems ex hypothesis, but not economic systems. This example can be displayed as in Figure 1.

The bottom arrows indicate that the behavior of the local unit is a characteristic of the interactions taking place within it. The individual, the lowest possible level of explanation, not only behaves according to some general

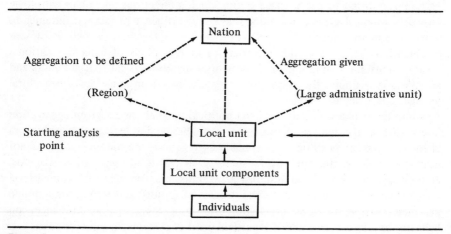

Figure 1.

factors, such as the conventional educational, occupational characteristics, but also behaves as a member of a local political unit, that is, his membership in the local unit makes a difference for his political behavior and the behavior of other members of the local unit. Knowing membership within the local unit improves the variance explained. Thus with respect to a particular type of local unit the individuals within it are components of a local system rather than an aggregation of individuals. The same is true for some other set of units, such as, for example, grommadas, townships, or wards. The wards and grommadas behave as components of the system of the local unit rather than as separate entities, each themselves a system.[5]

After rejecting individuals and the units within the local political unit as independent "systems," we can begin to test hypotheses about whether the local political units are components of other systems. We will confine ourselves to two alternatives of primary relevance for the study of local political systems today: states, or higher level units, and the nation. What is required are some precise statistical tests. These are only a basis for making inferences about effect of systemic factors, not an expression of the system interdependencies. The task is to explicate some possible statsitical tests.

We will first discuss the political dimensions where the points of aggregation are usually given, or set by the political systems itself and, second, the case where the points of optimal aggregation (regions) need to be determined.

Taking Polish powiats and voivodships and American counties and states, let us correlate (for a start, simple bivariate) the same kinds of variables across each of these two levels. If, for example, the correlation between education and membership in organizations is the same, then we can conclude that the system factors are nonoperative, that is the relationship between these variables is independent of the membership of the local unit in a larger political aggregation. There is no ecological effect. Of course, it would be desirable before reaching this conclusion that the variables examined constitute some sample of the political dimensions. But if across a sample of variables, and adding perhaps some multivariate analysis, there are no statistically significant differences—the two or more levels of possible systems are a single universe of units in which the same factors operate—we are in a position to generalize about the relationships as being "system free" or universal, reflecting some general social processes. The units under study are not systems. If relationships hold regardless of the level of aggregation then there is a basis for concluding that these relationships may reflect some general social phenomena, or that at least as far as these levels of aggregation are concerned, there are no systemic influences on the behavior of the variables.

What remains in this analysis is to check whether what is observed at these two levels is a process more general than a specific nation-state. Thus it is necessary to check whether the processes reflected in these variables are characteristics of a specific nation-state or are more universal. In order to determine this, however, cross-national data are required. With cross-national data, it would be possible to compare the correlations between these countries with the correlations within them. If they are the same, then the nation is not operative as a system, but more general processes continue to be reflected.

For a different set of variables different relationships would be observed at the two levels. We should reemphasize that what constitutes a system depends on the nature of the variables being examined. Here two possibilities must be faced. First, if the variance among regions, the higher levels, is less than the sum of the variances of local units within them, we can conclude that the local political units themselves constitute systems. They are free to vary on the dimensions under study despite their membership in higher level units. In another language we are asking to what extent the total variance observed at both levels is contributed to by the two competing levels. This can be determined by an analysis of co-variance among the variables. Second, if we find that the variance contributed by the higher level exceeds that contributed by the sum total of local unit variances, we have a system operating at the higher level. At this point the local unit as a system should be ignored in favor of the variance at a higher level. The local unit should be treated as a component of the higher level, the system of explanation, and the variance among the local units should be re-stated as the variance occurring within that system.

In both of the above cases, there is an alternative level of system, the nation. Even if we find that the variance at the local level is best explained in terms of the variances at that level and not at the next higher level, this does not preclude the possibility that the nation should be the point of analysis.

LEVELS OF ANALYSIS: A CROSS-NATIONAL PERSPECTIVE

In our example of two dimensions—political and economic—we probably will find different patterns in different countries. As an example, let us take the four countries and the level of local units studied in the International Study of Values in Politics: India (blocks), Poland (powiats), the United States (cities), and Yugoslavia (communes). There are several alternatives: blocks, powiats, cities, and communes are political and economic systems or they are components of some higher level political and economic systems. We can configurate these possibilities and hypothetically characterize each of the four countries.

The implication of these configurations, if true, would be different patterns of analysis in each of the countries. In Poland the relationships between economic and political variables should proceed at a higher level; in Yugoslavia, the predictions of the national leadership that the communes are both economic and political systems is true and cross-commune analysis is appropriate. In India, the agricultural mode of production constitutes a system at the block

		Political	
		Same Level	Higher Level
Economic	Same Level	Yugoslavia (communes)	India (blocks)
	Higher Level	U.S. (cities)	Poland (powiats)

(development) level, politically the units behave as components of larger regional systems. In the United States cities are not economic systems, but are political ones. In Poland and Yugoslavia, then, we can construct a data file with no "membership in systems" variables and proceed to study the processes at that level. In the United States and India we need to mix the data files, affixing regional economic scores to cities (membership in the region) and district (or some other unit) political scores to the blocks. These higher level scores are characteristic of that system which most heavily influences the variances on these particular dimensions. Analysis can now proceed, with, of course, the necessary adjustments for different degrees of freedom for the different variables.

CONCLUSION

The study of local political units contains some assumptions concerning their behavior as systems. We propose that these assumptions be tested and that adjustments be made if the evidence does not support them. If these assumptions are not tested, general processes, decomposed in the local political units, will be obscured or certain system characteristics, influencing what is observed at the local level, will be lost. The very idea of a local political system however, connotes membership in a larger political system, and the importance of that membership must be examined.

NOTES

1. There are numerous studies of local units, many of which are presented as case studies and some of which are put in a broader context for generalization.

2. For several examples of cross-community studies, see Clark (1968).

3. Various ecological factors influence the relationships. For a components analysis of variance see Stokes (1965).

4. Some procedures for doing this are discussed in Przeworski and Teune (1970). One example of this is elaborated in Ostrowski and Teune (1970).

5. One problem with individual studies of voting behavior is that treating individuals as components of a local or other kind of system is often excluded in favor of an "independent citizen" deciding in a context free situation. Some studies introduce system membership by scoring individual group memberships, but the analysis remains at the individual level. There is, of course, concern about "ecological" errors.

REFERENCES

CLARK, T. N. (1968) Community Structure and Decision-Making. San Francisco: Chandler.
OSTROWSKI, K. and H. TEUNE (1970) "Explaining within system differences: political systems as residual variables." Presented to the annual meeting of the American Political Science Association, Los Angeles, September.
PRZEWORSKI, A. and H. TEUNE (1970) The Logic of Comparative Social Inquiry. New York: John Wiley.
STOKES, D. (1965) "A variance components model of political effects," in J. Bern (ed.) Mathematical Applicants in Political Science. Dallas: Southern Methodist Univ. Press.

ABOUT THE AUTHORS

ABOUT THE AUTHORS

MICHAEL AIKEN is Professor of Sociology at the University of Wisconsin (Madison). His areas of interest include organizational behavior, sociological theory, and urban and community studies. His more recent work has concerned European comparative studies in the aforementioned areas of interest.

ROBERT R. ALFORD, Professor of Sociology at the University of Wisconsin (Madison), received his Ph.D. from the University of California (Berkeley). He is the author of several books, including *Party and Society: The Anglo-American Democracies* (1963), and *Bureaucracy and Participation: Political Cultures in Four Wisconsin Cities* (1969). He has written a number of articles for professional journals in the fields of sociology, political science, and public administration.

THOMAS J. ANTON is Acting Director of the Institute of Public Policy Studies and Professor of Political Science at the University of Michigan. He received his Ph.D. in Politics from Princeton, and taught at the Universities of Pennsylvania and Illinois before joining the Michigan faculty. He is currently working on an analysis of the Swedish political elite and on studies of politics in several metropolitan areas, including Stockholm.

TERRY NICHOLS CLARK is Associate Professor of Sociology at the University of Chicago and has taught at Columbia, Harvard, Yale, and the Sorbonne. He is the author of *Prophets and Patrons: The French University and the Emergence of the Social Sciences* (1973), *Community Power and Policy Outputs: A Review of Urban Research* (1973); and co-author and editor of *Community Structure and Decision Making* (1968), and *Gabriel Tarde on Communication and Social Influence* (1969).

ERIK COHEN is Senior Lecturer at the Hebrew University of Jerusalem. He has conducted sociological research on collective settlements and new towns in Israel and is currently engaged in urban anthropological studies of multi-ethnic communities. Author of numerous papers on collective settlements, urban communities and ethnic groups in Israel, he is preparing a book on the sociology of tourism.

ROBERT C. FRIED is Professor of Political Science and Director of the European Urban Research Project at the University of California (Los Angeles). He is author of *Planning the Eternal City* (1973), *Comparative Political Institutions* (1966), and *The Italian Prefects* (1963); the editor of *The Quality of Life in European Cities* (1973); and co-author of *Comparative Urban Performance* (1974).

PETER JAMBREK is currently on leave from the University of Ljubljana, Yugoslavia teaching sociology at the University of Zambia in Lusaka. He was born in Ljubljana and did his undergraduate work there before moving to the University of Chicago for both his M.A. and Ph.D. He has published widely in various Yugoslav professional journals; most of his articles deal with topics in social stratification, comparative community decision-making, and political development.

MARK KESSELMAN, Professor of Political Science at Columbia, is the author of *The Ambiguous Consensus* (1965), co-author of *Power and Choice in American Politics: A Critical Introduction,* as well as articles on French, American, and comparative politics in many foreign and domestic professional journals. He did his undergraduate work at Cornell, and received both his M.A. and Ph.D. from the University of Chicago. He is currently engaged in a study of children and politics in France and the United States.

DELBERT C. MILLER is Joint Professor of Sociology and Business Administration at Indiana University. His special fields of interest are industrial sociology and community power structures. He is the author of *International Community Power Structures* which describes community studies conducted in Seattle, Washington; Bristol, England; Cordoba, Argentina; and Lima, Peru. The chapter in the present volume is based on research work conducted in these four cities.

K. NEWTON took his first degree in sociology at the University of Exeter, England, and received his Ph.D. from the University of Cambridge. He taught political sociology at the University of Birmingham where he also carred out a study of politics in the city. He held an American Council of Learned Societies Fellowship at the University of Wisconsin, 1973-74 and is now engaged in research on local politics in Britain at Nuffield College, Oxford. He is the author of *The Sociology of British Communism* and co-author/co-editor of *Opportunities After O' Level.*

K. OSTROWSKI is affiliated with the Institute of Philosophy and Sociology of the Polish Academy of Science and with the University of Warsaw. He has recently published a book on participation in trade unions in Poland, and co-authored a paper with A. Przeworski on social mobilization in Poland. He is involved in questions of scientific and education policy for Warsaw.

EUGEN PUSIC, born in Yugoslavia, received his Doctorate in Law from the University of Zagreb. He has held various offices in public administration, including that of State Secretary for Health and Welfare. He teaches administration at the University of Zagreb and has published extensively in the areas of administrative and political science, social policy, and health administration.

CHARLES TILLY is Professor of Sociology and History at the University of Michigan. He received his Ph.D. in sociology from Harvard, and also studied at Balliol College, Oxford, and the Facultés Catholiques de l'Ouest, Angers. He is currently a member of the Mathematical Social Science Board, and of the committee of the Centre National de Recherche Scientifique (Paris) responsible for the transcription and dissemination of data from nineteenth-century French censuses.

HENRY TEUNE is Professor of Political Science at the University of Pennsylvania. He received his M.A. from the University of Illinois and his Ph.D. from Indiana University. The chapter in this volume is his third co-authored publication with K. Ostrowski, and it reflects a continued collaboration with Ostrowski in the Research Committee on Local Government and Politics of the International Political Science Association and the Social Ecology Committee of the International Sociological Association.

JORGEN WESTERSTAHL is Professor of Political Science at the University of Göteborg, Sweden. He has published books on Swedish trade union movement, political press, local politics, and objectivity in news reporting. He is Chairman and General Program Director of a common large-scale research program on local government and politics which has been developed by the political science departments of all five Swedish universities.

INDEX

INDEX